Informal Payments and Regulations in China's Healthcare System

Jingqing Yang

Informal Payments and Regulations in China's Healthcare System

Red Packets and Institutional Reform

Jingqing Yang
School of International Studies
University of Technology Sydney
Sydney, NSW
Australia

ISBN 978-981-10-2109-1   ISBN 978-981-10-2110-7   (eBook)
DOI 10.1007/978-981-10-2110-7

Library of Congress Control Number: 2016956911

Cover illustration: Cover design by Samantha Johnson

Printed on acid-free paper

This Palgrave Macmillan imprint is published by Springer Nature
The registered company is Springer Nature Singapore Pte Ltd.
The registered company address is: 152 Beach Road, #22-06/08 Gateway East, Singapore
189721, Singapore

To Suzhen, Bochan and Bozhi

CONTENTS

LIST OF FIGURES

ix

LIST OF TABLES

Introduction

If the reform of any sector that has ever been claimed a failure by a Chinese central government agency, it was the healthcare sector. In 2005, Ge Yanfeng, Deputy Head of the Research Department of Social Development of the Development Research Center of the State Council, announced that "the healthcare reform was basically unsuccessful" (Wang 2005b). His announcement was first published in *Chinese Youth*, a leading national newspaper controlled by the Chinese Youth League Central Committee. Later on, he published a jointly authored book elaborating the problems his team detected in the health reform. In the book, he and his team blamed the failure on excessive marketization, which led to increasing inequality, low efficiency, and proliferation of "unhealthy practices" in the healthcare system (Ge and Gong 2007).

The Ministry of Health (MOH) disagreed (Guo 2005). Gao Qiang, Minister of Health, when addressing a training workshop for provincial and municipal health department heads in November 2005, asserted that it was pointless to argue whether the health reform was successful or unsuccessful.[1] His speech was widely interpreted as a formal denial of the failure and provoked public outcries. Commentators accused the MOH for being arrogant and disconnected with reality, and disrespecting public opinions (Liu 2005).

Even though the MOH did not agree with Ge Yanfeng on that it was wrong to choose marketization as the policy direction for health reform, senior health officials, including Gao Qiang himself, admitted that the Chinese healthcare system was fraught with problems resulted from the

© The Author(s) 2017

J. Yang, *Informal Payments and Regulations in China's Healthcare System*,
DOI 10.1007/978-981-10-2110-7_1

healthcare reform.[2] Among these problems, a major concern of the Ministry, the central government, and the general public, were "unhealthy practices" that prevail within healthcare organizations and among individual healthcare professionals. Gao Qiang, in the Work Report addressed to the 2004 National Health Work Conference, admitted that the unhealthy practices are "jeopardizing the vested interest of the people, damaging the good image of the healthcare undertakings, impinging the flesh-blood relationship between the [Chinese Communist] Party (CCP) and the mass, and impeding health reform and development" (Gao 2004b). This remark manifested the CCP's concern that unhealthy practices in the healthcare system could jeopardize its legitimacy of ruling. The unhealthy practices that Gao Qiang mentioned in his report included drug kickbacks, prescription for commission, overcharge, over-provision, and "red packets." The first four unhealthy practices involve illegitimate transactions between individual doctors and organizations, be it hospitals or third-party organizations such as pharmaceutical companies. Although inappropriate incomes that doctors make from these activities ultimately come out of patients' pockets, doctors do not take money directly from patients. Usually, patients pay formally to organizations, which redistribute the payments formally or semi-formally or informally to doctors.

This book focuses on the fifth practice—red packet, which is different from the other four by nature. It represents doctors taking payments directly, unofficially, and illegally from patients. If the other four practices are organization-based misconducts, the red packet is an individual-centered misconduct that not only is endemic in China, but also wreaks havoc on healthcare systems worldwide.

INFORMAL PAYMENTS AROUND THE WORLD

Internationally, red packet is usually called "informal payment," but it is also known by other names, such as "under-the-table payment," "envelope payment," "illegal payment," "unofficial payment," and so on. In general, the practice is mostly found in former and current socialist countries. Evidence indicates that informal payments already existed in the former Soviet Union (FSU) and the Soviet bloc in the Central and Eastern Europe (CEE) and Central Asia (CA) before these countries commenced democratic and market transition in the early 1990s (Miller et al. 2000). The collapse of socialism and the abandonment of the "Semashko" healthcare systems for market-oriented healthcare systems only exacerbated the problem.

The "Semashko" healthcare system, named after the Nikolai A. Semashko (1874–1949), the founder of the "Soviet medicine," was established on a constitutional guarantee of universal health coverage for the entire population at the expense of the state (Field 2002a, p. 161). It featured a highly centralized hierarchical administrative, planning, and financing structure, with all the health workers employed by the state in salaried positions in public medical institutions. Private health services were virtually non-existent in these countries. Healthcare became a right of citizenship and an undertaking of the state (Field 2002b).[3]

The "shock therapy" that was adopted by the governments in this region witnessed quick disintegration of the old healthcare systems and deterioration of economy. Healthcare financing and governing were decentralized, market elements were introduced, and private practice was allowed again although it didn't rise to a dominant position in the systems (Kornai and Eggleston 2001a; Belli 2001; Field 2002b). Economic hardships that prevailed the region saw a sharp and constant decline of public spending on health. Public health facilities were considerably underfinanced. Health professionals were underpaid or even not paid. However, most of these countries did not abandon the constitutional guarantee of universal entitlement to free healthcare at the point of delivery. Informal payments become rampant in such an institutional and economic setting.

Throughout the 1990s, drastic reduction of public investment in healthcare was the major reason behind unruly informal payments in transition economies. In Russia, the new Russian Constitution which was promulgated in 1993 continued to stipulate that "provision of health care at state and municipal health institutions shall be free of charge" (Shishkin et al. 2003, p. 10). However, public expenditure on healthcare reduced by 26 percent between 1991 and 2001 (Shishkin et al. 2003). Public medical facilities suffered significant budget cuts and were forced to rely increasingly on user fees to compensate financial shortfall. Public health workers also took informal payments to supplement their meager, and sometimes unguaranteed, wages (Feeley et al. 1999). As a result, Russian patients had to pay out of pocket for constitutionally guaranteed "free" medical services. It was estimated that in 1997 informal payments made by patients amounted to 0.86 percent of Russia's gross domestic product (GDP), and 24 percent of total reported public health expenditures (ibid.).

Many other CEE countries faced the same problems. In Bulgaria, following the political changes in 1989, its healthcare system remained state owned and financed, and its citizens were continuously guaranteed free medical services by the Constitution. But public health funding declined drastically due to economic hardships. In the meanwhile, the change of regime inflated the public's expectations for health. The gap between the increasing expectations and low quality of healthcare due to falling investment had to be met by patients' out-of-pocket payments that were usually transacted informally to healthcare providers. Eventually, informal payments became "an important fact of life in health care" (Delcheva et al. 1997, p. 99). A 1994 survey in Bulgaria revealed that 43 percent of the respondents reported to have paid out of pocket for "free" medical services and drugs in the past two years. A high proportion of the informal out-of-pocket payments were made to doctors, nurses, and other healthcare personnel (ibid., p. 93).

In Hungary, a 1998 survey shows that the majority of the public believed doctors expected gratuities. The frequency and size of informal payments varied across types of medical services. Surgeons reported that they received informal payments from 73 percent of patients, while gynecologists received from 85 percent (Kornai and Eggleston 2001b, p. 170). It is estimated that at macro level, informal payments received by doctors could be "one-and-half times bigger than their official aggregate earnings" (Kornai and Eggleston 2001b, pp. 171–172). To put it in another way, nearly two-thirds of Hungarian doctors' total income came from informal payments (Kornai and Eggleston 2001a, p. 73). A commentator even lamented that informal payments "had so deeply penetrated the system that no reform seems likely to succeed" (Blasszauer 1997).

The healthcare systems of the CA countries which were part of the FSU before 1991 were also plagued with informal payments. Kazakhstan was among the first countries whose healthcare system drew the attention of international scholarship. In the early years of the transition period, Kazakhstan's state revenue dropped by 65 percent, which directly influenced the funding of healthcare. Insufficient funding led to "fuel debts, delays in wage payments and shortage of medical supplies" (Ensor and Savelyeva 1998, p. 43). Informal payments for "free" medical services which had been already endemic under the communism became even worse in the transition period. It is reported that doctors working in rural health facilities relied solely on patients' informal contributions for living due to wage arrears (Ensor and Savelyeva 1998). An estimation indicates that informal payments in the Kazakhstan's healthcare system could double the state expenditure (ibid.).

Lewis's (2000) synthetic review of existing studies demonstrates that informal payments were prevalent since the early 1990s in the public healthcare systems in nearly all the countries in the FSU bloc in CEE and CA, as well as in Vietnam. The frequency of informal payments ranged from 21 percent in Bulgaria up to 91 percent in Armenia, with the amount of informal payments usually exceeding formal payments (p. 18). The only exceptions were the Czech Republic and Slovenia, where the average incomes of doctors were above the national average and were kept pace with inflation. Informal payments were rare in these countries (p. 6). But this does not necessarily mean informal payments never existed. Both countries reformed their healthcare systems in the early 1990s. In Slovenia, one of the implicit aims of the privatization-centered healthcare reform was to overcome informal payments (Albreht and Klazinga 2009). Before the healthcare reform in 1992, informal payments to doctors were also widespread in Czech (Albert et al. 1992). It was estimated that, in 1988, informal payments to health personnel represented "a 25 % increase in health service expenditures," and the lost revenue from health workers' untaxed earnings "would have added up to 2 % toward the gross domestic product (GDP) devoted to health services" (Albert et al. 1992, p. 2462). Even in the late 1990s, informal payments still accounted for nearly 10 percent of the total out-of-pocket payments for healthcare in Czech (Central and Eastern European Health Network 2003, p. 27).

In the twenty-first century, with growing academic interest and increasing evidence, the scale of the phenomenon is better understood. Evidence shows that in spite of the health reforms that all the FSU, CEE, and CA countries undertook in the two decades since the fall of the Berlin Wall, the practice of informal payments seems to have survived in a stronger form in most of them (Chereches et al. 2011; Balabanova et al. 2012).

In the early 1990s, Russia launched reforms to transfer the public healthcare system into a decentralized and insurance-based system in an attempt to improve efficiency and equity (Gordeev et al. 2011). After two decades, the system is still "half-reformed," and the transition remains unfinished (Gordeev et al. 2011, p. 270). Many problems inherited from the Soviet era linger, including informal payments. According to a survey carried out in 2009, 1.4–4.3 percent of users of outpatient non-dental and check-up services reported to have paid informal payments; 12.7 percent of inpatients made informal payments; and 17 percent of users of dental services paid informally. On average, about 7.3 percent of Russian healthcare users reported paying informal payments (Gordeev et al. 2014). Another investigation reveals that informal payments have become more widely spread. In 2001, 5.4 percent of patients were affected by informal payments, while in 2008, 17.3 percent of outpatients and 22.8 percent of inpatients were affected (Kutzin et al. 2010a, b).

According to Short and colleagues (Short et al. 2007), significant transformation of Bulgarian healthcare systems only started in 1999 with the promulgation of the universal health insurance legislation. Modeled on the Australian Medicare system of "universal publicly funded health care insurance" (Short et al. 2007, p. 131), the legislation reaffirmed the Bulgaria's constitutional commitment to "free" healthcare for all citizens. Given the poor economic performance and financial crisis, however, such commitment was significantly handicapped. Out-of-pocket payments for "free" healthcare services continue to be pervasive. In an attempt to contain the grey economy in the healthcare sector, the Bulgarian MOH adopted a policy that allowed patients to pay fees for medical services by choice. This policy is interpreted as "the end of the former state socialist system of so-called 'free' health care" (Short et al. 2007, p. 133). But the policy failed to control informal payments to health personnel, as the ranges and amounts of officially sanctioned out-of-pocket payments are limited, and the salaries for public health practitioners remain low (Ivanova 2007). A recent survey shows that informal payments constituted 47.1 percent of total out-of-pocket payments in 2006 (Dimova et al. 2012).

Informal payments seem equally prevalent in Hungary as in Bulgaria in the 2000s. The study by Baji and colleagues (Baji et al. 2012) indicates that in 2006 and 2007, 9 percent of patients paid informally to general practitioners (GP) even if their practices were mainly private; 14 percent made informal payments to specialists for outpatient visits; and 50 percent had to pay informally to medical staff for inpatient care. In the case of inpatient care, the average amount of informal payments were 58 euros, which represented significant expenses for patients, as it equaled "13.7 % of the average net monthly salary and 20.5 % of the average pension in 2007" (Baji et al. 2012, p. 74). In early 2007, as part of the preparation for joining the eurozone, the Hungarian government launched a healthcare reform aiming at reducing healthcare deficit in the government budget and to control rampant informal payments. A key component of the reform was the introduction of co-payments, which were called "visit fee" (Baji et al. 2012). However, the reform and the "visit fee" had little effect on informal payments, only significantly reducing the probability of making informal payments among patients over 60 years of age in inpatient care, as the "visit fee" benefited medical institutions rather than medical staff. In March 2008, the "visit fee" was voted out in a nation-wide referendum, indicating that the population did not accept "visit fee" but was willing to pay informally and directly to medical staff (Baji et al. 2012).

In fact, in the 2000s, informal payments are reported in all CEE and FSU countries except for Czech and Slovenia, although the extent and magnitude vary across the countries (Rechel and McKee 2009; Kutzin et al. 2010a, b, p. 329; Afford and Lessof 2006). Even in Moldova, whose reformed healthcare model has been recommended to transition economies as exemplary model, informal payments "remain an important component of the underlying cost structure for the patients who visit the government sponsored healthcare facilities" (Mokhtari and Ashtari 2012, p. 190). A survey in 2008 reveals that around 25 percent of patients gave informal payments, although the figure represents a significant drop from 75 percent in 1999 (Mokhtari and Ashtari 2012).

Informal payments are also widely spread in developing countries in Asia (Lewis 2007; Killingsworth et al. 1999; Joselow 2007; Barber et al. 2004; Vian et al. 2012), Latin America (Di Tella and Savedoff 2001), Africa (Lewis 2007, 2010; Xu et al. 2006; Stringhini et al. 2009; Maestad and Mwisongo 2011), and even in some high-income countries such as Greece (Boutsioli 2010; Siskou et al. 2008) and Israel (Cohen 2011). But informal payments in transition economies have direct implications for the situation in China.

Informal payments in the Chinese healthcare system are inadequately reported in the international literature, but the magnitude of the practice is by no means inconsiderable. A large-scale survey conducted by Chinese scholars between 2008 and 2009 shows that 54.4 percent of patients reported making informal payments to their doctors. Among them, only 4.7 percent were motivated by pure gratitude, while 95.3 percent gave red packets for doctors' reciprocity. A large percentage (76.8 percent) expected doctors to reciprocate their informal payments with better services (Kong et al. 2011). Compared with its pervasiveness, however, the impact of the practice is more concerning.

THE IMPACT OF INFORMAL PAYMENTS

The informal payment is deeply ingrained in many healthcare systems and has massive adverse impact on healthcare. For health authorities and policy makers, a major concern is its grave repercussions on accessibility and equality of healthcare.

Informal payments, which are transacted in a "private, unregulated market within a public shell" (Lewis 2000, p. 9), restrict accessibility of healthcare, making even essential services unaffordable. In many countries, informal payments are "compulsory" payments, which discourage the poor from utilizing necessary health services or place a disproportionate burden on their shoulders. Szende and Culyer's (2006) study of informal payments in the Hungarian national healthcare system shows that income is not equally distributed across the population: "the poorest 40 % of the population earns less than 20 % of income earned by the country's population, while the richest 10 % earn close to 30 % of all income" (p. 268). The informal payment, however, is more equally distributed across income groups. That means the informal payment is particularly regressive, with the poor paying proportionally more in informal payment (Szende and Culyer 2006). In the case of urgent health services, informal payments may force a patient to forgo other essential expenditure. Even voluntary informal payments imply unequal access for equal needs (Kaitelidou et al. 2013). The deterring effect of informal payments on the poor has been reported in most countries in which the practice is reported widespread (Mishtal 2010; Parkhurst et al. 2005; see, e.g., Barber et al. 2004).

The adverse impact of the informal payment on the efficiency of healthcare systems and the allocation of resources is equally obvious (Lewis 2000). Due to their deterring effect, medical services are not consumed by those who would benefit most (Liaropoulos et al. 2008; Kaitelidou et al. 2013). The informal payment also creates perverse incentive that encourages medical practitioners to manipulate supply (supplier-induced or supplier-reduced demand), as in the case of caesarean sections (Liaropoulos et al. 2008; Delcheva et al. 1997). Informal payments thus impede efforts in health reform. Healthcare practitioners whose incomes are increased informally may "resist reform measures that aim to change the status quo" (Gaal et al. 2006, p. 259). Such negative attitudes toward reform weaken the government and its pursuit of public interests (Mokhtari and Ashtari 2012). Moreover, as informal payments can keep an underfunded and inefficient healthcare system functioning and justify the inadequate public investment in healthcare, the government's impetus for health reform is reduced (Lewis 2000).

Furthermore, informal payments are a component of informal economy. The transactions are not reported and cannot be tracked, and result in tax evasion on the part of healthcare providers. Shrinking tax base is detrimental to the government's health financing ability (Delcheva et al. 1997).

According to some studies, however, informal payments are not all bad things. A major advantage is the retention of poorly paid healthcare professionals in an underfinanced system that would otherwise collapse should they exited. This is the main thesis of the "inxit" theory (Gaal and McKee 2004a), which reasons that "informal payments can lure the physician to work in the public sector from which non-paying patients may also benefit" (p. 713). Taking Hungary as an example, Gaal and McKee (2004a) argue that informal payments not only benefit patients who are promised free or low-cost healthcare by the state, but also save the face of the government and keep intact the superficial integrity of ideology. Medical services funded by informal payments are better than no services.

The impact of red packets on healthcare equity in China is also widely acknowledged. The Chinese population is not covered by a universal health insurance. Due to the extensive commercialization of healthcare and shrinkage of publicly financed or work-unit-financed insurance schemes, out-of-pocket payments for medical services have been constantly on the rise since the early 1980s. For those who are not covered by any insurance, costs of medical services are already heavy. Red packets increase financial burden and deter patients from seeking treatment (Lu 2011; Xu 2006). But the utmost concern of Chinese scholars, as well as policy makers, is the moral hazards of red packets. In China's political rhetoric, the red packet is deemed as an "unhealthy" practice, which means it is morally wrong, but does not reach the level of corruption. As mentioned above, the health authority worried that uncontrolled red packets could result in rising public discontent and threat the legitimacy of the ruling of the CCP. The prevalence of red packets is viewed as fundamentally in conflict with the dominating ideology promoted in the Chinese healthcare system. The CCP has established that healthcare professionals have a moral and social responsibility to commit to the selfless service to the people. "Serving the people whole-heartedly" is the departing point and the moral height of the socialist healthcare system. Taking red packets is considered as contradicting this moral principle and damaging the image of socialist medicine. The practice also contributes to the deterioration of solidarity and trust of the society, impedes the public's acceptance of health reform policies, and ultimately subverts the government's efforts in improving healthcare efficiency and equity (Feng and Feng 1994; Li and Tong 1995; Li and Su 1997; Chen 2006b). In a nutshell, the potential political consequences impel the CCP and the government to take red packets seriously.

INFORMAL PAYMENTS AND RED PACKETS: DEFINITIONS

Informal payments are a widespread practice in the healthcare systems of many countries, but with regards to what constitutes an informal payment, there is no universal agreement. Several definitions have been posited. Some of them are used more often than others. But the application of these definitions to the phenomenon in China is not straightforward.

Ensor and Savelyeva's (1998) study of Kazakhstan is among the earliest attempts to define the phenomenon. Informal payments are described as "payments made to medical staff or institutions that are not officially required, but are either expected or demanded by providers," and "may be in money or in-kind" (p. 41). Three observations can be made about this definition. Firstly, the informality of such payments lies in that they are not officially required. They are made outside the official channel and are thus not officially sanctioned. Secondly, they can be made to either medical staff or health institutions, or both. Thirdly, the payment may be in money or in kind. In short, informal payments are unofficial payments for free medical services. This has become the mainstay of most definitions of informal payments.

Lewis (2000) defines informal payments as "(1) payments to individual and institutional providers, in kind or in cash, that are made outside official payment channels and (2) purchases that are meant to be covered by the health care system. The former encompass 'envelope' payments to physicians and 'contributions' to hospitals, and the latter the value of medical supplies purchased by patients and drugs obtained from private pharmacies that should be provided by government-financed health care services" (p. 1). This definition highlights the characteristics that have been identified by Ensor and Savelyeva, that is, an informal payment is made to either individuals or institutions, is in kind or in money, and is made outside official channels for medical services that are meant to be free. But Lewis's definition accentuates an aspect of the practice that is not clearly demarcated in Ensor and Savelyeva's definition. That is, payments to institutions include those for drugs and supplies that are covered by the publicly financed healthcare system. Lewis further emphasizes that informal payments to either individuals or institutions are a form of corruption, and thus illegal. She has used this definition in all her studies of informal payments (Lewis 2007, 2000, 2010).

Balabanova and McKee's definition (2002) reads more succinct: "Informal payments are defined as monetary or in-kind transaction between a patient and a health care professional for services officially free of charge in state health facilities" (p. 246). It not only includes the defining features of informal payments—unofficial payments for free services—but also limits the practice to the public sector.

The above two definitions, which have been widely used (Thompson and Xavier 2002; Falkingham 2004; Vian 2005; Baschieri and Falkingham 2006; Chereches et al. 2011; Kaitelidou et al. 2013; Tomini et al. 2012), captured a commonality in the phenomenon, that is, informal payments are made for healthcare services that patients are entitled to free of charge. Noticing this commonality, Gaal and colleagues (Gaal et al. 2006) intend to formulate a universal definition by selecting "terms of entitlement" as the key defining feature of informal payments. They state:

> Regulations are important insofar as they determine what services patients should receive in exchange for what, a concept that we call *entitlement*. The *terms of entitlement* describe those services that can be used by patients, what these services comprise, and how much out-of-pocket payment has to be paid. (p. 275, emphasis original)

They argue that "the reference point for determining whether a direct contribution is a formal or informal payment is the formal terms of entitlement, regardless of who sets them" (p. 276). The terms of entitlement can be set by the state, the insurer, and the healthcare provider, as long as the terms are formally established. Informal payments are thus defined as "a direct contribution, which is made in addition to any contribution determined by the terms of entitlement, in cash or in-kind, by patients or others acting on their behalf, to health care providers for services that the patients are entitled to" (p. 276). By identifying terms of entitlement as the defining feature, Gaal and colleagues take issue with other elements identified by other scholars and dismissed illegality, informality, and corruption as the defining characteristics. This definition is adopted by some scholars, who define informal payments specifically by the reference point of entitlement (Tatar et al. 2007; Ozgen et al. 2010; Gaal et al. 2010).

The applicability of this definition to informal payments to transition economies, however, is problematic. According to Gaal and colleagues, as long as the terms are formally or officially set by an institution, be it the state, the health facility, the insurer, or the individual healthcare provider, they become formal. Any payments beyond these terms are informal. But terms of entitlement set by different institutions (most likely at different administrative levels) can conflict with each other. At macro level, the clash between a ruling party's fundamental ideology and operative ideology (Seliger 1970) could lead to health policies that clash with the terms of entitlement guaranteed in the Constitution. For example, Aarva and colleagues (2009) report that in Russia the 1996 government resolution to allow local authorities to provide chargeable services in public healthcare facilities is in direct conflict with the constitutional guarantee of free healthcare and medicine. Such ideological conflicts also exist in China, which has been described as "signalling left, turning right" (Huang 2013a; Wu 1999).

At micro level, the formal pricing of services or medicine in a healthcare facility, or the terms of entitlement set by the facility, can contradict to the policies of health authorities. The Chinese healthcare authorities have been constantly pricing basic medical services below costs and controlling the prices of medicine covered by public health insurance schemes in order to maintain the affordability of medical services and control the budget of healthcare expenditure. These can be deemed as benefits that patients are entitled to. At the same time, the authorities introduced policies that allow healthcare facilities autonomy to provide special services and drugs that that are not on the official list covered by public insurance schemes. Health facilities usually have great latitude in determining the prices of these services and drugs. To maximize the profit, they formulate their own official schemes to encourage health professionals to prescribe special services and uncovered drugs to patients. Consequently, health facilities provide less services and drugs that patients are entitled to in the policy framework set by the health authorities, but more special services and uncovered drugs sanctioned by the terms of entitlement set by health facilities (Liu and Hsiao 1995; Liu et al. 2000; Yang 2006b). The boundary of entitlement is constantly manipulated by facilities in the Chinese healthcare system, making it less usable as a reference point.

The applicability of Lewis's and Balabanova and McKee's definitions to the phenomenon in China is more problematic. Both definitions explicitly or implicitly indicate that informal payments are made for services that are covered by public finance and thus supposedly free of charge, and both suggest that it is a practice that happens mainly in the public healthcare facilities. In China, over 90 percent of outpatient and inpatient visits occurred in public hospitals in 2010, and 90 percent of health professionals were employed in the public sector (China Health Year Book Editorial Board 2012, pp. 620–621 and 682). But unlike most of the countries mentioned above, China has never in its Constitution promised free health coverage to her citizens.

Article 93 of the first Constitution of the People' Republic of China enacted in 1954 stipulated that "working people of the People's Republic of China have the right to material aid in old age, and in case of illness and disability. To guarantee enjoyment of this right, the state provides social insurance, social relief and public health services and gradually expands these facilities."[4] It is clearly stated that only the working people, or the labors, have the right to such material assistance as health services. That is to say, such right was not citizenship-based, but was based on, in a broad sense, political classification of the population and, in a narrow sense, employment. Furthermore, the Constitution did not guarantee free healthcare. What it promised was aid to the working people.

The new Constitution that was enacted in 1982 and last amended in 2004 replaces the ideology-laden term of "working people" with the more politically neutral term of "citizen," but it continues to exempt the state from the commitment to free healthcare. Article 45 of the new Constitution states, "Citizens of the People's Republic of China have the right to material aid from the state and society in old age, and in case of illness and disability. The state develops social insurance, social relief and medical and health services that are required for citizens to enjoy this right."[5] Again the new Constitution does not promise free medical services to citizens. It only obliges the state, as well as the society, to provide medical aid to citizens if they are sick, but does not specify at whose expense. However, the state- and society-provided aid is expanded to include all citizens and thus becomes a type of universal aid.

In comparison, the Constitution of FSU clearly stated that citizens were entitled to free medical services. Article 120 of the Constitution adopted in 1936 stated, "Citizens of the U.S.S.R. have the right to maintenance in old age and also in case of sickness or loss of capacity to work. This right is ensured by the extensive development of social insurance of workers and employees at state expense, *free* medical service for working people and the provision of a wide network of health resorts for the use of the working people."[6] The Constitution of the Russian Federation adopted in 1993 after the fall of Berlin Wall reassures the state's commitment to free healthcare to citizens. Article 41 states, "Everyone shall have the right to health protection and medical aid. Medical aid in state and municipal health establishments shall be rendered to individuals gratis, at the expense of the corresponding budget, insurance contributions, and other proceeds."[7]

Universal coverage and free medical care to citizens are the cornerstones of the "*Semashko* model." Before 1989, variants of the Semashko model dominated the Soviet bloc in CEE and CA (Afford and Lessof 2006). But the Soviet healthcare model was never established in China, although the latter's healthcare system was set up with the help of Soviet experts (Lampton 1977). Up to the early 1980s, the majority of the Chinese population was covered by three welfare insurance schemes, and all these schemes were occupation-/status-based rather than citizenship-based.

The Labour Insurance established by the Labour Insurance Act promulgated in 1951 was designed to protect industrial workers. The provisions of the Act on health protection stipulated that the enterprise should cover the costs of consultation, treatment, surgery, hospitalization, and general medicine incurred in the course of seeking medical care by their workers and staff, but patients should bear the costs for expensive medicine (Article 13, Item A). The enterprise was obliged to cover only half the medical expenses of the dependents of a worker (Article 13, Item E). The other half had to be paid out of the worker's pocket. The Publicly Funded Health Insurance launched in 1952 covered the healthcare for formal employees of government work-units and institutional work-units in the sectors of education, health, culture, and so on (Zhou 1952). The insurance, however, did not cover the dependents of state employees (Tang and Meng 2004). Furthermore, both insurance schemes provided cover only for formal full-time employees mainly in the public sector. Their benefits to part-time, sessional, and seasonal employees were either limited or non-existent (Wong et al. 2006). As a matter of fact, both insurance schemes were occupational welfare rather than social welfare.

Rural Cooperative Medicine promoted in the 1960s provided health insurance to rural residents in a way that is similar to universal coverage, but it was not a unified system. Communes had different policies about financing and proportion of co-payments. Generally speaking, patients covered by Rural Cooperative Medicine still needed to pay for part of consultation fees and for drugs (Wilenski 1976, pp. 47–49).

In the late 1990s and 2000s, new health insurance schemes were established in urban and rural China, respectively, but none of these schemes provide universal coverage, and all require individuals' contribution to their health insurance accounts and co-payments at the point of delivery of medical services (Wong et al. 2006; Bloom and Tang 2004; Wagstaff et al. 2009; Hougaard et al. 2011). Furthermore, in the late 1990s and early 2000s when new health insurance schemes were not widely implemented, over 70 percent of the Chinese population did not have any health insurance (MOH Statistics and Information Centre 2004, p. 16). It was during this period, informal payments became rampant in the Chinese healthcare system. The combination of low health insurance coverage and widespread informal payments means that many patients have to make informal payments on top of formal payments that are officially charged by public medical institutions without any relief from insurance schemes. Considering these factors, paying for medical services and materials that are supposed to be free of charge can hardly be considered as a defining feature of informal payments in China.

By the same token, payments to healthcare organizations can hardly be considered as informal payments even if the payments include overcharges or illegal fees. In the Chinese healthcare system, patients receive formal, official receipts for whatever payments they make to public hospitals. But at organization level, over-provision and over-charging are widespread in the public health sector. Due to distorted pricing of medical services, drastically reduced revenue from the government, inappropriate incentive structure, and flawed regulatory framework, public hospitals have to rely on over-provision of medical tests and over-prescription of drugs to compensate the loss of revenue (Hao et al. 1995; Zeng et al. 2011; Liu et al. 2000; Wang et al. 2012). But over-payments by patients for over-provided tests and over-prescribed drugs are not informal payments, as they are paid directly to the hospital via official channels, most probably at the hospital fee office. The hospital may incentivize over-provision and over-prescription by giving proportional bonus to individual doctors for prescribing expensive, fee-paying tests and drugs, but the bonuses are formally paid into doctors' hands by the hospital (Yang 2006a).

Irrational overcharges are another type of over-payments from patients to medical institutions. Unlike payments incurred from over-provision and over-prescription which represent excessive provision of services and drugs that are expensive and mostly unjustifiable from a professional point of view, over-charging designates payments for services or drugs that are never provided in reality. Over-charging is a type of organizational fraud, but again, it is not informal payment, as patients, if for whatever reasons do not challenge the bill, pay the hospital via official cashier. The payments are formal and above the table, although the charges are illegal.

Drug kickbacks, which are bribes that pharmaceutical companies or their representatives give doctors for prescribing specific drugs, are another issue in question. Transactions of drug kickbacks have been identified as a type of commercial corruptions by Chinese healthcare authorities. From the patient's point of view, drug kickbacks mean they have to pay excessively for over-priced drugs. In China, nearly 80 percent of drugs are sold within hospitals (Chen and Yi 2011, p. 111). Drug kickbacks are usually linked to over-prescription. It means, on top of proportional bonuses that hospitals give individual doctors for prescribing certain types of drugs, representatives of those drugs also give bribes to prescribing doctors secretly. The bonuses and bribes drive up the retail prices of drugs in hospitals and force patients to pay substantial amount of extras. However, the excessive payments incurred from drug kickbacks are not informal payments either, as patients have to pay formally to hospitals first. Drug reps then share the revenue from drug sales with doctors in the form of kickbacks. In other words, drug kickbacks represent informal (and illegal) incomes for doctors, but for patients, they are formal payments.

In short, unofficial payments to health institutions are not a defining feature of informal payments in the Chinese healthcare system either.

The study of informal payments has to be country-specific (Tatar et al. 2007). Each country has different political, cultural, legal, and moral traditions that significantly influence what activities are acceptable and what are not. The definition of informal payments is determined by these factors.

As the red packet is a major policy concern of the Chinese government, the definitions made by health authorities become the guideline of official actions against the practice. Official definitions constitute an important reference point to identify red packets and are followed by health authorities and hospitals in practice. Available sources do not indicate that the MOH has ever tried to define what a red packet is. In 2004, it launched a specific campaign targeting the practice and a few other related unhealthy practices in the healthcare system. In response to the ministerial initiative, provincial governments formulated local anti-red packets policies and action plans. In their policies, several provincial health departments provided definitions, and all these definitions define red packets in a similar way. For example, in 2004, Guangdong Health Department enforced "The Provisional Rules on the Investigation and Punishment of Guangdong Health Facilities and Their Staff That Solicit or Take 'Red Packets' and Kickbacks" (hereafter the "Guangdong Rules") which defined the red packet as "economic interests such as cash, negotiable securities, credit cards, and shopping cards that are given to or received by [health personnel] as donations in the course performing duties" (Guangdong Provincial Health Department 2004). The definition tries to delimit the red packet by only specifying what it is, without differentiating the motivations, purposes, and timing of the transaction. That is, the regulation does not concern whether the transaction is motivated as a gift or a bribe and whether it is an ex ante or ex post transaction. As long as it occurs during the course when health personnel perform professional duties, any form of economic interests specified in the definition given to and taken by medical staff members qualifies for a transaction of red packet and warrants disciplinary intervention. As a result, the one-size-fits-all definition makes no difference between ex ante and ex post informal payments and denies genuine gratuities as a justifiable transaction.

It was particularly stated in the document that the "Guangdong Rules" was applicable to all types of medical and health institutions and their employees. This makes the rules problematic. It is true that the vast majority of the healthcare practitioners are salaried employees in the public sector and the vast majority of medical activities happen in public healthcare facilities. However, individual private practitioners are legal and active in the healthcare sector who rely on patients' direct fees for a living. It is apparently not as justifiable to prohibit them from taking "red packets" from patients.

Apart from official definitions provided by the government, Chinese scholars also made attempts to delineate the phenomenon. Feng Tongqiang and Feng Zhaodi (1994) define the red packet in the healthcare sector as "all kinds of money and goods that patients give medical staff gratis" (p. 13). This definition, one of the earliest provided by Chinese scholars, seems to indicate that red packets are a form of gratuities. Huang Yi (2004) defines the red packet as "money and goods that patients and their relatives give medical staff for the purpose of medical treatment and health recovery" (p. 49). This definition is formulated on the assumption that patients are officially required to pay for medical services directly to health institutions rather than to medical staff, who are not permitted to receive anything with monetary values from patients. But such assumption only holds true in the public sector, while in the private sector, especially in the rural areas where healthcare services are predominantly privatized and are provided by individual rural doctors, it is common and legal for patients to give money and goods directly to healthcare workers. Huang's definition reflects a public- and urban-centric mindset and fails to convey the unofficial and under-the-table nature of the practice.

In recent years, some Chinese scholars gained an international perspective in the study of red packets and started to link the red packet to the informal payment (*fei zhengshi zhifu*). Liu Lihang is one of them who attempt to establish a connection between the term "informal payment" and the term "red packet." She notes, "informal payments are in-kind or cash rewards paid to providers (individuals/organizations), which are gained outside formal payment channels. They are generally in the forms of cash, goods, services and gifts. If the informal payment is in the form of cash, it is customarily called 'red packet,' which is the money that patients give doctors for treatment or surgeries" (Liu 2009b, p. 60). This definition is close to the one provided by Lewis. Both characterize informal payments as those given to individuals and organizations beyond official payment channels, indicating Chinese scholars' attempt to align their research with international scholarship. However, confining red packets to only cash, Liu's definition greatly limits the scope of red packets, comparing with the definitions given by healthcare authorities.

There is no doubt that red packets are informal payments. The phenomenon in China even shares cultural similarity with the practice in other societies, that is, informal payments are usually delivered in envelopes. Lewis (2000) describes informal payments made to individuals and institutional providers outside official channels as "envelope" payments. In FSU, informal payment in the healthcare system was described as "envelope-passing medicine" (Field 1991, p. 52). In Hungary and Poland, informal payments are also delivered in envelopes (Kornai 2000; Chawla et al. 1998). The prevalence of "'fakellaki' (Greek for small envelope)" in the Greek healthcare system was reported since the mid-1990s (Liaropoulos et al. 2008, p. 74). In China, *hongbao* (red packet) literally means "red envelope." *Hong* (red) also carries the meaning of "dividend" and "profit." *Hongbao* thus means both "red envelope" and "dividend (money) in envelope."

Considering the similarity of the phenomenon of red packets to the practice of informal payments widely reported in other countries, and the particularity of the Chinese healthcare system, the present research defines the red packet as in-kind or cash contributions made by patients and their relatives to individual medical staff members in the public healthcare system outside official payment channels for the latter's provision of professional services. Red packets do not include those made to healthcare organizations. In this book, red packet and informal payment are used interchangeably.

Informal payments plague healthcare systems around the world, exacerbating health inequality and inefficiency and impeding health reforms. In China, rampant red packets not only aggravate inequality and inefficiency and corrupt the medical profession, but are also considered as a threat to the legitimacy of the CCP. To the health authority, they represent an "illness." To the medical profession, they tarnish its image. To the patients, they impose a much-hated burden. Then why has the practice become pervasive in the Chinese healthcare system?

The aim of this book is to examine the rise and prevalence of red packets in the Chinese healthcare system. Drawing on both documentary and empirical data, the research examines the political, economic, and social institutions carried forward from previous eras or emerged in the new age. It argues that the persistence of socialist health ideology, the continuity of bureaucratic organization of the medical profession, and the commercialization of healthcare have jointly created an institutional setting in which the red packet has become a tenacious ailment of the healthcare system and a political concern to the Party-state. Theoretically, the research draws on sociology of professions and studies of informal payments, which will be elaborated in the next chapter.

NOTES

1. News.sina.com.cn/c/2005-11-29/13298437894.shtml, accessed 24 May 2016.
2. News.sina.com.cn/c/2005-11-29/13298437894.shtml, accessed 24 May 2016.
3. An exception to the "Semashko" system in the Soviet bloc was the former Yugoslavian healthcare system, which had undergone drastic decentralization since the early 1950s. But private practice was also not encouraged and had been scheduled to phase out by 1985. Instead of nationalization, healthcare services were collectivized (Parmelee et al. 1982).
4. http://www.lawinfochina.com/display.aspx?lib=law&id=14754& CGid=, accessed 24 May 2016.

5. http://www.for68.com/new/201007/he60492159127010212383.
   shtml, accessed 24 May 2016.
6. Quoted from http://www.departments.bucknell.edu/russian/const/
   36cons04.html#chap10; emphasis added; accessed 24 May 2016.
7. http://www.constitution.ru/en/10003000-03.htm,   accessed
   24 May 2016.

BIBLIOGRAPHY

Aarva, Pauliina, Irina Ilchenko, Pavel Gorobets, and Anastasiya Rogacheva. 2009. Formal and informal payments in health care facilities in two Russian cities, Tyumen and Lipetsk. *Health Policy and Planning* 24(5): 395–405.

Afford, Carl, and Suszy Lessof. 2006. The challenges of transition in CEE and the NIS of the former USSR. In *Human resources for health in Europe*, ed. Carl-Ardy Dubois, Martin McKee, and Ellen Nolte. Berkshire, UK: Open University Press.

Albert, Alexa, Charles Bennett, and Martin Bojar. 1992. Health care in the Czech Republic: a system in transition. *Journal of American Medical Association* 267 (18): 2461–2466.

Albreht, Tit, and Niek Klazinga. 2009. Privatisation of health care in Slovenia in the period 1992–2008. *Health Policy* 90(2–3): 262–269.

Baji, Petra, Milena Pavlova, Laszlo Gulacsi, Homolyane Csete Zsofia, and Wim Groot. 2012. Informal payments for healthcare services and short-term effects of the introduction of visit fee on these payments in Hungary. *The International Journal of Health Planning and Management* 27(1): 63–79.

Balabanova, Dina C., and Martin McKee. 2002. Understanding informal payments for health care: the example of Bulgaria. *Health Policy* 62(3): 243–273.

Balabanova, Dina C., Bayard Roberts, Erica Richardson, Christian Haerpfer, and Martin McKee. 2012. Health care reform in the Former Soviet Union: Beyond the transition. *Health Services Research* 47(2): 840–864.

Barber, Sarah, Frederic Bonnet, and Henk Bekedam. 2004. Formalizing under-the-table payments to control out-of-pocket hospital expenditures in Cambodia. *Health Policy and Planning* 19(4): 199–208.

Baschieri, Angela, and Jane Falkingham. 2006. Formalizing informal payments: the progress of health reform in Kyrgyzstan. *Central Asian Survey* 25(4): 441–460.

Belli, Paolo. 2001. *Ten years of health reforms in former socialist economies: lessons learned and options for the future*. Cambridge, MA: Harvard Center for Population and Development Studies.

Blasszauer, Bela. 1997. Petty corruption in health care. *Journal of Medical Ethics* 23 (3): 133–134.

Bloom, Gerald, and Shenglan Tang (ed). 2004. *Health care transition in urban China*. Hants, UK: Ashgate.

Boutsioli, Zoe. 2010. The Greek hospital sector and its cost efficiency problems in relation to unexpected hospital demand: a policy-making perspective. *Review of European Studies* 2(2): 170–187.

Central and Eastern European Health Network. 2003. *Formal and informal household spending on health: A multicountry study in Central and Eastern Europe.* Harvard School of Public Health.

Chawla, Mukesh, Peter Berman, and Korota Kawiorska. 1998. Financing health services in Poland: new evidence on private expenditures. *Health Economics* 7(4): 337–346.

Chen, Wenling, and Lihua Yi. 2011. *2011 nian Zhongguo yiyao weisheng tizhi gaige baogao (2011 Report on Chinese healthcare system reform).* Beijing: Zhongguo Xiehe Yike Daxue Chubanshe (Chinese Union Medical University Press).

Chen, Xie. 2006b. Fansi 'hongbao' xianxiang de cunzai jichu ji duice (Reflection on the foundation of 'red packet' phenomenon and policies dealing with it). *Zhongguo yixue lunlixue (Chinese Medical Ethics)* 19(1): 55–57.

Chereches, Razvan, Marius Ungureanu, Ioana Rus, and Catalin Baba. 2011. Informal payments in the health care system—Research, Media and Policy. *Transylvanian Review of Administrative Sciences* 32(E): 5–14.

China Health Year Book Editorial Board. 2012. *China health year book 2011.* Beijing: Renmin Weisheng Chubanshe (People's Health Publishing House).

Cohen, Nissim. 2011. Informal payments for health care—the phenomenon and its context. *Health Economics, Policy and Law* 7(3): 285–308.

Delcheva, Evgenia, Dina Balabanova, and Martin McKee. 1997. Under-the-counter payments for health care: evidence from Bulgaria. *Health Policy* 42: 89–100.

Di Tella, Rafael, and William D. Savedoff. 2001. *Diagnosis corruption: fraud in Latin America's public hospitals.* Washington, DC: Inter-American Development Bank.

Dimova, Antoniya, Maria Rohova, Emanuela Moutafova, Elka Atanasova, Stefka Koeva, Dimitra Panteli, and Ewout van Ginneken. 2012. Bulgaria: Health system review. *Health Systems in Transition* 14(3): 1–186.

Ensor, Tim, and Larisa Savelyeva. 1998. Informal payments for health care in the Former Soviet Union: some evidence from Kazakstan. *Health Policy and Planning* 13(1): 41–49.

Falkingham, Jane. 2004. Poverty, out-of-pocket payments and access to health care: evidence from Tajikistan. *Social Science and Medicine* 58: 247–258.

Feeley, F. G., I. M. Sheiman, and S. V. Shishkin. 1999. Health sector informal payments in Russia. In *Technical Assistance in the Reform of Health Laws and Regulations in Russia.* Boston: Center for International Health, Boston University.

Feng, Tongqiang, and Zhaodi Feng. 1994. Dui hongbao xianxiang de sikao (Consideration of the phenomenon of red packets). *Zhongguo yiyuan guanli (Chinese Hospital Management)* 14(2): 13–15.

Field, Mark G. 1991. The hybrid profession: Soviet medicine. In *Professions and the state: expertise and autonomy in the Soviet Union and Eastern Europe*, ed. Anthony Jones, 43–62. Philadelphia: Temple University Press.

———. 2002a. The inelasticity of institutional patterns: an impediment to health care reform in post-communist Russia. In *Health care reform around the world*, ed. Andrew C. Twaddle, 160–178. Westport, Connecticut: Auburn House.

———. 2002b. The Soviet legacy: the past as prologue. In *Health care in central Asia*, ed. Martin McKee, Judith Healy, and Jane Falkingham, 67–75. Buckingham: Open University Press.

Gaal, Peter, Paolo Carlo Belli, Martin McKee, and Miklos Szocska. 2006. Informal payments for health care: definitions, distinctions, and dilemmas. *Journal of Health Politics* 31(2): 251–293.

Gaal, Peter, Melitta Jakab, and Sergy Shishkin. 2010. Strategies to address informal payments for health care. In *Implementing Health Financing Reform: Lessons from Countries in Transition*, edited by Joseph Kutzin, Cheryl Cashin and Melitta Jakab, 327. United Kingdom: World Health Organization.

Gaal, Peter, and Martin McKee. 2004a. Informal payment for health care and the theory of 'INXIT'. *International Journal of Health Planning and Management* 19(2): 163–178.

Gao, Qiang. 2004b. Yi 'Sange daibiao' zhongyao sixiang wei zhidao, jianchi kexue fazhan guan, jiakuai weisheng yiye gaige yu fazhan—zai 2004 nian quanguo weisheng gongzuo huiyi shang de jianghua (Guided by the Important Thought of 'Three Represents', following the Scientific Outlook on Development, speeding up the reform and development of health care—speech addressed to the 2004 National Health Work Conference). In *China Health Yearbook 2005*, 68–78. Beijing: Renmin Weisheng Chubanshe (People's Health Publishing House).

Ge, Yanfeng, and Sen Gong. 2007. *Zhongguo yigai: wenti, genyuan, chulu (Chinese health care reform: problems, reasons and solutions)*. Beijing: Zhongguo Fazhan Chubanshe (China Development Press).

Gordeev, Vladimir S., Milena Pavlova, and Wim Groot. 2011. Two decades of reforms. Appraisal of the financial reforms in the Russian public healthcare sector. *Health Policy* 102(2–3): 270–277.

———. 2014. Informal payments for health care services in Russia: old issue in new realities. *Health Economics, Policy and Law* 9(1): 25–48.

Guangdong Provincial Health Department. 2004. Guangdong sheng yiliao weisheng jigou jiqi gongzuo renyuan suoyao, shoushou 'hongbao', huikou zeren zhuijiu zanxing banfa (The provisional regulations on the investigation and punishment of Guangdong health facilities and their staff that solicit or take 'red packets' and kickbacks). Accessed 23 September 2010. http://www.lmrmyy.com/onews.asp?id=147.

Guo, Shaofeng. 2005. Weisheng Bu guan yuan fou ren yigai bu chenggong (Ministry of Health officials deny that medical reform is unsuccessful). *Xin Jing bao*

(New Beijing Post), 29 October. Accessed 25 October 2006. http://news. thebeijingnews.com/china/2005/1028/013@137019.htm.

Hao, Mo, Yanfeng Wu, Zhifeng Wang, Yichuan Zheng, Jincheng Wang, Yonglong Wang, Rangchun Sun, Jianping Zhou, Longxing Wang, Jinfu Wang, Haiyang Zhou, and Shuzhong Zheng. 1995. Shehui hudong: Yiliao feiyong guo kuai zengzhang de chengyin (Social interaction: The reasons behind fast rising medical costs). *Zhonghua yiyuan guanli zazhi (Chinese Journal of Hospital Management)* 11(9): 565–567.

Hougaard, Jens Leth, Lars Peter Osterdal, and Yu. Yi. 2011. The Chinese healthcare system: structure, problems and challenges. *Applied Health Economics and Health Policy* 9(1): 1–13.

Huang, Haifeng. 2013a. Signal left, turn right: central rhetoric and local reform in China. *Political Research Quarterly* 66(2): 292–305.

Huang, Yi. 2004. "Hongbao" xianxiang de zhidu fenxi—yi xiang yixue shehuixue de yanjiu (Institutional analysis of the phenomenon of red packets: A research of medical sociology). *Zhongshan Daxue yanjiusheng xuekan (shehui kexue ban)* (Graduate Journal of Sun Yat-Sen University [Social Sciences]) 25(3): 47–53.

Ivanova, Maria. 2007. Bulgarian doctors protest over crisis in health-care system. *Lancet* 369(9568): 1157–1158.

Joselow, Ethan. 2007. Informal payments for health services: Problems and policy proposals. Master of Public Health, Rollins School of Public Health, Emory University.

Kaitelidou, Daphne Ch., Christina S. Tsirona, Petros A. Galanis, Olga Ch. Siskou, Philipa Mladovsky, Eugenia G. Kouli, Panagiotis E. Prezerakos, Mamas Theodorou, Panagiota A. Sourtzi, and Lykourgos L. Liaropoulos. 2013. Informal payments for maternity health services in public hospitals in Greece. *Health Policy* 109(1): 23–30.

Killingsworth, James R., Najmul Hossain, Yuwa Hedrick-Wong, Stephen D. Thomas, Azizur Rahman, and Tahmina Begum. 1999. Unofficial fees in Bangladesh: price, equity and institutional issues. *Health Policy and Planning* 14(2): 152–163.

Kong, Xiangjing, Zhizheng Du, Mingjie Zhao, Yang Yang, and Yi Qin. 2011. Hongbao yu yi huan chengxin (Red packets and honesty in doctor-patient relationship). *Yixue yu zhexue (Medicine and Philosophy)* 32(5): 34–37&48.

Kornai, Janos. 2000. Hidden in an envelope: gratitude payments to medical doctors in Hungary. In *The paradoxes of unintended consequences*, ed. Lord Dahrendorf, Yehuda Elkana, Aryeh Neier, William Newton-Smith, and Istvan Rev, 195–214. Budapest: Central European University Press.

Kornai, Janos, and Karen Eggleston. 2001a. Choice and solidarity: the health sector in Eastern Europe and proposals for reform. *International Journal of Health Care Finance and Economics* 1(1): 59–84.

————. 2001b. *Welfare, choice, and solidarity in transition: reforming the health section in Eastern Europe, Federico Caffè lectures*. Cambridge and New York: Cambridge University Press.

Kutzin, Joseph, Cheryl Cashin, and Melitta Jakab (ed). 2010a. *Implementing health financing reform: Lessons from countries in transition, Observatory Studies Series*. Copenhagen: European Observatory on Health Systems and Policies.

Kutzin, Joseph, Melitta Jakab, and Cheryl Cashin. 2010b. Lessons from health financing reform in central and eastern Europe and the former Soviet Union. *Health Economics, Policy and Law* 5(2): 135–147.

Lampton, David M. 1977. *The Politics of Medicine in China, Westview Special Studies on China and East Asia*. Boulder, CO: Westview Press.

Lewis, Maureen. 2000. *Who is paying for health care in Eastern Europe and Central Asia?* Washington, DC: The World Bank.

————. 2007. Informal payments and the financing of health care in developing and transition countries. *Health Affairs* 26(4): 984–997.

————. 2010. Informal Payments and the Financing of Health Care in Developing and Transition Countries. In *IPC Working Paper Series*. Ann Arbor: International Policy Center, Gerald R. Ford School of Public Policy, University of Michigan.

Li, Peiling, and Wenqiao Su. 1997. Hongbao xianxiang zhi lunli fenxi (An ethical analysis of red packet phenomenon). *Zhongguo yixue lunlixue (Chinese Medical Ethics)* 1997(6): 51–52, 56.

Li, Weimin, and Xianfang Tong. 1995. Weisheng hangye 'hongbao' xianxiang de chansheng, weihai ji zhili duice (The emergence, hazards and rectification of 'red packets' in the healthcare system). *Lanzhou xuekan (Journal of Lanzhou)* 6: 43–44, & 62.

Liaropoulos, Lykourgos, Olga Siskou, Daphne Kaitelidou, Mamas Theodorou, and Theofanis Katostaras. 2008. Informal payments in public hospitals in Greece. *Health Policy* 87(1): 72–81.

Liu, Lihang. 2009b. Fei zhengshi zhifu, "hongbao" yu zhili—jiyu guoji yiliao fuwu lingyu de shizheng fenxi (Informal payments, "red packets" and governance—An empirical analysis from the perspective of international medical service sector). *Yixue yu zhexue (Medicine and Philosophy)* 29(10): 60–62, & 64.

Liu, Xingzhu, and William C. Hsiao. 1995. The cost escalation of social health insurance plans in China: Its implication for public policy. *Social Science and Medicine* 41(8): 1095–1101.

Liu, Xingzhu, Yuanli Liu, and Ningshan Chen. 2000. The Chinese experience of hospital price regulation. *Health Policy and Planning* 15(2): 157–163.

Liu, Yibin. 2005. Zhenglun yigai chenggong yufou you shenme buhao (Why should arguing whether health reform is a success or not be a problem?). *Zhongguo qingnian bao (China Youth)*, 30 November. http://zqb.cyol.com/content/2005-11/30/content_1210544.htm.

Lu, Zhengrong. 2011. Qianxi 'kanbing song hongbao' ji zhili duice (A study of 'giving red packet for medical treatment' and policies dealing with it). *Zhongguo yiyao zhinan (Guide of Chinese Medicine)* 9(24): 360–362.

Maestad, Ottar, and Aziza Mwisongo. 2011. Informal payments and the quality of health care: Mechanisms revealed by Tanzanian health workers. *Health Policy* 99 (2): 107–115.

Miller, William L., Åse B. Grødeland, and Tatyana Y. Koshechkina. 2000. If you pay, we'll operate immediately. *Journal of Medical Ethics* 26(5): 305–311.

Mishtal, Joanna. 2010. Neoliberal reforms and privatisation of reproductive health services in post-socialist Poland. *Reproductive Health Matters* 18(36): 56–66.

MOH Statistics and Information Centre. 2004. *Zhongguo weisheng fuwu diaocha yanjiu (Chinese health services investigation and study—an analysis report on the Third National Health Services Investigation)*. Beijing: Zhongguo Xiehe Yike Daxue Chubanshe (China Union Medical University Press).

Mokhtari, Manouchehr, and Mamak Ashtari. 2012. Reducing informal payments in the health care system: evidence from a large patient satisfaction survey. *Journal of Asian Economics* 23(2): 189–200.

Ozgen, Hacer, Bayram Sahin, Paolo Belli, Mehtap Tatar, and Peter Berman. 2010. Predictors of informal health payments: the example from Turkey. *Journal of Medical Systems* 34(3): 387–396.

Parkhurst, Justin Oliver, Loveday Penn-Kekana, Duane Blaauw, Dina Balabanova, Kirill Danishevski, Syed Azizur Rahman, Virgil Onama, and Freddie Ssengooba. 2005. Health systems factors influencing maternal health services: a four-country comparison. *Health Policy* 73(2): 127–138.

Parmelee, Donna E., Gail Henderson, and Myron S. Cohen. 1982. Medicine under socialism: Some observations on Yugoslavia and China. *Social Sciences and Medicine* 16: 1389–1396.

Rechel, Bernd, and Martin McKee. 2009. Health reform in central and eastern Europe and the former Soviet Union. *Lancet* 374(9696): 1186–1195.

Seliger, Martin. 1970. Fundamental and operative ideology: the two principal dimensions of political argumentation. *Policy Sciences* 1: 325–338.

Shishkin, S.V., Y.G. Bogatova, V.A. Potapchik, A.Y. Chernets, and L.A. Chirikova. 2003. *Informal out-of-pocket payments for health care in Russia*. Moscow: The Moscow Public Science Foundation: Independent Institute for Social Policy.

Short, Stephanie, Zdravka Dimitrova Toneva, and Valentin Dimitrov Hadjiev. 2007. On the inequitable impact of universal health insurance: The experience of Bulgaria in transition. *Health Sociology Review* 16(2): 130–145.

Siskou, Olga, Daphne Kaitelidou, Vasiliki Papakonstantinou, and Lykourgos Liaropoulos. 2008. Private health expenditure in the Greek health care system: where truth ends and the myth begins. *Health Policy* 88(2–3): 282–293.

Stringhini, Silvia, Steve Thomas, Posy Bidwell, Tina Mtui, and Aziza Mwisongo. 2009. Understanding informal payments in health care: motivation of health workers in Tanzania. *Human Resources for Health* 7(1): 53–62.

Szende, Agota, and Anthony Johr Culyer. 2006. The inequity of informal payments for health care: the case of Hungary. *Health Policy* 75: 262–271.

Tang, Shenglan, and Qingyue Meng. 2004. Introduction to the urban health system and review of reform initiatives. In *Health care transition in urban China*, ed. Gerald Bloom, and Shenglan Tang, 17–38. Hants, UK: Ashgate.

Tatar, Mehtap, Hacer Ozgen, Bayram Sahin, Paolo Belli, and Peter Berman. 2007. Informal payments in the health sector: a case study from Turkey. *Health Affairs* 26(4): 1029–1039.

Thompson, Robin, and Ana Xavier. 2002. Unofficial Payments for Acute State Hospital Care In Kazakhstan: A Model of Physician Behaviour with Price Discrimination and Vertical Service Differentiation. LICOS Centre for Transition Economics.

Tomini, Sonila, Wim Groot, and Milena Pavlova. 2012. Informal payments and intra-household allocation of resources for health care in Albania. *Health Services Research* 12: 17.

Vian, Taryn. 2005. Health care. In *Fighting corruption in developing countries: strategies and analysis*, ed. Bertram I. Spector, 43–64. Bloomfield: Kumarian Press.

Vian, Taryn, Derick W. Brinkerhoff, Frank G. Feeley, Matthieu Salomon, and Nguyen Thi Kieu Vien. 2012. Confronting corruption in the health sector in Vietnam: Patterns and Prospects. *Public Administration and Development* 32(1): 49–63.

Wagstaff, Adam, Magnus Lindelow, Shiyong Wang, and Shuo Zhang. 2009. *Reforming China's rural health system, Directions in development*. Washington, DC: World Bank.

Wang, Junxiu. 2005b. Guowuyuan yanjiu jigou: wo guo yi gai gongzuo jiben bu chenggong (State Council research institute: our country's medical reform is basically unsuccessful). *Zhongguo qingnian bao (China Youth)*, 29 July.

Wang, Ying, Jay J. Shen, Mei Sun, Charles B. Moseley, Jun Lu, Fang Lin, Xiaohong Li, Fengshui Chang, and Mo Hao. 2012. Why healthcare became som expensive in China? The transformation of healthcare financing during Chinese economic development. *International Journal of Public Policy* 8(1/2/3): 4–20.

Wilenski, Peter. 1976. *The delivery of health services in the People's Republic of China*. Ottawa: International Development Research Centre.

Wong, Chack-kie, Vai Io Lo, and Kwong-Leung Tang. 2006. *China's urban health care reform—from state protection to individual responsibility*. Oxford: Lexington Books.

Wu, Guoguang. 1999. Legitimacy crisis, political economy, and the Fifteenth Party Congress. In *Dilemmas of reform in Jiang Zemin's China*, ed. Andrew James

Nathan, Zhaohui Hong, and Steven Smith, 13–30. Boulder, CO: Lynne Rienner Publishers.

Xu, Ke, David B. Evansa, Patrick Kadamaa, Juliet Nabyongab, Peter Ogwang Ogwal, Pamela Nabukhonzod, and Ana Mylena Aguilar. 2006. Understanding the impact of eliminating user fees: utilization and catastrophic health expenditures in Uganda. *Social Science and Medicine* 62: 866–876.

Xu, Peng. 2006. 'Hongbao' xianxiang de zhidu jingji xue fenxi (An institutional economic analysis of the 'red packet' phenomenon). *Zhongguo weisheng ziyuan (China Health Resources)* 9(4): 147–149.

Yang, Jingqing. 2006a. The privatisation of professional knowledge in the public health care sector in China. *Health Sociology Review* 15(1): 16–28.

———. 2006b. Wage reforms, fiscal policies and their impact on doctors' clinical behaviour in China's public health sector. *Policy and Society* 25(1): 109–132.

Zeng, Yanbing, Ying Wang, Jun Lu, Fengshui Chang, Xiaohong Li, Mei Sun, Li Luo, Hong Liang, and Mo Hao. 2011. Niuqu de buchang jizhi kunrao yiliao jigou fazhan 30 nian (Distorted compensation mechanisms frustrated the development of medical institutions for 30 years). *Zhongguo weisheng ziyuan (China Health Resources)* 14(1): 50–51, & 56.

Zhou, Enlai. 1952. Zhongyang Renmin Zhengfu Zhengwu Yuan guanyu quanguo geji renmin zhengfu, dangpai, tuanti ji suoshu shiye danwei he guojia gongzuo renyuan shixing gongfei yiliao yufang de zhishi (Directive of the State Council of the Central People's Government on implementing public-funded medicine and prevention for state workers employed by people's governments at all levels, parties, associations and their institutional work units). *Renmin ribao (People's Daily)*, 28 June, 1.

CHAPTER 2

Socialist Medicine and Theories of Informal Payments

Informal payments are endemic in many healthcare systems around the world, including some developed countries and regions, but academic interests have overwhelmingly focused on post-socialist transitional economies, where the phenomenon is considered a major threat to equality and efficiency in healthcare delivery, and an impediment to health reform and transition. Numerous studies have been carried out to gauge and explain the phenomenon in these countries. Generally speaking, the research of informal payments can be divided into two periods—those conducted before the early 1990s, and those done after. The distinction lies in the perspectives that researchers employed to examine the phenomenon. Before the early 1990s, scholars of the FSU looked into the problem from the perspective of the sociology of professions with a focus on the political institutions and power relations in its authoritarian or totalitarian healthcare systems. In the post-socialist period up to present, economic and policy perspectives dominate the studies, which tend to analyze the economic institutions that give rise to the practice and its policy implications.

My analysis draws on both traditions, and endeavors to connect and extends them in an attempt to provide a more comprehensive understanding of the phenomenon in China in particular, if not on a broader scale. It begins with a premise that the prevalence of informal payment is predominantly contributable to the particular power relations between major actors in the Chinese healthcare system and has its roots in both the institutional legacy inherited from the pre-reform era and institutional changes brought about by the economic reforms instigated in 1978. In this chapter, I will first

© The Author(s) 2017   29
J. Yang, *Informal Payments and Regulations in China's Healthcare System*,
DOI 10.1007/978-981-10-2110-7_2

elaborate and compare the two traditions, and then contextualize my own study in the extant scholarship.

SOCIOLOGY OF WESTERN PROFESSIONS

The medical profession in a socialist state shares the same knowledge basis with its counterpart in the West, but the social, economic, and political institutions related to the functioning of the profession are significantly different from those in an open and democratic society. The difference is widespread, from the education, organization, and employment of medical professionals, the position of the profession in the political and the economic systems, to the relationship between the profession, the state, and the patient. The difference is largely attributable to the dichotomies in the political and power structures, ideology, and economic development in the two types of polity. In an open society, particularly in Anglo-American countries, the medical profession enjoys considerable autonomy and power in technical, economic, and political terms and high social prestige. In a socialist state such as the FSU and China, however, the profession is not as highly regarded and does not have as much autonomy and power. The fundamental difference in the power structure is decisive to the rise, spread, and governance of informal payments in former socialist countries, and red packets in China in particular.

Students of the medical profession in the Soviet Union drew on sociological theories of professions to analyze the institutions and power structures that produced informal payments, but they had to make modification, as the theories were developed to explain the social process of professionalization in the West in particular. Here I shall first look at the theories about professions in the West in order to provide a reference point for the apprehension of the theories of the medical profession in the Soviet Union.

Professionalization is one of the key features of modern Western society. As Parsons (1954 [1939]) noted it, "many of the most important features of our society are to a considerable extent dependent on the smooth functioning of the professions" (p. 34). Bell (1999) predicted in the 1970s the coming of a post-industrial society, and stated that professional and technical class would be the largest and predominant occupational group in the future, surpassing the working class. Perkin (1989) even termed post-industrial society as professional society, arguing that the developed world has entered such society which distinguished itself by its reliance on human capital produced by education and strategies of social exclusion.

Up to the mid-twentieth century, the sociology of professions was dominated by functionalism influenced by Durkheim, who claimed professions played vital roles in the economic and political arenas of a society. Economically, Durkheim criticized classical economists for their encouragement of unregulated competition and pursuit of self-interest which caused instability in society. He argued that only professions, due to their tendency to common morality and collegiality, and their comparative stability derived from homogeneous identity and shared interests bestowed on them by the division of labor offered the cure to the evil of modern economy. Professions, being the focus of a moral life, would create close associations between individuals, forcing them to think beyond themselves and taking into account social needs and social interests (Durkheim 1957, p. 16). "[T] his adherence to some thing that goes beyond the individual, and to the interests of the group he belongs to, is the very source of all moral activity" (ibid., p. 24).

Politically, Durkheim claimed that the French democratic system, whose foundation was influenced by Rousseau's theories on democracy, could not function properly because the state was in direct contact with individuals. Such a democracy had two risks. On the one hand, the state could be reduced to an entity merely reflecting the sentiments and ideas of the majority of individuals, losing its own identity and transcendent aims. On the other hand, the risk was also high that the state, due to the impossibility of communicating with and catering to the interests of every individual effectively, was likely to be dominated by a minority of the population. As a result, the interests of the majority of individuals were ignored, and those of the ruling minority were imposed on the majority. To redress the malaise of this type of democracy, an intermediary social structure was needed. As social developments had rendered regional groups less and less relevant as suitable voting groups, professions became more and more pertinent as a bulwark "to prevent the State from tyrannizing over individuals," and "individuals from absorbing the State" (Durkheim 1957, p. 106).

According to Durkheim, professions thus had two major functions in the society. Economically, they provided an urgently needed morality to the economic order so that self-interest could be regulated and disciplined, and peace could be brought to individuals under the roof of a collectivity (Durkheim 1957, p. 24). Politically, professions constituted the major part of an intermediary structure between individuals and the state to counterbalance the power of both in a democratically political life.

Durkheim's concept of professions is broad, including not only ordinary occupations and professions, but also guilds and corporative industrial bodies, as long as they form certain types of communities. In the late nineteenth century and early twentieth century when Durkheim lectured on professions (Kubali 1957), professions were not fully developed in France. That is why Durkheim strongly advocated the revival of professions and vehemently refuted the idea that professions, like their forefather guilds, were no longer relevant to modern society (Durkheim 1957).

In the early twentieth century, professions experienced strong development in Britain. Carr-Saunders and Wilson, in their seminal work *The Professions*, investigated the development of major professions and main aspects of this occupational category. They came to similar conclusions as Durkheim about the social and economic functions of professions. In the first place, professions were regarded as politically stabilizing elements in the society. Professional associations generated "modes of life, habits of thought, standards of judgement which render them centres of resistance to crude forces which threaten steady and peaceful evolution" (Carr-Saunders and Wilson 1933, p. 497). The crude forces that the authors were particularly worried about were the destruction brought about by revolutions as happened in America and Russia (ibid.). Even universal suffrage was only symbolic and could not guarantee genuine democracy. As they argued, the voting power of individual citizens was only a minor part of a citizen's political responsibility. A firmer democracy relied more on a citizen "as an element in a worthy public opinion on the issue of his specialty or occupation" (Carr-Saunders and Wilson 1933, pp. 499–500). That is, professional persons could make more valuable contribution to democracy based on their professional knowledge than on their voting power. However, such stabilizing function had to be rooted in the freedom of association. As they argued, free associations were central to professionalism and provided counterbalance to the oppressive nature of industrial organizations.

Secondly, professional morality was also emphasized as a defining feature in Carr-Saunders and Wilson's work. They pointed out that the obligation to serve whenever called upon without discrimination was widely recognized among professions in Britain. "When a man becomes a member of a profession, he undertakes an honourable calling. His duty is to serve the interests of the public" (Carr-Saunders and Wilson 1933, p. 421). In the professional world, "[t]he whole commercial attitude is condemned" (ibid., p. 430). Professionals were obliged to "give only the best service and to subordinate all personal considerations to the interests of the client" (ibid., p. 422). As a result, personal indifference to profit was perceived as a defining characteristic of professionalism. Like Durkheim, Carr-Saunders and Wilson believed that such morality would provide the necessary remedy to profit-driven business models. They were even optimistic that with the professionalization of business management in the future, administration of large concerns would be separated from their ownership, and professionalized administrators would be able to concentrate on the efficiency of management without much concern about profit (ibid., pp. 492–493).

Thirdly, due to their service orientation, a typical professional practitioner had to be a freelancer who set up business alone or form partnership with a small number of other practitioners to attract clients (Carr-Saunders and Wilson 1933, p. 446). Large bureaucratic organizations were particularly dismissed as incompatible with professional ideals. Organizations, particularly in the form of companies, not only were oppressive in nature, but also separated practitioners from their clients and diverted their loyalty to the company. British professions believed, it was said, that loyalty and direct service to clients lay at the basis of professional ethics (ibid., p. 447).

T.H. Marshall (1963 [1939]) noticed that the development of social services in Britain in the 1930s had changed the work patterns of the professions. More and more professions were assimilated into employment and worked as salaried employees in the public sector serving the community rather than individual clients. Unlike Carr-Saunders and Wilson who idealized individualistic freelance practice, Marshall believed that professions continued to play an important role in the political structure of the state even if they were assimilated into social services. The assimilation, according to Marshall, was a two-way process. On the one hand, the state exerted control over the professions. On the other hand, the professions professionalized social services, rendering the politicians' voice less relevant in the planning and operation of the services. Whether the professions worked freelance or were in employment, as Marshall pointed out, was no longer a defining character.

In response to the charge that the professions used code of ethics to disguise their pursuit for pecuniary gains, Marshall argued that ethical codes did not demand the professional to be indifferent to money and to be unambitious to extend their business. Echoing Carr-Saunders and Wilson, Marshall believed the major difference between the professions and the commercial world lay in that the former placed the welfare of their clients before pecuniary gains. "The professional man ... does not work in order to be paid: he is paid in order that he may work. Every decision he takes in the course of his career is based on his sense of what is right, not on his estimate of what is profitable" (Marshall 1963 [1939], p. 151). Commercialism was thus the natural foe of professionalism in private life (ibid., p. 162). Because of their indifference to material gains and their service orientation, Marshall bestowed on the professions the responsibility of organizing social efficiency and finding "for the sick and suffering democracies a peaceful solution of their problems" (Marshall 1963 [1939], p. 170).

Talcott Parsons (1954 [1939]) did not accept altruism and indifference to self-interest as the defining feature of the professions. He argued that the problem of self-interest was institutional rather than motivational. In this sense, doctors were not particularly more motivated by altruistic goals than business people in their services and their career. Because of the institutional norms governing the professions, however, doctors were compelled to place service to the society before the consideration of personal gains. That is, altruism was institutionalized in the professions so that professionals were bound to be rather than motivated to be altruistic.

Parsons did not deny the great functional significance of "disinterested-ness" to the modern professions, but he pointed out that the commonalities that the professions shared with other occupational groups, such as business and government, were more outstanding than the problem of self-interest. The institutional patterns determined that the three occupational groups shared common grounds in terms of rationality, functional specificity, and universalism. All the three relied on rationality in their work, performed specific function rather than diffused function, and emphasized universalism rather than particularism in social relationships.

Early sociologists tended to consider professions in terms of their relations to other social and political actors, and identify what functions they performed to make society stable. In the 1950s and 1960s, some functionalists turned their attention to the process of professionalization, looking at how aspiring occupations attempted to lift their status to professions and how professions interacted with the larger society and with other emerging professions. Their studies usually began with providing a list of traits of the professions in an attempt to identify what professions were and how they were different from ordinary occupations. William Goode is regarded as a prime advocate of this traits approach (Macdonald 1995). After surveying existing definitions of the term "profession" from a variety of sources, he specified two core characteristics of a profession; namely, "a prolonged training in a body of abstract knowledge, and a collectivity or service orientation" (Goode 1960, p. 903). Derived from the core traits were the autonomy, monopoly, strong political power in state and national political arenas, and high prestige and incomes that the professions enjoyed. Goode argued that a profession gained autonomy by proving to the society its ability to police itself, and was granted monopoly by showing that it was the "sole master of its special craft and that its decisions are not to be reviewed by other professions" (p. 903). The autonomy and monopoly that the larger society granted the professions was the corollary of their ability to demonstrate self-discipline and their mastery of a body of special knowledge and craft. Unlike previous sociologists, Goode did not take the service orientation and the altruism for granted. He argued that the power of the professions was a temptation for the practitioner to exploit the client, but the community of the profession refused to do so and exercised social controls over its members to ensure they did not do so in order to win the respect and trust of the larger society. In this sense, service orientation was a professionalization strategy rather than something natural to the profession.

Bernard Barber (1963), a follower of Parsons, took an even more mechanic approach toward the traits of the professions. He enumerated four essential traits: a body of "generalised and systematic knowledge"; "primary orientation to the community interest rather than to individual self-interest"; self-control through codes of ethics; and "a system of rewards (monetary and honorary) that is primarily a set of symbols of work achievement and thus ends in themselves, not means to some end of individual self-interest" (p. 672). Like Goode, he regarded the first two traits as the fundamental while the other two as derivative. That is, the autonomy and the system of rewards were corollary to generalized knowledge and service orientation. According to Barber, since the professions were more concerned about public interests than individual interests, members should be rewarded in various forms. While non-monetary rewards were an important form of recognition of their achievements, sufficient monetary income seemed more important for professionals to maintain the lifestyle and prestige for which other honors had positioned them (Barber 1963).

The logic of the functionalists and the trait theorists can be summarized as follows: because the professions command bodies of highly specialized knowledge which are of great value to and are much needed by the society, and because they are dedicated to the service of the public above and beyond their personal interests and gains, they are granted prestige, authority, and power which provide them not only with decent monetary rewards but also exclusive control over their own affairs against lay interference from both the general public and the state. However, the tendency of the functionalism, and especially the trait theory, to idealize the social functions of the professions, or to focus overwhelmingly on the "ideal type" of professions, was criticized as "ahistorical," failing to understand their "power relations in society—their sources of power and authority and the ways in which they use them" (Johnson 1972, p. 18). The trait theory was particularly criticized for the "adoption of the profession's own self-advertisement" (Freidson 1994, p. 3).

In the early 1970s, sociologists shifted their attention to the examination of the social processes that lead to the formation of the abovementioned attributes, and assessed the validity of the claims made by the functionalists and trait theorists. The publication of Eliot Freidson's *Profession of Medicine* in 1970 has been widely acknowledged as a groundbreaking work (Daniel 1990; Larson 1977). The work (Freidson 1970), which took what was later termed as a "power" approach to analyze the relations between the medical profession and the state (Freidson 1994), challenged the validity of the distinctiveness of the fundamental traits put forward by the trait theory; namely, prolonged training in a body of specialized and abstract knowledge and service orientation. With regard to the first criterion, Freidson pointed out that in fact there were no clear agreement among established and aspiring professions on the length and the degrees of specialization and abstractness of the contents of training. The three traditional professions of medicine, law, and the ministry varied significantly on the three dimensions, while some occupations, like nursing and pharmacy which were denied the status of professions, were not particularly inadequate in terms of the content and duration of training. What was critical here was not training as such, according to Freidson, but occupational autonomy and control over training (Freidson 1970, p. 79).

The service orientation was more problematic. If it referred to the orientation of individual members of an occupation, then, there was simply no empirical evidence to answer such questions as "what proportion of professionals manifests a service orientation and with what intensity"; "the degree to which a service orientation is more intense and more widely distributed among professionals than other orientations"; and "whether the distribution and intensity of a service orientation among professionals is greater than that among other types of workers" (Freidson 1970, p. 81). If service orientation was considered as an institutional attribute of a profession, then such a characteristic could be deliberately created. As Freidson put it:

The profession's service orientation is a public imputation it has successfully won in a process by which its leaders have persuaded society to grant and support its autonomy. Such imputation does not mean that its members more commonly or more intensely subscribe to a service orientation than members of other occupations. (Freidson 1970, p. 82; italics original)

If prolonged training in specialized knowledge and service orientation were not unique to the professions, then what was the defining character of a profession? It was legitimate, organized autonomy, as Freidson claimed, that distinguished a profession from an ordinary occupation. Such autonomy, in its essence, was the right to allow a profession to control its own work. The autonomy covered a broad spectrum, from a wholesome control of the social and economic organization of professional work at one extreme, as manifested in the medical profession of the USA, to the mere control of the technical core of the professional work without much control of the economic and administrative terms at the other extreme, as manifested in the Soviet medicine (Freidson 1970, pp. 39–43). For a profession, as long as it controlled the technique and was "free of the technical evaluation and control of other occupations in the division of labor, its lack of ultimate freedom from the state, and even its lack of control over socio-economic terms of work do not significantly change its essential character as a profession" (Freidson 1970, pp. 24–25). That is, "autonomy of technique is at the core of what is unique about the profession" (p. 45). It is in this sense that the medical profession of the Soviet Union is comparable with that in the USA and other types of polities.

Apparently, autonomy is the source of professional power, be it broad or limited. Then how does a profession establish its authority and derive its power from that authority? According to Freidson, professional authority does not lie in its claim to a body of arcane knowledge and its service orientation. "Professions are *deliberately* granted autonomy" (p. 72) by persuading the elite segment of the society of their values, competence, and virtues. Not only can service orientation be "deliberately created to persuade politically important figures of the virtues of the occupation" (p. 82), but the training can also be deliberately created to persuade the elite and the public of its importance (p. 79). In a Western society as represented by the USA and partially by the Britain, the success in persuasion not only granted the medical profession control over its technique, but also social and economic positions and reward that make it a powerful player in the social, political, and economic structure of the country. In the Soviet

Union, although the medical profession did not achieve as broad autonomy and power as its counterparts in the West, it nevertheless controlled the technical core of its work and exerted significant power in the bureaucracy of medicine (Freidson 1970). In a nutshell, in the West, the medical profession, and professions in general terms, has the autonomy to control both the professional technique and the social and economic organization of its work, while the Soviet medical profession could only control the technical core of its work.

Regardless of the source of the autonomy and power, sociologists discussed in the preceding texts agree that professions in Western societies enjoy tremendous power in their social, economic, and political structure. Evidence to support such agreement is abundant. Carr-Saunders and Wilson highly commended the service orientation and indifference to personal interest of the British professions, but they also elaborated on how the British Medical Association (BMA) resorted to collective bargaining and blacklisting to ensure its members get better paid when the National Health Insurance Bill was introduced in 1911. For example, the BMA refused to publish in the *British Medical Journal* any advertisements for posts of medical officers in services and under local authorities, and of practitioners under the National Health Insurance scheme, and warned its members against applying any positions if the status and pay were not disclosed or did not meet the scale of minimum salaries decided by the BMA. Its strategies were very successful, forcing some local authorities which did not disclose salary or offered lower salaries for medical posts to advertise in the lay press and eventually unable to attract any applications from qualified doctors (Carr-Saunders and Wilson 1933, pp. 98–99). The public thus viewed the BMA as governed by self-regarding motives and concentrating "too exclusively upon the material rewards of its members" (p. 102). The Fabian Society accused the BMA of always "considering the private pockets of the doctors who are their members" (p. 101). But the general practitioners who were members of the BMA benefited significantly from the collective power manifest in the BMA's negotiation and bargaining with the government and enjoyed high incomes and social status that their knowledge and skills did not match (p. 99).

Today, even though the vast majority of British doctors rely on the National Health Service for a career and remuneration, institutions exist to protect the interest of the profession so that doctors enjoy relatively high levels of income from the state, despite the state's "virtually monopsonistic power as the purchaser of doctor's services" (Ryan 1989, p. 19). The BMA continues to be a major regulatory body and negotiator on medical pay and market protection, while the General Medical Council (GMC), which was established under the Medical Act in 1858 and has long been dominated by elite doctors, is a state-approved self-regulatory professional institution controlling the admission, behavior, and disciplining of all doctors (Moran and Wood 1993). In Australia, the MediCare crisis in the 1980s also demonstrated the bargaining power of the Australian medical profession in its negotiation with the Commonwealth Government and its ability to bring the government to its knees (Daniel 1990). The incidents are perfect examples of the functioning of negotiation and bargaining between a profession and the state in the public sphere in a Western society.

Gift-giving, which is common in the patient–doctor relationship in the Western healthcare systems (Lyckholm 1998), is also indicative of the power of the medical professions in these societies. Although gifts in Western healthcare systems are very unlikely to be on the same scale as informal payments in China, and in the CEE and FSU countries, evidence indicates that they are by no means rare. Andereck and Weijer point out the "increasing tendency of hospitals to attract donor money with promises such as 'access to the best.'" "The implication here is that sizable donation will result in special attention or the ability to 'jump the queue.'" He continues to note that physicians are also involved in this practice, which may be detrimental to the healthy relationship and trust between the doctor and patient (Andereck and Weijer 2001, p. 76). In Huw Morgan's brief account of gifts that a British GP may receive during his or her long-term service in a place, three categories of gifts are identified. The gifts of the first category represent genuine expressions of gratitude. The second category is called routine gifts given in the festival seasons, such as Christmas. What is of concern is the third category, in which the gift is "used as some kind of bribe or pay off" (Morgan 1996). "The classical use of the manoeuvre is when an unnecessary home visit has been asked for" (ibid.). Many other reports also indicate the widespread presence of manipulative gifts in the predominantly Anglo-American healthcare systems (Drew et al. 1983; Gabbard and Nadelson 1995; Morse 1992).

The motivations that prompt a patient in Anglo-American societies to give doctors gifts overlap to a significant extent with those that impel a patient in the former and current socialist countries to give informal payments to doctors, although probably on a much lesser scale. What is striking is how the issue, be it gifts or informal payments, is dealt with in the Western societies. As the medical profession enjoys tremendous autonomy and associational power, the issue is largely treated as an internal one within the profession. As a result, doctors taking gifts from patients is not considered as a serious breach of ethical practice. For instance, the Code of Medical Ethics published by the American Medical Association (AMA) recognizes that "[g]ifts that patient offer to physicians are often an expression of appreciation and gratitude or a reflection of cultural tradition, and can enhance the patient-physician relationship" (American Medical Association 2004, p. 301). The Code does warn AMA members against gifts or cash which patients offer to secure preferential treatment, but claims that "[t]here is no definitive rules to determine when a physician should or should not accept a gift" (ibid.). Of course, this autonomy is not completely unchallenged. For example, in 1989–1990 and 2000, the US Congress "threatened punitive legislation to discourage abuses of gifts," but the profession was allowed to respond by tightening internal discipline and conducting educational campaign for its members (Greene 2000).

In summation, whatever the views the sociologists have about the sources and processes through which professions acquire power and authority, about their ethics and service orientation, and about the organization of professions, they take as an explicit or implicit departing point the existence of an intermediary social and political structure between individuals and the state in the West. Through this structure, professions are able to act collectively, negotiating and bargaining with the state, persuading the public and the elite, and influencing other organizations and occupations in order to protect and advance their own interests. It is this structure that allows the medical profession to exert countervailing power against the state and dominance over its clients and subordinate occupations. By the same token, informal payments in an open society are dealt with in a way that is completely different from that in an authoritarian society where such a structure is either non-existent or in a very preliminary stage, as demonstrated in such socialist countries as the Soviet Union.

THE MEDICAL PROFESSION IN THE SOVIET UNION

Sociological theories developed from the studies of professions in Western societies, particularly in the Anglo-American societies, seem inadequate to explain professions in socialist countries. In terms of medicine, the profession in both the Western and socialist countries, as well in all types of polities, is established on an almost entirely identical knowledge base (Freidson 1970). Professional activities at clinical level follow similar rules and standards developed on the roughly identical scientific principles. In the Soviet Union, the specialization of medicine was apparently different from the West due to the unique Soviet view toward "medico-scientific knowledge and skills" (Ryan 1978, p. 48), but the knowledge base (especially its arcane nature) and medical skills were not dissimilar from those in the West (Field 1957, 1967). Furthermore, the emergence of medical professions before the establishment of socialism in Russia was inspired by the profession's development in the West, and they were organized in a way similar to their counterparts in the West, and thus enjoyed similar power, autonomy, and prestige (Field 1967, 1976, 1988, 1991).

It is in terms of the knowledge base and history that comparisons can be drawn between the professions in the two types of polities, and sociological theories developed from the examination of the medical profession in the West are not completely irrelevant to the conditions of medical professions in socialist countries. These theories, however, are apparently limited in their explanatory power, because the political and economic structure of a socialist country is entirely different from, if not opposite to, that of the West. In the West, the medical profession emerged and developed in a market economy and democratic political system where open negotiation and collective bargaining are a norm, while in a socialist country, medicine is organized in a command economy and in a political environment of totalitarianism or authoritarianism where public space and freedom are significantly limited. In spite of the fact that socialist states in Europe as well as China have undergone market-oriented economic reform since the 1970s, and the Soviet Union and its bloc also embarked on democracy-oriented political reform, which led to the collapse of socialist ruling in these countries, the socialist legacy is still strongly felt. In China, socialism is continuously the official ideology of the country, and authoritarianism continues to underscore the political structure.

Fortunately, the limited applicability of the theories of the sociology of professions to socialist regimes is compensated by theories developed by scholars of the health system of the Soviet Union who drew on both the sociology of professions and studies of the Soviet political, economic and social systems. These scholars, represented by Mark G. Field, took into consideration the effect of the state ideology on the organization of medical profession and the power relations between the major actors in healthcare. Their studies showed that except for the common knowledge base, socialist medicine was virtually antithetical to the medicine in the West in all other aspects, especially the social and economic organization of the profession. In the first place, in the state ideology of the Soviet Union, the medical profession was not trusted as service oriented and indifferent to personal interests. Secondly, the entire medical profession was nationalized and bureaucratized. Doctors lost self-control but at the same time gained administrative and executive power embedded in their posts as state bureaucrats. Thirdly, as salaried employees of the state, powerless Soviet doctors did not have control over the economic terms of their work and were not well paid.

Ideology and the Soviet Medical Profession

In the FSU, the state ideology occupied the central position in the political system and shaped the policies and activities in almost every political, economic, and social sphere. The rise or fall of professions was determined by the central government and the communist party, according to ideology and centrally determined social, political, and economic agenda.

In the domain of healthcare, Field (1967) identified two levels of ideology. "There is, first and foremost, the basic, official ideology upon which the regime theoretically rests" (p. 30). This basic and official ideology was what was called Marxism–Leninism. "Second … is the 'ideology' of Soviet medicine, which might briefly be described as a set of principles derived, for the greater part, from Marxism-Leninism, but adapted and modified to serve as the ideological foundations of the Soviet health service and to justify and support that service" (p. 31).

Although not explicitly specified, Field further divided the "ideology" of Soviet medicine into two levels: one is the fundamental, and the other the operative. At the fundamental level, the keystone was the communist commitment to "serving the people."[1] This foundation, as Field (1967) pointed out, was established on the basis of vehement criticism of bourgeois medicine, which was blamed for its exploiting and oppressing nature and its ignorance of the health needs of the working class.

It was on the basis of this ideological keystone of "serving the people" that a set of eight operative principles were established to guide the setting of priorities, the making of health policies, the organization of health and medical services, and government and individual actions and activities in the Soviet healthcare system, or the *Semashko* system. Under these principles, public health and medical services were rendered the responsibility of the Soviet state and developed "within the framework of a single plan" (Field 1967, p. 44). The highly centralized healthcare system excluded private medical care and prioritized prevention. Health and medical services were delivered to the population at no direct cost (Field 1967, pp. 43–48). Healthcare was completely socialized. The entire healthcare resources, including human resources, were nationalized, centralized, and distributed according to centrally made plans. Medical professionals became cogs in the national healthcare machine. Meanwhile, despite being provided free healthcare services, citizens could only seek medical services in a single nationalized and centralized healthcare system where they had little choice but to succumb to the control of state medicine. The behaviors, choices, and even outlooks of both medical professionals and patients were hemmed in by the state.

A new type of doctor–patient relationship was hence established as guided by the ideology. As with medicine in the West, socialist medicine was claimed to be service oriented, but the latter usually claimed service to a much wider population. To this end, doctors were required in ideology to serve, rather than the limited scope of their clients or direct community, the entirety of the people, especially the workers and peasant classes who were usually underprivileged and poor and had limited access to medical services when the Soviet Union was established. To ensure that the medical profession understood the significance of the socialization of medicine and willingly materialized in practice the ideology of serving the people, doctors were required to be not only technically competent, but also politically learned in Marxism–Leninism (Field 1967, p. 33). Field (1991) observed:

The centerpiece of this process [i.e., "socialization" of medicine] was the removal of "capitalistic" medical practice whose earmark was the private practice of medicine and the fee-for-service payment. Socialized medicine meant that the cash nexus between patient and doctor would be eliminated. The doctor would no longer be dependent on the patient for a livelihood and would thus not be tempted to treat only the rich, or to exploit patients through unnecessary services. The elimination of "commercialism" in medicine, the payment by society to the physician on a salaried and predictable fashion, would permit the physician to be concerned only with the medical aspects of the work. The physician need not be, any more, a "business person." (pp. 50–51)

The socialization of medicine and the nationalization of the medical profession in the Soviet Union, and understandably in other socialist countries, were devised to let doctors concentrate on the service side of their practice rather than the business side. Patients' concern about affordability and accessibility was also removed as medical services were distributed to them gratis according to centrally planned schemes. That was what service means in socialist ideology. Caring for the interests of the working people was the core of the communist ideology and the major source of legitimacy of the communist party of any socialist country. As Ryan (1978) noted, "It is an ideological imperative for the Soviet government to emphasize that it makes medical care available to the whole population free of charge at time of use" (p. 28). "In the Soviet Union ... official ideology is entirely hostile to the concept of a market in medical care" (ibid., p. 30).

The Power of the Powerless: The Position of the Medical Profession in the Soviet Union

The medical profession in the former Soviet Union was powerless in the profession–state relationship but wielded tremendous power in the patient–doctor relationship. Bureaucratization of medicine in the authoritarian political system was the major reasons behind the power position of doctors in Soviet medicine.

As discussed above, professions in democracies serve as an intermediary institution which possesses significant countervailing power against the state. The medical profession is a prime example of such power. But in socialist and authoritarian regimes, the social and political space for the existence and functioning of such intermediary institutions is extremely compressed if not non-existent. In terms of medicine, while the profession in the West usually assumes significant autonomy and exercises tremendous organizational and political power in its relationship with the state and the public, doctors in the Soviet Union, as well in other (former) socialist countries, were, and still are, politically and organizationally powerless. A striking feature of the political and economic systems of a totalitarian country such as the Soviet Union is the concentration of power and authority in the hands of a limited number of political elites. The power and authority are executed through highly bureaucratized political and governing structure. In this hierarchical power pyramid, resources, especially scarce resources, human and material, are allocated by those on the top of the pyramid according to centrally formulated plans to lower levels of power and function through a downward chain along the hierarchically administrative ladder (Field 1957, pp. 9–10). Those on lower levels are usually on the receiving end. Light (1995) observed:

State dominance ... stands for a situation perhaps like that in the former Soviet Union, where doctors are employees—with relatively low status and pay—of a delivery system designed by the state. They have little budgetary control and the budget is small, thus limiting professional elaboration, which is so critical to institutional elaboration and charismatic development. The state controls supply, most of the resources, and even the division of labour. The professionals in high office are political appointments whose job is to carry out the interest of the state, not the profession. The organized profession in this extreme, ideal-typical case is outlawed. (p. 28)

Corollary to the bureaucratization and nationalization of the medical profession is that collective negotiation and bargaining is nearly non-existent in the public sphere in a (former) socialist country. The state, or the ruling party to be exact, assumes the absolute power in almost every sphere of politics, economy, and everyday life. Direct and formal negotiation and bargaining with the state is not tolerated, because no other interest groups outside the Party-state, or bureaucratic system are allowed any meaningful space and autonomy to form and exercise substantial collective power to promote their interests through negotiating and bargaining with the state.

Before the Bolshevik Revolution in October 1917, Russian doctors' position in society was little different from that of their counterparts in the West. "Physicians saw themselves as professionals and experts, charged with important responsibilities, and enjoying a high regard and status among the population" (Field 1988, p. 183). Their associations, the most eminent of which was the Pirogov Society, gained considerable independence from the government and was able to exercise tremendous associational power over their members and against the Tsarist state. With the coming to power of the Bolsheviks and the establishment of the totalitarian regime, the power that the medical profession and its associations had enjoyed in the "old regime" was no longer tolerated by the new government. Medical associations "were dissolved on the familiar ground that they were 'counter-revolutionary'" (Field 1988, p. 184). From then on, the Soviet medical professions were subject to the full control of the state and never had any corporate power again. As Field (1988) puts it, "*all* Soviet physicians, regardless of their rank, are employees of the state, trained and remunerated by the state, and subject to its discipline and directives" (p. 188; italics original). In another place, Field (1991) stated:

... the Soviet medical profession does not constitute an articulate interest group. It is generally incapable of affecting the conditions under which it works (hours of work, or rate of pay, for instance). It is therefore unable to organize independently of the regime and to exert a collective will, or to challenge its employer, the state. As such, politically the medical profession is inert ... Politically, the medical profession has been emasculated, defanged, eliminated. (pp. 49–50)

The rationale behind the nationalization of medical human resources was to prevent doctors from being "tempted to treat only the rich, or to exploit patients through unnecessary services" (Field 1991, p. 50). Ideologically, doctors were supposed to serve the masses of the people. But in reality, we see a different picture. The doctor–patient relationship was not one of serving and being served, but one of "ruling" and being ruled. That is, a public medical professional was a holder of government medical office, which was embedded with both professional and bureaucratic authority and power. As government officials, doctors were responsible to the state and to their work-units. The arrangement of their employment did not necessitate them to be accountable for the patients' interests. The absolute dominating position of doctors was likely to turn ordinary patients' challenge of doctors' authority into challenges of not only the professional authority but also the state's authority. Under such circumstances, absolute obedience from patients was expected and evident, while irresponsibility, indifference, negligence, unresponsiveness, and bureaucracy toward patients were characteristic of public medical institutions. In this context, the new mode of payment, namely, dependence on the state for income, failed to produce the ideologically intended outcome. Patients did not receive "better or more attentive care" (Field 1991, p. 51). On the contrary, the state employment of the medical profession, although depriving the latter of any corporate power, conferred on doctors almost unchallenged professional and bureaucratic power at clinical level. They dominated not only other affiliated health occupations, such as nursing, but also non-elite patients and clients, that is, the populace. As state functionaries, they wielded mixed power of the state and the profession. Although this power cannot be used to challenge the state, it could well be used on most of the patients under the doctor's professional jurisdiction. Field (1988) notes that "the Soviet physician exercises over his patient and subordinates the kind of absolute power that would hardly be possible nowadays in other more pluralistic settings" (p. 189).

Field (1988) identified three elements in the power equation of the Soviet doctor. The first element was the usual jurisdictional authority entrusted to the bureaucratic professional. In essence, this is the same type of power exercised by bureaucrats generally, and by Soviet bureaucrats in particular, over those with whom they officially deal. In one sense, the bureaucratic power of the official over the client, customer, applicant, or patient may be seen as *compensation* for the lack of power and the subordination the bureaucrat experiences from his or her superiors. This situation apparently exists from top to bottom in Soviet society, including the medical sector (p. 189).

Field (1988) went on to note that in Czechoslovakia the "doctor-patient relationship was defined as a 'totalitarian' one, reflecting a 'totalitarian' society" (p. 189). This is exactly the state power and authority that were imparted in the medical bureaucratic positions that Freidson elaborated in the above.

The second element was the very "professional" authority that derived from the doctor's mastery of a body of esoteric knowledge and his or her capacity to intervene in a life-and-death situation. In the Soviet society, as well as in all other societies, "the physician is held to know more by virtue of his education and experience than the patient. Indeed, were it not for this asymmetry of knowledge, there would be no need to consult a medical specialist" (Field 1988, p. 190).

The third element was the emotional dependence of patients on doctors in a condition of illness and trauma. The dependence gave doctors more power over patients, and made the latter feel emotionally powerless and indebted to doctors' services. "Thus, the doctor/patient encounter is endowed with more affective meaning than that of most others" (Field 1988, p. 190).

The bureaucratic plus specialized power that doctors enjoyed was further strengthened in the Soviet Union by the suppression of patients' rights. Patients, usually in the position of a supplicant, did not, or were not allowed to, question doctors' authority, and were very much at the latter's mercy. In the Soviet scheme, "the customer or patient is rarely right" (Field 1988, p. 190). "At least, one does not find in the Soviet Union either a movement or organization dedicated to promote patients' rights, to challenge physicians' judgements, or to institute suits against them for malpractice..." (Field 1991, p. 54). The miserable situation of patients was compounded by doctors' inability to control their work terms. They had to see a large number of non-elite patients every day, "so that patients tend to be processed in an assembly-line fashion" (Field 1991, p. 51). "Given the powerful position of the physician vis-à-vis the patient and the press of work, it is not surprising that physicians are often criticized in the Soviet media for their rudeness and callousness" (Field 1988, p. 193). Field continued, "Soviet physicians have shown an extraordinary ability, bred in the bureaucratic crucible, to neglect the interests of their patients … this neglect takes the form of the indifference, 'nine-to-five medicine,' formalism, cruelty, and mercenary attitudes that are exhibited by the salaried Soviet doctors" (Field 1991, p. 51).

Low Salaries and Informal Payments

A direct fallout of the lack of corporative power and the absence of formal negotiation and bargaining mechanisms on the life of the majority of doctors in a socialist country is that the salaries paid to doctors are usually very low. Ryan (1989) stated:

> Since the economic interests of employees were deemed to be a reflection of the national interest as defined by the Party, there could be no place for wage bargaining. The salaries paid to Soviet doctors thus represent the Party's valuation of their services and, more generally, the degree of priority attaching to health care provision in a centrally-planned economy.

> Lacking the autonomy enjoyed by their colleagues in the West—and hence the opportunity to strike their own bargains over pay—Soviet doctors have received rises only when the authorities have seen fit to increase remuneration for all employees in this sector. By the same token, the timing of rises mirrors a government policy decision and not a widespread sense of frustration over pay among health care personnel (pp. 20–21).

Up to the late 1980s, the salaries for doctors had been lower than manual and blue-collar workers in heavy industry, manufacturing, and elsewhere (Ryan 1989, p. 21). In 1990, "average compensation for the salaried physician is only 70 percent of the average salary of a nonfarm worker" (Rowland and Telyukov 1991, p. 82).

Without collective bargaining power to negotiate with the state over salaries, doctors in (former) socialist countries usually have to settle down with whatever the state set for them. But the absence of bargaining power does not mean that the medical profession is powerless in all spheres. As medical bureaucrats, doctors dominate ordinary patients, which constitute the vast majority.[2] Their overwhelming power and authority in the doctor–patient relationship and their virtual role as bureaucrats open up a space for the abuse of the power. One form of the abuse is for doctors to require "gifts" from patients.

Ryan (1989) pointed out, "To restrict reference to official salary levels would be naïve in view of the abundant evidence that a variety of informal transactions have served to enhance a doctors' command over resources" (p. 25). To compensate the low incomes, doctors were involved in a so-called "envelope-passing medicine," requesting extra fees for medical services beyond those set by public health providers. Field (1991) reports that in the Soviet Union such under-the-table payments were so common that "74 percent of patients [had] resorted to such payment for medical attention" (p. 52). "Physicians openly solicit payments, particularly for surgical operations" (Field 1988, p. 194). Diagnosis and prescription may not be performed "according to criteria that are rooted in medical knowledge," but according to the means of the patient. The link between low wages and extortion of "gifts" was evidently recognized by Soviet officials in the late 1970s and the 1980s. Eduard Shevardnadze declared in a 1983 report about the Georgian healthcare system, "There is every justification for saying that many instances of bribe-taking, illegal private practice and outright violations of a doctor's duty remain in the shadows … Really it's no secret that, to speak frankly, wages for this category of workers are low …" (quoted in Ryan 1989, pp. 29 and 31).

While in the relationship with the state the medical profession was completely powerless, in the doctor–patient relationship, it was the patient who did not have much power. The official arrangement of the health service did not allow ordinary patients to choose their doctors, and the way that the health service was delivered. They were completely subordinate to doctors' clinical power and authority. In reality, doctors opposed giving patients the power to choose their doctors on the ground that patients did not have the knowledge to make the right choice (Field 1988). In this context, informal personal monetary contributions to doctors became one of the limited means for patients to buy some choosing power, to gain some levy to counterbalance doctors' clinical power and to exert influence on the latter. The informal payment met "the drive to have a choice, to gain some sense of control over the care received, to manipulate the bureaucracy, instead of the other way around" (Field 1991, p. 53). "Such payments, incidentally, may also express a belief that whatever is available free of charge is of no great value" (ibid.).

Now we can draw a picture of the power relations between the profession, the state, and the public (or patients, to be exact) in a (former) socialist state. On the one hand, the medical profession, lacking in organizational power to advocate and protect its interests in the face of the state, is subject to the government's control in particularly economic and work terms, as well as in almost every other aspect. No formal and open negotiation space and bargaining mechanisms is existent to allow the profession to counterbalance the state's intervention and control. As exemplified in the case of Soviet medicine, the political powerlessness of doctors was reflected in the fact that they were ideologically obliged to serve the people and the "fee-for-service" pattern of entrepreneurial medicine was replaced by the socialistic pattern of bureaucratic medicine. On the other hand, as public employees in government health agencies, their professional power was protected by the state. In fact, publicly employed health professionals in a socialist state could be regarded as an extension of state governance (Johnson 1995), with the state authority and power embedded in their public positions. This power and authority again did not allow individual patients to formally and openly negotiate anything more than the system bestowed on them. The absolute, unchallenged power and authority of Soviet doctors rendered patients the most powerless in the health bureaucratic system.

Informal payment, which is fee-for-service in nature, turns the "socialistic" doctor–patient relationship back into a "capitalistic" one and poses a threat to the legitimacy of the rule of the Communist Party which claims in ideology that the party and all its organs serve the interests of the people. In practice, the informal payment is supposed to empower patients in their relationship with doctors, offsetting doctors' bureaucratic practice and increasing their accountability and responsiveness. It is in this sense that informal payment is extremely important in the understanding of the doctor–patient relationship in a (former) socialist country.

The sociological perspective discussed above presents a clear analytical framework to explain the emergence of informal payments in the Soviet healthcare system. The politically powerless and economically underprivileged medical profession is subordinate to the power and command of the Party-state, which has an ideological obligation to serve the people. In the meantime, the medical profession possesses tremendous bureaucratic and professional power and authority that are almost unchallenged by their patients. In such a context, corruption seems inevitable. Informal payments become a natural result of the Soviet power structure.

The sociology of the Soviet medical profession reveals that the informal payment was inexorable fallout of the power interactions between the medical profession, the state, and patients, but it was yet to investigate the question of how the informal payment had in turn influenced the power interactions between these actors. The students of the former Soviet Union seem to have balked at the macro level of the phenomenon. The corpus of the sociological studies of Soviet medicine produced little discussion on how the payments were transacted at clinical level, and how the transactions influenced the power relationship between doctors and patients at micro levels. A probable reason for the dearth of scholarship in this area was attributable to the apparent difficulty of doing this kind of research in a totalitarian/authoritarian society. Another puzzle that needs answer is how the informal payment is regulated in a totalitarian/authoritarian system. In the Soviet Union, taking informal payments from patients was illegal and politically incorrect. For this reason, the regime must have some regulatory systems investigating, monitoring, and controlling professional graft. Then how did the system work and why did it fail to reign in the practice? Furthermore, with the transition into market economy and the adoption of democracy in the political systems, former socialist countries in the CEE and FSU have undergone tremendous institutional changes which have reshaped the power structures in all types of social and political relationships. The establishment of market economy, for instance, has particularly strong implications for the power relations between medical professionals and patients, as patients' rights and their power as consumers of health services have been increasingly recognized. But the sociological study of the Soviet medicine failed to extend into the post-socialist era and examine how the power relations between doctors, patients, and the state have evolved from both old and new institutions, and how the relations have helped perpetuate the practice of informal payments in a new institutional setting. The study of informal payments in the post-socialist era assumes a different line with overwhelming emphasis on behavioral, economic, and policy implications of the practice in the CEE and FSU countries.

INFORMAL PAYMENTS IN TRANSITION ECONOMIES: THE ECONOMIC AND POLICY PERSPECTIVES

With the fall of the communist regimes in the Soviet Union and its bloc in the CEE, studies of the medical profession in socialist countries and informal economic activities in the healthcare systems from the analytical perspective of the sociology of professions have become less articulate. Instead, the problem of informal payments has been increasingly addressed as economic and policy issues in transition economies.

From 1989 to 1990, socialism in these countries collapsed almost overnight. Since then the CEE and FSU countries have undergone profound transformation from socialist to democratic polities (Bunce 1999). The transition of healthcare systems in these countries, however, has not necessarily followed a democratizing trajectory. A major problem that many of these countries have long faced is the decrease in health investment due to the poor performance in economy, the decline in state revenues, and commercialization of healthcare. The state budget is no longer able or available to fund universal health coverage, leaving health facilities relying more and more on user fees for operative funding and payroll. Meanwhile, the state monopoly in healthcare resources is yet to be liberalized. Several studies report that in at least some of these countries, strict state regulation of pricing of medical services is still enforced and has kept the prices of medical services below costs (Pažitný and Zajac 2005). Underpaid or even not paid health professionals have to resort to informal payments for basic or extra incomes.

Informal payments are widespread, but research on the issue is extremely inadequate, due to its informal nature. In many countries, informal payments have been defined as a form of corruption and claimed as illegal. As a result, participants in this informal economy are reluctant to inform any serious research, even if they are the victims of the practice (Gaal et al. 2006). To date, the majority of the limited research on the phenomenon is exploratory in nature.

Based on the predominantly exploratory investigations, several scholars have made attempts to look at the issue from a more generalized perspective (Ensor 2004; Thompson and Witter 2000). "State capture" is one of the earliest theories about informal payments. Lewis (2000, 2002) defines informal payments in healthcare as a form of systemic corruption, although she readily admits that in the FSU countries in CA, grateful patients rewarding doctors with gifts is a long-standing practice. Lewis argues that due to market failure, government intervention in healthcare provision is necessary, but she points out that, as there is an excessive supply of doctors in this region, and the governments are either unwilling or unable to reduce the capacity, government intervention turns healthcare provision into government failures (Lewis 2000). In these countries, the public sector continues to enjoy a monopoly over healthcare services. The monopoly power, she states, "has assisted the state capture and state monopoly of health care sector" (ibid., p. 7). As doctors usually lead government health ministries and control and staff medical facilities, they can exert considerable influence on policy-making process to serve their interests and discourage competition. The state capture is exacerbated by lack of accountability evidenced by the low possibility of being caught and the light punishments for misconduct. In the CEE and FSU countries, the monopoly power is apparently derived from the fact that the medical profession is by large a governmental organ. As Lewis suggests, doctors in public employment are public servants. Their public posts are embedded with state power.

Lewis's proposition about the powerful doctors who "can exert considerable influence on the policy-making process to serve their interests" does not seem to conform to the findings by other students of the Soviet Union healthcare system, and is logically flawed. If doctors can exercise considerable power collectively, it is reasonable to believe they should raise their incomes and/or legalize informal payments through formal, official channels, rather than continuing the distortion of fees. At least they can pressure the state into paying doctors normal salaries, which cannot be guaranteed in some CEE and FSU countries. The very fact that low-paid doctors have to rely on informal payments for a living in some former socialist countries belies their power to influence policy-making. It is true that in the (former) socialist countries government agencies of health administration are usually staffed by officials with a medical background or even practicing doctors. As health officials, however, they do not necessarily represent the interests of doctors. They work for the government, not the profession. Defining informal payment merely as a form of corruption represents an over-simplistic approach toward the issue.

Peter Gaal and his colleagues (Gaal et al. 2006) disagree with Lewis over her definition of informal payments as a form of corruption. They argue that the situation surrounding the phenomenon is far more complicated than a simplified approach can capture. For example, informal payments to institutions often include such things as bringing one's own linen and food and paying for medicine out of pocket. These activities on the part of the patient can hardly be associated with corruption motivated by greedy public servants. Apart from the difficulty of pinpointing the legal nature of informal payments as corruption, they further point out that it is unfair to blame doctors for corruption if the state lets the profession down in the first place. In many of these countries, decreasing salaries and even non-payment are common. Underpaid or unpaid doctors have to leave the healthcare system if their access to informal payments is denied. Their "exit" will lead to the collapse of the healthcare system, and virtually no service will be available to the public. This is definitely not a desirable outcome. In opposition to Lewis's accusation against public doctors for beating the system, they argue that "it is the system (the government) that has beaten it first. Patients and doctors simply adapted to the rules of the game to survive" (Gaal et al. 2006, p. 270). Contrary to Lewis's view of deeming public doctors as public servants abusing the state authority and power embedded in their posts, Gaal and colleagues view the medical profession as a victim of government policies and the poor performance of the state economy, and developed the "inxit" theory to explain the phenomenon.

The theory of "inxit" (Gaal and McKee 2004b) is built on two key assumptions. "The first is that the underlying cause of the problem is shortage associated with the Semashko system" (p. 165). "The second key assumption is that informal payment is a reaction by dissatisfied patients and physicians to shortage—a manifestation of deteriorating organizational/system performance" (p. 165). Drawing on Stiglitz's theories, Gaal and McKee argue that health providers tend to exploit their monopolistic market position for extra profit and physicians tend to extract rent by "capitalizing information asymmetry" (ibid., p. 166). Meanwhile, the market deters those who cannot afford it from accessing healthcare. The situation necessitates government intervention, which can correct both problems through public finance.

Public finance, however, can lead to government failure in two aspects. Firstly, public finance is a good device to contain costs, but it can also result in inadequate provision of healthcare if that function goes too far. Using its monopolistic power, the state can decide the level of healthcare that is available to individuals. For the purpose of cost containment or other economic reasons, the state may be pressured or choose to reduce public finance and create shortage of supply. At the same time, public finance tends to keep doctors' salary low as a means of cost containment. Low salary in turn is likely to demoralize health professionals and lead to decline in performance and low satisfaction among doctors. Secondly, public finance is purported to ensure that everybody has access to healthcare, regardless of financial means. Patients are thus encouraged to over-consume medical services. If excessive demand is not met, shortage inevitably occurs. As a result, shortage becomes the economic hotbed of informal payments.

The shortage that Gaal and McKee discuss here is not one of provision of basic or primary services. Generally speaking, most (former) socialist countries, after decades of development in education, economy, and infrastructure, have the human and material resources to meet the demand for basic medical and health services. There are reports of overstaff and excess capacity in the healthcare systems of the CEE and CA countries (Lewis 2000). One of the achievements in healthcare that the FSU often showed off to the rest of the world was the number of doctors it had in absolute and relative terms (Ryan 1989). The shortage is in fact a shortage of quality. In Gaal and McKee's words, "shortage was manifested in diluted service quality" (Gaal and McKee 2004b, p. 172), or "performance decline" (ibid., p. 171).

Gaal and McKee argue that cost containment and excess demand do not necessarily lead to the emergence of informal payments. In this connection, Hirschman's "exit, voice and loyalty" theory is introduced to explain their second assumption. Facing low performance, Hirschman believes that doctors and patients are pressured into actions to find solutions. The solutions are summarized as "exit," "voice," and "loyalty." "Exit" refers to patients and doctors opting out of the public sector. For patients, this option includes seeking medical services in the private sector. For doctors, the option can be finding employment in other sectors. "Voice" refers to actions that patients and doctors take to articulate their dissatisfactions in order to pressure the authority to bring changes to the system. "Loyalty" is an inert option to get by with the system when "exit" is not available and "voice" is either useless or dangerous.

On the basis of Hirschman's three options, Gaal and McKee developed the concept of "inxit"—an option between "exit" and "voice." "It resembles voice inasmuch as the dissatisfied persons do not leave the organization (system) but seek to change its activities, not through open complaints, but using informal methods, such as payments or connections. These mechanisms resemble the exit option, insofar as they are depersonalised and secure benefits for only the persons concerned. Informal payments can be regarded as an exit mechanism, but within the organisation. Thus it is an informal/internal exit, hence the term 'inxit'" (Gaal and McKee 2004b, p. 167).

"Inxit" is therefore a private coping strategy for both patients and doctors in dealing with the shortage of quality in the system.

Informal payment transaction works on perceptions on both patients and doctors. Patients set a minimum but reasonable level of performance that they expect low-paid doctors to conduct and the expected level of service they want to get, and decide whether they want or have the means to pay the gap. On the other hand, low-paid doctors would determine the level of commitment and quality of their work in accordance with the level of their payment and very likely in comparison with the levels of payment, workloads, and work intensity of other occupations, and would formulate a price for extra services. If the patient's and the doctor's contemplation meets, the deal is sealed. Apparently, the mechanism works more closely to market principles, a subversion of the purpose and goal of government intervention.

Gaal and McKee go on to apply the "inxit" model to the healthcare system of Hungary. The system is described as an exclusive state monopoly over medical human resources, health insurance, and patient choices. The totalitarian regime created a closed system in which gives little room for public voices, and no formal bargaining channels. Both professionals and patients are not encouraged to complain. The Hungarian healthcare system has equity as its prime objective, but its financial system and investment policy could not afford the objective. The unrealistic objective and the investment reality reduce the healthcare to poor quality and prompt endemic informal activities within the system. The situation is aggravated by the lack of power of the profession in terms of setting their economic terms. Their salaries are kept low for political purposes and cost containment. However, the profession also possesses some countervailing power against the state monopoly. By using their low performance to meet patients' high expectations and rising demands for quality services, and by the state support of their professional monopoly over medical services, the profession can actually force the regime to tolerate informal activities, if it wants the system to run without challenging the ideology. While formal bargaining power and negotiation space for the profession and the patient do not exist, informal negotiation and bargaining mechanisms nevertheless operate well in the healthcare system.

Here we can see a connection between the "inxit" theory and the power theory developed by Mark Field and other scholars of the Soviet Union. "Exit" is only possible in a liberalized economy where there exists a private medical sector that is at least of the same magnitude and power as the public sector. In former socialist countries, private economy was ideologically discouraged. The private sector was either non-existent or, if there was some residue, was extremely insignificant. The state monopoly over medical resources and opportunities and the extremely immature private market made "exit" impractical. "Voice" is only possible when there are formal mechanisms for open negotiation, and there exist interest politics and collective bargaining. Again, as shown above, they did not exist in former socialist countries. In their transition periods, these countries continue to exhibit authoritarianism to various degrees. Formal and open negotiation space is still constrained, if not non-existent. In Gaal and McKee's words, "the regime left little room for the public's voice to be heard. The channels of voice were strictly controlled, and complaints were regarded as an assault against the ruling regime" (Gaal and McKee 2004b, p. 171). Under these circumstances, "loyalty" and "inxit" become the only options for both patients and doctors. While "loyalty" exemplifies a passive response to the unavailability of "exit" and "voice," "inxit" represents informal negotiation and bargaining between the patient and the doctor.

But the "inxit" theory takes the power theory a step further, although it is an implicit step. As mentioned above, the power theory did not examine what impact that informal payments could bring on the power relations between the profession and the state. The "inxit" theory suggests that through informal payments, the medical profession can exert countervailing power against the state. Admitting that informal payments are illegal in Hungary, Gaal and McKee continue to argue:

> The legality or illegality of a particular action certainly influences an individual's willingness to do it, but does not guarantee total compliance with the law. Indeed, the individuals' own judgment may be different from legal proscriptions, and if the whole or at least the majority of society think differently, regulations become illegitimate and enforcement becomes difficult, or even impossible. (p. 169)

Obviously, in the power hierarchy in Hungary, the medical profession has not been completely powerless in the face of the state, and has not been always on the receiving end of the top-down power transmission. By resorting to informal practices, doctors can take advantage of their monopolistic position, abuse their professional and bureaucratic power, and exert countervailing power through informal channels to force the state and the public to accept and legitimize their illegal activities. Illegal practices thus become legitimate and acceptable norms. As they point out, informal payments had been tolerated by the communist regime up to 1989, when they were further formalized by the state as they were included in the taxable income of doctors (Gaal and McKee 2004b, pp. 172 and 174). This is a significant concession that the medical profession wrings out of the state, and demonstrates the countervailing power that the medical profession exercises in the informal negotiation space.

Quoting Hirschman, Gaal and McKee (2004b) argue that the existence of an "exit," for instance, a private alternative, may not be a good option for socialist countries facing declining performance in healthcare. In the first place, the "exit" of patients and doctors deprive the public sector of a chance to improve, should they stay and complain. Secondly, the existence of a private choice for both patients and doctors undermines the state's monopoly of medical human resources and pressures the government into increasing doctors' salaries in order to retain them in the public sector. Resources allocated to improve the infrastructure and other facilities are hence diverted, which may consequently cause performance decline and force the "quality-conscious" patients to "exit." The existence of a private alternative without the "exit" of doctors from the public sector is also problematic, as it leads to absenteeism.

In comparison with the private alternative, "inxit" is actually a better choice for the state, for "informal payment can lure the physician to work in the public sector from which non-paying patients may also benefit. The theory suggests that 'inxit' may be preferable to 'exit' if benefits spill over to other users of public services" (Gaal and McKee 2004b, p. 173). That is, as long as doctors choose or have no choice but to stay in the public sector, but can compensate their low incomes with informal incomes from patients' contributions, the public healthcare system will continue to function. This helps not only public patients who are promised free or low-cost healthcare by the state, but also the government which saves face and the superficial integrity of ideology.

The economic and policy studies of informal payments in post-socialist countries have made many interesting and profound discoveries, especially in the spheres of policy and behavioral patterns and choices, but also leave many questions unanswered. All the former socialist countries in the FSU and CEE have undergone transitions to market economies and some kind of democratic political systems, but it is rarely discussed how the institutional changes have exacerbated informal economies in the healthcare systems. Why in a market economy do patients still not have the kind of consumer power and rights to countervail the medical profession? In a relatively democratic environment after the transition, does there exist an open space for collective bargaining and negotiation? Why is "voice" still not politically permissible or useful? In a considerably liberalized economic system, why are medical professionals still monopolized by the state? What power has the medical profession gained against the oppressive power of the state? Has an intermediary structure formed in these societies which consists of freely incorporated social, professional/occupational, business, and other types of associations and organizations that can exert collective power to counterbalance the state's intervention and dominance over individuals? More importantly, are these theories applicable to red packets in China?

RED PACKETS IN CHINA: THE MORAL PERSPECTIVE

As mentioned before, research of informal payments has to be country-specific. China is also in transition, but it has taken a path different from other post-socialist countries. In the first place, China has effectively dampened attempts at political democratization up to date. It remains an authoritarian, single-party regime and retains socialism as its fundamental ideology. Secondly, in spite of the ups and downs in economy, China did not experience the economic hardships that other post-socialist countries have done and has performed comparatively well in terms of transiting to a market economy. That means the institutions that China inherited from before it embarked on economic reform and those that emerged during the reform are markedly different from other post-socialist countries. Consequently, red packets are bound to emerge from a unique institutional setting that deserves a distinctive approach to examine.

Health reforms in China have been a focus of academic interests. Numerous studies have been carried out to evaluate health policies and reforms, social welfare changes, and their impact on the population and society (Anson and Sun 2005; Bloom and Tang 2004; Wong and Chiu 1998; Wagstaff et al. 2009; Huang 2013b). But the power relations between the medical profession, the state, and the public in the new era are yet to attract academic interest. Red packets to doctors have also attracted increasing academic interests in recent years. Compared with the studies of the issue in the CEE and FSU countries, however, the scholarship generated within and without China on the issue of informal payments in the Chinese healthcare system is not as impressive in terms of quantity and quality.

International studies of red packets are not profuse. Among the limited number of investigations, the emergence of red packets is usually attributed to doctors' low wages (Bloom et al. 2001), distorted pricing of medical services (Hsiao 2008), or profit-oriented activities in hospitals (Hougaard et al. 2011). As to the institutional origins of these causes, and how they give rise to red packets, there is scant scholarship.

Compared with international scholarship which tends to explore the economic and policy reasons behind red packets, Chinese scholars usually approach the issue from moral perspectives. There is a substantial body of short publications (ranging from one to five pages in academic and non-academic Chinese journals) discussing the practice from roughly the same perspectives and of similar caliber. Generally speaking, this type of literature emphasizes the moral incorrectness for doctors to take red packets, arguing that in spite of the enthusiastically pursued marketization and capitalism in all economic sectors in China, doctors should resist the moral erosion stoked up by "money worship" and "unhealthy practices" in the society.[3]

Liu Hongjun's comment is emblematic of this perspective. He opines that red packets "vulgarize the normal doctor-patient relationship, turning it into money-for-service relationship. The practice, being secretive, widespread and extremely morally erosive, brings tremendous harm to the construction of medical ethics and good practice, and adversely affect the image and development of hospitals" (Liu 2001, p. 103). Liu specifies seven reasons that have given rise to red packets. The first is that health professionals misunderstand socialist market economy and health reform, equating the market economy with profit pursuit. He accuses some medical professionals for ignoring the fundamental differentiation between commodity exchange theories and professional ethics and viewing the doctor–patient relationship as one of demand-supply or buy-and-sell. The second is the endemic unhealthy practice in the society. The third, which Liu argues is the key reason, is attributed to the "corrupt thoughts of the West" which erode the morality of Chinese medical professionals at a time when their income is unfairly low due to the state's incapability of fairly compensating their work. The fourth is blamed on the monopoly of the public sector and information asymmetry. The fifth is attributed to the imperfection of the healthcare system, which leads to a shortage of medical services in some regions and creates high demand for highly competent specialists and some specialties. To ensure the accessibility to desired medical services, patients are forced to pay extra fees. The sixth is blamed on the inadequate moral education of medical professionals conducted by the state. Liu contributes the seventh reason to the poor legislation, weak enforcement, and flawed administrative structure.

Liu prescribes three solutions. The first is to raise the moral standard of medical professionals by educating them with Marxism, Mao Zedong's thoughts, Deng Xiaoping's theories, and Jiang Zemin's idea of "Three Represents," so that they would realize the socialist market economy needs them to sacrifice selflessly. Secondly, legislation, regulation, and enforcement must be strengthened so that the offenders are duly punished. The third and last solution is to urge the government to compensate doctors fairly (Liu 2001).

Liu's approach to the issue is shared by numerous commentators who blame the prevalence of red packets predominantly on corrupt morality of the medical profession while treating the government's deleterious policies toward healthcare organization and provision as secondary reasons (Wang 1998; Li and Su 1997; Tong 2002; Lu 2011; Sha 2015). Consequently, strict regulation, enhanced moral education, and the obedience of the medical profession to the government are emphasized as solutions, while the government is pardoned for neglecting its duty to the people and the profession.

This "politically correct" moral perspective offers little help to a profound understanding of the institutional grounds on which the practice flourishes, but the popularity of such opinions nonetheless indicates the powerlessness of the Chinese medical profession and distorted "voice" in the public space, phenomena that are not unfamiliar to the students of the Soviet Union or post-socialist countries. China is a transitional socialist country. Institutionally, it is indebted to the bygone Soviet Union. In the meantime, it strives to establish new institutions that are also embraced by transitional post-socialist countries and faces problems that also haunt the latter. It is in this connection that the sociology of Soviet medicine and the theories of informal payments developed from the studies of transition economies become relevant and provide a valid analytical framework for red packets in the Chinese healthcare system. Then why do the old institutions persist? How have new ones risen? And how have the old and the new created an institutional setting in which red packets become endemic? These are the questions that this research seeks to answer.

NOTES

1. "Serve the people" (*wei renmin fuwu*) is in fact a term in Chinese Communist Party's ideology, but it expresses the same ideological commitment of the ruling communist parties in both China and the Soviet Union and is thus used here for its succinctness and for consistency with the following discussions in Chap. 2.
2. In a socialist state, patients are stratified according to their positions. Privileged people, who are top party and state officials, have access to top-quality medical resources, including human resources. It is highly unlikely that doctors can dominate these patients (Field 2002b; Ryan 1989, p. 25).
3. It is interesting to notice that the word "shehui" (society) always denotes the "informal" public spheres outside the "formal," state-controlled spheres, and contains derogatory implications.

BIBLIOGRAPHY

American Medical Association. 2004. Code of medical ethics: current options with annotations, 2004–2005 ed. Chicago: AMA Press.

Andereck, William, and Charles Weijer. 2001. Should physicians accepts gifts from their patients? *Western Journal of Medicine* 175(August): 76–77.

Anson, Ofra, and Shifang Sun. 2005. *Health care in rural China—lessons from HeBei Province*. Hants, UK: Ashgate.

Barber, Bernard. 1963. Some problems in the sociology of professions. *Daedalus* 92 (4): 669–688.

Bell, Daniel. 1999. *The coming of post-industrial society: a venture in social forecasting*. New York: Basic Books. Original edition, 1973. Reprint, 1999.

Bloom, Gerald, Leiya Han, and Xiang Li. 2001. How health workers earn a living in China. *Human Resources for Health Development Journal* 5(1–3): 26–38.

Bloom, Gerald, and Shenglan Tang (ed). 2004. *Health care transition in urban China*. Hants, UK: Ashgate.

Bunce, Valerie. 1999. *Subversive institutions: the design and the destruction of socialism and the state*. In *Cambridge Studies in Comparative Politics*, ed. Peter Lange. Cambridge: Cambridge University Press.

Carr-Saunders, A.M., and P.A. Wilson. 1933. *The professions*. Oxford: Oxford University Press.

Daniel, Ann. 1990. *Medicine and the state: Professional autonomy and public accountability*. Sydney: Allen and Unwin.

Drew, Jennifer, John D. Stoeckle, and J. Andrew Billings. 1983. Tips, status and sacrifice: Gift giving in the doctor-patient relationship. *Social Science and Medicine* 17(3): 399–404.

Durkheim, Emile. 1957. *Professional ethics and civic morals.* Translated by Cornelia Brookfield. Edited by W. J. H. Sprott, *International Library of Sociology and Social Reconstruction.* London: Routledge and Kegan Paul Ltd.

Ensor, Tim. 2004. Informal payments for health care in transition economies. *Social Science and Medicine* 58: 237–246.

Field, Mark G. 1957. *Doctor and patient in Soviet Russia.* Cambridge, MA: Harvard University Press.

———. 1967. *Soviet socialized medicine: an introduction.* New York: The Free Press.

———. 1976. Health as a 'public utility' or the 'maintenance of capacity' in Soviet society. In *Social consequences of modernization in communist societies,* ed. Mark G. Field, 234–264. Baltimore and London: The John Hopkins University Press.

———. 1988. The position of the Soviet physicians: the bureaucratic professional. *The Milbank Quarterly* 66 (Supplement 2: The Changing Character of the Medical Profession): 182–201.

———. 1991. The hybrid profession: Soviet medicine. In *Professions and the state: expertise and autonomy in the Soviet Union and Eastern Europe,* ed. Anthony Jones, 43–62. Philadelphia: Temple University Press.

———. 2002b. The Soviet legacy: the past as prologue. In *Health care in central Asia,* ed. Martin McKee, Judith Healy, and Jane Falkingham, 67–75. Buckingham: Open University Press.

Freidson, Eliot. 1970. *Profession of medicine: a study of the sociology of applied knowledge.* Chicago and London: The University of Chicago Press. Reprint, 1988.

———. 1994. *Professionalism reborn: theory, prophecy, and policy.* Cambridge: Polity Press.

Gaal, Peter, Paolo Carlo Belli, Martin McKee, and Miklos Szocska. 2006. Informal payments for health care: definitions, distinctions, and dilemmas. *Journal of Health Politics* 31(2): 251–293.

Gaal, Peter, and Martin McKee. 2004b. Informal payment for health care and the theory of 'inxit'. *International Journal of Health Planning and Management* 19: 163–178.

Gabbard, Glen O., and Carol Nadelson. 1995. Professional boundaries in the physician-patient relationship. *Journal of American Medical Association* 273 (18): 1445–1449.

Goode, William J. 1960. Encroachment, charlatanism, and the emerging profession: psychology, medicine, and sociology. *American Sociological Review* XXV: 902–914.

Greene, Jay. 2000. CME focus on professional development, ethics of gifts. *American Medical News* 43(25): 10.

Hougaard, Jens Leth, Lars Peter Osterdal, and Yu. Yi. 2011. The Chinese healthcare system: structure, problems and challenges. *Applied Health Economics and Health Policy* 9(1): 1–13.

Hsiao, William C. 2008. When incentives and professionalism collide. *Health Affairs (Millwood)* 27(4): 949–951. doi:10.1377/hlthaff.27.4.949.

Huang, Yanzhong. 2013b. *Governing health in contemporary China, China policy series*. New York: Routledge.

Johnson, J. Terence. 1972. *Professions and power*. London: Macmillan Press.

Johnson, Terry. 1995. Governmentality and the institutionalization of expertise. In *Health professions and the state in Europe*, ed. Terry Johnson, Gerry Larkin, and Mike Saks, 7–24. London and New York: Routledge.

Kubali, Huseyin Nail. 1957. Preface. In *Professional ethics and civil morals*. Edited by W. J. H. Sprott, ix–xi. London: Routledge and Kegan Paul.

Larson, Magali Sarfatti. 1977. *The rise of professionalism: a sociological analysis*. Berkeley, Los Angeles and London: University of California Press.

Lewis, Maureen. 2000. *Who is paying for health care in Eastern Europe and Central Asia?* Washington, DC: The World Bank.

———. 2002. Informal Health Payments in Central and Eastern Europe and the Former Soviet Union: Issues, Trends and Policy Implications. In *Funding Health Care: Options for Europe*, ed. Elias Mossialos, Anna Dixon, Josep Figueras, and Joe Kutzin, 184–205. Buckingham, Philadelphia: Open University Press.

Li, Peiling, and Wenqiao Su. 1997. Hongbao xianxiang zhi lunli fenxi (An ethical analysis of red packet phenomenon). *Zhongguo yixue lunlixue (Chinese Medical Ethics)* 1997(6): 51–52, 56.

Light, Donald. 1995. Countervailing powers: a framework for professions in transition. In *Health professions and the state in Europe*, ed. Terry Johnson, Gerry Larkin, and Mike Saks, 25–41. London and New York: Routledge.

Liu, Hongjun. 2001. Qianyi yiyuan 'hongbao' xianxiang de chengyi jiqi duice (A brief discussion of the causes and solutions of 'red packet' phenomenon in hospitals). *Guoji yiyao weisheng daobao (International Medical and Health Guiding News)* 2001(7): 103–104.

Lu, Zhengrong. 2011. Qianxi 'kanbing song hongbao' ji zhili duice (A study of 'giving red packet for medical treatment' and policies dealing with it). *Zhongguo yiyao zhinan (Guide of Chinese Medicine)* 9(24): 360–362.

Lyckholm, L. 1998. Should physician accept gifts from patients? *Journal of American Medical Association* 280(22): 1944–1946.

Macdonald, M. Keith. 1995. *The sociology of the professions*. Thousand Oaks: Sage. Reprint, 1999.

Marshall, T. H. 1963 [1939]. The recent history of professionalism in relation to social structure and social policy. In *Sociology at the crossroads and other essays*, ed. T.H. Marshall, 150–170. London: Heinemann.

Moran, Michael, and Bruce Wood. 1993. *States, regulation, and the medical profession, law and political change*. Buckingham, Philadelphia: Open University Press.

Morgan, Huw. 1996. Gifts. *British Medical Journal* 312(7023): 128.

Morse, Janice M. 1992. The structure and function of gift giving in the patient-nurse relationship. In *Qualitative health research*, ed. Janice M. Morse, 236–256. Newbury Park: Sage.

Parsons, Talcott. 1954[1939]. The professions and social structure. In *Essays in sociological theory*, ed. Talcott Parsons, 34–49. New York: Free Press.

Pažitný, Peter, and Rudolf Zajac. 2005. Health care reform in Slovak Republic. *The William Davidson Institute Policy Brief #9*. Accessed 14 June 2006. http://wdi.umich.edu/files/Publications/PolicyBriefs/2005/Pazitny_Peter_09w.pdf.

Perkin, Harold. 1989. *The rise of professional society: England since 1880*. London: Routledge.

Rowland, Diane, and Alexandre V. Telyukov. 1991. Soviet health care from two perspectives. *Health Affairs* 10(3): 71–86.

Ryan, Michael. 1978. *The organization of Soviet medical care*. Special Edition ed, *Aspects of social policy*. New York: Professional Seminar Consultant, Inc. Original edition, Basil Blackwell & Mott.

———. 1989. *Doctors and the state in the Soviet Union*. London: Macmillan Press.

Sha, Rula. 2015. "Hongbao" xianxiang yuanyin fenxi yu sikao (Analysis and consideration of the reasons behind "red packet" phenomenon). *Zhongguo weisheng zhiliang guanli (Chinese Health Quality Management)* 22(3): 94–97.

Thompson, Robin, and Sophie Witter. 2000. Informal payments in transitional economies: implications for health sector reform. *International Journal of Health Planning and Management* 15: 169–187.

Tong, Chunping. 2002. Qiantan 'hongbao' xianxiang ji duice (Brief discussion of the phenomenon and solutions of 'red packets'). *Zhongguo yixue lilun yu shijian (Theory and Practice of Chinese Medicine)* 2002(11): 1492–1493.

Wagstaff, Adam, Magnus Lindelow, Shiyong Wang, and Shuo Zhang. 2009. *Reforming China's rural health system, Directions in development*. Washington, DC: World Bank.

Wang, Yankun. 1998. Dangqian yiyuan hongbao xianxiang de chengyin yu duice (The reasons and countermeasures against the current red packet phenomenon in the hospital). *Jinzhou Yixueyuan xuebao (Journal of Jinzhou Medical College)* 19(4): 69–70.

Wong, V.C.W., and S.W.S. Chiu. 1998. Health-care reforms in the People's Republic of China. *Journal of Management in Medicine* 12: 270–286.

CHAPTER 3

Institutional Changes and the Power of Chinese Medical Professionals

As in other (former) socialist countries, the endemic informal payment in the Chinese healthcare system is attendant to the power relations among the major actors, namely, the state, the medical professions, and the patient. The year 1949, when the Chinese Communist Party rose to power, represents a dividing point for medical professions in terms of growth and relationships with the patient and the state. This chapter will first present a brief account of the medical professions before 1949 and then explore the institutions and institutional changes that have influenced the doctor–patient and profession–state relationship in the pre-reform period (1949–1977).

CHINESE MEDICAL PROFESSIONS AND THE REPUBLICAN STATE

In terms of the emergence and development of modern medicine, the Republican era (1912–1949) is extremely important. The functioning of traditional medicine in China can be traced back thousands of years in history, and the rise of modern Western-style in China came long before the period, but it was in this era that medicine became modernized, and medical occupational groups professionalized. Development in medicine after 1949 is in great debt to the achievements in the medical and health sector before 1949.

Historians usually divided the Republican China into three periods: the Beiyang regime (1912–1928), the Nationalist regime (1928–1937), and

© The Author(s) 2017   67
J. Yang, *Informal Payments and Regulations in China's Healthcare System*,
DOI 10.1007/978-981-10-2110-7_3

the wars period (1937–1949). The Sino-Japanese war between 1937 and 1945 and the following civil war between the Nationalist and Communist forces disrupted to a considerable degree the normal functioning of the Chinese medical profession, and the Chinese healthcare system to a larger degree. The period between 1912 and 1937 became the golden age for the Chinese medical professions. During this period, a Durkheimian-style inter-mediary social structure between individuals and the state existed and was active. Medical professions, as well as other professions, guilds, trade unions, and native place associations (*tongxiang hui*), enjoyed considerable political and economic autonomy and power. Public space, despite being constantly eroded throughout the period, was comparatively ample and functioning. Professions were able to negotiate and bargain collectively with the govern-ment through formal and open channels. In most cases, they could influ-ence the making and implementation of regulations and laws in their favor and boycott state initiatives that were deemed adverse to professional interests. The relationship between medical professions and the state is described as one of "symbiotic dynamics" (Xu 2001). On the one hand, medical professions sought after the state's intervention in terms of stan-dardization of curriculums of medical schools and registration of practi-tioners. On the other hand, they vehemently resisted unfavorable governmental regulations and excessive political intervention into profes-sional affairs. The freedom and autonomy that professions enjoyed allowed them to control their work and economic terms to a significant degree.

With the introduction of modern Western medicine into China in the late Qing dynasty, learned societies of doctors started to form. In 1886, missionary doctors formed a learned society—Chinese Medical Missionary Association (CMMA). In the beginning, the CMMA only recruited foreign doctors as members. From 1903 onward, it gradually allowed Chinese doctors to join. In 1915, when the CMMA had its regular meeting, a group of Chinese doctors decided to form a separate association consisted of Chinese practitioners only, hence the Chinese Medical Association (CMA; *Zhonghua Yixue Hui*) (Yin 2013). Members of the CMA were mainly graduates of British and American medical schools or missionary medical schools in China. In 1931, the CMMA merged into CMA. The new entity assumed the name of CMA. Chinese members were appointed to major positions of the association. In 1915, another medical associa-tion—the Medical and Pharmaceutical Society of the Chinese Republic (MPSCR; *Zhonghua Minguo Yiyao Xuehui*)—was inaugurated by medical graduates trained in Germany and Japan (Xu 2001, p. 133; Yin 2013,

p. 71). Both CMA and MPSCR were scholarly societies by nature, but in their early days, with the absence of professional associations, they were also engaged extensively in professional affairs on behalf of their members. Medical professional associations appeared rather late. The first association of this type was established in Shanghai in 1925. Named Shanghai Medical Practitioners' Association (SMPA; *Shanghai Yishi Gonghui*) and consisted of members graduated with formal credentials from recognized medical educational institutions within and without China, it engaged extensively in professional affairs and exerted significant influence in the political and professional arenas. In 1929, joining forces with the CMA and MPSCR, SMPA initiated and inaugurated the National United Association of Medical Practitioners (NUAMP; *Quanguo Yishi Lianhe Hui*) (Yin 2013, p. 71). Although these associations were not particularly sizable, they were able to recruit increasing number of practitioners to join them. For example, SMPA had only about 80 members when it was inaugurated. In 1949, its membership reached 3208 (Shanghai Health Annals Editorial Committee 1998).

Before and during the Republican era, Western-style doctors were considerably outnumbered by traditional native doctors who formed more associations. In the first decade of the twentieth century, there were about eight hundred thousand traditional practitioners active in both cities and the countryside (Wang 2011a, p. 3). Facing the challenge from the Western-style medicine, some reform-minded doctors of Traditional Chinese Medicine (TCM) started to take positive strategies to seek modernization of traditional medicine. In 1885, the first school of traditional medicine was created in Ruian, Zhejiang, which represented a breach from the traditional way of master-apprentice training (Wen 2008, p. 34; Zhu 2008, pp. 79–80). In the following years, several other schools of native medicine were opened in Zhejiang and Shanghai (Wen 2008, p. 34). A few modern TCM hospitals were also established, marking the revolution of practicing mode (Wen 2008). More importantly, modern-minded TCM practitioners started to form learned societies, which represented the first attempt of professionalization and modernization (Wen 2008). For example, the Chinese Medical Society (*Zhongguo Yixue Hui*) established in 1909 in Shanghai created new curriculums for its medical training institute which integrated Western medical knowledge, especially anatomy into textbooks (Lei 2014, pp. 71–74).

In the Republican era, more associations of native medicine were established, especially in Shanghai. In 1912, the Chinese Medical and Pharmaceutical United Association (CMPUA; *Zhonghua Yiyao Lianhe Hui*) was inaugurated. A few months later, the Shenzhou Medical and

Pharmaceutical General Association (SMPGA; *Shenzhou Yiyao Zonghui*) was established which became the most popular entity representing ordinary TCM practitioners. With its headquarter in Shanghai, it set up branches in other provinces and boasted a membership of over six thousand and played an instrumental role in organizing collective actions against persecution and hostile regulations of the government (Xu 2001, p. 133). Another important association of TCM was Shanghai Society of Traditional Chinese Medicine (SSTCM; *Shanghai Zhongyi Xuehui*) established in 1921. Composed of renowned practitioners, it had a much smaller membership, but was equally influential due to the individual reputation of its members (Xu 2001). All these were learned societies whose aims were to promote scholarly research and exchange among members, although they were actively engaged in activities to promote professional interests. The Shanghai Traditional Chinese Medicine Association, which was established in 1928 and later on renamed as Shanghai National Medicine Union (SNMU; *Shanghai Guoyi Gonghui*), was the first and most powerful professional association of TCM.

The mushrooming learned and professional associations of medicine operated in a fashion and in a social and political environment that resembled what Durkheim expected for professions. They formed an intermediary social structure and force between the state and individuals, protecting individuals from the tyranny of the state and preventing the individuals from dominating the state. The conflict between the profession of TCM and that of Western-style medicine under the Beiyang regime is illustrative of the dynamics in the public space.

When the Beiyang government rose to power, it immediately devoted itself into the enterprise of modernizing China. Education was regarded as one of the institutions that urgently needed changes. In late 1912, the "New Education Act of the Republic of China" and associated regulations on specialized medical school and pharmaceutical school were promulgated. Education of traditional medicine was not mentioned in the Act and regulations, which means that TCM was excluded from the modern educational system and schools of traditional medicine were not recognized by the government. In response to inquiries from TCM practitioners, Wang Daxie, Minister of Education, said he was determined to abolish traditional medicine and stop using traditional drugs (Wen 2008, p. 45). Wang's attitude toward traditional medicine was disquieting and compelled professional TCM associations into joint actions. In 1913, the newly founded SMPGA sent a telegram to Yuan Shikai, President of the

Beiyang government, requesting the inclusion of education of traditional medicine into the new educational system. As the government took actions to redress the issue, the SMPGA called on associations of traditional medicine across the country to form a joint delegation. Representing traditional doctors of 19 provinces, the delegation went to Beijing to petition the State Council and the Ministry of Education in 1914 (Xu 2001, pp. 135–136), and forced the government to soften on its anti-TCM ground. In reply to the petition, the State Council confirmed it had no intention to abolish traditional medicine (Zhao 1989, p. 142). Although the Ministry of Education rejected the delegation's request for separate regulation on the education of native medicine and did not support TCM legally, administratively, and financially, it compromised its stance on abolishing traditional medicine and formally recognized several private schools by putting them on a national register (Zhao 1989; Wen 2008; Lei 2014, p. 99).

When the Nationalist Party rose to power and formed government in Nanjing, establishing a new healthcare system characteristic of state medicine was regarded as an important area of national reconstruction (Yip 1995; Lucas 1982). Again TCM was put under spotlight for its alleged incompatibility with science and modernity. The "Provisional Regulations on Doctors" enforced in January 1929 did not mention traditional medicine. In February, the MOH appointed a Central Commission of Health consisted of health officials and leaders of associations of Western-style medicine. Its task was to lay down the blueprint for the construction of state medicine, and discuss other important issues concerning the modernization of medicine in China. The future of traditional medicine was an important agenda item. Yu Yunxiu, former president of SMPA, and first president of the NUAMP to be created in late 1929, proposed a six-step plan to abolish TCM, which was largely accepted by the Committee whose resolution was published in the *New Medicine and Society*, a journal of the SMPA (Xu 2001, pp. 193–196).

TCM doctors responded to the resolution of the Central Commission of Health with collective actions organized by professional associations. In March 1929, over 40 associations of traditional medicine and traditional drug trade convened a joint meeting in Shanghai to discuss the strategies to contend the resolution of the Central Commission of Health. In the meeting, the participating associations agreed to establish the Shanghai Federation of Medical and Pharmaceutical Associations (SFMPA; *Shanghai Yiyao Tuanti Lianhe Hui*) to lead the fight with the authority. The SFMPA emphasized "organized collective action to persuade the government to come to their side" and prevented individuals from dealing with the outside on the issue (Xu 2001, p. 197).

In the national conference organized by the SFMPA shortly after, the National Federation of Medical and Pharmaceutical Association (NFMPA; *Quanguo Yiyao Tuanti Zong Lianghe Hui*) was created and sent a delegation to Nanjing to lobby the government. The lobbying was successful. The delegation had audiences with several heavyweight political figures and ministers in the central government and received promises from them that the government had no intention to abolish traditional medicine (Xu 2001, pp. 196–200).

The victory of traditional medicine was ephemeral. Shortly after the delegation returned from Nanjing, the Ministry of Education decreed that all TCM schools must not use the title of *xuexiao* (school) and refused to place them on the national register, excluding them from the educational system (Xu 2001, p. 204). The associations of traditional medicine immediately went into action by organizing another round of collective actions to persuade and lobby the government for equal status with Western-style medicine. This round of organized collective endeavors resulted in the establishment of the Institute of National Medicine, a government-funded organization charged with the responsibility to reconstruct traditional medicine with scientific methods (Xu 2001, p. 209), an indication of the success of collective petition and negotiation through open, public channels.

Even when the state stepped up its control over civil organizations, professional associations were still able to organize collective resistance to protect their organizational and professional autonomy. Under the regime of the Nationalist government, the intrusion of the state into professional domain, and into the civil society in general, was mounting and blatant. All occupational and social organizations were required to apply to the Nationalist Party headquarters for permission to associate and were subject to inspections by the Nationalist Party. All associations must pledge to follow the Three Principles of the People (*sanmin zhuyi*), the core of the ideology of the Party, and were subject to the supervision and instruction of the Party organs (Xu 2001, pp. 99–100; Yin 2008, pp. 73–74). In the case of medical associations, the Party must be notified of any meetings and elections and would send officials to monitor these events on site (Yin 2008, p. 74).

The state's attempt to interfere with the organization and operation of medical associations were met with strong resistance and public criticism from practitioners. In 1929, the MOH called for feedbacks on a draft "Medical Associations Act," which postulated that the government was the supervisory superior of all medical associations, and laid down detailed clauses with regard to the government's supervisory and administrative power and responsibility in the incorporation, registration, election, and operation of associations, with little concern for the interests of members. The draft received widespread criticisms. Medical professionals were extremely concerned about the relationship between the state and the profession that the authority intended to institutionalize, blaming it for excessively emphasizing the state power and oppressing medical power, and for turning medical associations into affiliated organs of the government. The barrage of criticisms forced the government to shelf the Act for a long period until 1943, when a new "Medical Practitioners Law" (*yishi fa*) was enacted which covered the organization and operation of associations (Yin 2008, p. 75; Wen 2008, p. 157). The new law did not assert the state's interference in the associational life of professions as before.

These incidents demonstrated the existence of an ample and functioning public space in which the exercise of organized civil power and the action of collective negotiation with the government was not only tolerated but also effective. The exercise of state power was mitigated and in some cases countervailed by collective actions of the professions. In this milieu, medical professionals were able to maintain autonomy to a significant degree, particularly in terms of economic and practicing autonomy.

Throughout the Republican period, medical professionals had significant control over their work and economic terms. Most of the medical practitioners practiced privately in a fee-for-service mode. Despite its efforts to promote state medicine, the government could only afford very limited number of positions in public employment, and these positions were not particularly attractive in terms of salaries and work patterns. Graduates fresh from local or overseas Western-style medical schools might work for public and private health facilities as salaried employees, an option that many young practitioners chose to start their career. Then many would transfer to independent and private practice which allowed them to determine their own fee patterns and work terms (Yin 2013, pp. 44–59, 2008, pp. 37–50). In addition, TCM practitioners were entirely excluded from the public employment. As a result, the vast majority of medical professionals were private practitioners.

Private doctors enjoyed significant control over their practice and had the leeway to set their service charges according to such elements as their qualifications, reputation, demand, competition, and so on. The Republican government made attempt to regulate the fee schedules of private practitioners, but its efforts were not only compromised but also ineffective. In 1929, in order to make medical services affordable to the ordinary people, the Nationalist Party Shanghai headquarter demanded the Shanghai Bureau of Health to issue a policy setting a ceiling on the fees that Western-style doctors could charge their patients. Viewing the initiative as an excessive interference of the government with the profession's economic autonomy, the SMPA petitioned the MOH, demanding the latter to pressure the Shanghai Bureau of Health to revoke the policy. The Shanghai health authority did not revoke the policy, but compromised by allowing significant increases in the service rates. In reality, however, doctors never followed the regulated fee schedules (Xu 2001, pp. 145–146; Yin 2013, pp. 126–134).

Professional ethics was another sphere where medical professions enjoyed significant autonomy. In Confucianism, medicine was regarded as "benevolent skills" (*renshu*). Practitioners were expected to uphold the spirit of service and take as the ultimate object and reward the saving of patients' life. Personal gains should not be taken into consideration when treating patients (Jonsen 2000, pp. 36–38; Qiu et al. 2008, pp. 17–19). Doctors "must be learned and skilled, generous and compassionate, continent and restrained, courteous and courtly, and attentive to the needs of rich and poor, noble and commoner" (Jonsen 2000, p. 38). Altruism was always advanced as the highest ideal of medical practice. However, as traditional medicine was only professionalized in the early twentieth century, there was never in the Chinese history a professional organization to promote the exercise of ethical conducts in practice and to ensure doctors to follow principles and ideals of morality. It was not until 1930 was the first code of ethics—the *Pledge of National Medicine* (*guoyi gongyue*)—for doctors of traditional medicine formulated by the SNMU (Yin 2013, pp. 134–135).

The *Pledge of National Medicine* contained 18 rules regarding members' morality and appropriate behaviors toward each other and patients and with Western-style medicine. In terms of doctors' relationship with patients, the *Pledge* required that doctors should be responsive and considerate and provide convenience to the poor and emergency. Doctors were demanded not to make exaggeration in advertisement and not to make immoral profits. They should not speak harshly to patients and prescribe injudiciously, as it was against the principles of benevolent medicine (Yin 2013, p. 135). The *Pledge* did not make further insistence on TCM doctors upholding the service ideal and altruism, but only stipulated the basic ethical behaviors, and left space for individuals to pursue the highest moral standards. Service orientation was not accentuated as an indispensable part of professionalism.

The emergence of the modern conception of professional ethics in medicine is always attributed to Song Guobin's seminal *The Ethics of Medical Practice* published in 1933 (Jonsen 2000, p. 39; Qiu et al. 2008, p. 19; Yin 2013, pp. 194–195). Song studied medicine in France and was a medical professor at Zhendan University in Shanghai. As a leading figure of the SMPA, he authored several important works on ethics, including the *Tenets of the SMPA* and the *Graduation Oath of the Medical School of Zhendan University*. The *Tenets of the SMPA*, adopted in 1931, included ten principles stipulating appropriate conducts for members in terms of advertisements, competition, privacy, obligation to the patient, and standards of practice. It particularly emphasized the doctor's obligation to serve patients regardless of their economic status, and disapprove immoral profits (Yin 2013, p. 135). But Song also accentuated doctors' legal rights to fees. Noting that doctors should be detached and charitable and keep away from commercialism and money worship, he stressed that medical profession was an occupation which provided a source of livelihood for the practitioner. Medicine was not charity, and doctors had indispensable right to fees (Yin 2013, pp. 196–197).

In reality, however, professional associations had little control over the conducts of individual practitioners. Unethical conducts were reportedly widespread among both TCM and Western-style doctors. In the eyes of the public, doctors were not professionals but business people who placed profit above service (Yin 2013, p. 194). Complaints about doctors substituting vitamin injections for other medications (Yip 1995, p. 160) and prescribing expensive medicine for drug kickbacks (Xu 2001, p. 54) were not uncommon.

The doctrine that advocated equal treatment to all patients regardless of their social and economic status was hardly followed in practice, either. Doctors were criticized for behaving remarkably differently toward the rich and the poor, and to a significant degree neglected their obligation to the latter (Yin 2013, p. 194). However, doctors complained that the ideal was unrealistic in a new age when the costs of education and setting up practice markedly exceeded those before. Medicine was an occupation by nature whose economic function as a way of providing livelihood superseded its social function as benevolent service to the people. Doctors should not be ashamed of their purpose and activities to recover costs and make a profit. Song Guobin, for example, advised that doctors should not feel embarrassed about demanding fees from patients as it was the just reward for their services. If the latter refused to pay, doctors should ask the association to intervene. If the association failed, legal procedures should be pursued (Yin 2013, pp. 198–199). Charity toward the poor and the underprivileged was, in the main, the responsibility of the state rather than the profession (Yin 2013, p. 197).

There was no evidence to indicate the existence of informal payments per se in the Republican period, although many TCM practitioners, albeit in private practice, did not openly charge fees for services. Rather they took customary "red packets" that patients offered as a token of gratuity (Zhou and Zhang 2003). On surface, this was an attribution to the ethical doctrine against using medicine for profit, as advised by great doctors in history (Yin 2012). Western-style doctors in private practice would publicize their fee rates that they deemed suitable for their qualifications and reputations and acceptable to medical market. Informal payments for their services were not necessary. On the contrary, some doctors even offered fee discounts in competition for businesses (Yin 2012, 2013). Because of the professions' autonomy in economic terms and work patterns, especially their control over fee rates, there was no need for them to charge fees informally. Institutionally, informal payments were not necessary.

In summary, in the Republican era doctors of TCM and Western-style medicine underwent comparatively successful professionalization and formed, in conjunction with other social and economic corporations, an intermediary structure between the state and individuals. The existence of public space, albeit shrinking throughout the period, and the comparatively loose state control, albeit gradually intensified, allowed considerable collective bargaining, negotiation, and persuasion. Medical professionals, through their associations, were able to wield their power through organized collective actions to resist policies and regulations they deemed unfavorable to them and to influence the state to implement measures in their interest. They were also organized to lobby the government to support their hostile actions against other occupational groups.

The autonomy and power of the medical professions were not only reflected in the ability to influence and resist government policies collectively in an open process, but also in the diverse types of employment and practitioners' ability to determine their own terms of economy and work. China under the Nationalist government was basically a market economy with the private sector a major contributor to the economy. Although the state made increasing efforts to establish state medicine, especially between 1928 and 1937, the majority of medical professionals remained in the private sector. The economic autonomy that private practice afforded allowed practitioners to charge their patients above board in accordance with market principles, leaving informal payments a groundless practice. But the public and the state were apparently concerned about other types of widespread unethical conducts and particularly the failure of the professionals to meet the ideal of serving the people regardless of their social and economic status. Entrepreneurial medicine was seemingly the major obstacle to the availability of modern medicine to the mass. Dr. Chen Zhiqian, who received medical training in Peking Union Medical College and was renowned for his successful experiment of social medicine in Ding county in Hebei Province in the 1920s and 1930s, criticized reputed Western-style doctors for using the most prettiest equipment and words to serve the rich only, and blamed ordinary returned medical graduates for promoting the foreign model of private practice vehemently, pursuing profits only, and serving the privileged specifically (Hu 2011, p. 66). When the Communist Party came to power, professional ethics, especially the service orientation, became the major concern of the new Party-state.

Medical Professions and the Socialist State: 1949–1978

Toward the later period of the Nationalist regime, authoritarianism was on the rise. Public open space was constantly suppressed. The state interference with civil society gained momentum (Xu 2001). However, as Chu Anping famously predicted in 1947, under the Nationalist regime, freedom was a question of "more" or "less," while, "if the Communist Party comes to power, freedom will become a question of 'have' or 'have not'" (Chu 1947, p. 6). After 1949, public space was drastically squeezed, and economy was nationalized. Institutional changes introduced by the new regime under new ideology significantly altered the power relations between medical professions, their patients, and the state. These changes led to the establishment of new economic and work terms for medical professionals, and gave rise to informal economies in the healthcare sector.

The Transitory Survival of Old Institutions

In the first half of the 1950s, private economy was not suppressed. In spite of its aim to establish socialist economy and politics in China, the CCP took

a gradualist approach toward national economy and protected and encouraged capitalist elements for the sake of national reconstruction even to the
extent of curbing workers' aggressive demand for pay rises and for their
attempt to set scores with factory owners (Bo 1991, pp. 46–66;
MacFarquhar 1997, p. 25). Politically, the CCP promoted united frontline
policy to ensure a wide base of support from extensive social classes and
political forces. Administratively, the CCP relied heavily on the bureaucratic
and technical personnel of the Nationalist government to make the new
regime functional (MacFarquhar 1997). These measures created a comparatively lenient environment in which medicine continued its business in the
new regime.

Private fee-for-service practices continued and enjoyed significant economic autonomy in the first few years of the PRC. Due to the constraint in
resources and finance and the rapidly increased demand, the government
found it difficult to implement state medicine and had to support private
practice as a major alternative for users that could not be handled by the
public healthcare system (Lampton 1977, p. 34). The First National Health
Conference, which was held in August 1950 in Beijing, set the tone for
public–private relationship in healthcare. In his concluding report, He
Cheng, the First Vice Minister of Health and the actual responsible leader
of the MOH, stated that, as the distribution of healthcare resources could
not meet the needs of the masses, private medical services were necessary
and should not be prejudiced against. Health authorities at all administrative levels were required to assign public preventative and curative tasks to
private medical practitioners or organizations and reduce or exempt their
business taxes if they fulfilled the tasks as required (He 1951c). This
initiative was formalized in an MOH decree promulgated in April 1951, in
which governments at all levels were demanded to cooperate with private
practices and divide tasks between the public and the private sectors, so that
both the public and the private medical institutions could contribute accordingly to the healthcare enterprise. For those who accepted military, preventative, and public health tasks, provided free hospitalization and clinic
consultation to the poor, and charged fees according to standards set by the
government, their business taxes were exempted (Ministry of Health 1951a).

Nevertheless, the new government believed that individual private practices were economically unsustainable and thus encouraged individual practitioners to unite and set up shareholding group practices. In 1951, the
MOH issued two directives encouraging the establishment of united medical organizations, allowing significant economic autonomy for private

united medical organizations (State Council 1951a; Ministry of Health 1951b). With the encouragement of health authorities, private practice expanded extensively in the early years of the PRC. In 1952, 84.6 percent of medical practitioners were in the private sector (n.n. 1958, p. 332). In Hubei Province, the number of united clinics rose from 915 in 1952 to 5533 in 1957, and the number of private clinics increased from 289 to 1145 during the same period (Hubei Local History Compiling Committee 2000, pp. 126–127).

Politically, elite Western-style doctors continued to wield significant power and dominated policy making at central and local levels. The new MOH was led and staffed by independently minded Western-style doctors who had both professional qualifications and military experiences with the red army. Their perception of healthcare problems in the new era was different from that of political leaders, but the outcomes of policy making reflected more of professional concerns rather than political concerns. Western-style doctors who were active in the Republican era also contributed significantly to the health policy making. In fact, policies concerning medical education and research bore significant resemblance to that advocated by the CMA in its proposal made to the Nationalist government in mid-1949, before the establishment of the PRC and the inauguration of the new MOH (Lampton 1977, Chap. 2).

The Loss of Professional Autonomy and Organizational Power

In spite of their lingering economic autonomy and political influence, however, the organizational power of the medical professions was significantly compromised since the very beginning of the PRC. They no longer constituted an intermediary structure between the state and individuals. In the first place, the professions were denounced as ideologically backward and needed strenuous work to improve their thought.

"Serve the People": The Health Ideology

Ideology is at the core of institutions. Institutional changes are thereby inevitably pre-conditioned by ideological changes. With the CCP coming to power in 1949, communist ideology dominated the politics of China. One of the core values that the CCP claimed to uphold consistently and vehemently was its commitment to serving the people. In spite of numerous amendments and re-writing to reflect the political priorities and trends of different periods, the CCP Constitution has always required its members to understand the identification of the Party's interests with the people's interests, and the demanded that members serve the people wholeheartedly. This commitment was obligatory not only for all Party members but also for non-Party members who served in the Party-state organs, and constituted the ideological foundation of all "normative health policy" and "action policy" (Lampton 1977, p. xviii).

The CCP's commitment to the people's health in the early years of the PRC was apparently drawn from the thinking and instructions of the major leaders of the CCP, especially Mao Zedong. The best representation of Mao's idea toward healthcare is reflected his article "On Memorizing Bethune" (Lynteris 2013). Dr. Norman Bethune (1890–1939) was a Canadian surgeon and a member of the Canadian Communist Party who came to assist the Chinese Communist army in the anti-Japanese War, and died of blood poisoning received from treating Communist soldiers on 12 November 1939. Bethune won his renown mainly due to an article by Mao, in which Mao speaks extremely highly of Dr. Bethune's absolute selflessness. Mao says:

> Comrade Bethune's spirit, his utter devotion to others without any thought of self, was shown in his great sense of responsibility in his work and his great warm-heartedness towards all comrades and the people. Every Communist must learn from him.
>
> We must all learn the spirit of absolute selflessness from him. With this spirit everyone can be very useful to the people. A man's ability may be great or small, but if he has this spirit, he is already noble-minded and pure, a man of moral integrity and above vulgar interests, a man who is of value to the people. (Mao 1939, pp. 337–338)

Although Mao's article was intended to address communists and communist health workers, with the establishment of communist ruling in China, his call for learning from Dr. Bethune became a political demand for all health professionals, regardless of their Party membership.

The CCP insisted that the most fundamental difference between its government and all previous governments and regimes laid in that it was a political party which placed the people at the center and served the interests of the people. Such rhetoric was particularly loud in healthcare. From the very beginning, "serve the people" was established as the cornerstone of the new healthcare system, and the departure point for all health policies. When Zhu De, Vice Chairman of the PRC, addressed the First National Health

Conference in 1950, he emphasized that the old reactionary government did not care about the life and death of the people, but "our people's government ... is committed to the nearly 500 million people" (Zhu 1951, p. 6). He commended the health workers of the communist army for their self-sacrifice in order to complete tasks just because they had embraced "serving the people" as the outlook on life. He further called for all military and civilian health workers to unite their conscience and perception and unanimously establish "serve the people" as the outlook on life (Zhu 1951).

According to Lampton, there are two types of health policy: normative policy and action policy. Normative policy, representing "a set of long-term goals and values supporting more short-term programs," was formulated in the First National Health Conference and has not changed significantly since then. It has four "enduring dimensions": "(1) Emphasis on preventive medicine. (2) Promotion of the union of traditional and western medicine. (3) Provision of health services for 'the broad masses.' (4) Utilization of mass health campaigns and mobilization of the people to solve their own health problems" (Lampton 1977, p. xviii). But these four dimensions are not of equal importance. Dimension three—serving the "broad masses"—is the most important, while the other three are secondary and derivative. Li Dequan (Health Minister) and He Cheng emphasized repeatedly that the kernel of health work was to serve the people and the masses in particular. To achieve this fundamental goal, it was better to take proactive action to prevent the spread of disease and to prevent the people from getting sick than to passively treat them when they were sick; it was better for Western-style doctors to join forces with traditional doctors so that there would be more health personnel to serve particularly peasants and workers who had little access to health services before; and it was better to involve the people to actively participate in health campaigns to improve their health awareness, foster healthy lifestyles, and take their health into their own hands. The distribution of health resources (including human resources), the establishment of grassroots healthcare organizations, and medical education policy were also designed to serve this ultimate purpose. Even the governmental support of individual private practice and united clinics were meant to serve the people better (He 1951c; Li 1951).

"Serve the people" was not just the ideological basis of all other health policies. It was also the ideological foundation of the CCP's relationship with healthcare professionals. This ideological commitment provided the government with the ideological justification to suppress the organizational power of medical professions.

The Loss of Organizational Power

After 1949, the medical professions swiftly lost their organizational power. The loss was particularly conspicuous in two areas. Firstly, medical associations were unified and subject to strict governmental supervision and control and were thus defanged. Secondly, the Party-state was deeply involved in associational affairs and controlled the membership of medical associations. For professions, this represented a great loss of organizational power and political muscle.

Immediately after 1949, all medical professionals associations were disbanded. Shanghai made a good example of how medical professions lost their organizational power. Before 1949, there were many medical and health professional associations in Shanghai, representing a wide variety of disciplines, such as nursing, midwifery, dentistry, private hospitals, pharmacy, Western-style medicine, traditional medicine, and so on. Among them, the most powerful and distinguished associations were SNMU and SMPA. In 1951, however, all the associations in the medical and health sector were disbanded and were required to join together to form one association only—Shanghai Health Workers' Association (SHWA). Professionals and non-professional practitioners of all medical and health disciplines and trades were organized into parallel sub-committees under the umbrella of SHWA. There was little doubt that the marriage was forced politically; as during the preparation period between October 1951 and September 1952, the would-be members were organized to study politics and policies, and to receive socialist and patriotic education. According to the brief account of the history of the SHWA in Shanghai Health Annals, its major responsibility since its inauguration appears to have been organizing political studies to ensure political obedience.[1]

The famous CMA survived, mainly because it was not a professional association but a scholarly society. Even so, its autonomy was significantly compromised. Established in 1915 as a society purely for Western-style doctors, it was deeply involved in the movement aiming at abolishing traditional medicine in the Republican era (Xu 2001, p. 192). Since 1954, however, it started to admit TCM practitioners. In 1956, it admitted 702 TCM doctors, more than the number of Western-style doctors it did in that year (Anonymous 1956b).

With the loss of organizational power and disappearance of public space, medical professionals became powerless in fending off the Party-state's interference in professional autonomy in economic, work, and even technical terms.

The Loss of Economic Autonomy

Although private practice was permissible in the early years of the PRC, that did not mean the CCP accepted bourgeois medicine. The CCP claimed what set itself from all the previous regimes was its commitment to serving the people selflessly. Before 1949, the CCP did not have the capacity to train medical professionals and had little control over medical and educational institutions. The vast majority of qualified medical professionals worked in the cities and regional localities under the control of the Nationalist government. After 1949, the CCP believed that these doctors must have acquired bourgeois mindsets and behaviors which prevented them from serving the people under the new regime. As the modernization project could not proceed without qualified human resources, the CCP had to rely on "old" health professionals, but they must be transformed through political learning and ideological reform to make them useful for the new system (He 1951c).

For this purpose, an edited book which contained over ten articles by communist leaders such as Mao Zedong and Zhu De, and leading healthcare officials such as He Cheng, was published several times by local governments of the CCP regime to educate health workers. The preface of the book claimed the aim of the book was to "profoundly criticize the previous and remaining capitalist medical thoughts" in order to "establish the proletariat standpoint and the ideology and practice of serving the people" among health personnel (Editor 1951). One of the articles, whose author was unnamed, described bourgeois medicine as established on the basis of private practice, which necessitated the doctor to consider personal gains when treating diseases. The more patients, the higher income. All bourgeois medical organizations were thus opponents of any programs of social medicine. "To cling to their uncertain position, bourgeois doctors are ready to sell their soul at any time" (Unknown 1951, p. 63). He Cheng, in a speech addressing a health research conference, divided medical personnel into two types. One type of doctors exploited the suffering of patients for profits, while the other sympathized with patients. The former were the seller of technique and were thus selfish. He claimed that "some 'old' medical personnel, working in the 'old' society, embarked on the road of degeneration because of the influence of the 'old' political, economic, and cultural institutions" (He 1951a, p. 45). When selling their medical skills, these doctors were turning the noble medical morality into commodity for sale (He 1951a).

As a result, private practitioners and private medical organizations, although being permitted to continue their business, had to participate in political learning campaigns in order to eliminate their bourgeois mentality and profit-driven behaviors and establish proletariat ideology. As He Cheng demanded, "private practitioners should pro-actively change their old practice, study politics, establish the mentality of serving the people, correct the idea of pursuing profit only, and go to the masses. Only so can they develop and have a future" (He 1951c, p. 13). For example, as a response to the ideological demand to transform private practitioners, Tianjin government held a health conference in the wake of the First National Health Conference. Participants included government officials and medical practitioners in both the public and private sectors. The conference passed four resolutions. One was to require private hospitals and clinics to provide free medical services to the poor. It is reported that the conference was an occasion of extensive and profound education for the private sector and assisted private institutions to eliminate the viewpoint of purely for profit. The conference accentuated the policy of serving the worker, the peasant, and the soldier. The participants from the private sector are alleged to have said that "previously we only treated the rich, and looked down upon the poor. Now we must change to treat the poor and love the labouring people" (Tianjin Government 1951, p. 9). In response to the demand for free services to the poor, private practitioners expressed that the percentage set by the government was not high and could be raised further. They also passed a bill to unify the rates of services across all private hospitals and clinics (Tianjin Government 1951).

Some medical workers employed in the public organizations were also criticized for inappropriate mentality. Doctors who were concerned about their income, welfare, and work conditions were criticized for pursuing fame and gain, "poisons that the 'old' society left with us" (He 1948 [1951], p. 52). Such doctors did not care about their work, but were only concerned about "better food, better housing, and better attire, which is hedonism of landlord and bourgeoisie" (ibid.). They needed to purify their thought through intensive political studies in order to rid of bourgeois ideology (He 1948 [1951], Zhu 1954). In short, the pursuit of personal gain was vehemently denounced as ideologically incorrect. Medical service providers in both the private and the public sectors thus lost in ideology the bargaining ground to protect their own interests. While private economy was tolerated, the mentality of private ownership had to be eliminated. Along with the dismissing of the rights to pursue economic gains was the loss of economic autonomy on the part of individuals and businesses in the health sector.

Loss of Autonomy in Work Terms

Closely associated with the diminishing economic autonomy was the mounting ideological denunciation of the professional autonomy in terms of work patterns. This seems inevitable as the CCP took over all the public medical institutions left behind by the defeated Nationalist government, and confiscated most of the missionary hospitals and medical organizations sponsored by foreign funding (Peng 2013). To support the Korean War between 1950 and 1952, the government encouraged qualified private practitioners to join public institutions and work for the country (State Council 1951a). In the first few years of the 1950s, most of the medical professionals with formal education were in fact worked in the public sector as salaried employees. Transferring from individual private practice to salaried positions in the public sector, many doctors may not adapt well and tend to retain their old work patterns. This tendency was criticized as bourgeois individualism. Zhu Xianyi, an eminent doctor and president of Tianjin Medical College, criticized doctors for pursuing freedom and autonomy in practice. He said:

> In the old society, medical personnel could open up business. To pursue the highest income from practice, they concentrated in big cities. They had the freedom to set excessively high fees; they had the autonomy to decide consultation hours. They were careless about the suffering of patients and took rest for three months during the summer. They did not answer emergency call at night, and did not travel far for home visit. Medical workers who were used to such kind of life is not easy to accept the disciplinary constraint of public hospitals... They think subjecting themselves to the organization and obeying disciplines are intrusion of their "individual freedom." They do not understand that socialist reconstruction is created by organized and disciplined collective work, and is the utmost achievement of collective wisdom. Individualism is the enemy of socialist reconstruction. (Zhu 1954)

A major governmental interference in professional work patterns came in the policy of unified job allocating system. Again this was implemented under the grand auspices of serving the people. In 1950, the central government started to centrally allocate jobs for tertiary graduates (Davis 2000, pp. 256–257). In the healthcare sector, it was announced in the First National Health Conference in 1950 that the government would assign jobs to all graduates of medical schools and they would work for three years in the first place in the countryside, factories, mines, and arm forces before they were allowed to come back to work or continue to study in cities (He 1951c, p. 11). This initiative was confirmed in the State Council's "Act of Education Reform" promulgated on 1 October 1951, which decreed that the government assign jobs to all graduates of tertiary educational institutions, public and private alike (Zhou 1951a). Until 1953, the private sector was still able to receive some tertiary graduates. According to the 1953 State Council graduate distribution decree, among the 31,974 graduates, 184 were released into the private sector. But of the 1975 medical and pharmaceutical graduates, none seems to have been given jobs in the private sector (State Council 1953). From 1954, the private sector was entirely excluded from the tertiary job distribution system (State Council 1954).

In general, graduates welcomed the unified job assignment system. Firstly, most graduates were "idealistic and patriotic" and enthusiastic about serving the nation (Davis 2000, pp. 259–260). Secondly, with the diminishing private sector, the best jobs could only be found in the public sector (Davis 2000, p. 257). But tertiary graduates completely lost choice of jobs, which were rationalized by the government. "Like scarce bricks, scarce doctors, engineers, and teachers were to be distributed by a rational plan, not by personal preferences, or the capitalist code of supply and demand" (Davis 2000, p. 261). Those who were not satisfied with allocated jobs and refused unified job allocation were usually under the bombardment of ideological work and subject to intensive political study in order to make them overcome "individualism" and to accept that their individual interests must be aligned with national interests (Davis 2000, p. 258; Lian 1953).

Even the central government admitted that the unified job allocation system was not a perfect matchmaker. In spite of its constant emphasis on "matching training to employment" (*xue yong yizhi*) (see, e.g., State Council 1954), it was not uncommon that graduates were assigned to wrong posts (Davis 2000, p. 259). Warning against waste of human resources featured all State Council decrees on unified job allocation throughout the period between 1953 and 1957 (State Council 1953, 1954, 1955, 1957). The MOH complained that personnel departments did not investigate adequately the human resources needs of the work-units in their jurisdiction and the training of new graduates, and distributed jobs blindly.

Overstaff or staff doing jobs they were not trained to do were common in some work-units. Some other work-units even hoarded tertiary graduates as scarce resources and refused to release those whose training did not match the post to work-units which could use them better (The MOH Department of Cadre 1956; Yu and Gao 1957). In the whole process of job allocation, graduates' preferences were barely considered. They were required to put the national interests above individual interests and "serve the people wholeheartedly, and willingly and happily accept assigned jobs" (Ministry of Education, Ministry of Internal Affairs, and National Planning Commission 1963, p. 103). After they were assigned jobs, they could hardly change them. Any resistance to the unified job allocation or "unrealistic" expectations of individual freedom was criticized as individualism, egocentric, or mentality of the "old society" (Lian 1953). Those who rejected or resigned from assigned posts could face harsh punishment and unemployment (Ministry of Tertiary Education and Personnel Bureau of the State Council 1956).

With the completion of the Three Great Socialist Transformations in 1956, private medical practices were increasingly viewed as non-socialist work modes and were under mounting pressure. With the launch of the Great Leap Forward in 1958, the whole country was caught in political fanaticism. Private ownership in any form was no longer accepted as supplementary to socialism. Private medical practice was swiftly integrated into the public healthcare delivery system. In Guangzhou, among the 1316 individual private practitioners practicing in the six municipal districts at the end of 1957, only 200 continued to practice privately at the end of 1958. By 1959, 95.4 percent of private practitioners that had practiced either individually or in private united clinics were integrated into institutions of public or collective ownership, or *da lianhe* (grand united clinics) as they were called in those days (Guo 2011, p. 13). Similar movement occurred across the country. But the integration of private practitioners and united clinics into grand united clinics and public employment quickly inflated the workforce of public healthcare system, significantly increased the financial pressure derived from the enlarged payroll, and wreaked havoc on the public healthcare system.

The chaos was partially reverted in 1962 when the top leadership of the country realized the fiasco of the Great Leap Forward and set to remedy the disaster by rationalizing the economy. Private practices were permitted again.[2] In general, the period between 1962 and 1965 witnessed relatively lax governmental control over private health economy. Some degree of freedom in work terms for private practitioners was allowed, although limited to only the less qualified of health human resources. The majority of health workforce, particularly those with formal qualifications, continued to be employed publicly in the highly bureaucratized healthcare system.

Order in healthcare did not last long. During the Cultural Revolution, private practice was completely eliminated. Salaried doctors in the public sectors were even more heavily impacted. As Mao Zedong demanded the health policy to be re-focused on rural healthcare, a large number of urban doctors and their families were sent to work in the countryside (Qian 1992, p. 56). Between December 1967 and March 1970, 2193 medical workers were transferred from Beijing to less developed regions. Among them, 1672 medical personnel, together with nine hospitals and three medical schools, were moved to Gansu and Qinghai provinces; 791 medical workers were sent to remote suburbs in the mountainous areas to work as barefoot doctors (Wang 2001, p. 914). The medical profession now completely lost control over work terms. Private practice was entirely banned, while in the public sector, work terms succumbed to political willfulness.

Political Interference in Technical Autonomy
Another area in which political interference in professional authority and autonomy was ideologically justified was professional technique or skill. Freidson (1970) argues that in socialist countries, medical professionals did not enjoy economic autonomy and have little control over work terms, but they controlled their technique to the similar degree as their counterparts in the USA and Great Britain. The autonomy and monopoly in technique means that the doctors' professional work was not to be evaluated by laypeople, and was thus the defining feature of professional autonomy (pp. 42–43). But this was not true in China. In the early years of the PRC, the state's interference in technical autonomy of medical workers was justified in ideology. For example, the interference in the traditional medicine was justified on the ground that it had to be modernized by integrating scientific elements into its education and practice. That is, TCM needed to reform and learn from the Western-style medicine. To unite the traditional and Western-style medicine meant in the first place to modernize the former (Wilenski 1976, pp. 31–37). Consequently, the technical content and core knowledge of the TCM were subject to the interference of another discipline and became a subordinate profession. This policy established in ideology the dominance of the modern Western-style scientific medicine over TCM although this policy was soon criticized and abandoned (Croizier 1965).

The Western-style medicine was not exempt from political interference either. Western-style doctors were advised that if they did not improve their political awareness, the advancement of their technique would be impeded. The idea of putting technique above everything else was particularly targeted.

Doctors with the view of putting technique above everything else (*danchun jishu guandian*) were accused of claiming "medicine has nothing to do with politics" and "those studying natural science does not need to study politics" (He 1948 [1951], p. 54), or believing that medicine transcended class struggle (Zhu 1954). Ideologists asserted that the development of medical science was determined by social systems. The "old" society emphasized passive and curative medicine and developed technology to serve the exploitative classes of landlords and capitalists, while socialist medicine, aiming at serving the people, would develop both preventative and curative medicine. The demarcation would have an impact on medical science and control of certain diseases. Furthermore, putting technique above everything else would lead doctors to focus exclusively on the disease and ignore the patient as a social person and the social origins of the disease. Such ignorance would significantly lower the efficacy of doctors' technique and narrow their professional vision (He 1948 [1951], 1951b). If medical workers did not eliminate their bourgeois mentalities, their contribution to the socialist reconstruction would be significantly limited (Zhu 1954). He Cheng, paraphrasing Mao Zedong's ideas, insisted that technique must follow politics (He 1951b).

It was propagated that as long as medical professionals established correct ideology and served the people wholeheartedly and selflessly, their technique would advance significantly. If they did not follow the ideology of "serving the people," particularly workers, peasants, and soldiers, their technique and skill would be greatly limited. In 1957, Li Dequan, addressing the Fourth Meeting of the First People's Congress, asserted that the Party could lead health science and technology and refuted those antithetical views as rightists' attack on the Party and the people's healthcare enterprise (Li 1957a). The new political order in medicine is perfectly exemplified in the story of saving the life of Qiu Caikang.

Qiu Caikang was a worker of Shanghai Steel Factory who was burnt by molten steel in May 1958. With 89.3 percent of his body surface burnt, medical experts with bourgeois outlook did not attach any hope to the saving of his life (Lynteris 2013, p. 68). Armed with correct ideology and revolutionary enthusiasm, Guangci Hospital, which was affiliated to the

Shanghai Second Medical College, brushed aside the pessimism of bourgeois experts and saved the worker's life. The story was widely circulated on media. The Shanghai Second Medical School CCP Committee interpreted the success as having "proved, once again, that a proletarian party, and only such a party, is capable of leading every kind of work, including the extremely exacting science of medicine, that today, even the seemingly most complicated work of healing, only by departing from individual effort alone and following the mass-line can more and better results gained faster and more economically" (quoted in Lynteris 2013, p. 68).

In summation, in the pre-reform period, the medical profession lost its autonomy and organizational power. With the disbanding of incorporated professional associations active in the Republican era, the organizational and collective power of the profession was completely annihilated. Its ability to serve as a buffer zone between the state and individual professionals disappeared. Professional autonomy in economy, work patterns, and technique were attacked as bourgeois mentality and practices, and as ideologically incompatible with socialist medicine. The profession's control over education, recruitment of novice, and entry to the profession were in the hands of the government although related policies were usually made most of the time by elite professionals in administrative positions. Health human resources, especially quality resources, were entirely nationalized and absorbed into public employment. The medical profession became organizationally powerless.

But medical professionals were not completely powerless. While losing professional autonomy and collective power, they gained another power—bureaucratic power.

Bureaucratization of the Medical Professions

Nationalized doctors were not just assigned salaried positions in public employment. They gained a new status—cadre, and the power and authority associated with it.

Doctors' Cadre Status

On the one hand, the CCP claimed to be a proletariat party for workers and peasants and oppressed intellectuals frequently in the pre-reform era. On the other hand, it always accorded the educated, especially those with formal tertiary education, with higher social status, more opportunities of upward social mobility, and better economic and welfare benefits. After

1949, qualified medical and health professionals with formal education were nationalized and worked in public employment. As mentioned above, graduates of medical colleges were allocated public employment in public work-units through the unified job distribution system and were not allowed to seek employment by themselves. In the public sector, there were three kinds of work-units—administrative, institutional, and entrepreneurial work-units (Yang and Zhou 1999, pp. 38–39). Employees of these work-units generally have two types of identity—cadre and worker (ibid., p. 40). Cadre (*ganbu*) is an ambiguous term. In its narrow sense, it refers to public office holders, that is, officials above certain administrative ranks in responsible positions in all types of work-units, especially in administrative/governmental units. In a broad sense, it refers to an employment identity which was acquired through education (mainly at tertiary level), military service, or promotion from worker status (which was rare) (ibid., p. 42). Among the three paths, education was the most common way to acquire the cadre identity. Since the beginning of the PRC, tertiary students have automatically acquired the cadre identity on graduation. The "old" intellectuals who received their education in the Republican era were mostly absorbed into the public system and accorded cadre identity as long as they did not oppose the CCP (Harding 1981, pp. 35–37). The majority of public employees with general cadre identity were employed by institutional work-units, including universities and health organizations. In terms of human resources management, public employees with worker status were managed by government organs of labor; officials above certain administrative ranks were managed by CCP organs of organization (*zuzhi bu*); and employees with general cadre identity were managed by government organs of personnel (*renshi bumen*) (Feng 2010, p. 72). Many of the last type of public employees, including professionals in public health and medical organizations, fell into the category of technocrats, or *jishu ganbu* (technical cadre), to use the CCP terminology. In a sense, doctors were not medical professionals, but medical bureaucrats.

The cadre identity means more privilege than other identities. For one thing, in the Chinese bureaucratic system, no one can be promoted to a responsible administrative position without a cadre identity. For a worker to be promoted to a cadre, he or she has to acquire the cadre identity first either through education or through political merits, or both. But a tertiary graduate is automatically granted this identity, which means he or she has acquired the prerequisite for promotion to a position of certain administrative ranks and also means his or her salary and welfare entitlement are more favorable.

As state cadres, doctors had higher incomes than other social classes. As state employees, doctors did not have much say about their incomes. The consequence of nationalization of health human resources is that the wage rates of doctors have been set by the state since the early 1950s. However, in spite of political adversity against intellectuals, a social stratum to which medical professionals belong, doctors were well paid in the pre-reform era. The Communist government implemented its first significant across-the-board wage reform in 1956 (State Council 1956b). A major achievement of this reform is the establishment of a thirty-grade general wage scale, corresponding to thirty grades of administrative responsibility covering all occupational categories in all regions. The highest salary grade for the Beijing region (a category six region) was 644 *yuan* per month (that was Mao Zedong's salary), and lowest was 23 *yuan*. Different occupational categories (including administrative positions) occupied different spectra on the scale. Each occupational category was further divided into hierarchical ranks. Medical technicians (including doctors and nurses) had six professional levels and twenty-one wage ranks, covering grades six to twenty-six (Chen 2006a; Korzec and Whyte 1981). For a rank 1 Chief Doctor, the monthly salary was 333.5 *yuan*, while for a rank 4 Assistant Doctor (the lowest for Doctor ranks), the monthly salary was 62 *yuan* (State Council 1956a).

In comparison, technical workers were divided into ten ranks, covering grades nineteen (99 *yuan* per month) to twenty-eight (27.5 *yuan* per month) on the scale. Industrial workers had eight ranks, covering grade nineteen (99 *yuan* per month) to twenty-six (33 *yuan* per month). Service personnel in state organs had six ranks, covering grade twenty-five (37.5 *yuan* per month) to thirty (23 *yuan*) (Korzec and Whyte 1981). Compared with the working class, doctors' salaries were higher. If compared with peasants, the disparity was much wider. For example, in 1956, the average net income per peasant in Shangdong Province was only 86.72 *yuan* for the whole year, about 11.6 percent of the lowest level of salary for Assistant Doctor (i.e., 62 *yuan* per month).[3]

In terms of social capital and incomes, medical and health personnel with formal qualifications apparently occupied a much more favorable position than workers and peasants and enjoyed higher social esteem. They acquired a "social status" that, in Weberian terms, was anchored in bureaucracy. This status over the governed derived predominantly from "socially and economically privileged strata because of the social distribution of power" and was linked to the "possession of educational certificates" (Weber 1946, p. 200). Therefore, like their counterparts in the former Soviet Union, they became a "hybrid" profession—professionally powerless and bureaucratically powerful (Field 1991)—and became bureaucratic in their practice. On the one hand, the employment model of the profession rendered the medical professionals powerless organizationally, politically, and economically. On the other hand, the close affiliation with the Party-state also empowered the profession, which shared the state power by representing the state authority in the medical field, as its counterpart in the FSU.

Bureaucratic Power
As discussed above, the Chinese medical profession had little power in its relationship with the Party-state. Unlike autonomous professions in the Anglo-American societies which wielded tremendous corporate power to prevent the state from tyrannizing individuals, individual practitioners in China were directly exposed to the tyranny and violence of the Party-state. Work-units were predominantly Party-state organs and institutionally did not function as the intermediary structure of the society, but a cog of a huge state bureaucracy. Within this machine, individual doctors were usually powerless as professionals.

Although powerless in the face of the Party-state, public doctors in medical work-units gained additional power against ordinary patients—bureaucratic power. On top of their cultural authority that derived from the command of a body of "esoteric, scientific knowledge" which they applied "to the care and treatment of the sick" (Daniel 1990, p. 1), their cadre status acquired in the medical bureaucracy and in the hierarchical structure of the Chinese society accorded them higher social esteem and bureaucratic dominance over common patients. That is, as medical cadres, their relationship with patients took on a dimension of *guan* (officials) vis-à-vis *min* (the commoners), especially when patients were from the classes of peasants, workers, and the mass (*qunzhong*, i.e., plebeian urban residents living outside work-unit blocks, who usually did not have formal employment[4]).

In a shortage economy, public doctors served as gatekeepers of the entire public healthcare systems and controlled the redistribution of scarce medical resources. In a socialist system, the people are supposed to own the entire national resources and productive materials by proxy of the state. In reality, only the government, representing the state, has the power and right to utilize, distribute, and redistribute resources and products in terms that are decided by the government, and this is done through the omnipresent bureaucracy. Healthcare bureaucracy is charged with the responsibility of managing and distributing the vast medical resources and property. Doctors are the fingertips of the visible bureaucratic hand which are in actual contact on a day-to-day basis with the people and distribute medical resources to them. As a member of the people—the nominal owner of the state medical property and resources—what, how much, and at what price a patient can get from the public healthcare system is left at the discretion of doctors who are the frontline guardians of the public property and resources. This discretion gives doctors significant power over patients, especially when scarcity in public medical resources prevails, and the alternative non-public sector is extremely limited or non-existent.

In the course of delivering medical services to the beneficiaries of public health insurance and labor insurance, Chinese doctors' professional autonomy was further constrained due to retrenchment in healthcare spending, but their bureaucratic power was increased. This type of bureaucratic power "derived from the hierarchies of the organization, as embodied in the formal authority, and rules and procedures in organizations" (Zhou et al. 2012, p. 85). When seeking medical services from doctors in a bureaucratic setting, patients were in principal subalterns while doctors were medical cadres in superior and supervising positions responsible for the distribution of state resources.

Since its establishment in 1952, the public medical insurance (PMI, *gongfei yiliao*) has been in deficit all the time, which has been caused by poor design and management (Wu 2014). In the first decade, PMI, funded by the budget of government at all levels, covered the fees generated from consultation, surgery, hospitalization, and medicine. The insured, who were employees and retirees of governmental and institutional work-units and political organizations (namely, those with cadre status), and university students (the future cadres), only paid out of pocket for meals in and transportation to hospitals (Zhou 1952; Ministry of Health 1952, 1953). In the early years, the coverage of the PMI expanded rapidly, with the number of beneficiaries increasing from 4 million in 1952 to 7.4 million in 1957 (Wu 2014). The PMI was under great financial pressure.

To make things worse, behaviors of users and providers under PMI were poorly disciplined and monitored. Waste and "frivolous" use of medicine was widespread as both the patient and the doctor shared the same thinking: "the state will pay" (Lampton 1977, p. 165). Over-prescription of medicine, especially expensive drugs and herbal medicine, was identified as the major reason behind the skyrocketing PMI deficit (Huang 1957; Shanxi

Provincial Health Department 1957; Jiangxi People's Committee 1957). Doctors were criticized for not following medical principles and involved personal considerations, such as personal relationship (*renqing*) and "face" (*mianzi*) into the performance of professional services and the discharge of their bureaucratic responsibility, prescribing excessive medicine to PMI beneficiaries if the latter had higher bureaucratic ranks, or colleagues, friends, and relatives of doctors (Huang 1957; Hunan People's Committee 1957). Doctors' submission to beneficiaries' irrational requests was blamed as one of the major reasons of uncontrolled deficit.

To return the PMI to balance, local governments started to introduce co-payments since 1957 (e.g., Jiangxi People's Committee 1957), a measure that was adopted by the central government in 1965 (CCP Central Committee 1965). Apart from financial means, a more frequently used approach was to improve management and tighten bureaucratic discipline and supervision. In this regard, doctors' bureaucratic responsibility was strengthened. Doctors were required to eliminate personal elements and considerations in their work, stick to rules and principles, and take "impersonal" (*bu jiang qingmian*) attitudes toward their patients (Wang and Zhou 1965; Jiangxi People's Committee 1956). However, this should not be mistaken as a demand for improving professionalism. On the contrary, the idea of "pure medicine," which argued that treating patients was the business of doctors, while deficit was the business of accountants, was also criticized as ideologically incorrect (Henan Shan County Health Office and Henan Shan Country Bureau of Finance 1965). Through thought work (*sixiang gongzuo*), doctors were expected to raise their political awareness of protecting state property, strengthen their sense of responsibility, follow the rules, and explain the rules to patients and educate them (Henan Shan County Health Office and Henan Shan Country Bureau of Finance 1965; Jiangxi People's Committee 1957; Hunan People's Committee 1963; Tianjin Bureau of Finance 1965). While they should not delay the treatment of patients, they must take full responsibility toward state property and not waste a single cent of the public money (Shanxi Provincial Health Department 1957; Anhui People's Committee 1958). In some places, task forces composed of accountants, pharmacists, and doctors were set up to check PMI prescriptions to ensure doctors did not over-prescribe or prescribed expensive drugs that were not covered by PMI drug list (Henan Shan County Health Office and Henan Shan Country Bureau of Finance 1965; Jiangxi People's Committee 1956). In company with the limitation of professional autonomy, local governments also decreed that doctors' "correct" decisions must be followed. Cadres who pressured doctors into over-prescription or prescribing expensive drugs would be criticized and educated, and the prescription would not be reimbursed. Hospitalized beneficiaries who refused to follow doctors' order to discharge from hospitals would be reported to their work-units and would face criticism. The costs arisen from over-stay would be paid by patients out of their pockets (Hunan People's Committee 1963; Jiangxi People's Committee 1957).

Furthermore, as state cadre, doctors were also required to perform some kind of health "policing" functions like their counterparts in the FSU (Field 1991, pp. 53–54). A major responsibility in this regard was their authority to sign sick leave certificates (*bingjiatiao*).

Workers' rights to 8-to-10-hour workday and to rest and recreation were recognized in China's Constitutions, but in reality, workers' rights were frequently ignored. Overtime, paid or unpaid, was endemic in industry. The CCP's ambition to modernize China in a short timeframe in order to demonstrate the advancement of socialism as a way to organize industrialization, and to respond to pressures of the Cold War, usually led to irrational planning of production at all levels. Productive goals and tasks were set at an impractically high level, which, compounded by poor management, was far beyond the capacity of enterprises. As the fulfillment of these goals and tasks bore not only economic consequences, but, more importantly, also political consequences, overtime became the most useful strategy for enterprises to achieve the goals imposed on them as a command by the state. Overtime was particularly worrying during the Great Leap Forward and the Cultural Revolution (Zhu 2009).

Workers usually did not have much bargaining power in the enterprise (Jia 2012). They were told that "state plan is the law" (Lin 2013, p. 151) and completing the state productive plan demonstrated their political loyalty and contribution to the state building. Refusal to work overtime was regarded as "political backward," and may face criticism or even disciplinary actions (Hu 1956; Editor 1955; He 1956). As excessive overtime was illegal, in many factories and mines, workers were forced to "volunteer" their overtimes as contributions to the state (Lu 1956; Yao and Bai 1955; Editor 1955; Zhi 1955). During the Great Leap Forward and the Cultural Revolution, monetary compensation for overtime was regarded as contradictory to workers' status as "masters" of the country. Their selflessness and obligation to collectivism were emphasized and praised. Political mobilization and rewards replaced economic rewards for overtime (Lin 2013). Under the political and administrative pressure, overtime became endemic and tremendously damaged the health of workers. In this circumstance, sick leave inevitably increased and was virtually the only politically and administratively feasible way for workers to gain rest and recovery from the vicious overtime. Granting sick leave was the responsibility of doctors.

The Labor Insurance Act enforced in 1951 provided that workers were entitled to paid work-related and non-work-related sick and injury leave. Leave up to six months would be fully paid by the enterprise. For leave exceeding six months, the payment would be drawn from labor insurance fund (Provision 13) (State Council 1951b). In 1957, the MOH and the All-China Federation of Trade Unions jointly approved "Provisional measures of granting workers and staff sick, injury, and maternity leave." It provided that leave certificates had to be issued by medical institutions and signed by doctors. In general, doctors were given the authority to sign off a sick leave of no more than 5 days, and no more than 15 days consecutively for the same illness. Although doctors' discretion in terms of the length of sick leave was limited, this regulation respected doctors' professional autonomy in deciding whether an employee should be granted sick and injury leave. But in reality, doctors' professional autonomy and discretion were highly limited while their bureaucratic and administrative role was emphasized.

Bureaucratized doctors, especially those worked in medical institutions operated by enterprises, were charged with the responsibility of ensuring high turnout rates, particularly when the state-allocated productive tasks inflated. This responsibility could be discharged by promoting health and safety practices and providing preventative medicine to employees or, perhaps more often, by controlling the "standards" for and the number of sick leaves. In the latter case, doctors were pressured to follow administrative orders rather than their professional principles when signing off sick leave certificates. In a report published on *Laodong* (*Labor*) in 1956, workers of Shanghai Transport Co. complained about unbearable overtime. They were particularly unhappy about the company doctor who assisted the administration to force the workers to work overtime.

Not only the Second Factory of the Company publish articles on bulletin boards calling workers to work overtime, but its doctor, under the instruction of the administration, also found a lot of excuses to restrict workers taking sick leaves. The body temperature (of workers) had to reach 40 degrees to be granted a sick leave certificate. Worker Wu Hanzhang, who had stomach disease and lower back pain and was unfit for work, requested a sick leave. The doctor said, "(your) body temperature is normal, so no sick leave." He further said,

"Stomach disease doesn't count as a disease, and lower back pain is nothing—if you think it is a pain, it is; if you don't think it is a pain, it is not." (Hu 1956)

A eulogy dedicated to a beloved mother who worked as a doctor in a munitions factory provided another glimpse into the institution of granting sick leave in the 1970s:

I remember during the Cultural Revolution, in 1973, when she worked as a factory doctor in the hospital of the Mail Box 25 Factory in Chengdu, workers laboured very hard. Many workers tried to get some rest. Some of these workers were indeed sick and so tried hard to get sick leave certificates in order to take some rest. Many doctors did not sign sick leave certificates for minor illnesses. My mother thought that they were all ordinary people. When sick, they deserved rest. So many workers who were sick or had cold lined up in front of my mother's office for sick leave certificates for a three-day off. In those days, doctors usually only had the right to grant a sick leave of three days.[5]

Lack of further evidence, it is difficult to gauge the extent of bureaucratic interference with doctors' professional discretion to grant sick leave, but there seems little doubt that such interference did exist, especially in enterprise settings. Doctors' obligation and authority to exercise organizational control over employees' sick behaviors and benefits were prioritized over their professional discretion. It is highly likely that they had to follow internal bureaucratic rules rather than their expertise to decide whether a worker was fit for work and whether a worker deserved a sick leave. Such "policing" power derived from doctors' positions as state medical officials who were responsible for the distribution of sick leave as a type of scarce state-owned resources and as a means to ensure productivity of an enterprise in order to fulfill tasks allocated by the state. In this circumstance, it is no surprise that the "Provisional measures of granting workers and staff sick, injury, and maternity leave" placed the doctor's responsibility to the state before that to workers and staff (Item 15).

Bureaucratic Medicine
Max Weber identified impersonality as one of the distinctive characters of the ideal type of modern bureaucracy, which is dominated by "a spirit of formalistic impersonality: '*Sine ira et studio*', without hatred or passion, and hence without affection or enthusiasm. The dominant norms are concepts of straightforward duty without regard to personal considerations" (Weber

et al. 1978, p. 225). Bureaucratic activities are governed by rules rather than by personal elements such as feelings toward superiors, colleagues, and clients. A more decisive aspect of bureaucratic impersonality lies in that the loyalty of a bureaucrat is no longer attached to a person, but to an office, and to its "impersonal and functional purposes" (Weber et al. 1978, p. 959). Weber argues that "[b]ureaucracy develops the more perfectly, the more it is 'dehumanized,' the more completely it succeeds in eliminating from official business love, hatred, and all purely personal, irrational, and emotional elements which escape calculation" (Weber et al. 1978, p. 975).

While Weber praises impersonality as representative of the rationality of bureaucracy and rule of law and promoting productivity, many sociologists find this character is double-edged. Robert Merton (1968) argued that the emphasis on impersonality and "the categorizing tendency" developed from "the dominant role of general, abstract rules" may cause conflicts between bureaucrats and the public (p. 256). Clients, who understandably considered their situations as special, often felt offended by such "categorical treatment" (p. 256). Merton pointed out that "[t]he impersonal treatment of affairs which are at times of great personal significance to the client give rise to the charge of 'arrogance' and haughtiness' of the bureaucrat" (p. 256). "The bureaucrat, in part irrespective of his position within the hierarchy, acts as a representative of the power and prestige of the entire structure. In his official role he is vested with definite authority. This often leads to an actually or apparently domineering attitude, which may only be exaggerated by a discrepancy between his position within the hierarchy and his position with reference to the public" (Merton 1968, p. 257). As public organizations were usually of monopolistic nature, the public or clientele had no alternative agencies to obtain similar services. The monopolistic position of public organizations further strengthened the authority of the bureaucrat, and enlarged the tension between ideology and fact: "the governmental personnel are held to be 'servants of the people,' but in fact they are often superordinate, and release of tension can seldom be afforded by turning to other agencies for the necessary service" (Merton 1968, pp. 257–258). In the interactions between officials and clients, "petty tyranny" becomes a daily norm in all bureaucratic organizations even in industrialized, democratic societies in the West (Herzfeld 1993).

Medicine is supposed to be personal services for the special needs necessitated by the conditions of the patient. Traditionally, doctors act as agents of patients and are required by professional ethics to put the patient's interest on top priority (Mechanic 1976, pp. 14–15). In a bureaucratic setting, however, medicine is inevitably affected by the negative aspects of the characters of bureaucracy, which leads to the rise of bureaucratic medicine that is characteristic of impersonalized relationship between the medical professional/bureaucrat and the patient/client. As Weber expected of an official in a typical bureaucratic institution, doctors' loyalties shifted "from the individual patient providing the fee to the organization" (Mechanic 1976, p. 15). This shift may lead to the strengthening of technical quality of medical services, but "patients are dealt with more impersonally. Patients are more likely to feel that physicians are inflexible, less interested in them, and less willing to take time to listen to them. There is a tendency in such organizations to give relatively less attention to the patients' concerns and relatively more attention to the problems of organization and work demands" (Mechanic 1976, p. 15).

In the pre-reform China, bureaucratized medicine demonstrated an even stronger tendency to impersonality and oversight of patients' interests. In the totalitarian period of China, work-units were state functionaries which managed, utilized, distributed, and redistributed resources, products, and benefits that were in the possession of the Party-state. For employed individuals, the work-unit meant far more than a job. They acquired from it their careers, resources, welfare, status, social life, identity, and so on (Li and Li 2000). China's healthcare system was operated through work-units, such as hospitals and clinics. In such a work-unit, each doctor was an individual representative of state authority, namely, the authority to practice and govern, although they also formed part of the human resources of the hospital and were in the possession of the state. The professional power and authority that a doctor exercised in his or her work was granted by the state through state employment. Without state authorization, any individual practitioner cannot practice legally. In addition, the work-unit redistributed to individuals resources and opportunities the state entrusted to it, in accordance with pre-set plans. These resources and opportunities were usually scarce and were not available to people outside the work-unit system. As a result, the work-unit system had a "totalitarian" control over its employees. The latter relied entirely on the work-unit for nearly everything, from physical resources to career rewards. Such reliance had a profound impact on the doctor–patient relationship.

In practice, public doctors faced patients directly, but institutionally, both doctors and patients did not deal with each other directly. Their interaction took place through the curtain of the work-unit. Patients were not clients of medical professionals, but medical tasks assigned by the state to medical work-units; doctors were not medical professionals but medical officials carrying out the duties entrusted to them by the state through work-units. Medical personnel were not accountable to patients, but to their work-units because of their dependence on the latter for all physical and nonphysical resources, benefits, and rewards. Institutionally, patients' satisfaction and choice had little relevance to the rewards to doctors and had little influence on their behaviors and career. Unlike private practitioners or self-funded united clinics which relied predominantly on patients' satisfaction and acceptance for business and professional rewards, public doctors in work-units were rewarded not by the quality of their services to patients, but by formal and informal factors decided by work-units and the political system that in most cases had little to do with their professional performance. Organizationally, public doctors had no incentive to orient themselves to the service of the patient. This inevitably led to the prevalence of bureaucratic medicine, or bureaucratism in medicine. The delivery of healthcare through medical work-units particularly enlarged the impersonal nature of bureaucratic medicine. As the work-unit severed the professional-client relationship between doctors and patients, medical bureaucrats emphasized even more on their obligation to following impersonal rules than on their loyalty and service to individual patients.

From the very beginning of the PRC, complaints about the inflexibility of official rules in the healthcare system were widespread. An example of this was that in an unnamed hospital, a prescription had to be signed by seven to eight persons, including an intern, a doctor, a responsible doctor, a chief doctor, a prescription maker, a chemist, a pharmacist, and a nurse before the patient could get his prescribed medicine (Wang 1950). Patrons of public hospitals were particularly unhappy about the rigid and over-elaborate rules in relation to fees, which required upfront fees must be paid before any service was provided. Many readers complained on newspapers that medical personnel wouldn't budge a little in case of emergencies, even if patients' companies begged them to provide treatment and promised to get money immediately. Many unnecessary deaths resulted from the delay of treatment due to doctors' insistence on following bureaucratic rules of paying upfront fees (Editor 1952; Xu and Li 1952). There were also complaints about medical organizations sticking to the boundaries of systems and buck-passing practices to the point of callousness. For example, readers complained on the *People's Daily* that the Transport Hospital rejected a gas poisoned patient from the Central Youth League School in Beijing on the ground that the School was not part of the system that the hospital belonged to (Editor 1952). The patient later died due to the delay. Similar cases were abundantly reported on newspapers.

In spite of the frequent anti-bureaucratism movements staged between 1949 and 1966, in the healthcare system, as in other sectors, bureaucratism was mostly addressed by rationalization that aimed at "more bureaucratization" (Harding 1981, p. 14). In 1953, the MOH launched a study movement particularly targeting bureaucratism in healthcare. In the mobilization speech delivered on 19 February 1953, He Cheng criticized health administrative departments for lack of execution, supervision, and inspection, and for commandism, and blamed medical personnel for indifference to the suffering of the masses and for negligence and numerous malpractices. He emphasized that bureaucratism was not limited to health officials, but a problem of doctors and nurses as well (He 1953). When the movement was implemented locally, however, hospitals responded with more bureaucratism and formalism, putting aside time to study governmental documents and political works of the top leadership with little concrete methods and measures to improve the efficiency and effectiveness of the bureaucracy, still less response to the demands of the vast population (Shanxi Provincial Health Department 1953, Jiangxi Provincial Health Department 1953).

The bureaucracy-initiated and bureaucracy-centered solution demonstrated a strong tendency toward strengthening rules and institutions and inadequate attention to the masses in general and to patients in particular. There was no doubt that enhanced bureaucratic structure, tightened discipline, improved training of staff, and increased specialization benefits users of the healthcare system and lowered the rate of malpractice. At the same time, however, the medical bureaucracy became increasingly impersonal and organization-centric, which inevitably led to the negligence of the political demand of serving the people. In a broad sense, public healthcare was urban-biased, rural population being provided with far less resources. In its narrow sense, rules, regulations, and procedures developed by medical organizations and authorities focused predominantly on the advancement of medicine as science and a career for medical staff. Patients' interests were secondary considerations. The bureaucratic medicine alienated its clientele and caused tension in the relationship between medical personnel and patients. Doctors and nurses complained about patients being rude and aggressive and distrusting medical workers (Li 1957b; Zhou 1957), while patients complained about medical workers being arrogant and condescending and indifferent to their sufferings (Kang 1957). In some cases, such tension could lead to violence, with medical workers being physically assaulted most of the time (Editor 1956, 1957).

Such situation was a far cry from the harmonious relationship that the top leadership of the CCP, particularly Mao Zedong, expected, and convinced him that bureaucracy could not effectively solve bureaucratic problems all by itself (Yang 2013). The Great Leap Forward in medicine represented a change to "radical approach" (Harding 1981, p. 15) toward bureaucratic problems, which aimed at destroying the bureaucracy in order to release medicine from bureaucratic constraints and to make it serve the people better. Revolutionary elements of the healthcare system were mobilized to turn the system upside down. Established rules and institutions were abandoned or radically changed, hierarchy broken down, and specialization denounced.

Toward the mid- to late 1958, when the fever of the Great Leap Forward was at its highest temperature, rules and procedures established before were criticized as facilitating medical staff and hospitals rather than patients and encourage doctors and nurses to "love the disease, not the patient" (Guan 1958; Yang 1958a; Wang 1958a). They were antithetical to the principle of serving the people, and thus must be revolutionized. "Revolution" happened mainly in three areas. The first was outpatient office hours. In response to complaints about rigid consulting hours and long waiting time for seeing a doctor, hospitals extended clinic time from the normal one 8-hour shift to 24-hour three shifts, or other patterns, such as 12 or 13 hours or two 8-hour shifts, to facilitate after-hour visits of employees of other sectors and people traveling from afar. Secondly, senior doctors, who preferred inpatient wards as inpatients provided a better opportunity to build up their medical skills and academic career, were demanded to attend outpatient clinics as a way to demonstrate their political willingness to serve the masses. Thirdly, doctors and nurses were sent in teams by their hospitals to factories, organizations, and countryside to serve the working people in their workplaces (Zhang 1958; Yang 1958b; Wang 1958b; Fan 1960; Zhu 1958).

In the bureaucratic medical institutions, hierarchy had two dimensions—administrative and technical. While the administrative hierarchy was regarded as necessary, technical hierarchy was criticized as bourgeois inequality. Senior doctors and medical researchers were leashed at for monopolizing research resources and opportunities, suppressing junior doctors and nurses in research and practice, bullying and denigrating subordinates, and even appropriating the research outcomes of subordinates (Qiu et al. 1958). To break down authority and technical hierarchy, the

Beijing Union Hospital, one of the best hospitals in China, sent senior doctors to outpatient departments and involved junior doctors and nurses in medical research. This was termed "technical democracy" (Guo and Xiong 1958).

Specialization is one of the defining characteristics of bureaucracy and medical profession. During the Great Leap Forward, however, the barrier between specialties and even professions was pulled down as a reform to destroy technical hierarchy and professional dominance (Lampton 1977, p. 167). In some major hospitals in Beijing, nurses were encouraged to practice medicine along with doctors, while the latter were praised for practicing caring and acupuncture. Pharmacists and pathologists were required to study and practice caring, midwifery, and TCM. Everyone was supposed to be versatile. Doctors, nurses, and medical workers were required to join forces to "form" one occupation (Guo and Xiong 1958; Editor 1958).

As in other sectors, the Great Leap Forward created chaos in healthcare. Fortunately, the political frenzy did not last long. In July 1959, the MOH held a national forum of hospital work in which the impact of the Great Leap Forward on hospitals was the focus. Although the conference did not challenge the "correctness" of the Great Leap Forward and some of the reforms it brought about to the system, it made some attempts to restore bureaucracy. The conference pointed out that quality of medical services must not be sacrificed and the norms ensuring the quality must not be eliminated. The workloads of medical workers should be rational in order to guarantee sufficient time for rest, recreation, and study. More importantly, the conference recommended that the abolition or creation of norms and regulations must be taken seriously to ensure order and efficiency, indicating a latent strong push for the restoration of bureaucratic practice (Editor 1959).

Along with the conclusion of the Great Leap Forward in early 1961, bureaucratization was quickly restored in the healthcare system. Convenience for the patient was no longer considered as an important principle to organize healthcare delivery. Priority was predominantly given to the construction of bureaucracy and institutions which were viewed as the ultimate guarantee of efficiency and effectiveness. A central theme in the administration of hospitals was to create and improve rules and regulations, strengthen hierarchical structures of responsibility, and observe these norms strictly. This was regarded as the most important way to improve the quality of medical services (Ji 1961; Anonymous 1961a; Tan 1963). The impersonality of bureaucracy again dominated the healthcare system and led to the resurgence of bureaucratic medicine and increasing alienation of patients. An incident can illustrate the frustration of the patient faced with the impersonal bureaucratic system. A doctor, whose name was Yu Zhongfu, was reported to have recalled an incident before the Cultural Revolution:

> It was a noon, the time was 11:35, when an old worker carried his sick child who was short of breath to seek treatment at Nanchang No. 3 Hospital where Yu Zhongfu worked. Because he was five minutes late [for the morning outpatient session], he couldn't register for a doctor. And because the body temperature of the child was one degree below the requirement for "emergency," the hospital [emergency department] rejected the child. The old worker had to wait with his child in his arms until afternoon. But, when doctors came back to work in the afternoon, his child was already dead. The old worker was angry and made a complaint against the "hospital of the lord." Yu Zhongfu did not care much about it at that time. (Xinhua News Agency Reporter 1969)

Despite the latent alienation of the clientele of the healthcare system, medical professions were largely left alone to carry out the business in their own way during the relatively stable period between the Great Leap Forward and the launch of the Cultural Revolution. Political interference did exist but was limited, and the political zeal was mainly directed at spurring medical institutions to serve the broad masses in an economic manner.

The Cultural Revolution represented a major disruption of the health bureaucracy and the bureaucratic organization of medical services. The function of the MOH was nearly paralyzed, especially in the early stage of the Revolution (Lampton 1977, Chap. 9). "Rationalization" was again criticized as bourgeois mentality. Any norms that were not established to give convenience to workers, peasants, and soldiers were considered as counter-revolutionary and must be eliminated and replaced. Again outpatient clinic hours became an issue. In Beijing TCM Hospital, early morning, noon, evening, and night shifts were added to the normal shifts, and the daily number of outpatients was not limited. Patients could receive medical services immediately at any time of the day (Xinhua News Agency reporter 1971). Another area of "de-bureaucratization" was, again, the breakdown of technical hierarchy and barriers between professions, and even specialties. In some medical work-units, doctors were asked to do nursing, while nurses to do pharmaceutical work (Anonymous 1969). There were even suggestions to reform work clothes in hospitals so that doctors, nurses, and workers could not be distinguished by what they wore. This suggestion argued that the current work clothes reflected a hierarchical system established in light of "foreign" (*yang*) rules and doctrines and strengthened the sense of hierarchy, reputation, and profit among employees. Eliminating the distinction in clothes, nurses would feel confident to practice medicine without arousing the suspect of patients while doctors would not feel losing face if they were asked to do the job of nursing or cleaning (Zhou 1966).

In summation, the pre-reform period witnessed an oscillation between bureaucratization and de-bureaucratization in healthcare organizations. During the phases of bureaucratization, rules and regulations were formulated or reconstructed and observed closely; professional, technical, and administrative hierarchical structures were in place administering the boundaries between employees of different occupations and positions; and attention to technical details of medical work was strongly emphasized in hospitals. While the bureaucratization tended to bring efficiency and effectiveness to the healthcare system, its strong tendency to rotate around rules and regulations could alienate patients and led to public outcries over the impersonality of bureaucratic medicine. Furthermore, bureaucratic medicine, with its over-reliance on modern technology and standards, was strongly biased toward urban population. Claiming "serving the people" as the core of the CCP's health ideology, Mao Zedong was constantly unsatisfied with the urban bias of the healthcare delivery and the bureaucracy-centered rather than people-centered healthcare organization, and challenged bureaucratic medicine by emphasizing political standards and the significance of the CCP ideology to medical work. The attack on bureaucratism in medicine could temporarily tear down the hierarchical structure of healthcare organization and forced the delivery of healthcare to swing away from bureaucracy to the patient. But de-bureaucratization tended to disrupt the normal function of hospitals, led to the decrease of efficiency and quality and created confusion and disorder. More importantly, de-bureaucratization tended to redistribute medical resources that concentrated in urban areas and created shortage of quality medicine.

Shortage of Quality Medicine
In the pre-reform era, China's healthcare infrastructure and resources expanded significantly. In terms of human resources, the entire workforce in the healthcare system increased from 541,200 in 1949 to 2,593,500, representing an increase of 4.8 times. Among them, qualified Western-style doctors increased from 38,000 in 1949 to 293,000 in 1975, an increase of

Table 3.1   Number of professional staff of the whole country

	1949	1957	1965	1975
Total	541,200	1,254,400	1,872,300	2,593,500
Western-style doctors	38,000	73,600	188,700	293,000
Western-style para-doctors	49,400	135,700	252,700	356,100
TCM doctors	276,000	337,000	321,400	228,600

Source: China Health Yearbook (2002), p. 457

Table 3.2   Number of health organizations and beds of the whole country

	1949	1957	1965	1970	1975
Total (health organizations)	3670	122,954	224,266	149,823	151,733
Hospitals	2600	4179	5746	5964	8399
Total (beds)	84,600	461,800	1,033,300	1,261.500	1,764,300

Source: Adapted from China Health Statistics Yearbook (2009), pp. 3 and 65

7.7 times (see Table 3.1). During the same period, the number of healthcare institutions expanded from 3670 to 151,733, an increase of more than 41 times. The number of hospitals at and above country level increased more than 3.2 times from 2600 in 1949 to 8399 in 1975. The number of hospital beds increase from 84,600 to 1,764,300 during this period, a staggering increase of 20.9 times (see Table 3.2). The administrative and operating costs funded by the state budget increased by 4.7 times between 1953 and 1975, similar to the speed of expansion of healthcare workforce (see Table 3.3), which means the increase of healthcare budget for administrative and operational costs just covered the increase of payroll in healthcare. But the healthcare capital construction investment, which was the budget for the building of hospitals and increase of hospital beds, lagged far behind the growth.

The comparison of Tables 3.2 and 3.4 indicates that between 1957 and 1965, the number of beds more than doubled, but the capital investment by the state during the eight years (0.752 billion yuan) was just slightly more than the total investment of the previous five years (0.648 billion yuan). In average, the level of capital investment between 1957 and 1965 was about 73 percent of the average yearly investment in the First Five-Year Plan period. It only caught up with the pace of expansion of beds between 1966 and 1970. The jump of capital investment during the Fourth Five-Year Plan

Table 3.3 Healthcare operational budget in the pre-reform era

	Healthcare operational budget ¥ billion	National budget ¥ billion	% of healthcare operational budget in national budget
1st 5-year plan (1953–1957)	1.455	134.568	1.08
2nd 5-year plan (1958–1962)	2.334	228.867	1.02
Adjustment period (1962–1965)	1.884	120.498	1.56
3rd 5-year plan (1966–1970)	4.45	251.86	1.77
4th 5-year plan (1971–1975)	6.562	391.96	1.67

Source: China Health Yearbook (2002), p. 503

Table 3.4 Healthcare capital construction investment in the pre-reform era

	Health capital construction investment ¥ billion	National total capital construction investment ¥ billion	% Health in National capital construction investment
1st 5-year plan (1953–1957)	0.648	58.847	1.1
2nd 5-year plan (1958–1962)	0.485	120.609	0.4
Adjustment period (1962–1965)	0.267	42.189	0.63
3rd 5-year plan (1966–1970)	0.329	97.603	0.34
4th 5-year plan (1971–1975)	0.9	176.395	0.51

Source: China Health Yearbook (2002), p. 504

by 2.74 times on the Third Five-Year Plan may represent a policy shift from cities to the countryside and increased funding to beef up the infrastructure of rural health facilities. It is worth to note that between 1960 and 1975, the number of beds in rural hospitals increased by 13.4 times, from 46,300 to 620,300 (Ministry of Health 2009, p. 65). However, the proportion of capital construction investment in healthcare against the national capital construction investment in all sectors only represented a moderate rise by 50 percent.

As Lampton (1977) pointed out, healthcare was underfunded in the pre-reform era as it was not considered as important as other economic sectors. Hospitals were financed by balance allocation, which means that they were not fully funded by the state. Hospitals generated revenues from providing services by charging fees on users covered by public insurances or paying out of pocket. The gap between the revenue and costs was financed by public funding (Qian 1992, p. 977). As a result, the operation and development of a hospital depended on how much revenues it could generate from providing services and the supplementation of public funding to fill the revenue gap. But in the pre-reform era, this financing model had many problems. As discussed above, the increase of administrative and operational budget just kept pace with the increase of workforce in the healthcare sector, while capital construction investment lagged behind the expansion of the sector most of the time. This means hospitals had to generate more revenue to finance their development and expansion, but this was politically problematic.

As mentioned before, China has never established a *Semashko* healthcare system providing free medical services to its citizens. At the same time, the CCP adopted "serving the people" as the core of its healthcare ideology, the same as the Soviet medicine. Then how to materialize this ideology when the regime had to redistribute the limited healthcare resources to ever-increasing demand for healthcare and the expansion of population base? In general, two strategies were used. One was to reduce medical service fees, and the other was to expand healthcare infrastructure economically.

Reduction of medical service fees was frequently used as a strategy to contain the expenditure of the PMI and Labor Insurance (LI), and to increase affordability to fee-paying users. As one commentator indicated, whenever there was a complaint about soaring public insurance expenses, hospitals were required to reduce their fees (Liu 2009a). But overspend was usually viewed as an issue of public insurance management and was rarely openly cited as a reason behind reduction of medical service fees. In media, fee reduction was always described as voluntary action on the part of hospitals to increase affordability of medicine in response to the call of serving the people.

Between 1956 and 1966, there were four rounds of reduction of medical service fees, which were motivated similarly by the political commitment to the ideology of serving the people (Anonymous 1958; Zheng et al. 1987; Anonymous 1956a). These rounds of fee reduction significantly decreased hospitals' revenues from the provision of medical services, but the government did not change the level of subsidy. As a result, hospitals' losses were not adequately compensated (Zheng et al. 1987; Cai 1981). It must be noted that during the same period, the state's budget of capital construction investment was kept at a very low level, but the number of beds increased considerably. The expansion during the period of retrenchment was made possible by another political and economic demand, that is, "hard work and thrift" (*qinjian jieyue*). Since the mid-1950s, a continuous theme in hospital management was "operating hospitals industriously and thriftily" (*qinjian ban yuan*). A typical model of this type is illustrated by Xingtai City Hospital. It was reported that to meet the mounting demands for medical services in the city, the Hospital increased the number of beds by threefold without receiving a single cent from the state. The staff of the hospital was mobilized to empty staff dormitories and offices and turn them into wards, and recycle wastes, such as tables, stools, basins, and broken beds that were found in the hospital's storages. Doctors and nurses mended broken furniture to furnish the newly created wards, using private sewing machine to make quilts and bed sheets out of old curtains and mosquito nets, and repaired old and dilapidated houses into wards. Through the efforts of the entire staff members, the number of beds of Xingtai City Hospital increased from 12 to 50 (Anonymous 1957).

Such a pattern of expansion was highly praised and repeated throughout the pre-reform era, especially during the peak times of political interference of medicine. During the Great Leap Forward, increasing the beds under the guidance of "hard work and thrift" philosophy became a predominant mode of expansion. In 1958, medical organizations in Shanghai added 2000 beds without any state investment (Xinhua News Agency 1958). The First Affiliated Hospital of Shengyang Medical College added four hundred beds by squeezing more beds into one ward, turning doctors' and nurses' offices and patient entertainment areas into wards, and set up "simply equipped wards" (*jianyi bingfang*) for peasants with limited economic means (Lin 1958). Hospitals also saved expenses by repairing broken medical equipment, or making equipment themselves, recycling cotton and bandages, or even mending broken surgery gloves for reuse in medical procedures (Anonymous 1961b). Provision of sub-standard medical services and facilities was praised as a victory over bourgeois medicine and represented the spirit of "serving the people," and were used as major strategy to cope with under investment in both urban and rural areas (He 1966).

Sending urban health workers to reside in the countryside or to work in rotating medical teams also diluted the quality of medical services in cities while providing sub-standard medical services to rural people. From 1958, rotating medical teams consisted of urban medical personnel were organized to provide mobile medical services to factories and villages. Since 1965, rotating medical teams to the countryside were organized in a considerably larger scale. In the first half of 1965, three rounds of rotating medical teams were organized, involving over a hundred thousand medical professionals and workers across the country. In some provinces, urban hospitals organized "mobile hospitals" equipped with the "whole sets" of medical personnel and equipment to provide services to rural population (Xinhua News Agency 1965). Since 1966, rotating medical teams was no longer considered a politically sufficient form to respond to Mao's call to place the emphasis of health work on the countryside. Numerous medical professionals and workers were relocated from urban centers to rural centers at county and commune levels permanently to strengthen the health work in rural areas (Yu 1966; Anonymous 1966). The access of the rural population to medical services was thus increased, but the quality of the services was usually poor. For one thing, rural cooperative medicine was established and operated under the principle of "hard work and thrift." Any attempt to follow the standards of urban medicine was criticized as bourgeois and "gibberish" (Editor 1965).

The "hard work and thrift" approach apparently had negative impact on the quality of medical services. Spreading the resources for one person to more people doubtlessly increased accessibility and affordability. Given the retrenchment and periodically political requirement to reduce prices in healthcare, however, what each person received was diluted amount of benefit and reduced quality. While for the rural population, it was a change from "having nothing" to "having something," for the urban residents, especially those ordinary public employees covered by public health insurances, the quality of medical services was watered down and became scarce. While quantitative expansion still fell short of meeting the mounting needs of the population, the quality was unfortunately sacrificed, especially in urban areas.

In summation, throughout the pre-reform era, users of the Chinese healthcare system were faced with two problems—bureaucratic medicine and shortage. The bureaucratization of medical workforce through the work-unit system turned medical professionals into medical bureaucrats and alienated their clientele. Medical workers were no longer accountable to patients, because they relied completely on the bureaucracy/work-unit for career and livelihood. Granted the cadre status, doctors enjoyed higher social status. Employed in bureaucracy, they were devoted more to bureaucratic and professional rules and regulations and the functioning of bureaucracy than to the service of clients. This impersonality of their services was one of the major sources of conflict between patients and doctors. The solution was political interference with professional and bureaucratic work. The political demand to "serve the people" was continually imposed on medical workers to counter bureaucratic impersonalism and to improve their accountability to patients. The political interference, however, tended to create chaos in the system and influenced adversely efficiency and effectiveness and usually short lived. Whenever the political interference was abated, there was a strong rebound of bureaucratic practice and attitude among doctors which would lead to the next round of political interference. As a result, patients were frequently faced with either impersonal service or chaos.

Shortage of medical resources, especially quality resources, posed a more consequential problem to users. The number of healthcare facilities rose tremendously under the CCP regime, but capital investment in the construction of healthcare infrastructure remained at a very low level since 1958. That means the expansion of healthcare was achieved at the expense of quality. While access to and affordability of healthcare were improved significantly, the improvement was still unlikely to catch up with the increase of demands for medical services from both urban and rural population. The bureaucratic tendency to urban-biased curative medicine was always in odd with Mao's political and ideological commitment to the countryside, and was under constant political pressure to divert resources from urban centers to rural areas. Portioning out urban health resources to rural areas made quality medical resources in urban areas even more scarce. Compounded by the widespread impersonality in the course of seeking medical services, users of medical services, particularly users with some resources in urban areas, took the issue in their hands and addressed it beyond the official means available. This attempt led to the rise of "backdoor" medicine.

"Backdoor" Medicine
"Backdoor" medicine thrived on personalism and particularism that was inherent in Chinese society and surged particularly in the wake of the Great Leap Forward and during the Cultural Revolution. Scholars have long noticed that the traditional Chinese society was relationally structured with emphasis on ubiquitous personalism and particularism (Gold 1985; Weber 1968; Parsons 1951). Fei Xiaotong (Fei et al. 1992) relates that by nature, Chinese society, which was fundamentally rural, was a society of acquaintances (*shuren shehui*). He created the concept of "differential mode of association" (*chaxu geju*) to describe China's social structure, which worked in the way of water ripples: from the inside out (p. 63). "In the pattern of Chinese organization, our social relationships spread out

gradually from individual to individual, resulting in an accumulation of personal connections. These social relationships form a network composed of each individual's personal connections. Therefore, our social morality makes sense only in terms of these personal connections" (p. 70). He continued to point out the absence in the Chinese society of a universal "love" without distinctions as embedded in Christianity (p. 76). He noted, "[a] society with a differential mode of association is composed of webs woven out of countless personal relationships. To each knot in these webs was attached a specific ethical principle... Therefore, all the standards of value in this system were incapable of transcending the differential personal relationships of the Chinese social structure" (p. 78). That is, in this social structure, "love" and ethical standards were relationship-based and thus particularistic. As Fei said, "[i]n such a society, general standards have no utility" (p. 78).

The CCP was apparently aware of the particularism in the society and has made constant efforts to promote universalism to replace particularism under its regime. Ezra Vogel (1965) observed that the Chinese Communist regime successfully weakened private and particularistic friendship in three aspects among the people in its first 15 years of rule. First, through frequent political and economic campaigns, the CCP encouraged people to provide to the authority information which could "cause friends to suffer" (p. 46), and thus created a fear of friendship and avoidance of intimacy. Secondly, through concerted attack on nepotism and the use of personal influence, and placing the power of decision about "placement in schools or jobs in the hands of committees rather than single individuals" (p. 53), individuals were unable to utilize their positional advantage in an organization to provide others from the same locality, the same school, or the same clan with opportunities for schooling or employment (p. 54). Thirdly, individuals had much less resources of private wealth and thus could not provide "sizable economic assistance to others" (p. 54). In place of personal friendship which was accused of as a "feudalistic" relationship, the CCP, according to Vogel, successfully diffused a new morality—comradeship, "which stresses friendliness and helpfulness between all citizens" (p. 46). "The new morality does not distinguish between people on the basis of personal preferences. Like the Protestant ethic in which all are equal under God, comradeship is a universalistic morality in which all citizens are in important respects equal under the state, and gradations on the basis of status or degree of closeness cannot legitimately interfere with this equality" (p. 46).

There is no doubt that the CCP suppressed the particularistic relationship among the citizens and diffused a universalistic morality in its place, but some scholars apparently disagreed with Vogel on whether the CCP's efforts were successful. Gold (1985), drawing on personal observations and a wide assortment of publications, suggested that contrary to Vogel's conclusions, the CCP was unlikely to have penetrated the society so deeply as to root out particularistic friendship and replace it with a universalistic comradeship, and, in spite of placing the power of decisions in the hands of committees, individual members could still do favors for people related to them through personal and/or particularistic connections, namely, *guanxi*.

In the healthcare system, particularistic ethic, in spite of being under constant pressure of rectification, did not disappear during the pre-reform era. On the contrary, it flourished, especially in the decade of the Cultural Revolution. One of the reasons that had led to the surge of *guanxi* was closely related to the promotion of the ethos of universalistic particularism in the healthcare system.

Universalistic particularism was motivated by the ideal of comradeship and represented by the attempt to universalize particularism. This endeavor was embedded in the recurrent political demand that the health personnel apply "particularistic" principles to all patients, as reflected in the slogan of "treating patients as families" (*dai bingren ru qingren*). Health workers were required to apply universally and equally an emotional quality that was characteristic of a familial relationship toward all patients, be they relatives or strangers. Such a universalistic relationship was beyond comradeship. It was "comradeship plus kinship" (*tongzhi jia qinren*). Basically it was an anti-rationalism mentality emphasizing self-sacrifice and emotional commitment to the well-being of "strangers." When praising the achievement of the Second Affiliated Hospital of Wuhan Medical College in rescuing a transport worker Cheng Debao who was severely injured in an accident, Liu Yangqiao, the incumbent CCP secretary of Hubei Province, gave three reasons behind the success. The third reason was related to the attitude of service, that is, "a working people's attitude of serving the people wholeheartedly and honestly... Comrades of the Second Affiliated Hospital of Wuhan Medical College demonstrated this attitude in the process of rescuing the life of Cheng Debao. Because of this attitude, the relationship between people becomes a relationship of family (*qinren de guanxi*). Nurse comrade Lin Yuying said, 'Socialist society is a big warm family.' Indeed, in our new society, the relationship between people is no longer an ordinary relationship, but a relationship of family" (Liu 1960).

In the healthcare system, the attitude of this conditional universalistic particularism was largely encouraged by a persistent political demand that politics command technology (*zhengzhi tongshuai jishu*), but this demand constantly met strong resistance that derived from other sets of ethics, namely, bureaucratic impersonality and social particularism. The former emphasized the observation of bureaucratic rules and technological standards rather than how patients felt, while the latter impelled the practitioners to give special considerations to people in their social networks. The exercise of universalistic particularism in the healthcare system was highly dependent on political frenzy and was thus most evident during such periods as the Great Leap Forward and the early stage of the Cultural Revolution. As a result, universalistic particularism was usually unsustainable and tended to create chaos and put a strain on medical resources. Once political pressure was not imminent, it was neglected or at least took a secondary position in the medical bureaucracy. In its place were bureaucratic impersonality and social particularism which always demonstrated a tendency to differentiate patients and treat them differently.

The intermittent promotion of the unreliable universalistic particularism and the persistent and alienating bureaucratic impersonality, compounded by another, more deleterious factor—shortage—forced the patient to rely on particularistic relations for quality services, that is, seeking medical services through one's social networks. In the pre-reform era, this meant seeking medical services through "backdoors," or *zou houmen*.

Zou houmen is securing scarce goods, services, and opportunities through informal channels, and involves the abuse of two types of power—prerogative and redistributive power. Prerogative is embedded in one's official position or privileged status. In the difficult times, the government usually provided senior officials and eminent social figures (e.g., famous intellectuals) at local and central levels with specially supplied goods and services so that they could live better-off lives than commoners. But senior officials could abuse their prerogative and take more than what they were legitimately entitled to, a conduct that was antithetical to the CCP's ideological commitment to serving the people and equality. The Great Leap Forward created chaos in economy and markedly reduced in its wake the supply of consumer goods and daily necessities, which were rationed and sold by coupons. The shortage of supply was exacerbated by government officials, taking advantage of their positions and power, appropriating more supplies than permissible by policies (Zhou and Ru 2015). In 1960, the central government launched a campaign targeting "backdoor" corruption in the retail and finance sectors. The campaign, which is called "Movement Combating Obtaining Goods and Commodities through 'Backdoor,'" had as one of its major objectives reducing the quota of specially supplied goods to government officials, and preventing officials from abusing their prerogative and power (Zhou and Ru 2015; Zhong 2009). In 1963, "backdoor" corruption and abuse of prerogative were again targeted in a new round of "Five Anti" (*wu fan*) movement in cities (Wang 2011b). But in spite of these campaigns, "backdoor" corruption became worse and worse among officials. During the Cultural Revolution, the scope of "backdoor" corruption went beyond goods and services. Government officials were widely involved in obtaining through "backdoor" opportunities for related people to get employment, enter university, or join the army (Li 2011).

Zou houmen was not limited to the privileged with governmental power or prerogative. In the wake of the Great Leap Forward when the entire private sector was eliminated, general public employees who were in charge of redistributing public goods and services became the major force of "backdoor" activities. The positions of these employees could be as high as the head of a department store, or as basic as a butcher. Their redistributive power could be as grand as concerning goods and commodities of millions of *yuan*, or as tiny as cutting a piece of pork in front of a line of buyers with pork coupons in their hands. It was revealed that 70 to 80 percent of employees in public retail shops were involved in "backdoor" activities (Zhong 2009). In some shops, every single employee participated in the activities (Zhou and Ru 2015). For ordinary frontline shop assistants, redistributive power meant that they could withhold scarce goods and consumer products for or disclose their availability to relatives or people that had particularistic connections with them. It must be noted that the prerequisite for *zou houmen* was *la guanxi*—to establish underhand connections. Without *guanxi*, the "backdoor" would not open. As a doggerel of that time said, "having money in hand is not as good as knowing a shop assistant" (Li 2010, p. 176).

Even during the Cultural Revolution when the CCP's attack on the private aspect of people's life was at its peak, China did not cease to be a society of acquaintances. Particularly due to the absence of private wealth as well as a dearth of public resources, people had to resort to particularistic relationships to survive the daily hardship. People who were charged with the responsibility of distribution of or had access to public resources were engaged in covert and informal redistribution or exchange of public services or consumer products through personal *guanxi* networks (Yang 1994). It was in this context that medicine became the most sought-after occupation. The most sought-after occupations in the 1960s and 1970s were doctors, drivers, and shop assistants, and in that order.[6] Shop assistants could obtain scarce goods and daily necessities, drivers of public cars or trucks could give a "free" ride to acquaintances, but doctors could do more. Generally speaking, doctors could provide many benefits to their relatives and acquaintances through "backdoor." In the first place, the medical certificates that they signed off could bring life-changing opportunities to the recipients. Toward the later years of the Cultural Revolution, many "educated youths" sent to the countryside did everything possible to return to cities. For those from influential or resourceful backgrounds, their parents could arrange them to be transferred to formal public employment in factories or institutional work-units, or enrolled in universities (Cai 2003). For the children of ordinary families, critical medical conditions became the major excuse for returning to cities. To prove that they were seriously sick, they needed the medical certificates signed off by doctors. There were two ways to get the certificate—self-inflicted injury or "backdoor." The first approach was usually used by the most desperate and lest resourceful youths, and could be very dangerous. For those who or whose family had some *guanxi* at hand, obtaining medical certificates through "backdoors" was the only way to get themselves out of the countryside (He 2015; Bonnin 2013). As an official retired from the long-gone Guangzhou Municipal Educated Youth Office recalled, in those days, doctors were the most sought after, as they could issue medical certificates to "prove" that a healthy "educated" youth was sick and should be brought back to city, or they could "prove" that a sick youth was physically fit for employment in an urban work-unit after returning from the countryside.[7] It is believed that the informal activities attempting to get "educated" youths back to cities set start a wave of pervasive corruption that are still lingering today (Bonnin 2013). Doctors were a major player in this wave although initially they offered their help mainly out of their obligation to such particularistic relationship as kinship and friendship.

Sick leave certificate was another arena where doctors could exercise their combined bureaucratic and professional power informally and illegitimately. As discussed before, doctors could yield to the pressure of the management of the work-unit and sign off as few sick certificates as possible to ensure high turnout for timely completion of production tasks. But they could also abuse this power in another way by signing off sick leave certificates for people coming from the "backdoor" so that they could get paid leave although they were not unwell or not sick enough for a leave. Walder's study of Chinese factories revealed that in the Cultural Revolution, it was common for workers to establish *guanxi* with factory doctors and exchange gifts or favors for sick leave certificates (Walder 1986, pp. 210–219). For those who did not have *guanxi* or something to exchange, doctors could be very strict.[8]

Through "backdoor," one could get scarce resources and good attitudes. The constant low level of public investment in healthcare also led to the scarce supply of quality medicine, hospital beds, and even X-ray films. The distribution of these resources was mainly in the hands of doctors. If a patient had a relative who was a doctor, he or she could have relatively easy access to these things. Otherwise patients had to establish *guanxi* with doctors first before they could obtain drugs that were in high demand and short supply or get hospitalized sooner.[9] Doctors were also criticized for taking different attitudes toward patients. As discussed above, the major characteristic of bureaucratic medicine was impersonalism. During the Cultural Revolution, bureaucratic impersonalism quickly degenerated into rudeness and insolence.[10] But for those coming from the "backdoor," doctors were usually kind and pleasant.[11]

The "backdoor" was not for charity. It was an exchange network redistributing among acquaintances scarce goods and services that were nationalized and controlled by the Party-state. Doctors were major participants and redistributors in this network, and their involvement was not for free. In most situations, when they illegitimately dispensed medicine and services under their control through the "backdoor," they expected recipients to return favors. Sources indicate that, in spite of the political persecution targeting the educated class, ordinary doctors usually lived a better-off life in the 1960s and 1970s, as they could receive scarce goods and services through their "backdoor" network.[12]

In conclusion, since the early PRC regime, the medical professions ceased to function as an independent and intermediary structure of the new regime. Both the Western-style medicine and TCM were completely nationalized and bureaucratized, especially after the mid-1960s when private practices were entirely eliminated. The bureaucratized medicine demonstrated a strong tendency toward bureaucratic impersonalism to patients in spite of the recurrent political campaigns demanding medical professionals to serve the people wholeheartedly. Political turmoil and exacerbated shortage caused by consistent low level of public investment made quality medical services and medicine dearth. Prevalence of bureaucratic medicine and widespread shortage compelled users of the healthcare system to resort to social connections and "backdoor" practices for quality supplies and services. The economic reform, which was to a large degree meant to redress serious issues arisen from command economy, brought about institutional changes that would lead to the even wider diffusion of informal payments in the healthcare system.

NOTES

1. http://shtong.gov.cn/node2/node2245/node67643/node67661/node67750/node67882/userobject1ai65381.html, accessed 2 May 2016.
2. See, for example, http://www.fjsq.gov.cn/ShowText.asp?ToBook=3207&index=454&, accessed 23 October 2014.
3. *Shandong sheng qing ziliao ku* (Shandong Provincial Infobase) http://www.sdsqw.cn/bin/mse.exe?seachword=&K=a&A=18&rec=62&run=13, accessed 2 December 2014.
4. See Yang and Zhou 1999, p. 80.
5. http://jinian.zupulu.com/jiwen/show?jwid=54227, accessed on 29 December 2014.
6. There were several versions of this most-sought-after occupation list, which was usually spread in the form of folk doggerels. In Guangdong Province, the top three occupations were doctors, drivers, and butchers. In north China, they were doctors, drivers, and shop assistants. In all the versions, doctors always ranked the first among the top three.
7. http://news.163.com/06/0922/09/2RK7N61V00011SM9.html, accessed 15 May 2016.
8. See, for example, http://cdn.q2n.cn:8000/zbcms/2012/0811/26604.shtml, accessed 15 May 2016.
9. See, for example, http://m.kdnet.net/share-650409.html?id=650409&boardid=5, accessed 10 May 2016; http://www.hj01.com/home.php?mod=space&uid=6343&do=blog&id=594, accessed 10 May 2016; http://blog.sina.com.cn/s/blog_3fab9d250102vgnd.html, accessed 8 May 2016.
10. http://view.news.qq.com/zt2012/lianse/index.htm, accessed 10 May 2016.
11. http://m.kdnet.net/share-650409.html?id=650409&boardid=5, accessed 10 May 2016.
12. See, for example, http://cdn.q2n.cn:8000/zbcms/2012/0811/26604.shtml, accessed 15 May 2016.

BIBLIOGRAPHY

Anhui People's Committee. 1958. Guanyu gaijin gongfei yiliao yufang guanli de guiding (Regulations about improving the management of the public medical insurance and prevention). *Anhui zhengbao (Gazette of Anhui Government)* 4: 8–9.

Anonymous. 1956a. Weisheng bu yanjiu jiangdi yiliao shoufei biaozhun (The Ministry of Health is studying the possibility of reducing medical service fees). *Jiankang bao (Health News)*, 13 July, 1.

———. 1956b. Zhonghua Yixuehui xishou dapi zhongyi ruhui (Chinese Medical Association absorb numerous TCM doctors). *Jiankang bao (Health News)*, 17 July, 1.

———. 1957. Xingtai shi yiyuan qin jian jian yuan reqing gao (Enthusiasm for building Xingtai Hospital with industry and thrift). *Jiankang bao (Health News)*, 18 January, 1.

———. 1958. Gedi jiangdi yiliao shoufei jianqing bingren fudan (Medical service fees are reduced in many places to relieve patients of their burdens). *Jiankang bao (Health News)*, 9 August, 3.

———. 1961a. Jianli jianquan yiliao zeren zhi (Establish and strengthen medical responsibility system). *Jiankang bao (Health News)*, 2 September, 1.

———. 1961b. QInjian ban yuan dali zhiyuan shengchan (Run the hospital with industry and thrift and support production vigorously). *Jiankang bao (Health News)*, 14 June, 3.

———. 1966. Shandong Hubei Shanghai yi pi yiwu renyuan xiaxiang luohu (Medical personnel from Shandong, Hubei and Shanghai settled down in the countryside). *Jiankang bao (Health News)*, 23 March, 1.

———. 1969. Guangzhou shi Hongshu weisheng yuan yi hu renyuan gaibian yiliao zuofeng (Doctors and nurses of Guangzhou Red Book clinic changed their practices). *Renmin ribao (People's Daily)*, 13 January, 3.

Bo, Yibo. 1991. *Ruogan zhongda juece yu shijian de huigu (Review on several significant policies and events)*. 2 vols. Vol. 1. Beijing: Zhonggong Zhongyang Dangxiao Chubanshe (CCP Central School Press).

Bonnin, Michel. 2013. *The Lost Generation: The Rustification of China's Educated Youth*. Translated by Krystyna Horko. Hong Kong: The Chinese University Press.

Cai, Renhua. 1981. "Zuo" de sixiang daozhi yiyuan yue ban yue qiong (The "leftist" thought makes hospitals poorer and poorer). *Yiyuan guanli (Hospital management)* 2: 50–52.

Cai, Tianxin. 2003. Li Qinglin shang shu Mao Zedong yu zhiqing zhengce tiaozheng (Li Qinglin's letter to Mao Zedong and the adjustment of the educated youth policies). *Zhonggong dangshi yanjiu (CCP history study)* 4: 30–35.

CCP Central Committee. 1965. Zhonggong Zhongyang pi zhuan Weisheng Bu dang wei 'guanyu ba weisheng gongzuo zhongdian fangdao nongcun de baogao' (CCP Central Committee's approval and circulation of the Ministry of Health's 'Report on placing the emphasis of health work in the countryside'). Accessed 12 January 2015. http://news.xinhuanet.com/ziliao/2005-02/02/content_2538494.htm

Chen, Mingyuan. 2006a. *Zhishi fenzi yu Renminbi shidai (Intellectuals and the era of Renminbi)*. Shanghai: Wenhui Chubanshe (Wenhui Press).

Chu, Anping. 1947. Zhongguo de zhengju (China's political situation). *Guancha (Observation)* 2(2): 3–8.

Croizier, Ralph C. 1965. Traditional medicine in Communist China: science, Communism and cultural nationalism. *China Quarterly* 23: 1–27.

Daniel, Ann. 1990. *Medicine and the state: Professional autonomy and public accountability*. Sydney: Allen and Unwin.

Davis, Deborah S. 2000. Social Class Transformation in Urban China: Training, Hiring, and Promoting Urban Professionals and Managers after 1949. *Modern China* 26(3) (July 2000):251–275.

Editor. 1951. Preface. In *Yiwu gongzuozhe de daolu (weisheng renyuan sixiang xuexi wenjian) [The path of medical workers (Ideological learning document for health personnel)]*. Unkown: Unknown.

———. 1952. "Yiwu renyuan zhong yanzhong de bufu zeren de zuofeng bixu kefu (Medical personnel must overcome serious irresponsible practice in their work)." *Renmin ribao (People's Daily)*, 18 June, 6.

———. 1955. Bixu jianjue fandui lanxing jiaban jiadian (Firmly oppose reckless overtime). *Laodong (Labour)* 12: 12.

———. 1956. Beijing shi renmin daibiao dahui weisheng gongzuo daibiao tichu zunzhong yiwu gongzuo zhe deng yijian (Health representatives of Beijing Municipal People's Congress put forward such proposals as respecting medical workers). *Jiankang bao (Health News)*, 21 August, 1.

———. 1957. Dui bingren duo zuoxie gongzuo (Do more work on patients). *Jiankang bao (Health News)*, 11 January, 1.

———. 1958. Shoudu yiwu jie gongchan zhuyi fengge zai chengzhang (Communist fashion is growing in the medical circles of the Capital). *Jiankang bao (Health News)*, 16 July, 1.

———. 1959. Jixu jiaqiang Dang dui yuyuan gongzuo de lingdao (Continuously strengthen the Party's leadership in hospital work). *Jiankang bao (Health News)*, 22 July, 1.

———. 1965. Shehuizhuyi nongcun yiyuan yao zheyang de zhengguihua (Socialist rural hospital needs formalization like this). *Renmin ribao (People's Daily)*, 12 November, 1.

Fan, Quan. 1960. Zuo xin xingshi zhong de xin yiwu gongzuo zhe (Become new medical workers in the new situation). *Jiankang bao (Health News)*, 9 April, 7.

Fei, Xiaotong, Gary G. Hamilton, and Wang Zheng. 1992. *From the soil, the foundations of Chinese society: A translation of Fei Xiaotong's Xiangtu Zhongguo, with an introduction and epilogue.* Berkeley: University of California Press.

Feng, Junqi. 2010. Zhong xian ganbu (Cadres of Middle County). PhD, Department of Sociology, Beijing University.

Field, Mark G. 1991. The hybrid profession: Soviet medicine. In *Professions and the state: expertise and autonomy in the Soviet Union and Eastern Europe,* ed. Anthony Jones, 43–62. Philadelphia: Temple University Press.

Freidson, Eliot. 1970. *Profession of medicine: a study of the sociology of applied knowledge.* Chicago and London: The University of Chicago Press. Reprint, 1988.

Gold, Thomas B. 1985. After comradeship: personal relations in China since the Cultural Revolution. *The China Quarterly* 104: 657–675.

Guan, Jian. 1958. Zhengzhi tongshuai jishu yiqie wei bingren (Politics command techniques; all for patients). *Jiankang bao (Health News),* 18 April, 1.

Guo, Caixia. 2011. 20 shiji 50 niandai lianhe zhensuo shimo—yi Guangdong Sheng wei li (United clinics in the 1950s—A study of Guangdong Province). Master of Science, Medical History and Literature of TCM, Guangzhou University of Chinese Medicine.

Guo, Shaojun, and Shiqi Xiong. 1958. Da po "quanwei" he "dengji zhi" (Break "authoritativeness" and "hierarchy"). *Jiankang bao (Health News),* 15 November, 2.

Harding, Harry. 1981. *Organizing China: The problem of bureaucracy, 1949–1976.* Stanford, CA: Stanford University Press.

He, Caihuo. 1956. Jiaban jiadian de jiubing fufa (Overtime again). *Renmin ribao (People's Daily),* 24 July, 2.

He, Cheng. 1948 (1951). Dui jishu guandian de jiantao (Criticizing technical viewpoints). In *Yiwu gongzuozhe de daolu (weisheng renyuan sixiang xuexi wenjian) [The path of medical workers (Ideological learning document for health personnel)],* 49–61. Unknown: Unknown.

———. 1951a. Yiwu gongzuozhe de daolu (The path of medical workers). In *Yiwu gongzuozhe de daolu (weisheng renyuan sixiang xuexi wenjian) [The path of medical workers (Ideological learning document for health personnel)],* 42–48. Unknown: Unknown.

———. 1951b. Yong Mao Zhuxi de sixiang wuzhuang weisheng renyuan de tounao (Arm health workers' brain with Chairman Mao's thoughts). *Zhongyi zazhi (Journal of Traditional Chinese Medicine)* 1(2): 3–5.

———. 1951c. Zai diyi jie quanguo weisheng gongzuo huiyi shang de zongjie baogao (Concluding report of the First National Health Conference). *Zhongyi zazhi (Journal of Traditional Chinese Medicine)* 1(1): 8–15.

———. 1953. Guanyu weisheng renyuan xuexi yuandong de dongyuan baogao (Mobilization speech on health personnel study movement). *Zhongyi zazhi (Journal of Traditional Chinese Medicine)* 2(4): 1–6.

He, Juncai. 1966. Tuchu zhengzhi, wei geming ban yiliao weisheng shiye (Give prominence to politics and run healthcare for revolution). *Guangdong yixue (Guangdong medicine)* 4(2): 70–73.

He, Qianqian. 2015. *Xiaxiang na xie nian (The years in the countryside)*. Hong Kong: Guoshi Chubanshe.

Henan Shan County Health Office, and Henan Shan Country Bureau of Finance. 1965. Shan xian gongfei yiliao guanli gongzuo de ji dian jingyan (Lessons from the management of the public medical insurance in Shan County). *Caizheng (Finance)* 7: 17–19.

Herzfeld, Michael. 1993. *The social production of indifference: exploring the symbolic roots of Western bureaucracy*. Chicago: University of Chicago Press.

Hu, Bicheng. 1956. Jingren de jiaban jiadian (Astonishing overtime). *Laodong (Labour)* 8: 55.

Hu, Yi. 2011. *Song yi xia xiang: xiandai Zhongguo de jibing zhengzhi (Sending medicine to the countryside: The disease politics of modern China)*, New Sociology Series. Beijing: Shehui Kexue Chubanshe (Social Science Publishing House).

Huang, Yun. 1957. Dangqian gongfei yiliao jingfei guanli zhong de wenti he gaijin yijian (Current problems of public medical insurance fund management and suggestions for improvement). *Caizheng (Finance)* 3: 13–15.

Hubei Local History Compiling Committee. 2000. *Hubei Provincial Annals: Health* Vol. 1. Wuhan: Hubei Renmin Chubanshe (Hubei People's Publishing House).

Hunan People's Committee. 1957. Hunan sheng renmin weiyuanhui pizhuan weisheng ting 'guanyu gongfei yiliao jingfei yanzhong chaozhi qingkuang ji jiejue yijian de baogao' de tongzhi (Hunan People's Committee's notice of approving and circulating the Health Department's 'Report on the situation of considerable overspending of the public medical insurance fund and suggested solutions'). *Hunan zhengbao (Gazette of Hunan Government)* 11: 367–368.

———. 1963. Hunan sheng remin weiyuanhui pi zhuan weisheng ting guanyu Hunan Sheng ganbu yiliao wenti de ruogan yijian (Hunan People's Committee approves and circulates the Health Department's suggestions on cadre medical (insurance) issues in Hunan Province). *Hunan zhengbao (Gazette of Hunan Government)* 9: 184–186.

Ji, Ji. 1961. Gaijin yiyuan gongzuo tigao yiliao zhiliang (Improve hospital work and the quality of medical services). *Jiankang bao (Health News)*, 30 August, 1.

Jia, Wenjuan. 2012. Cong reqing laodong dao nongxu zuojia: "Dayuejin" qian hou richang shengchan zhong de guojia kongzhi yu jiceng shijian—yi dui Guangzhou TY chang de kaocha weili (1956–1965) (From working enthusiastically to cheating: state control and grass-roots practice in everyday production before and after the "Great Leap Forward"—A case study of Guangzhou TY Factory (1956–1965)). *Kaifang shidai (Open Times)* 10: 5–21.

Jiangxi People's Committee. 1956. Jiangxi sheng renmin weiyuanhui pi zhuang sheng weisheng ting 'guanyu jiujiang zhuan shu ben nian shang ban nian gongfei yiliao yufang jingfei chaozhi wenti de jiancha baogao' de tongzhi (Jiangxi People's Committee's notification of approving and circulating the Provincial Health Department's 'Report of investigation of overspending of the public medical insurance fund in Jiujiang Special District in the first half of the year'). *Jiangxi zhengbao (Gazette of Jiangxi Government)* 21: 41–45.

———. 1957. Guanyu gaijin gongfei yiliao yufang gongzuo de yijian de pifu (Reply to suggestions on improving public medical insurance and prevention work). *Jiangxi zhengbao (Gazette of Jiangxi Government)* 20: 46–48.

Jiangxi Provincial Health Department. 1953. Jiangxi sheng weisheng renyuan xuexi yundong zongjie baogao (Summary report of Jiangxi health personnel study movement). *Jiangxi zhengbao (Gazette of Jiangxi Government)* 14: 1–6.

Jonsen, Albert R. 2000. *A short history of medical ethics.* New York: Oxford University Press.

Kang, Ding. 1957. Ji suo buyu, wu shi yu ren (Don't impose on others what you yourself don't desire). *Jiankang bao (Health News),* 22 March, 4.

Korzec, Michel, and Martin King Whyte. 1981. Reading Notes: The Chinese Wage System. *The China Quarterly* 86(June 1981): 248–273.

Lampton, David M. 1977. *The Politics of Medicine in China, Westview Special Studies on China and East Asia.* Boulder, CO: Westview Press.

Lei, Sean Hsiang-lin. 2014. *Neither donkey nor horse: medicine in the struggle over China's modernity, Studies of the Weatherhead East Asian Institute, Columbia University.* Chicago & London: The University of Chicago Press.

Li, Chunhua. 2011. Fasheng zai Wenge qijian shangshan xiaxiang gongzuo zhong buzheng zhifeng de shiliao (Historical materials concerning the unhealthy trends in the work of going and working in the countryside during the Cultural Revolution). *Heilongjiang shi zhi (Heilongjiang history and annals)* 6: 36–38.

Li, Dequan. 1951. Guanyu quanguo weisheng huiyi de baogao (Report on the National Health Conference). *Zhongyi zazhi (Journal of Traditional Chinese Medicine)* 1(1): 5–8.

———. 1957a. Dang neng lingdao weisheng kexue jishu (The Party can lead health science and technology). *Jiankang bao (Health News),* 12 July.

Li, Jianzhong. 2010. Nanyang xian gongxiao hezuoshe yanjiu: 1949–2010 (A study of Nanyang Supply and Marketing Cooperative: 1949–2010). PhD, History, Nanjing University.

Li, Minsheng. 1957b. Zheyang chuli duima, gongzheng ma? (Is it right and just to deal with it like this?). *Jiankang bao (Health News),* 11 January, 2.

Li, Lulu, and Hanlin Li. 2000. *Zhongguo de danwei zuzhi: ziyuan, quanli he jiaohuan (Resources, power and exchange in the Chinese work uni organization), Series of Contemporary Sociology Study.* Hangzhou: Zhejiang Renmin Chubanshe (Zhejiang People's Publishing House).

Lian, Feng. 1953. Zuo hao jin nian gaodeng xuexiao biye tongxue tongyi fenpei de sixiang dongyuan gongzuo (Do well the work of ideologically mobilizing this year's tertiary graduates for unified job assignment). *Renmin jiaoyu (People's Education)* 7: 6–8.

Lin, Chaochao. 2013. Shengchanxian shang de geming: 20 shiji 50 niandai Shanghai gongye qiye de laodong jingsai (Revolutions on the production line: Labour competition in Shanghai industries in the 1950s). *Kaifang shidai (Open Times)* 1: 146–164.

Lin, Zhaoqian. 1958. Shenyang Yixueyuan yi yuan zheng gai Qian hou (Before and after the rectification and reform in the First Affiliated Hospital of Shenyang Medical College). *Jiankang bao (Health News)*, 28 February, 3.

Liu, Hongqing. 2009a. Gongfei laobao yiliao: jian xing jian yuan de jiyi (The public medical insurance and the labour insurance: a fading memory). *Zhongguo shehui baozhang (Chinese Social Security)* 10: 42–45.

Liu, Yangqiao. 1960. Jiuhuo Cheng Debao shuoming le sheme (Saving the life of Cheng Debao, what does it indicate). *Jiankang bao (Health News)*, 11 May, 2.

Lu, Fengcheng. 1956. Jiaban jiadian re ren chou (Annoying overtime). *Renmin Ribao (People's Daily)*, 2 November, 2.

Lucas, AnElissa. 1982. *Chinese medical modernization: Comparative policy continuities, 1930–1980s.* New York: Praeger.

Lynteris, Christos. 2013. *The spirit of selflessness in Maoist China: Socialist medicine and the new man.* Basingstoke: Palgrave Macmillan.

MacFarquhar, Roderick. 1997. *The Politics of China: the eras of Mao and Deng*, 2nd edn. New York: Cambridge University Press.

Mao, Zedong. 1939. In memory of Norman Bethune. In *Selected works of Mao Tse-Tung*, 337–338. Beijing: Foreign Languages Press.

Mechanic, David. 1976. *The growth of bureaucratic medicine: An inquiry into the dynamics of patient behavior and the organization of medical care, health, medicine, and society.* New York: Wiley.

Merton, Robert King. 1968. *Social theory and social structure.* 1968 enl. ed. New York: Free Press.

Ministry of Education, Ministry of Internal Affairs, and National Planning Commission. 1963. Gaodeng xuexiao biyesheng tiaopei, paiqian zanxing banfa (Provisional methods of distribution and dispatch of tertiary graduates). In *Renshi gongzuo wenjian xuanbian (Selected collection of personnel work)*, ed. Personnel Bureau of the Ministry of Internal Affairs, 97–106. Beijing: Ministry of Internal Affairs.

Ministry of Health. 1951a. Guanyu tiaozheng yiyao weisheng shiye zhong gongsi guanxi de jueding (Decision on adjusting the public-private relationship in the medical, pharmaceutical, and healthcare enterprise). *Renmin ribao (People's Daily)*, 19 May.

———. 1951b. Guanyu zuzhi lianhe yiliao jigou shishi banfa (Enforcement methods for organising united medical organisations). *Zhongyi zazhi (Journal of Traditional Chinese Medicine)* 1(2): 2.

————. 1952. Guojia gongzuo renyuan gongfei yiliao yufang shishi banfa (The implementation methods of the public medical insurance for state personnel). Accessed 6 January 2015. http://www.chinalawedu.com/falvfagui/fg22598/24166.shtml.

————. 1953. Guanyu gongfei yiliao de ji xiang guiding (Several rules about the public medical insurance). Accessed 3 June 2014. http://china.findlaw.cn/fagui/p_1/185483.html.

————. 2009. *2009 Zhongguo weisheng tongji nianjian (2009 Yearbook of Chinese health statistics)*. Beijing: Beijing Xiehe Yike Daxue Chubanshe (Beijing Union Medical University Press).

Ministry of Tertiary Education, and Personnel Bureau of the State Council. 1956. Guanyu jiejue gaodeng xuexiao biyesheng fenpei gongzuo hou tiaozheng gongzuo wenti de baogao (Report on solving the problem of job changing after tertiary graduates being assigned jobs). *Zhonghua Renmin Gongheguo Guowuyuan gongbao (Gazette of the State Council of the People's Republic of China)* 41: 1055–1056.

no name. 1958. *Woguo de guomin jingji jianshe he renmin shenghuo (Our country's national economic reconstruction and people's life)*. Beijing: Tongji Chubanshe (Statistics Publishing House).

Parsons, Talcott. 1951. *The social system*. 1967 reprint ed. London: Routledge and Kegan Paul.

Peng, Xuebao. 2013. Jianguo chuqi zhonggong suqing waiguo zai hua wenhua shili yanjiu (A study of the Chinese Communist Party's elimination of foreign cultural forces in the early years of the PRC). PhD, Department of the CCP History, The Party School of the Central Committee of the CCP.

Qian, Xinzhong. 1992. *Zhongguo weisheng shiye fazhan yu juece (The development and policy of Chinese public health)*. Beijing: Zhongguo Yiyao Keji Chubanshe (Chinese Medical and Pharmaceutical Science and Technology Press).

Qiu, Renzong, Ziyang Chen, and Shaojun Guo. 1958. Chongpo yixue kexue yuejing de zhangai—dengji zhi (Break the barrier to leap-forward in medical science—hierarchy)." *Renmin ribao (People's Daily)*, 5 November, 7.

Qiu, Xiangxing, Fuchuan Sun, and Mingxu Wang (ed). 2008. *Yixue lunli xue (Medical ethics)*, 3rd edn. Beijing: Renmin Weisheng Chubanshe (People's Health Publishing House).

Shanghai Health Annals Editorial Committee. 1998. *Shanghai Health Annals*. Shanghai: Shanghai Shehui Kexue Chubanshe (Shanghai Social Sciences Publishing House).

Shanxi Provincial Health Department. 1953. Shanxi Sheng weisheng renyuan xuexi jihua (Study plan for Shangxi health personnel). *Shanxi zhengbao (Gazette of Shangxi Government)* 10: 77–79.

———. 1957. Guanyu dujue gongfei yiliao zhong de langfei xianxiang de tongbao (Circular on eliminating waste in public medical insurance). *Shanxi zhengbao (Gazette of Shanxi Government)* 1: 48–50.

State Council. 1951a. Guanyu chongshi guofang jianshe zhong de weisheng renyuan de jueding (Decision on replenishing health personnel in the reconstruction of national defence). *Zhongyi zazhi (Journal of Traditional Chinese Medicine)* 1(2): 1.

———. 1951b. Zhonghua Remin Gongheguo Laodong Baoxian Tiaoli (The PRC Labour Insurance Act). In *Laodong baoxian shenghuo fuli wenjian xuan bian (Selected documents of labour, insurance, life, and welfare)*, 83–93. Taiyuan: Shanxi Labour Bureau.

———. 1953. Guanyu 1953 nian shuqi quanguo gaodeng xuexiao biyesheng tongchou fenpei gongzuo de zhishi (Decree regarding the unified job distribution for tertiary graduates in the summer of 1953). *Shanxi zhengbao (Gazette of Shanxi Government)* 17: 45–48.

———. 1954. Guanyu 1954 nian shuqi quanguo gaodeng xuexiao biyesheng tongchou fenpei gongzuo de zhishi (Decree regarding the unified job distribution for tertiary graduates in the summer of 1954). *Shanxi zhengbao (Gazette of Shanxi Government)* 16: 81–84.

———. 1955. Guanyu 1955 nian shuqi quanguo gaodeng xuexiao biyesheng tongchou fenpei gongzuo de zhishi (Decree regarding the unified job distribution for tertiary graduates in the summer of 1955). *Zhonghua Renmin Gongheguo Guowuyuan gongbao (Gazette of the State Council of the People's Republic of China)* 13: 452–456.

———. 1956a. Gelei renyuan de gongzi biaozhun (Wage standards for personnel of all trades). In *Zhonghua Renmin Gongheguo jingji dang'an ziliao xuanbian: 1953–1957 (Selected economic archival documents of the People's Republic of China: 1953–1957)*, edited by Chinese Academy of Social Sciences and Central Archive House, 497–527. Beijing: Zhongguo Wujia Chubanshe (Chinese Pricing Press).

———. 1956b. Guanyu gongzi gaige de jueding (Resolution regarding wage reform). Accessed 5 March 2016. http://news.xinhuanet.com/ziliao/2004-12/30/content_2393793.htm.

———. 1957. Guanyu 1957 nian shuqi quanguo gaodeng xuexiao biyesheng tongchou fenpei gongzuo de zhishi (Decree regarding the unified job distribution for tertiary graduates in the summer of 1957). *Zhonghua Renmin Gongheguo Guowuyuan gongbao (Gazette of the State Council of the People's Republic of China)* 33: 703–705.

Tan, Zhuang. 1963. Tan tigao yiliao zhiliang wenti (On issues of improving medical service quality). *Jiankang bao (Health News)*, 7 December, 2.

The MOH Department of Cadre. 1956. Heli di fenpei he shiyong gaodeng yi yao yuan xiao biyesheng (Rationally assign and use graduates of medical and pharmaceutical colleges). *Jiankang bao (Health News)*, 17 July 3.

Tianjin Bureau of Finance. 1965. Guanyu wo shi gongfei yiliao guanli cunzai de wenti ji gaijin yijian de baogao (Report on the problems in the management of the public medical insurance in our city and improvement suggestions). *Tianjin zhengbao (Gazette of Tianjin Government)* 9: 5–7.

Tianjin Government. 1951. Benfu xiang zhengwuyuan guanyu Tianjin shi weisheng huiyi de baogao (The government report to the State Council on Tianjin Health Conference). edited by Tianjin Government. Tianjin: Tianjin Government.

Unknown. 1951. Sulian yisheng de sixiang zuofeng (The thought and practice of Soviet doctors). In *Yiwu gongzuozhe de daolu (weisheng renyuan sixiang xuexi wenjian) [The path of medical workers (Ideological learning document for health personnel)]*, edited by Unknown, 62–74. Unknown: Unknown.

Vogel, Ezra F. 1965. From friendship to comradeship: the change in personal relations in Communist China. *The China Quarterly* Jan–Mar(21): 46–60.

Walder, Andrew G. 1986. *Communist neo-traditionalism: Work and authority in Chinese industry*. Berkeley: University of California Press.

Wang, Dazhong. 2011a. Wo guo zhongyi congye renyuan zhiye guizhi chutan (Preliminary study on the practice regulations of our country's Traditional Chinese Medicine practitioners). Masters, Social Medicine and Health Management, Nanjing University of Chinese Medicine.

Wang, Dingkun. 1958a. Pipan zichan jieji geren zhuyi zhengqu zuo you hong you zhuan de renmin yiwu gongzuozhe (Criticize bourgeois individualism, and strive to become a both red and competent medical worker). *Jiankang bao (Health News)*, 28 May, 5.

Wang, Kangjiu (ed). 2001. *Beijing weisheng zhi (Beijing health annals)*. Beijing: Beijing Kexue Jishu Chubanshe (Beijing Science and Technology Publishing House).

Wang, Kejin. 1950. Buyao wujie zhengguihua (Don't misunderstand formalization). *Renmin ribao (People's Daily)*, 19 March, 6.

Wang, Shaohua, and Miao Zhou. 1965. Jiaqiang gongfei yiliao guanli de ji xiang cuoshi (Several measures to enhance the management of the public medical insurance). *Caizheng (Finance)* 11: 16–18.

Wang, Yonghua. 2011b. Jiangsu sheng xin "wu fan" yundong shu lue (A brief account of the new "Five Anti" Movement in Jiangsu Province). *Lianyungang Shifan Gaodeng Zhuanke Xuexiao xuebao (Journal of Lianyungang Teachers College)* 2: 85–91.

Wang, Zhaohuai. 1958b. Tuidong yiyuan gongzuo yuejin zai yuejin (Push hospital work to leap forward and forward further). *Jiankang bao (Health News)*, 1 October, 3.

Weber, Max. 1946. *From Max Weber: Essays in sociology*. Translated by Hans Heinrich Gerth and C. Wright Mills. New York: Oxford university press.

————. 1968. *The religion of China: Confucianism and Taoism, A Free Press paperback.* New York: Free Press.

Weber, Max, Guenther Roth, and Claus Wittich. 1978. *Economy and society: an outline of interpretive sociology, 2 vols.* Berkeley: University of California Press.

Wen, Yang. 2008. *Yizhi yu chaoye—Minguo zhongyi yizheng (Transplant and transcend—Administration of traditional medicine in Republican China).* Beijing: Zhongguo Zhongyiyao Chubanshe (Chinese TCM Publishing House).

Wilenski, Peter. 1976. *The delivery of health services in the People's Republic of China.* Ottawa: International Development Research Centre.

Wu, Wenjun. 2014. Xin Zhongguo chuqi gongfei yiliao zhidu jianshe yanjiu—jiyu fan langfei de shijiao (A study of the construction of public health insurance institutions in the early years of the New China—From the perspective of anti-waste). *Jishu jingji yu guanli yanjiu (Technological economy and management study)* 7: 86–90.

Xinhua News Agency. 1958. Buyong guojia touzi zengshe bingchuang er qian zhang (Add two thousand hospital beds without state investment). *Jiankang bao (Health News),* 21 May, 1.

————. 1965. Chengshi weisheng bumen ba gongzuo zhongdian zhuanxiang nongcun (Urban health departments shift the focus of their work to the countryside). *Renmin ribao (People's Daily),* 27 September, 1.

Xinhua News Agency Reporter. 1969. Yi chang sixiang lingyu li de da geming (A great revolution in the ideological domain). *Renmin ribao (People's Daily),* 30 December, 4.

————. 1971. Cong renmin liyi chufa, wei renmin de jiankang fendou (In view of people's interests, and for the health of the people). *Renmin ribao (People's Daily),* 14 August, 3.

Xu, Xiaoqun. 2001. *Chinese professionals and the republic state: the rise of professional associations in Shanghai 1912–1937,* ed. William Kirby, *Cambridge Modern China Series.* Cambridge: Cambridge University Press.

Xu, Xinen, and Xianzhang Li. 1952. Chedi gaizao sixiang, renzhen wei renmin fuwu (Transform thought thoroughly, serve the people genuinely). *Renmin ribao (People's Daily),* 16 January, 6.

Yang, Jisheng. 2013. Daolu, lilun, zhidu—wo dui Wenhua Dageming de sikao (Path, theory, institution—my thinking about the Cultural Revolution). *Jiyi (Remembrance)* (104). Accessed 19 May 2016. http://prchistory.org/wp-content/uploads/2014/05/REMEMBRANCE_No104.pdf.

Yang, Mayfair Mei-hui. 1994. *Gifts, favors and banquets: the art of social relationships in China.* In *The Wilder House Series in Politics, History and Culture,* ed. David Laitin, and George Steinmetz. Ithaca and London: Cornell University Press.

Yang, Xiaomin, and Yihu Zhou. 1999. *Zhongguo danwei zhidu (China's work-unit system).* Beijing: Zhongguo Jingji Chubanshe (Chinese Economy Publishing House).

Yang, Zhenya. 1958a. Tianjin yiwu jie zai shuang fan yundong zhong (Tianjin medical circles in the double-anti movement). *Jiankang bao (Health News)*, 18 April, 3.

———. 1958b. Yiliao shiye guanli zhong de jige wenti (A few issues in medical administration). *Jiankang bao (Health News)*, 23 August, 3.

Yao, Shangwen, and Shangqian Bai. 1955. Yi ge yikao jiaban jiadian wancheng renwu de gongcheng duan (An engineering unit that relies on overtime to complete tasks). *Renmin ribao (People's Daily)*, 6 November, 6.

Yin, Qian. 2008. Study on medical practitioners in the period of the Republic of China (1912–1937)—Take Shanghai as a focus. PhD, Institute of Modern Chinese University, Central China Normal University.

———. 2012. Shenfen xunqiu yu juese chongtu: jindai yisheng zhenjin wenti tanxi (Identity search and role conflict: a study of the consultation fees of modern doctors). *Huanzhong Shifan Daxue xuebao (Renwen shehui kexue ban) (Journal of Huazhong Normal University (Humanities and social sciences))* 51(1): 92–98.

———. 2013. *Minguo shiqi de yishi quanti yanjiu (1912–1937)—yi Shanghai wei taolun zhongxin (A study of medical groups in the Republican era [1912–1937]— with Shanghai as the focus)*. Beijing: Zhongguo Shehui Keshi Chubanshe (Chinese Social Sciences Publishing House).

Yip, Ka-che. 1995. *Health and National Reconstruction in Nationalist China—the Development of Modern Health Services, 1928–1937*. Ann Aorbor, MI: The Association for Asian Studies.

Yu, Chaoan. 1966. Sichuan san qian duo yiwu renyuan xiaxiang luohu (In Sichuan more than three thousand medical personnel settled in the countryside). *Jiankang bao*, 15 January, 1.

Yu, Qihua, and Mingyuan Gao. 1957. Yinggai heli shiyong renli (Use manpower rationally). *Jiankang bao (Health News)*, 8 March, 2.

Zhang, Kai. 1958. Po mixin cha hongqi sixiang yuejin gongzuo yuejin (Banish blind faith, put in red flags, thought leaps forward, work leaps forward). *Jiankang bao (Health News)*, 5 July, 1–2.

Zhao, Hongjun. 1989. *Jindai zhong xi yi lunzheng shi (A modern history of the debate and struggle between traditional Chinese and western medicine)*. Hefei: Anhui Kexue Jishu Chubanshe (Anhui Science and Technology Publishing House).

Zheng, Zhijun, Li Wang, Nan Liu, and Chuanrong Yu. 1987. Yiliao shoufei zhidu bianqian de huigu yu zhanwang (Review of and outlook for medical service fee system). *Zhongguo weisheng jingji (Chinese Health Economics)* 2: 32–34.

Zhi, Ge. 1955. Fandui renyi jiaban jiadian (Oppose unrestrained overtime). *Laodong (Labour)* 9: 17.

Zhong, Jianying. 2009. Ershi shiji liushi niandai de fan shangpin "zou houmen" yundong (The movement combating obtaining goods through "backdoor" in the 1960s). *Zhonggong dangshi yanjiu (CCP history study)* 7: 56–63.

Zhou, Enlai. 1951a. Guanyu gaige xuezhi de jueding (Resolution of Education Reform). *Renmin jiaoyu (People's Education)* 4(1): 53–54.

————. 1952. Zhongyang Renmin Zhengfu Zhengwu Yuan guanyu quanguo geji renmin zhengfu, dangpai, tuanti ji suoshu shiye danwei he guojia gongzuo renyuan shixing gongfei yiliao yufang de zhishi (Directive of the State Council of the Central People's Government on implementing public-funded medicine and prevention for state workers employed by people's governments at all levels, parties, associations and their institutional work units). *Renmin ribao (People's Daily)*, 28 June, 1.

Zhou, Hong, and Jun Zhang. 2003. Yisheng xianglai shou "hongbao"? (Doctors have always taken "red packets"?). *Dushu (Reading)* 9: 122–128.

Zhou, Quanhua, and Lu Ru. 2015. 20 shiji 60 niandai chu fandui shangpin "zou houmen" yundong tanxi (An exploration of the movement combating obtaining goods through "backdoor" in the 1960s). *Dangdai Zhongguo shi yanjiu (Contemporary China History Studies)* 22(4): 55–67.

Zhou, Sihui. 1966. Gongzuofu yigai gaige (Uniforms should be reformed). *Jiankang bao (Health News)*, 2 February, 3.

Zhou, Sumin. 1957. Chuli gong xiu jiufen yi fen qing shi fei (Distinguish right from wrong when handling disputes between workers and patients). *Jiankang bao (Health News)*, 5 February, 2.

Zhou, Xueguang, Yun Ai, and Hong Lian. 2012. The limit of bureaucratic power in organizations: The case of the Chinese bureaucracy. In *Rethinking power in organizations, institutions, and markets*, ed. David Courpasson, Damon Golsorkhi, and Jeffrey J. Sallaz, 81–111. Bingley, UK: Emerald Group.

Zhu, De. 1951. Wei qunzhong fuwu bing yikao qunzhong shi weisheng shiye fazhan de zhengque daolun (Serving the masses and relying on the masses is the right way to develop health enterprise). In *Yiwu gongzuo zhe de daolu (Road for medical workers)*, edited by Health Department of the People's Government of Hubei, 5–8. Changsha: Health Department of the People's Government of Hubei.

Zhu, Deming. 2008. *Minguo shiqi Zhejiang yiyao shi (Zhejiang medical and pharmaceutical history in the Republican era)*. Beijing: Zhongguo Shehui Kexue Chubanshe (Chinese Social Science Publishing House).

Zhu, Ling. 2009. Nongcun qianyi gongren de laodong shijian he zhiye jiankang (Working hours and occupational health of rural migrant workers). *Zhongguo shehui kexue (Chinese Social Sciences)* 1: 133–149.

Zhu, Xianyi. 1954. Yiwu renyuan xuexi Zongluxian ying jianjue kefu zichan jieji xixiang (Medical personnel should resolve to overcome bourgeois ideology when studying the General Line). *Zhongyi zazhi (Journal of Traditional Chinese Medicine)* 3(2): 1–3.

Zhu, Zemin. 1958. "Jiating bingchuang" shi yiliao weisheng gongzuo de yi xiang chuangju ("Home hospital bed" is a pioneering undertaking in medical and health work). *Renmin ribao (People's Daily)*, 4 July, 7.

CHAPTER 4

Health Reform and the Rise of Informal Payments After 1978

Informal payments in the Chinese healthcare system gradually became widespread since the 1980s throughout the 1990s and 2000s. The surge of the practice is closely related to the economic reform launched in the late 1970s and the health reform that began in 1985. The economic reform and the health reform have brought about numerous institutional changes to the healthcare system and the economic systems of the country. However, some old institutions persisted until today. The change and the persistence intertwined and jointly created an institutional setting that gave rise to informal payments. In this chapter, I shall first look at institutional persistence, and then institutional changes in the healthcare system, and, in broader terms, in the political and economic milieu, in an attempt to reveal how informal payments emerged from contradictory ideologies and policies.

Institutional Persistence

An ultimate indicator of institutional persistence is reflected in the Chinese Communist Party's (CCP) continuous grasp on power and its persistent efforts to justify its rule. Tony Saich pointed out that while the reform launched by Deng Xiaoping in 1978 "affected every aspect of life in China and left no institution untouched," it "left the pillar of one-party rule untouched" (Saich 2011, p. 67). The Third Plenum of the Party's Eleventh Central Committee held between 18 and 22 December 1978 marked the launch of the economic reform which was intended to subordinate "all other considerations to the task of modern economic development" (Meisner 1999, p. 435). But the democratic movement that gained momentum in the early months of 1979 prompted Deng Xiaoping to proclaim, on 30 March 1979, the "Four Cardinal Principles" (*si xiang jiben yuanze*) as the political boundaries that the reform should be carried out within. The "Four Cardinal Principles" demanded "adherence to the socialist road, proletariat dictatorship, the leadership of the Communist Party, and Marxism, Leninism, and Mao Zedong Thoughts" (Deng 1983, p. 151–152). Deng considered the "Four Cardinal Principles" as the root of reform and the direction of the Party (Deng 1983, pp. 242–243), determined to retain the reform in the economic domain only. The ideological dominance of Marxism and Mao's thoughts and the political dominance of the CCP must not be challenged and changed. The "Four Cardinal Principles" were soon enshrined in the Constitution of the People's Republic of China (PRC) in 1982 and in the CCP's Constitution in 1992.

Of the principles, Deng deemed the adherence to the leadership of the CCP as the most important and, according to Meisner (1999), "the only enduring one" (p. 347). Throughout the 1980s and 1990s, Deng consistently emphasized that "the core of the Four Cardinal Principles is the adherence to the leadership of the Party" (Deng 1983, pp. 301 and 317) (see also Deng 1993, pp. 195 and 248; Leng and Wang 2004, p. 1363). Deng did not provide legal or moral justification for the legitimacy of the persistent leadership of the CCP. Instead, he sought justification predominantly from the Party's historical legacy, and the threat of use, and the use in reality, of the coercive power and violence of the Party-state to ensure the perpetuated leadership.

Post-Deng CCP leaders tend to justify the CCP's ruling on moral grounds. Jiang Zemin's "'Three Represents' Important Thought," which justifies the legitimacy of the ruling of the CCP on the basis that the Party represents the advanced productive force, represents the advanced culture and most importantly, represents the fundamental interest of the vast majority of the people. He claims that the entire work of each member of the Party is to serve the people wholeheartedly and to realize, protect, and advance the interest of the people (Jiang 2006a, pp. 2–4). "Serving the people" also constitutes the core of the theory of "Scientific Outlook on Development," Hu Jingtao's contribution to the CCP's canon. In his report at the 17th National Congress in 2007, Hu explained this core of his theory as to put people first. "We must always put people first. Serving the people wholeheartedly is the fundamental purpose of the Party, and its every endeavor is for the well-being of the people. We must always make sure that the aim and outcome of all the work of the Party and the state is to realize, safeguard and expand the fundamental interests of the overwhelming majority of the people."[1]

The realization of the Chinese Dream and the rejuvenation of the Chinese Nation that Xi Jingping envisaged after he succeeded Hu Jintao again rely on vigorous pursuit of the Party's fundamental purpose of serving the people. In a speech made in June 2013 at the working conference of the Program of Mass Line Education and Practice, Xi said,

> In this new era, in order to realize the Chinese Dream and the objectives set by the 18th CPC National Congress, we must remain close to the people, rely on them, and fully mobilize their initiative, enthusiasm and creativity. We have launched the campaign of mass line education and practice with the aim of reminding all Party members that their fundamental purpose is to serve the people wholeheartedly, unite the people through the Party's fine tradition, and work hard with them to realize the objectives set by the Congress (Xi 2014, p. 403).

As the ruling party, the CCP not only demands its members to serve the people. In fact, it demands the whole citizenry observe this moral principle. In 1996, the Sixth Plenary of the Central Committee of the 14th CCP National Congress passed "The resolution on many important issues regarding strengthening the construction of socialist spiritual civilization." In this "Resolution," serving the people was established as the core of socialist moral construction and the cardinal principle for social, occupational, and family ethics.[2] In 2001, the "Resolution" was operationalized with the publication of "The implementing guidelines for the construction of citizen's ethics," which demands that the construction of socialist ethics always take "serve-the-people" as the core and collectivism as the principle. The document asserts that "serve-the-people" is the outstanding characteristic that distinguishes socialist morality with that of other social systems and is a moral requirement not only for the CCP members and cadres but also for the broad masses of the people. It is at the center of ethics for individuals, occupations, and family.[3] That is, every single citizen of China is required by the CCP to take "serve-the-people" as the starting point of their moral considerations and ethical behaviors in all their social, economic, and political roles. In such a context, it is no surprise that "serve-the-people" persists as the guiding principle of medical ethics.

"Serve-the-People" and Medical Ethics

In the pre-reform era, medical ethics was not a particular concern of health policy makers and practitioners. Apart from the "Working Rules for Comprehensive Hospitals" and "Duties of Working Staff of Comprehensive Hospitals" promulgated in 1958, in which there were some ethical requirements for hospital employees of all occupations and positions, there was not a national code of ethics specific for medical professions and employees. Since the early period of the reform era, policy makers, health administrators, and health professionals started to consider a code of ethics to regulate the relationships between colleagues, and between professionals and patients. In June 1981, the First Medical Ethics Conference was held in Shanghai jointly convened by the publisher of the journal of *Medicine and Philosophy*, CMA (Chinese Medical Association) Shanghai Branch, and Shanghai Research Institute of Dialectics of Nature (Xu 1981). In this conference, it was generally agreed that professional behaviors of health practitioners should be guided by the principle of serving the people wholeheartedly, healing the wounded and rescuing the dying, and practicing revolutionary humanitarianism that had always been advocated by Mao Zedong (Shanghai Research Institute of Dialectics of Nature 1981, p. 8). On 23 August 1981, *Jiankang bao* published an article entitled "The core of socialist medical ethics" (*Shehuizhiyi yide de hexin*), which argued that "to prevent and cure diseases, to heal the wounded and rescue the dying, and to serve the people wholeheartedly, is the fundamental characteristic of socialist medical ethics that distinguishes it from those of all exploitative societies" (Lu and Fan 1981). This article set the tone for the socialist medical ethics that has been followed throughout the reform era until today.

The Ministry of Health (MOH) has been instrumental in promoting the socialist medical ethics. Three months after the first conference on medical ethics, the MOH enforced the "Rules for Hospital Workers," which had only eight rules. Rules 1 to 3 are of particular relevance to the current research. Rule 1 required hospital workers to "love the motherland, love the CCP, love socialism, and stick to Marxism and Mao Zedong's Thoughts." Rule 2 demanded the workers to "study politics diligently, and to perfect professional work in order to be both red and specialized." Rule 3 encouraged them to "carry forward the revolutionary humanitarianism of healing the wounded and rescuing the dying, to sympathize with and respect patients, and to serve the people wholeheartedly."[4] In 1982, the MOH renewed the "Duties of Working Staff of Hospitals" which was first enforced in 1958 and continued to charge the head of a hospital with the responsibility of "educating the staff to establish the thought and medical ethics of serving the people wholeheartedly."[5] In 1988, the MOH formulated and enforced the code of practice for medical personnel in particular (Ministry of Health 1988). The code contains 13 items. Item 1 elaborated the premise and purpose of the code. It states, "The 'Code of Medical Ethics and Implementing Methods' is particularly formed to enhance the construction of socialist spiritual civilization in the healthcare system, to improve professional ethics of medical personnel, to better the quality of medical services, and to serve the people wholeheartedly." Item 3 prescribed the ethical conduct in particular in seven sub-items. The first four of the seven good practices required doctors

(1) To heal the wounded and rescue the dying and practice revolutionary humanitarianism. To think for the patient all the time and to try every possible way to free the patient of disease and pain.
(2) To respect the integrity and rights of patients and treat them equally regardless of nationality, sex, occupation, status and wealth.
(3) To provide services with good manners ...
(4) To be clean and honest in serving the public, to obey rules and laws, and not to abuse medicine for personal gain.

These seven rules are further itemized and standardized in the guidelines for establishing the ethics evaluation system for doctors, published in 2007 by the MOH (Ministry of Health 2007). The guiding principles for the "Guidelines" are stated to be derived from Deng Xiaoping's theory of preliminary stage of socialism, Jiang Zemin's "important thought of 'Three Represents'," and Hu Jintao's socialist outlook on honor and shame and the scientific outlook on development.[6] The professional conduct of doctors is evaluated in light of the seven sub-items provided in the 1988 code of practice. The evaluation contents for each sub-item are given in detail. For sub-item 1—"to heal the wounded and to rescue the dying, and to serve the people wholeheartedly"—doctors are expected to "strengthen the study of political theories (i.e. the ideological contributions of all the CCP top leaders) and professional ethics, in order to establish the conscience of healing the wounded and rescuing the dying, centring on patients, and serving the people wholeheartedly; and to carry forward the Bethune spirit assiduously."

The Bethune Spirit

During the reform era, the selflessness spirit represented by Norman Bethune remains as the optimum symbol for serving the people and ultimate role model for public employees. In 1979, Deng Xiaoping called upon the members of the CCP and medical workers to become "Bethune-style revolutionaries and Bethune-style scientists" (Deng 2005). Jiang Zemin also called upon leading cadres to follow the role model of Bethune (Jiang 2006b).

Throughout the reform era, Norman Bethune has always been the ultimate role model for health workers. In 1981, the MOH launched a campaign in which employees in the healthcare system were called to follow the Bethune Spirit and serve the people wholeheartedly and altruistically (He 1981, p. 50). In 1997, a Bethune Spirit Research Association was established in Beijing. Qian Xinzhong, former Health Minister who launched the 1981 campaign of studying Bethune, was elected the president of the Association,[7] which organized workshops and forums to study and promote the Bethune Spirit among health practitioners. This Association was re-incorporated in 2014 as a national organization. The honorary president is Chen Zhu, who retired from the position of Health Minister in 2013. The incumbent president is Yuan Yonglin, a former director of the Health Division of the PLA General Logistics Department.

The Bethune Spirit is not just a fine memory of the CCP and healthcare leaderships but an active requirement for the entire medical and health occupations. The year 2004 marked the 65th anniversary of Bethune's death and the publication of Mao Zedong's famous article of "On Memorizing Bethune." The MOH, jointly with other central CCP organs and the Health Division of the PLA General Logistics Department, held a seminar of commemoration, in which senior health leadership urged the health professions, whose reputations were tarred by endemic unhealthy conducts, to uphold the Bethune Spirit and subordinate their interests to the people's interests (Deng 2005). The China Medical Doctors Association (CMDA), Chinese Hospital Management Association, Chinese Medical Association, and Chinese Caring Association jointly issued a proposal calling workers of all health occupations to take Bethune as their model, always place the interest of patients on top and serve patients.[8]

The Party-state's effort to uphold the Bethune Spirit is best demonstrated in the establishment of the Bethune Medal in 1991, which was meant to award the best deeds and most ethical conducts of professionals and set up examples for others to emulate. According to its selection criteria, the awardee must "follow the Four Cardinal Principles, support reform and opening-up policies and guidelines, obey laws and regulations, and serve the people wholeheartedly" (*China Health Year Book* Editorial Board 1983, p. 60). The Medal was first awarded in 1994 to Zhao Xuefang, a gynecologist of Changzhi People's Hospital in Shanxi Province. She was praised for "taking as her noble duty of relieving patients of their illness and hardship and serving the people wholeheartedly...and demonstrating the lofty quality of selfless sacrifice" (Su 1994). Most of the latest awardees who won the Medal in 2012 also received the same praise from the authority. For example, Deng Qiandui, a village doctor from Yunnan Province, is praised for "materializing the belief in serving the people in actual deeds."[9] Another winner, Xia Guicheng, a TCM gynecologist is also commended for the lofty spirit of "sacrificing himself to the patient selflessly" and "serving the people wholeheartedly."[10]

"Unselfish sacrifice" is a moral standard that is more emphasized in the promotion of the Bethune Spirit than serving the people. The apex of the application of this moral standard was in the period of SARS in 2003. Medical professionals were called upon to "sacrifice selflessly" in the battle against SARS. Those who contracted the disease through treating the infected were highly commended for their courage, the willingness to selflessly sacrifice themselves to serve the people (Chen and Liu 2003; Chongqing Municipal Health Department 2003; Liu 2003; Ministry of Health 2003). In May 2003, five health professionals who died of saving the lives of SARS patients were awarded posthumous Bethune Medal. In an official announcement, they were praised for "exercising the sublime thoughts of the 'Three Represents' and serving the people wholeheartedly" and "treating patients as families" (*China Health Year Book* Editorial Board 2004, p. 73).

Universal Particularism and "Treating Patients as Families"

Universal particularism as reflected in the moral and emotional requirement for doctors to "treat patients as families" is even more emphasized after 1978 than before. Especially in the early years of the reform, the requirement was widely regarded as a component of socialist medical ethics which set medicine in China on a higher moral ground than capitalist medicine (Liu 1983). In an article published in 1981, socialist medical ethics was described as "healing the wounded and rescuing the dying, and practicing revolutionary humanitarianism; being extremely responsible to medical works and being extremely warm to patients; treating patients as families, exercising civility and etiquette, and living a pure and honest life" (Sui and Zhang 1981). The first university textbook on medical ethics published in 1983 listed three requirements under the principle of "serving the people." The second requirement demanded medical practitioners to "care for the illness and hardship of the people" and "treat patients as families and treat them better than families" (Qiu et al. 1983, p. 33).

The universal particularism is understandably promoted as a fundamental component of the Bethune Spirit. Bethune is believed to have said that doctors and nurses "must regard each patient as your brother, as your father, because, in practice, they are closer than your brother and father—because they are your comrades" (Qiu et al. 1983, p. 44). Before 2012, the majority of the awardees of the Bethune Medal were selected for predominantly moral reasons. In the tributes published on the MOH website, they were always praised for not only serving the people wholeheartedly but also, more specifically, treating patients as families. For example, the tributes to all the six winners of the Bethune Medal in 2003 that were published on the MOH website contained the wording of "treating patients as families."[11] Five of the seven winners in 2008 were commended as well for treating patients as families.[12]

But as Qiu Xiangxing elaborates in the latest edition of the widely used textbook *Medical Ethics*, "treating patients as families" is the loftiest moral standard that is only embodied in some model doctors (usually with CCP membership) and extremely eminent practitioners. And it is true that most of the awardees of the Bethune Medal and the recipients of the title of model health workers are CCP members. They are examples occupying the highest moral ground for ordinary practitioners to emulate. For the vast majority of medical workers, however, their ethics and behaviors are apparently subject to various constraints and practices, among which are tenacious organizational institutions and social norms inherited from the pre-reform era.

Organization of Health Professionals in the Reform Era

The insistence on the CCP leadership, the core of the Four Cardinal Principles, is not just hollow ideological rhetoric and vain thought work. It is vigorously pursued and implemented in reality. In the organization of health human resources, this principle is strongly followed to the extent that health professions are yet to allow any power and freedom to organize themselves in Durkheimian style in their relationships with the state and the individual. If we examine health professions in light of trait theories, it is apparent that they are not professionalized yet as their associational power and life have by no means developed to a stage that empower them collectively and grant them bargaining strength in their industrial relationship with the Party-state.

It must be admitted that the political space for associations has been greatly liberalized, and a civil society is arguably in the formation in the reform era. Compared with the totalitarian regime dominating most of the pre-reform era, an authoritarian regime gradually matured since 1978 which loosened the state's grip on associations. Several studies argue that China has entered an age of state corporatism from the early 1990s onward (Unger and Chan 1995, 2015; Gu 2001). Quoting Schmitter's (Schmitter 1979) classical definition, Unger and Chan (1995) defined corporatism as

> a system of interest representation in which the constituent units are organized into a limited number of singular, compulsory, noncompetitive, hierarchically ordered and functionally differentiated categories, recognized or licensed (if not created) by the state and granted a deliberate representational monopoly within their respective categories in exchange for observing certain controls on their selection of leaders and articulation of demands and supports (p. 30).

Depending on to whom the leadership of a peak association is beholden to, corporatism can be divided into two categories—state corporatism and societal corporatism (Unger and Chan 2015). State corporatism features top-down control in which the "weight of power...lies heavily on the side of the state" (Unger and Chan 2015, p. 180). Leaderships of state corporatist associations are accountable more to the state than to their memberships. A "dictatorial government may even take charge of creating and maintaining all of the corporatist associations and may grant itself the power to assign and remove their leaders at will" (Unger and Chan 2015, p. 180). On the other end of the spectrum of corporatism is societal corporatism in which "the leaders of the peak associations are beholden to their memberships" (Unger and Chan 2015, p. 180). Unger and Chan tracked two peak business associations in Beijing and found in the early 1990s that these associations obtained substantial independence and autonomy against the state and that the leaderships, albeit appointed by the government, identified themselves with the associations more than with the state. But this trend of societal corporatism was reverted in the 2000s as their follow-up investigation revealed that the leaderships changed their discourse and stressed that their jobs were to assist the government and fulfill "the government's core work" (Unger and Chan 2015, p. 189). This rolling back indicates the "government wants to prevent the development of any association that can muster even a soft challenge to the government's unilateral control..." (Unger and Chan 2015, p. 190).

If the 1990s was the "golden age" for societal corporatist arrangements, then the association for Chinese doctors missed it. The CMDA was corporatized in 2002 following the passage of the "Law of the People's Republic of China on Medical Practitioners" in 1999, which provided the legal ground for medical professions to form a peak association to represent them. According to its constitution, which was amended and enforced by its third national congress in 2012, CMDA receives guidance, supervision, and administration from the MOH. The constitution claims as the CMDA's major functions to safeguard practitioners' lawful rights, integrity, and safety in practice and to strengthen self-discipline, to provide continuous education of members and disseminate medical knowledge and innovations, and to engage in international exchange with foreign counterparts. The constitution also claims that CMDA will carry out investigations on the development and expectations of the medical professions, but the purpose is to provide the government with scientific evidence to facilitate the latter to make "policies, laws and regulations in relation to the administration of medical professions and medical services."[13] In short, CMDA is purported to facilitate the state's administration of medical professions. This is clearly reflected in the organization of CMDA. First, only those who demonstrate political loyalty and follow the Party's lines, principles, and policies can be elected as president, deputy president, and general secretary, and their election must be approved by the MOH before they can take their positions. Second, any amendment to the constitution has to be approved by the MOH. Third, the salaries, insurance, and welfare packages for formal employees in CMDA are set according to the standards for employees of state institutional work-units. Fourth, government funding constitutes a major source of budget of CMDA.[14] Unsurprisingly, the leaderships of CMDA have all come from health bureaucracies. For example, the first president of CMDA, Dr. Yin Dakui, had been one of the Vice Ministers of Health before he retired (because he had reached the maximum age limit for ministerial positions) and was "elected" as the CMDA president. It is fair to say that from its inception, the CMDA was created by the MOH. The incumbent president of CMDA, Dr. Zhang Yanling, had a military background. He was the Director of Health Division of PLA General Logistics Department before he retired from that position and was "elected" as CMDA president. These institutional arrangements provide the health authority with an exclusive channel to exercise targeted control of and influence on medical professions, in addition to the work-unit system that is still in use. Safeguarding the interests of medical professionals that the association asserts to represent takes only secondary position.

Empirical research also confirms that CMDA is a state corporatist establishment representing the government more than its membership. Xuebing Cao's investigation (Cao 2011) of two hospitals in Beijing and Guangzhou, respectively, reveals that in the eyes of frontline doctors, CMDA "has no industrial relations functions" (p. 86) and were deemed as a pure academic society "with no influence at all on work conditions or pay" (p. 86). In this sense, CMDA is considered to be no different from CMA, the learned society of medicine that has a history of nearly a century, and Cao's fieldwork shows that doctors are usually confused with the two. While doctors are increasingly discontented with their incomes, and it is the CMDA's claimed scope of functions to represent their doctors' interests, in reality profession-wide collective bargaining has never been allowed. No professional associations, including the CMDA, have ever acquired any right to represent their members in a collective way to bargain and negotiate with employers, especially when the government is the employer (Cao 2011). It is revealed that doctors are even not clear whether their CMDA membership is registered with the national corporate or local branches, as their memberships are likely to be registered by hospitals as work-unit memberships and their membership fees are automatically deducted from their wages by the hospitals.

Collective bargaining for wages is not completely non-existent in the healthcare system but only happened in small and fragmented scales. In 2000, the Ministry of Labour and Social Security published the "Collective wage bargaining provisional methods," which served as a trial guideline on wage negotiation between workplace unions and employers.[15] The "Collective contract provisions" enacted by the same ministry in 2004 expanded collective bargaining from incomes only to a broader scope including other welfare benefits and entitlements such as training, sick and maternity leave, and so on. It was specified in the "Provisions" that it applied to both industrial enterprises and institutional work-units that were managed and operated as enterprises.[16] But Chinese documentation shows that until 2008, collective bargaining did not make much progress in the industries in the private sector, still less in the public sector.

The advancement of collective bargaining gained some fresh impetus in 2008 when former Premier Wen Jiabao, in his Work Report to the 11th National People's Congress, stated that promotion of collective bargaining was a national labor policy and a key task of the central government's work.[17] Since then, there have been sporadic reports on collective bargaining in the healthcare sector. A widely reported exemplary case took place in Nanjing where medical staff of a village-level community medical service center carried out a collective bargaining with the management of the center for wage patterns and redistribution of revenues between staff and the management (Wang 2008). But such collective bargaining was only limited to work-units. To be exact, it was a negotiation between the union formed only by employees of a particular work-unit or business entity, usually of low level or in the private sector, and the management of that work-unit or a medical entity in the private sector. Collective bargaining never happened on a sector-wide scale, even if the sector is that of a city. However, even this work-unit-based collective bargaining in the public healthcare sector did not flourish. For example, in 2013, Sichuan Provincial Government announced "Sichuan Province industrial collective wage bargaining method," which excludes doctors and teachers of the public sector from the collective bargaining mechanism even though their incomes are comparatively low because, as a senior government official explained, they "are fed by public finance" (*chi caizheng fan*) (Lai 2013). This provincial policy is congruent with the latest development of collective bargaining policy at national level. The "CCP Central Committee's resolution on several key issues regarding global deepening of reform" passed in the Third Plenum of the 18th CCP National Congress in 2013 only mentioned that collective bargaining will be advanced in industrial enterprises. For the wage, allowance, and subsidy systems of administrative and institutional work-units, the CCP Central Committee only promised to carry out reform. This position was reiterated implicitly in the "Suggestions on constructing harmonious industrial relations" jointly issued in March 2015 by the CCP Central Committee and the State Council. The "Suggestions" advised that the promotion of collective bargaining and collective contract systems should target predominantly non-public industrial sector.[18]

In summation, medical employees of the public sector have never been granted any power to bargain collectively with their ultimate employer—the Party-state. Profession-wide collective bargaining organized and represented by the CMDA, the peak association of all medical professions in China, has never happened. In other words, the CMDA does not serve the function of an intermediary structure between individuals and the state. The CMDA is part of the state, while the majority of individual practitioners are still confined within the work-unit system and continuously bureaucratized instead of professionalized. The lack of power of CMDA and the absence of collective bargaining mechanism means that health employees have no control over their economic terms and their employment. The amount and patterns of their formal incomes are entirely determined by the Party-state without much input from both individuals and organizations. As a result, doctors' wages are deliberately kept low for politically motivated financial purposes, namely, to keep the general health budget under control.

Public Doctors' Wages
In the reform era, public doctors experienced many wage increases and three major wage reforms, with another reform in the making, but these increases and reforms have failed to lift their formal incomes to the level that the vast majority of doctors in the public sector are satisfied with. Since the very early stage of the economic reform, health workers started to complain bitterly about their low incomes and the consequent hardships. In 1979, *Jiankang bao* published several readers' letters, including one signed by 63 employees from the Affiliated People's Hospital of Beijing Medical College, a major hospital in the capital city. These letters complained of low wages, highly intensive workloads, constant exposure to health risks, and poor health. The doctors were particularly discontented with the fact that their incomes were much lower than industrial workers who not only earned higher wages but were also paid bonuses and a wide variety of allowances and stipends (Ma et al. 1979). *Jankang bao* conducted a survey of health technicians' wages and welfare in Beijing hospitals. The results, which were published in the same issue of *Jiangkang bao*, confirmed the dire situation of doctors. It revealed that employees in the healthcare system had more wage ranks than industrial workers, which means it usually took longer time for them to climb up the wage ladder. More importantly, since 1978, bonus system was reinstated in the industrial sector, which led to the significant increases of incomes to employees of productive work-units. But a similar system was not established in institutional work-units. Doctors consequently had less extra incomes from bonuses and allowances and relied almost entirely on their fixed wages for a living (Chen 1979).

The first significant wage reform in the public sector in the reform era was implemented in 1985, which abrogated the 30-grade wage scale that had been in use for almost 30 years since 1956, and introduced a structured wage scheme. Wages for public employees were divided into two categories: one for for-profit state-owned enterprises and organizations and the other for non-profit institutions. The salaries for medical professionals fell into the category for the non-profit institutional work-unit. In the new scheme, a doctor's salary was structured to have four components: base wage, position wage, standing stipend, and bonus. For personnel of any profession, the base wage was the same: 40 *yuan* per month. The standing stipend was 0.5 *yuan* per month for each year of service. What differentiated salaries depended on position wages, while standing stipends and bonuses were highly contingent.

For a Chief Doctor (*zhuren yishi*), the highest rate of wage he or she could earn was 355 *yuan* plus standing stipend, which was no more than 20 *yuan* per month, providing he or she had worked for forty years (Ministry of Health 1985c).[19] In other words, while in 1957, a top-level Professor/Chief Doctor could receive 333.5 *yuan* salary per month, his or her colleagues in 1985 could receive a fixed monthly salary of 375 *yuan* from the state (providing they had given service in the professional position for forty years), representing a nominal increase of 12.4 percent. However, the purchasing power of the 1985 salaries dropped significantly due to inflations over the past 30 odd years (Chen 2006a, Zheng 2004). Take, for example, the prices of crops and pork. In 1957, the average price for one ton of crops was 220 *yuan*, while in 1985, the price for the same amount of crops was 383.3 *yuan* (National Statistics Bureau 1986, p. 639). It means in 1957, a top rank doctor could buy 1.5 ton of crops with his or her monthly salary, while in 1985, he or she could buy only 0.98 ton, representing a drop of nearly 35 percent of purchasing power. In 1957, 100 kilograms of pork cost 118 *yuan*, while in 1985, the same amount cost 274.9 *yuan* (National Statistics Bureau 1986, p. 639). While the monthly wage of a top rank doctor could afford roughly 283 kilograms of pork in 1957, his or her wage in 1985 was only enough for 136 kilograms, a drop of over 50 percent of purchasing power. In terms of real wages, the 1985 reform in fact reduced the incomes for medical professionals (see also Lin 1999).

Throughout the 1990s up to 2006, the government implemented several wage reforms. Doctors' low wages improved. The 2006 round of wage reforms featured a substantial change to the wage structure and wage increases (Ministry of Personnel and Ministry of Finance 2006a). The structure of the fixed position wage plus flexible stipend was replaced by position grades, wage levels, performance wages, and stipends. Position grades and wage levels constitute the basic wage of a position. Specialized technical positions applicable to doctors are divided into 13 grades and 65 levels. Grade 1 appointments have to be approved by the Ministry of Personnel and thus have only limited applicability in reality. Normally, the wage grades for senior specialized technical positions are between seven and two and cover Chief Doctor and Associate Chief Doctor. Their salary ranges from 1247 *yuan* per month (Grade 7, Level 16) to 4500 *yuan* (Grade 2, Level 65). Middle-level positions (i.e., Responsible Doctor) match grades 8 to 10 with salary rates ranging from 861 (Grade 10, Level 9) to 3380 *yuan* (Grade 8, Level 65). Grades 11 and 12 are set for junior professionals (that is, Doctor). Wages for these positions range from 715 (Grade 12, Level 5) to 3220 *yuan* (Grade 11, Level 65) (Ministry of Personnel and Ministry of Finance 2006b).

It must be pointed out that during the same period, many welfare benefits to which employees of work-units were previously entitled disappeared. In their places were commercial fee-paying goods and services. The disappeared benefits that have the most significant financial impact on doctors include housing, healthcare, and education. In the pre-reform era and until the mid-1990s, these were provided to work-unit employees either for free or at highly subsidized rates, although the availability was not always guaranteed, especially of subsidized housing. Since the late 1990s, housing and education (especially tertiary education) have been commercialized. With the skyrocketing real estate prices and ever-rising fees for tertiary education, the purchasing power of the raised salaries of medical professionals has been greatly compromised.

As a result, despite the wage reforms, public doctors have been mostly dissatisfied with their incomes. In the 1980s and 1990s, doctors usually complained that they, as a major component of intellectual workers, earned less than manual workers in the industry and individual proprietors in the private sector, a phenomenon that was termed *nao ti dao gua* (reversed correlation of mental and physical jobs) (Liu and Cai 1998). In the 2000s, doctors more often complained that their income levels were lower than university staff or public servants and much lower than their colleagues in the West (CMDA 2015). From 2002 onward, the CMDA had conducted five surveys of medical professionals on their perceptions of workloads, pressures, practicing environments, and incomes. All these surveys revealed that doctors were discontented with their formal incomes. The 2009 Survey revealed that over 77 percent of respondents complained that their incomes were lower than university teachers, and nearly 92 percent believed that their incomes were not commensurate with the efforts they had put into their work (CMDA 2015). The outcome of the 2011 Survey was even more concerning. Over 95 percent of doctors believed their incomes were incommensurate with their hard work (CMDA 2015). The 2014 Survey, which was conducted after the New Health Reform was launched in 2012, showed that nearly 66 percent of doctors were not satisfied with their incomes (CMDA 2015). The figure represents a significant drop from previous results, indicating some positive effect of the new reform. However, as CMDA interprets it, the fact that over half of practitioners were still not satisfied with their incomes was equally concerning (CMDA 2015).

In spite of the widespread dissatisfaction, doctors do not seem to demand too much. A study completed in 2006 investigated the real incomes and expected incomes between two groups of employees under the age of 40. One group consisted of practicing doctors, and the other group was composed of former doctors who voluntarily left medical positions and found employment in other sectors between 2001 and 2004. The research revealed that respondents of both groups expected an average monthly income of 9000 *yuan*. In reality, those who had chosen to quit the medical profession earned an average income of 8500 *yuan* per month in other sectors, while those who had continued to practice as doctors only made 2700 *yuan* a month in average (Zhang et al. 2006). The difference is huge and appalling. Another report published in 2012 showed that 70 percent of medical professionals expected an annual income level of over 100,000 *yuan*, while in reality, only 4.7 percent reached that level (Sun and Cao 2012).

Health reforms have failed to raise doctors' incomes to levels that most of them would perceive reasonable, and their low incomes are to a great degree resulted from the absence of a collective bargaining mechanism in the economic and political structure and the lack of corporate power on the part of the medical profession. Although the reforms have liberalized many economic domains, the medical profession is largely not liberalized. Up to date, the majority of Chinese doctors are employed in the public sector and retain the status of state cadre.

Doctors as State Cadres

In the early years of the reform, private medical practices re-emerged with the permission of the government and served as supplement to public medicine, providing medical services to a population who had limited or even no access to the healthcare organized by the government (Yang 2008). From then on, the private sector has been expanding rapidly, especially in the rural area where medical practices at village level are nearly completely privatized (Anson and Sun 2005; Ge and Gong 2007). But the reform left the urban healthcare system largely intact with public establishments continuing to dominate the sector (Anson and Sun 2005, p. 15).

In terms of quantity, the number of privately funded hospitals has caught up in the past decade. In 2005, 82.8 percent hospitals were public owned and operated, while only 17.2 percent were private hospitals. In 2013, private hospitals accounted for 45.8 percent of the total number of hospitals, while the percentage of public hospitals dropped to 54.2 (National Health and Family Planning Commission 2014, p. 10). But the quality of private hospitals lagged far behind the public ones. Hospitals are divided into three levels according to the number of beds, equipment, employment, and functions. Level 3 represents the top hospitals, while level 1 constitutes less sophisticated hospitals. There are also many hospitals whose quality and configuration do not meet the standards for even level 1 hospitals and are thus unranked. As of 2013, among the 13,396 hospitals in the public sector, there were 1693 level 3 hospitals (12.6 percent) and 5944 level 2 hospitals (44.4 percent). Among the 11,313 privately owned hospitals, however, there were only 95 level three hospitals (0.8 percent) and 765 level 2 hospitals (6.8 percent). The majority of private hospitals were unranked (6764, or 59.8 percent) (National Health and Family Planning Commission 2014, p. 12). Although the number of private hospitals is almost level with that of public hospitals, the magnitude of the private sector is no match for the public sector. In terms of the number of hospital beds, the public sector accounts for 84.4 percent of the total, while the private sector only provide 15.6 percent. It is clear that in terms of quantity and quality, healthcare resources concentrate in the public sector.

As the majority of hospital beds concentrated in the public sector, so do human resources. The majority of licensed medical and health professionals and paraprofessionals are employed in the public sector. As of 2013, among the 1.5 million odd doctors and assistant doctors working in hospitals, 86.4 percent were employed in the public sector, while only 13.6 percent were in the private sector (National Health and Family Planning Commission 2014, p. 43).

The public healthcare system also monopolizes the career path of medical professionals and excludes those in the private sector. Publicly employed doctors can apply for promotion along a ladder of seniority—from Doctor (junior title), Responsible Doctor (middle title), through Associate Chief and Chief Doctor (senior titles). These titles not only entail increasing incomes but also represent a doctor's capacity and professional status. But these titles have long been denied to the private sector, which means privately employed doctors are not eligible to receive official promotion through this professional-title system. The system is only open to those with "cadre" status, and only those who are employed in the public sector have this status (Ding et al. 2015). For the sake of career development, doctors generally shun the private sector. It has been revealed that private hospitals are usually staffed by young graduates fresh from medical schools who cannot find employment in the public sector or old doctors who have retired from public employment (Kang et al. 2015). In general, doctors employed in the public sector are usually much better qualified and trained than those working in the private sector. Senior doctors are almost entirely concentrated in public hospitals.

Up to date, doctors formally employed in the public sector retain the cadre status and continue to function as medical bureaucrats. In the reform era, especially from the late 1990s onward when the state reformed its public personnel system and expanded the tertiary education system, the government has implemented policies to deliberately play down the importance of cadre status. With the rapid rise of a private sector and its ever expanding capacity of employment, the attraction of public employment has abated significantly. But in the healthcare system, as the state continues to monopolize quality resources, especially the professional-title system and other career opportunities such as overseas professional training opportunities and academic activities, public employment has always been eagerly pursued.

Graduates from medical universities, as well as all public universities, maintain their probationary cadre status. The most important document to evidence this status is the *baodao zheng* (report certificate) they receive on graduation. Xuzhou Medical College, in an online posting on 5 June 2015, emphasizes to its fresh graduates the importance of the "report certificate." The posting reveals that a "report certificate" is uniformly printed by the state and signed by the provincial education department and is only available to graduates who were recruited under the state's uniform recruitment plan and graduated under the state's employment plan. The "report certificate" serves at least seven functions. The last is that the certificate is the proof of the graduate's cadre status. "Without the 'report certificate,' the graduate will lose [his/her] cadre status and become a social working person (worker status). A talent center [*rencai zhongxing*] will not be able to accept the graduate's personal records [*dang'an*]."[20] The posting further advises,

> The report certificate has been in use for many years until today. In current talent markets [i.e., employment markets], some private companies and foreign companies express they do not require the report certificates of graduates, but any employer who is serious about students should take the report certificate seriously. For graduates from general tertiary educational organizations in China, under current system, the report certificate has significant implication for your post-graduation life.[21]

In spite of the Party-state's efforts to reform the institutional work-unit personnel system, up to the time when this research was being carried out, cadre status remained a crucial identity for public doctors on which their welfare, pension, entitlements, and career progress are dependent. In 2000, the Party-state introduced a reform aiming at liberalizing the rigid state personnel system and bringing more democracy and transparency to the system, more autonomy and accountability to the institutional work-unit, and more mobility to individual employees. One of the aims of the reform was to transform state-controlled status-based employment and management (*shenfen guanli*) into work-unit-controlled position-based employment and management (*gangwei guanli*) (Ministry of Organization and Ministry of Personnel 2000; Ministry of Organization; Ministry of Health, and Ministry of Personnel 2000). To put it in plain language, employment in the public sector has long been centrally managed by the Party-state according to centrally formed employment plans. Individual work-unit usually did not have the right to decide the number of employees according to its own needs and demands. Staff and workers were assigned to an institutional work-unit by the government rather than hired from human resources market and were paid in light of a uniform wage scheme by the government rather than by the work-unit. The reform was intent on granting individual work-units the authority and power to decide what positions they needed to perform their functions and tasks and fill these positions by contracting the most suitable and ablest persons irrespective of their status (Liu 2010).

But there is a catch. The reform to the system must not challenge the CCP's control over both the leadership of a work-unit and its staff. The Party's insistence can be summed up in two principles, namely, *dang guan ganbu* (the Party controls cadres) and *dang guan rencai* (the Party controls the talented). The latter is of particular interest as it concerns the employment of the vast majority of staff in institutional work-units. In the first Talent Work Conference (*Rencai Gongzuo Huiyi*) held in Beijing in 2003, former President Hu Jintao accentuated this principle as the core of the reform to the personnel system.[22] In 2012, the CCP General Office issued a document entitled "Advice on further strengthening the Party's control of talent work," which operationalized the principle (CCP General Office 2012).

The Party-state's tenacious hold on the employment of the talented results in the lagging behind of the change to related institutions, in particular the personnel archive management system (*renshi dang'an guanli*) which retains and updates individual cadres' personal records and organizations' comments and opinions on cadres' behaviors and performances (Yang 2011; Chen 2007). Another area that has hindered the reform is the welfare and pension system which was predominantly funded by governmental budgets until January 2015 when the State Council announced a resolution to socialize the pension system of institutional work-units (General Office of the State Council 2015b). But the implementation of the resolution may take a long time as it may meet strong resistance from employees of institutional work-units who consider it unfair. A major reason is that the resolution does not include employees of governmental and Party work-units, whose pensions are continuously funded by state budgets.[23] Compounded by a variety of factors, including those discussed above, the reform to the personnel system of institutional work-units advanced extremely slowly, and cadre status continuously carries weight with public employees, including those in the healthcare system. In May 2015, the State Council promulgated guidance on reform to urban public hospitals, in which the central government affirms that it will deepen the reform to the personnel system, implementing contracting system and position management system and shifting from status management to position management (General Office of the State Council 2015a), an exact reiteration of what it promised to do in 2000.

As publicly employed doctors continue to hold cadre status and work in medical work-units, their function as medical bureaucrats persists. As Zhu Hengpeng (2014), a researcher from the Chinese Academy of Social Sciences, criticizes, "our (public) doctors are not autonomous professionals, but 'state cadres' with staff status (*bianzhi shenfen*) of institutional work-units. Or in plain language, they are 'work-unit persons,' not 'social persons'." Then it is not a surprise that after over three decades of economic reform, bureaucratic medicine remains a strong feature of the public healthcare system.

Bureaucratic Medicine

There is no doubt that after more than three decades of economic reform and the so-called marketization of healthcare, doctors' clinical behaviors and the patterns of their interactions with patients have significantly changed. It is also clear from the above discussion that the CCP has made consistent efforts to advance the principle of serving the people and to promote universalistic particularism in healthcare system. As the structure of healthcare organization remains basically intact, however, it is equally evident that some old practices and norms survived, including bureaucratic medicine. Throughout the reform era, patients continue to face bureaucratic impersonalism.

Bureaucratic medicine seems to have never disappeared. Complaints about low quality, long waiting time, poor attitude, negligence, and rent-seeking behaviors were rife in national and local newspapers. Since the early 1980s, health professionals and workers have been widely accused of being "distant" (*sheng*), "callous" (*leng*), "brusque" (*ying*), "confrontational" (*ding*), and "shunning" (*tui*) toward patients (Gong 1981; Jiang 1993; Liu 1991; Yan 1998; Yang 1985; Zhang 1980).

Health authorities and public hospitals have never turned a blind eye on the issue of poor service attitudes and have made waves of efforts to address it. But poor attitudes seem persistent. For example, in 1995, the management of the First Affiliated Hospital of Kunming Medical College, which was one of the best hospitals of Yunnan Province, in an attempt at medical ethics construction and improvement of service attitudes, decided to enforce among the staff the use of civilities (*wenming yongyu*) such as "*qing*" (please), "*nin*" (the polite form of "you"), "*duibuqi*" (sorry), and "*xiexie peihe*" (thanks for cooperation) and ban the use of such curt and irresponsible remarks as "don't know, go talk to my leader"; "the disease is not treated in this unit, go find a unit that can treat you"; "your case (surgery, or disease) is no good"; and so on (Dang 1995). In 1998, the director of the hospital admitted that the problem was not solved and the service attitudes of the medical staff were still "very poor." Patients were attracted to its modern and sophisticated technology but at the same time were scared of the distant, callous, and harsh attitudes of the medical staff (Yang 1998). The director vowed to redress the attitude issue in one year.

But bureaucratic medicine was far more enduring than he anticipated, persisting well into the new millennium. In 2001, the hospital was publicly named by the Provincial Health Department for refusing to admit a pregnant woman to emergency because she did not meet the emergency criteria, even though she passed out in the waiting area in the hospital's lobby bleeding substantially. Her husband had to call the ambulance center and had her transferred to another hospital to save her life (Wu 2001). Another scenario described in a post on a major online community—Tianya—exposed a series of appalling incidents that a female blogger encountered when seeking medical advice and treatment to the flu in the hospital in 2012. The blogger blamed the hospital for being extremely bureaucratic and impersonal. To receive an injection, the blogger said she had to run between the doctor's office, pharmacy, fee office, and injection room several times because of unclear and inadequate instructions. When returning to the fee office the third time asking for a receipt for the payment of medicine as required by the injection room, the fee collector behind the windows allegedly said, "I have given you the receipt. You must have lost it. It is not my business." When the blogger countered, the collector said, "Go talk to my leader."[24] It seems that after over 15 years, the hospital staff are yet to learn how to use civilities.

The case of the First Affiliated Hospital of Kunming Medical College is not isolated. In fact, it reflects the tenacity of bureaucratic medicine in the entire public hospital system. The health authority is not inactive in this regard. Since 1997, the MOH has launched a series of campaigns promoting patient-centered healthcare, including the 100-Exemplary Hospitals (1997–2001), Hospital Management Year (2005–09), Long March to Medical Quality (2009–11), and "Three Goods and One Satisfaction" (2011–present). A major task of these campaigns is to improve service quality and attitudes and to rid of distant, cold, brusque, confrontational, and shunning behaviors in public hospitals. With the launch of the Hospital Management Year campaign in 2005, the MOH explicitly required that in public hospitals, civilities and polite manners must be adopted, and the phenomena of distance, coldness, brusqueness, confrontation, and shunning must be rooted out (Zhou 2005). The establishment of doctors' ethics assessment system in 2007 also included service attitudes within the assessment criteria. Doctors are required to "dress neatly, conduct in a dignified manner, use standard civilities for service, adopt good service attitudes, and have no 'distant,' 'cold,' 'brusque,' 'confrontational,' and 'shunning' phenomena" (Ministry of Health 2007).

The effect of these policy and administrative efforts seems limited. Numerous empirical investigations of patients' perceptions of medical services provided by public medical organizations at all levels indicate that the cost of medical services and poor attitudes of medical staff have always been the top two aspects that that patients have found most dissatisfied with (Xu et al. 2009; Lu et al. 2010; Leng 2002; Leng and Li 2008; Wang and Xu 2006; Huang et al. 2009). The outcomes of investigations focusing particularly on patients' perceptions of their relationship with doctors are more illustrious, and they reveal that patients are almost overwhelmingly most dissatisfied with the service attitudes and communicative manners of medical staff. The Fourth National Health Services Investigation conducted by the MOH in 2008 showed that 51.4 percent of respondents were not satisfied with the attitudes of doctors, followed by over-provision of services (23 percent) and low professional capacity (13.5 percent) (Center for Health Statistics and Information 2010, p. 154). When asked what they expected doctors to improve most, most respondents expected medical staff to improve their professional ethics and attitudes (ibid., p. 162). Another research (Lu et al. 2010) conducted independently around the same time revealed similar results. The research listed five reasons that were potentially attributable to the tension between doctors and patients, including over-provision of services, inappropriate informed consent, doctors' bad mood, unsatisfactory outcome of treatment, and dissatisfying services. More respondents (36.8 percent) placed dissatisfying services over other options (p. 44).

Patients' complaints registered with hospitals demonstrate from another perspective the fact that the bureaucratic manners are always central to patients' concerns in their interactions with doctors. A study of 56 medical disputes in Anhui Province between 1991 and 1995 showed that 52 of them were complaints about medical staff's cold attitudes, harsh language, and lack of communication (Shao et al. 1998). Investigations carried out in the new millennium indicate that such phenomenon is still widespread. Doctors' unkind manners are usually the top reason that causes patients to lodge complaints with hospitals, no matter whether they are major general hospitals (Li 2009; Wu and Lin 2006; Lei et al. 2014), specialized hospitals (Sun et al. 2008; Qiu et al. 2013), community hospitals (Li and Sun 2013), county hospitals (Jin et al. 2006), or village and township health centers (Diao and Xia 2015). In general, the complaints accuse doctors for lacking the sense of service, callousness, brusqueness, impatience, disrespect for patients, dressing patients down, using discriminative language, and sometimes verbally abusing patients (Qiu et al. 2013; Huang 2014; Wu and Lin 2006; Jin et al. 2006; Lei et al. 2014). Even a health law textbook warns medical university students that nearly 80 percent of medical disputes are caused by the poor service attitudes or callous and brusque language of medical staff (Zhao 2005, p. 46).

Some commentators attempt to explain patients' dissatisfactions away by claiming that callousness is a necessary evil of emotional detachment embedded in professional impersonalism or it is inevitable due to heavy workloads that doctors have to carry (see, for example, Li 2005). It is arguable that professional impersonalism and heavy workloads may have played a role in the formation of doctors' "distant," "cold," "brusque," "confrontational," and "shunning" manners. At the same time, it is also clear that these malpractices are not limited to the public healthcare sector. In fact, they prevails the entire public sector, including governments and their agencies, indicating that they are closely associated with the bureaucratic nature of these institutions. An Office of Redressing Unhealthy Trends (ORUT)[25] was established in particular in 1991 in an attempt to redress across the entire public sector the endemic "unhealthy" practices, including both poor service attitudes and rent-seeking activities such as "eating" (*chi*, that is, demanding help-seekers to take responsible officials to meals), "taking" (*na*, that is, taking goods of small value from help-seekers), "blocking" (*ka*, that is, intentionally setting up barriers for help-seekers), and "soliciting" (*yao*, that is, soliciting bribes).[26] Considering the state's monopolistic control over medical resources and the status of the majority of doctors as medical bureaucrats, it is fair to argue that doctors' poor service attitudes and their distant, callous, brusque, confrontational, and shunning manners are more associated with bureaucratic medicine than other factors.

Society of Acquaintances

For patients, bureaucratic medicine is not insurmountable. The two most efficient ways to bypass the callous, impersonal bureaucracy are *guanxi* and red packets. Most of the time, they have to be used together. Here I will examine *guanxi* first.

As a social norm, particularism continues well into the reform era until today as China remains a society of acquaintances. Resources are frequently redistributed according to the degrees of closeness in personal relationships. Social connection thus becomes a major determinant of what one can get from a particular system and how one is treated by others in the system (Xiao et al. 2009; Yu 2006). In the public healthcare system, seeking medical services through *guanxi* is a common practice among patients. It is nothing but backdoor medicine in the new era (Dai 1995). A recent investigation (Qu et al. 2010) reveals that 9.3 percent of patients utilized *guanxi* to arrange a visit to doctor every time, 45.6 percent utilized *guanxi* sometimes, while 15.7 percent wished to but cannot find *guanxi* when seeking medical services. Only 29.6 percent claimed they had never used or wished to use *guanxi*, while 70.4 percent used or intended to use *guanxi* in seeking services. The major reasons that motivate patients to utilize *guanxi* to seek medical services include ensuring commitment of doctors, reaching reputed doctors, jumping the queue, having better service attitudes, and avoiding over-provision of services. This investigation confirms the results of another research carried out in 2005, which revealed that around 72 percent of patients organized visits to hospitals through *guanxi* for generally the same reasons (Wu 2006). But what is more interesting about Qu, Tian, and Zhou's research (2010) is that 73.8 percent of doctors prefer providing services to patients referred to them through *guanxi*. While 41.5 percent of doctors hoped to expand their *guanxi* networks through acquaintance-referred patients, 40.4 percent of doctors also believed *guanxi* patients could increase their incomes. While the research did not specify whether the increased incomes were generated through formal or informal channels, other studies indicate that red packets were included (Qu 2010; Dai 1995).

In summation, institutional persistence leads to the continuity of fundamental healthcare ideology and the bureaucratic organization of medical professions. With its persevering insistence on the fundamental ideology of serving the people, the CCP continues to promote universal particularism in the healthcare system, demanding doctors to treat every patient equally and passionately as they do a family member. But the enduring bureaucratic organization of the medical professions perpetuates bureaucratic medicine, which continues to offset the Party-state's endeavor to advance universal particularism. Medical staff of the public healthcare system remains notorious for not only bureaucratic indifference but also appalling manners and attitudes toward patients. Fortunately, China remains a society of acquaintances, giving patrons of the public healthcare system an opportunity to bypass bureaucracy through *guanxi*. Backdoor medicine continues to be a major informal social norm for patrons to seek quality medical services in the state-monopolized healthcare system.

INSTITUTIONAL CHANGES

It is clear that the public healthcare system does not just perpetuate the institutions that existed in the pre-reform era. Reforms to some old institutions and the establishment of new institutions have significantly changed the landscape of healthcare in China. Major institutional changes in two areas have made significant contribution to the rise of informal payments in the public healthcare system, in companion with the persevering backdoor medicine. The first major institutional change is the political recognition of the value of doctors' cultural capital. The second relates to the abandonment of the idea of "organizing medicine with hard work and thrift (*qinjian ban yi*)" and the adoption of commercialization of medical services as a predominant strategy to sustain the rapid expansion of medical institutions.

The Political Recognition of Doctors' Cultural Capital

Cultural capital, conceptualized by Pierre Bourdieu (1986), refers to knowledge, skills, education, as well as other symbolic indicators of social class such as tastes, linguistic traces, and dispositions that possessors of such capital distinguish themselves from other social groups. It can be passed on across generations and can be converted to social capital and economic capital. In its institutionalized form, it refers to credentials and qualifications that the formal educational system bestows on the possessor. Doctors graduated with credentials issued by formal educational institutions through lengthy period of study and socialization apparently possess cultural capitals that can be transmitted into economic capitals and that set them apart from other social groups. In China, however, the distribution, acquisition, and transmission of cultural capital are largely controlled and determined by the Party-state, which even decides what counts as cultural capital. Since 1949, the cultural capital of medical professions has been always subject to the interference of the CCP, which decides how cultural capital should be institutionalized, who are allowed to acquire it, and how it can be converted to other types of capital, especially economic capital.

In the CCP's terminology of human resources, the category of professionals does not exist. People with higher education, regardless of their occupations, have been placed in the category of "intellectuals." Medical doctors, due to their education, have always been categorized into this social stratum and are subject to the CCP's policies toward intellectuals. Intellectual policies changed drastically under different leaderships. Since the establishment of the PRC, the leadership of the Party-state had a clear understanding that China's modernization relied on the input of knowledge workers and endeavored to expand the corps of intellectuals. It is mainly because of this understanding that personnel with higher education were usually better paid than others in the pre-reform era. However, the early leadership of the CCP had a strong suspicion about intellectuals' class affiliation and loyalty. Since 1951, many thought campaigns have been waged to force intellectuals to admit they were ideologically flawed and must undergo substantial re-education before they deserved better use by the new regime (see, for example, Zhou 1951b, 1956).

Up to 1965, tertiary education, especially health education, had generally followed the line of professionalization (Sidel and Sidel 1973, pp. 111–126) thanks to the influence of Soviet medicine, although the Soviet medical education model may not have lived up to the standards of professionalization in the West. Started by Mao Zedong's "June 26 Directive," however, the medical profession underwent deprofessionalization during the Cultural Revolution. Mao particularly criticized the higher education of medicine, claiming that lengthy training for doctors was useless and a waste of time (Milton et al. 1977, p. 151).

Following Mao's directive, the tertiary medical curriculum was drastically shortened. The admission of medical students was evaluated by political rather than academic standards (Sidel and Sidel 1973, pp. 111–126). In other words, the cultural capital of a doctor was significantly devalued although such educational arrangement increased the social mobility for lower social stratum.

This trend has been reversed under the leaderships of the reform era. Higher education in medicine has been returned to the pre-Cultural Revolution model, namely, the orthodox Soviet model. The curriculum is prolonged. Admission is determined by academic rather than political standards. What is more important for the development of intellectuals is that the suspicion that the CCP had about them has been gradually eroded and has disappeared. In the meantime, the ideological position of intellectuals has been on the constant rise.

The reform era is full of politically good news for intellectuals. Even in 1977, one year before the reform officially started, intellectuals started to feel the change. In that year, Deng Xiaoping (1995) volunteered to "take charge of the work in science and education" (p. 61). In a talk with two members of the CCP's Central Committee on 24 May 1977, Deng (1995) allegedly said,

We must create within the Party an atmosphere of respect for knowledge and respect for the educated (*rencai*). The erroneous attitude of not respecting intellectuals must be opposed. All work, be it mental or manual, is labour. Those who engage in mental work are also workers (p. 54).

Hereafter, "respecting knowledge, respecting the educated" has been widely cited in China's political rhetoric. The important message delivered in the talk is actually the "rise" of intellectuals' ideological status in relation to the working class. Medical professionals' cultural capital is recognized in the Party-state ideology. Formal knowledge,[27] rather than informal knowledge or folk knowledge that were valued in the Cultural Revolution, is again recognized and institutionalized as the key driving power behind social progression.

Bourdieu points out that cultural capital has the potential to be converted into economic profits and is constantly so in capitalist societies. But China lacks formal institutional arrangements that would allow medical professionals to convert their cultural capital into economic gains through legally sanctioned mechanisms. As discussed above, the Party-state insists on medical professionals upholding the ethical ideal of unselfish sacrifice. The persistence of bureaucratically organized medical professions, the absence of a bona fide market of healthcare human resources, and the prevalence of state corporatism deny doctors any opportunity to openly bargain with the state for economic terms that would materialize their cultural capital. Consequently, there is a significant gap between their high potential of cultural capital and their low economic position bestowed on them by the Party-state, a difference that cannot be made up through formal institutions.

Commercialization and the Profit-driven Behaviors of Medical Organizations

The healthcare system expanded significantly in the pre-reform era, but the expansion was largely achieved through "hard work and thrift" as government investment in healthcare was kept low. In the reform era, government investment in healthcare in proportion to the total healthcare expenditures declined even further until recently, while healthcare facilities expanded significantly in terms of both quantity and quality. The expansion has been achieved not through the observation of the principle of "hard work and thrift," which was abandoned in the early stage of the reform, but through commercialization of health and medical services. Medical organizations are encouraged to follow "market" principles to operate their services in a pseudo-market for medical services and to generate revenues in the midst of excessive state regulation, especially in the pricing of medical services.

The profit-driven expansion significantly reduced the equality, accessibility, and efficiency of healthcare and became a major source of social unrest (Wang 2003; Zhou 2008; Zhu 2010). A popular opinion is to blame these problems on marketization of medical services, as represented by the 2005 report, which claimed that the health reform was a failure (Ge and Gong 2007). In spite of its popularity, however, some scholars dismissed the opinion as "groundless" as a genuine market for medical services had never been established in China (Zhu 2010; Gu et al. 2006; Zhou 2008). The second opinion is more convincingly argued as it is apparent that the healthcare system is dominated by state-owned and operated medical facilities. Private medical organizations are treated unequally and handicapped in many ways, especially in taxation. Public hospitals are considered as not-for-profit organizations and are exempt from taxes, while private organizations are usually classified as for-profit and have to pay taxes (Ministry of Health et al. 2000). Public doctors are denied the right to collective bargaining, which is usually available to employees in the private sector, but at the same time, they have exclusive access to the professional titles, which have long been denied to the practitioners in the private sector. It is in this sense that Gu et al. (2006) argue that public hospitals are not much different from the institutional work-units in the era of the command economy, and their relationship to government agencies remains unchanged (p. 34).

The absence of the genuine market in the healthcare sector is also demonstrated in hospitals' lack of pricing power. China's health facilities have some degree of economic autonomy, but they have little say with regard to setting the prices for most of their medical services and products (Eggleston and Yip 2004; Liu et al. 2000; The World Bank 1997). Before 2000, the State Price Bureau was responsible for the administration of prices for medical services and products and set most of them well below cost. In 2000, the central government devolved the pricing authority to the provincial or municipal price bureaus (National Development Planning Commission and Ministry of Health 2000). Hospitals had some autonomy to decide their service prices to meet the real costs but within the boundaries that the local price bureaus formulated. It would be a mistake, however, to exaggerate that autonomy. For example, the Shenzhen Municipal Government declared in July 2007 that hospitals only have the "autonomy" to set prices lower than the government's guiding prices but are not allowed to charge more than them (Yang 2007).

The strict control has resulted in price distortion in consultation and service fees. A frequently used device to increase the healthcare accessibility is for the government to mark down the value of medical services in order to keep prices low (Hsiao 1995; Liu et al. 2000; Wong and Chiu 1998). The Chinese government reduced medical service fees several times from 1958 to 1978. Consequently, in the early years of the reform era, the revenues from providing services were not enough to recover the costs of services (Ministry of Health 1981). The device is still used in the present day. According to a study of unit costs of major health services in Shandong Province in 1994, the regulated hospital fees only allowed an average cost recovery rate of 50 percent. Only 4 percent of services had their fees set above costs (Liu, Liu, and Chen 2000). Ten years later, the situation was not much improved. A survey of 32 hospitals in Zhejiang Province in 2003 reveals that the regulated fees for 92.9 percent of surgical procedures could not cover the costs (Gu 2003). Payment for the technical component of surgeries is very low, accounting for only 10 percent of the total payment for a surgical procedure (Duan 2007). Setting medical service prices low seems to have been a major resort to contain cost, to appease the increasingly dissatisfied public, pursuant to the CCP's ideological commitment to serving the people. But the effect of overregulation is readily offset by the government's encouragement of commercialization.

Medical services have never been fully liberalized and marketized, but market elements have nonetheless been institutionalized since the early stage of the reform. In the late 1970s and early 1980s, health facilities suffered shortages of staff, beds, and surgical facilities resulting from funding shortage (Wang 2003). To address these problems, the State Council endorsed applications made by the MOH to allow hospitals to charge higher service fees to patients covered by public health insurance (Ministry of Health 1981). The policy represents the first attempt on the part of the MOH to bring healthcare closer to economic principles. In the following years, more and more market elements were introduced to the healthcare system. 1985 is usually considered as the beginning of the first round of health reform in China (Cao and Fu 2005) when a groundbreaking document by the MOH was approved by the State Council. Entitled "Report on several policy issues concerning reform of the health work," the MOH demanded more economic and personnel autonomy for hospitals and firm implementation of fixed budget administration. The "Report" acknowledged that the current fee schedules for medical services were not reasonable and also admitted that it would be difficult to adjust these schedules, indicating that it would not be possible to allow hospitals to recover costs of general services. However, the "Report" approved that hospitals could charge higher fees for the use of new equipment and the provision of new medical services and techniques to recover costs. Hospitals with newly built or renovated or expanded buildings could charge higher fees. Hospital wards could be graded according to equipment and furnishing and priced differently (Ministry of Health 1985b). In 1988, public hospitals were demanded to implement all forms of contracted responsibility systems and were encouraged to set up special clinics to provide higher quality services for patients who could afford higher out-of-pocket fees. In terms of services using new technology and equipment, hospitals were also allowed to charge fees according to real costs (labor costs excluded) (Ministry of Health et al. 1988). In short, hospitals were permitted and encouraged to generate and increase incomes through various forms of services and to associate self-generated income with the benefits and welfare of staff. "Hard work and thrift" is no longer emphasized as the guiding principle of healthcare delivery and expansion. Pursuing profits has become the common goal of public health providers (Ge and Gong 2007).

In company with policy encouragement to pursue profits, the Party-state constantly reduced funding to public hospitals by changing funding patterns. Until 1979, the expenses of public hospitals had been financed in accordance with the pattern of "full budget management, targeted subsidies, and fixed lump sum budget" (*quan'e guanli, dingxiang buzhu, yusuan baogan*), in which the entire payroll, one percent of welfare, and two percent of union fees were fully covered by government funding (Zhu 2010). In 1979, a new funding pattern was implemented which was summarized as "full budget management, fixed subsidies, and surplus to be retained (by hospitals)" (*quan'e guanli, ding'e buzhu, jieyu ziliu*) (Ministry of Health, Ministry of Finance, and National General Bureau of Labour 1979). In this pattern, government no longer covered the payroll of a hospital. Instead, the amount of government subsidies (or funding) was decided by the number of beds that a hospital had. Purchase of major equipment, expenses for major renovations, and retirement funds were subsidized separately according to the financial capacity of local governments. In 2000, this pattern was slightly changed. The government promised fixed budget for community medical centers, while continued targeted budgets for public hospitals at the country level and above (Ministry of

Finance, National Planning Commission, and Ministry of Health 2000). Government subsidies covered construction of new public hospitals and developmental construction of existing hospitals, expenditures for retirement pensions, scientific research, and so on. But again payroll was not funded. This pattern was in force until very recently.

Government subsidies constitute one of the three major revenue sources for public hospitals but always the smallest one. According to a study of economic operations of Shanghai public hospitals between 2002 and 2009, government subsidies accounted for only 5 percent to 6.8 percent of average annual revenues of a level 3 hospital and about 8.9 to 12.5 percent of the annual revenues of a level 2 hospital (Li et al. 2011). In many places, government subsidies cannot even cover the basic payroll of health facilities (Bloom et al. 2001). That means hospitals have to generate the majority of their revenues through the other two sources—drug sales and medical service fees. Since the 1950s, hospitals were permitted to charge extra fees on drugs sold through hospital pharmacies to compensate operational expenses (Xu 2009). In general, hospitals are not allowed to charge more than 15 percent of the purchase price of a medicine, but in reality, it is common for hospitals to go over that limit (Li et al. 2011). In average, drug sales incomes account for over 40 percent of a public hospital's revenues (Li et al. 2011). In some hospitals, the percentage can reach over 55 percent, up to over 60 percent (Xu 2009). Incomes generated from drug sales constitute a major source of hospital's funding for payroll (He and Yuan 2010). Hospitals thus have a strong incentive to overprescribe drugs to supplement significantly inadequate government funding and, in many cases, to compensate the losses from providing medical services (Xu 2009; Li et al. 2011).

The third source of revenues is the incomes generated from providing medical services. As mentioned above, the health authority has placed strict control over the pricing of basic medical services, which has led to widespread losses on the part of hospitals. But hospitals can charge higher fees if patients use new diagnostic equipment or pathological tests or receive treatment by new technologies. This creates another incentive for hospitals to promote these services in order to reduce losses if not make a profit.

Low government funding, distorting pricing mechanisms, and sanctioned drug sales as a major compensation for operational losses encourage over-prescription and over-provision in hospitals. But such revenue-generating strategies can only be realized through the cooperation of medical staff, who seem to have no choice but to cooperate. As government funding may not even be enough to cover medical staff's basic wages promised in the wage schemes, hospitals have to incentivize their staff to prescribe more drugs and profitable medical services to generate revenues. A widely used strategy is "prescription for commission" (*kaidan ticheng*), namely, the hospital gives doctors commissions for prescribing drugs and medical tests. The more they prescribe, the more they earn.

"Prescription for commission" is usually linked to doctors' floating stipend or performance wages, depending on the wage schemes. In many hospitals, especially minor hospitals, it constitutes the major part of doctors' formal incomes (Chai 2014). Usually, a substantial part of the doctor's normal wage is converted into contingent wage. As hospitals have been given increasing power over the administration of medical professionals, many have formulated internal wage policies that link doctors' income closer to their performance than the health authority allows. For example, Shenyang TCM Hospital enacted a new wage scheme in 2003. It features a "redistribution according to secondary performance assessment" paradigm. All the doctors and nurses are only guaranteed 30 percent of their wages (most probably referring to their position wage or basic wage) and are required to find their own "ways" in their work to earn the rest of the 70 percent or more. A position with a normal monthly wage of 1700 *yuan* is only paid around 700 *yuan*, including a 500 *yuan* fixed wage. The rest of the salary has to be earned through prescription of drugs, medical tests, and other services. At the same time, there is an entire scheme of kickback rates for prescriptions. For instance, doctors get 11 percent for prescribing herbal medicine, 10 percent for pathology tests, 13 percent for injections and bandage changes, 17 *yuan* for CT, and so on. Consequentially, doctors of some popular departments could pocket up to 10,000 *yuan* extra money per month as a reward for prescribing drugs and services, while others from the least popular departments could only receive 100 to 200 *yuan* "commission" from the hospital (Cong 2004).

Wage schemes like this have been widely adopted to motivate doctors and as a means to increase revenues for the hospital (Ji and Wang 2005; Tang 2004). Those who refuse to cooperate may suffer significantly in economic terms. In 2006, six doctors sued their employer—Changning TCM Hospital in Hunan Province—for underpaying (Xie 2006). They complained that as they were reluctant to prescribe expensive drugs, which had high commission rates and high-tech medical tests, they could not meet the revenue-generating targets set by the hospital management for each doctor and had been paid only basic wages without any bonuses or performance wages for three years. As a result, their incomes were even lower than the caretakers of the hospital. In another case, a doctor from a township hospital sued his employer for short paying (Min and Wang 2007). A public institution, the hospital received nearly no budget from the government. Facing a reduced number of patients and declining revenues, the head of the hospital decided to convert the entire wage (including basic wage) of his doctors into floating wage and link it to their economic performance, namely, the quantity of prescriptions. As a result, this doctor had not received his basic wage for several years, which put his life in hardship. In yet another case, Hu Weimin, a cardiologist who was acclaimed for upholding the principle of serving the people wholeheartedly and selflessly and put preventive medicine before curative medicine, not only suffered economically and but was also physically assaulted by his colleagues for refusing the hospital's "prescription for commission" scheme and revealing it to the public (Ouyang 2005; Tang and Li 2003).

The MOH decreed to ban "prescription for commission" in 1998, but the practice survived to date as hospitals cannot find a more efficient mechanism to ensure the unity of doctors' interests and hospitals' survival and development (Chai 2014). In 2013, the MOH issued "nine 'no's" to reiterate its banning on such practices as red packets, drug kickbacks, and prescription for commission (National Health and Family Planning Commission 2013), indicating that these practices are still endemic in the public healthcare system.

Hu Weimin's case mentioned above is interesting in that it illustrates the intense contradiction between the ideological demand for doctors to serve the people wholeheartedly and unselfishly and the financial and organizational constraints that strangle any attempt to materialize the ideology. Doctors who put patients' interests first or at least uphold the professional ideal of service are highly likely to be economically disadvantaged or even punished. In extreme cases, they may face persecution within hospitals. On the other hand, the profit-driven activities encouraged by the health authority and promoted in hospitals have brought significant benefits to doctors who cooperate or even collude (as prescription for commission has been illegalized) with their hospital management. If hospitals encourage and reward their doctors for over-prescription and over-provision, even if such practices are not sanctioned by the Party-state, then why doctors should feel shame of taking red packets?

RED PACKETS: AN OVERVIEW

Throughout the reform era, the problem of the scarcity of quality medical resources has never been properly solved in spite of the rapid expansion of the sector in terms of both quantity and quality. With the advancement of economic reform and increasing disposable incomes, users' expectations for quality also rise. Furthermore, the continuity of bureaucratically organized medical services perpetuates the shortage of good service attitudes and manners. To get a hand on quality resources and ensure good services or even take advantage of the public system for inappropriate personal gains, users resort to *guanxi* and/or monetary incentives to award doctors for preferential services or inappropriate advantages. As doctors have been denied associational power to negotiate with the Party-state for control over the economic terms of their professions and the work terms of their employment and not given a true market in which their cultural capital can be materialized, taking advantage of their bureaucratic role as the manager and distributer of public medical resources (including their service attitudes and manners) to seek rents becomes a natural choice. Red packets have emerged in such a setting.

In the early years of the reform, backdoor medicine continued to dominate the informal redistribution of medical resources and services, but red packets started to emerge as an important supplementary means. According to research conducted in the early 1980s, doctors were not the only public employees who were deeply involved in backdoor medicine. General staff, such as receptionists who were responsible for distributing doctors' register tickets, pharmacists who could get their hands on expensive imported drugs, and even caretakers of bicycle parking lots who knew receptionists, pharmacists, doctors, and nurses (Zhong 1982), got involved in backdoor medicine. Doctors were apparently more capable of carrying out backdoor medicine due to their positions as frontline practitioners of medical services and distributors of health resources. The same research revealed that some doctors could buy, solicit, or even withhold the prescription forms of publicly insured patients so that they could use the forms to prescribe new, expensive, and imported medicines or tonics for themselves or people who were not covered by public insurance. Doctors were also reported to sign off deceptive diagnostic certificates to help people of *guanxi* to get paid sick leaves, to receive extra amount of rationed food, to get urban household registration, to join the army, or to go to university. The allocation of hospital beds was another type of public resources that doctors controlled.

It was disclosed in a 1981 investigation that in a hospital with 580 beds, 46 percent of the 9215 inpatients were hospitalized through informal channels. Furthermore, the investigation revealed that about 10 percent of doctors (mainly surgeons) used their medical skills for backdoor medicine (Zhong 1982). Investigation of another hospital indicated that while 74 percent of the operations were performed according to their grades of complexity, 25 percent were not done in accordance with grading standards. Chief Surgeons and Responsible Surgeons were found doing operations lower than the degrees that they should do. According to the researcher, this was most probably the consequence of backdoor medicine. The researcher also confirmed that backdoor medicine and other inappropriate conducts could bring direct or indirect monetary benefits to doctors. For example, the drugs obtained through prescription forms for public insurance could be sold in the black market for cash. Hospital beds allocated to acquaintances or low-grade operations conducted by senior surgeons for acquaintances could allow doctors to exchange hospital resources or their services for favors or benefits of monetary values (Zhong 1982).

Gifts and meals of "stranger"-patients offered to doctors as expressions of genuine gratitude for medical services or allocation of resources were also popular and equally plentiful if not more. For patient and their beloved ones who traveled from afar to seek quality medical services in major cities, the mere action of the patients being hospitalized could prompt them to offer gifts and meals to thank doctors for allowing them access to such scarce resources as inpatient beds. Numerous reports praised doctors for declining gifts and meals from patients (see, for example, Pang 1980; Yang 1981; Deng 1981). These reports of commendation, however, indicated from another perspective the prevalence of the practice of doctors' taking gifts from patients and having meals paid by patients or their relatives. For example, commenting on a report commending the outpatient unit of a hospital for not taking gifts from patients, a reader (Han 1981) provided an opposite example. A doctor complained to his friend, "I suffered a huge loss after being transferred to an administrative position last year. When I was a doctor before, I had received too many food gifts in each festival to be consumed. But in the last Lantern Festival, I didn't receive even a single piece of *yuanxiao* (a type of sticky rice dumpling consumed particularly for the Lantern Festival)." The reader urged colleagues not to give preferential benefits to those who offered gifts while refused those who did not. However, we have a reason to believe that far more doctors took gifts from patients, be they acquaintances or "strangers," than those declined.

During this period, gifts in cash emerged, although may not be wide-spread.[28] It was in this milieu that in March 1982, the MOH launched its own campaign parallel to the "All People Civility and Politeness Month" campaign, demanding hospitals to address concerning issues in five areas. The fourth area was to improve service attitudes. Hospitals were required to establish the thought of serving the people wholeheartedly among medical personnel. Doctors should treat patients equally and must not ask patients to help them with private matters. They should decline patients' gifts and speak politely to patients (Editor 1982). The fact that declining gifts was included in the campaign indicated the diffusion of the practice.

The reforms to the healthcare system, which reduced and fixed government budget for hospitals but encouraged limited commercialization of medical services, were interpreted as government sanctioning the pursuit of profits by organizations as well as by individuals. "Privatization" of professional knowledge and skills by individual professionals for personal gains, be it sanctioned by the authority or not, became a widespread phenomenon among doctors.[29] More and more medical professionals took a market view of their services, arguing that as the government could not compensate them in light of the true value of their work, it was fair for them to take red packets from patients as supplementary compensation according to market principles (Guo and Jiang 1995; Xu 2006; Wang 1998; Chen 2006b; Fu 1993; Huang 1993). The backdoor medicine quickly evolved from an informal arrangement through which particularism was accorded to acquaintances into a practice in which particularism was extended to those who paid extra money informally and directly to doctors for their services.

The CCP has made great efforts to contain the practice since the 1980s. In 1993, MOH enforced the first decree against the red packets in particular (Ministry of Health 1993). The decree demanded that medical staff follow professional ethics closely and uphold the spirit of serving the people wholeheartedly and must not take red packets given to them in any manner. If they could not decline them, red packets must be handed to the authority. Anyone who did not hand in red packets or solicited them would be severely punished. In 1995, MOH issued an additional decree prohibiting doctors from not only taking red packets but also accepting gifts from or having meals paid by patients (Ministry of Health 1995). The Law on Medical Practitioners enforced in 1999 made it illegal for doctors to take advantage of their professional positions to receive or solicit money and goods from patients or pursue other inappropriate interests (1999). In 2004, MOH launched a country-wide campaign targeting red packets and drug kick-backs. All these policies and regulatory efforts, however, failed to contain the practice. The red packet has become a latent but endemic norm in the healthcare system (Sha 2015). The promulgation of the "Nine 'no's' to enhance the construction of professional ethics in medical and health industry" in 2013 (National Health and Family Planning Commission 2013) reiterated the prohibition on nine illegal practices that had long been banned in the healthcare system, including red packets. The decree itself tells its own story.

It is undeniable that the reform has brought tremendous changes to China, but it also evident that many institutions formed in the command economy before 1978 persisted after the watershed. The public healthcare sector is a field in miniature of conflictions of old and new institutions. The CCP's tenacious hold on power and its unchallengeable dominance in the society entails the continuous absence of public space in which medical professions, as well as other business and societal groups, are denied the right and power to form an intermediary structure between the Party-state and individuals. The absence of the public space means any meaningful, open negotiation and bargaining between the Party-state and incorporated associations of the society do not exist. As in the pre-reform era, medical professions remain powerless in their relationship with the Party-state. The direct effects of lack of power on the part of medical professions are that their organization, status, work and economic terms, and ethics are all determined by the state, despite the creation of CMDA that is alleged to represent the interests of doctors.

In the reform era, the Party-state continues to uphold the ideology of serving the people and requires medical professionals to treat patients as families, but the organization of medical professions perpetuates doctors' status as state cadre. Bureaucratic medicine characteristic of indifference and poor service attitudes continues to prevail in the public healthcare system, leaving *guanxi* to continue to be a major means for users of the public medical system to bypass bureaucratic medicine that is contradictory to universal particularism advanced by the CCP. At the same time, the impact of institutional changes on the medical profession is equally obvious. The CCP's recognition of doctors' cultural capital significantly boosted the cultural authority of the profession and gave it a high market potential, but the Party-state did not provide a formal, market mechanism to allow doctors to cash in on the policy change. What is more concerning is the commercialization of medical services and the change of government funding patterns. With the diminishing public funding, medical organizations are left with little choice but to encourage and incentivize their medical employees to overprescribe drugs and overprovide medical services, completely offsetting the CCP's efforts to champion the principle of serving the people selflessly. In a nutshell, doctors are now profit-driven medical bureaucrats. Widely engaged in organizationally sanctioned but morally controversial profit-driven activities, doctors are unlikely to find it morally problematic to take some money directly and secretly from patients. Red packets emerged in such institutional settings and have become endemic.

NOTES

1. http://en.people.cn/90001/90776/90785/6290140.html, accessed 22 June 2015.
2. http://www.people.com.cn/GB/shizheng/252/5089/5106/5182/20010430/456601.html, accessed 28 June 2015.
3. http://www.china.com.cn/chinese/2001/Oct/69881.htm, accessed 28 June 2015.
4. *Jiankang bao*, 18 October 1981: p. 1.
5. http://www.law-lib.com/law/law_view.asp?id=44985, accessed 2 July 2015.
6. These principles cover the ideological contributions of all the leaderships since the reform. All have been enshrined in the CCP Constitution and can be found on the following official website of the CCP: http://english.cpc.people.com.cn/.
7. See the Association's website: http://www.bqejsyjh.com/NewsLook.asp?p=1&SID=108&NewID=1373&FID=69, accessed 15 July 2015.
8. http://news.xinhuanet.com/newscenter/2004-12/22/content_2365168.htm, accessed 15 July 2015.
9. http://www.nhfpc.gov.cn/xcs/2012b/201301/a875f7ec3b1343319f98fc64d7968426.shtml, accessed 17 July 2015.
10. http://www.nhfpc.gov.cn/xcs/2012b/201301/ae28e749fec8495590af92b095593277.shtml, accessed 17 July 2015.
11. See http://www.moh.gov.cn/mohbgt/s6376/list.shtml (accessed 2 August 2015). In 2013, the Ministry of Health was replaced by the National Health and Family Planning Commission (NHFPC). The same information can also be found on the latter's website (http://www.nhfpc.gov.cn/xcs/s6376/list.shtml, accessed 2 August 2015).

12. See http://www.moh.gov.cn/mohbgt/s6376/list.shtml, accessed 2 August 2015.
13. CMDA Constitution (http://www.cmda.net/xiehuijieshao/shzc. html, accessed 14 August 2015).
14. CMDA Constitution (http://www.cmda.net/xiehuijieshao/shzc. html, accessed 14 August 2015).
15. http://www.labournet.com.cn/gongzixieshang/zc1.html, accessed 17 August 2015.
16. http://big5.gov.cn/gate/big5/www.gov.cn/zwgk/2005-08/ 15/content_22926.htm, accessed 18 August 2015.
17. http://www.npc.gov.cn/huiyi/dbdh/11/2008-03/19/content_ 1421002.htm, accessed 17 August 2015.
18. http://www.gov.cn/guowuyuan/2015-04/08/content_2843938. htm, accessed 17 August 2015.
19. The bonus, which was the floating part of wage, was not guaranteed. It depended on how much the work-unit could save from the state budget or how much revenue a work-unit could generate from providing services.
20. http://xzmc.university-hr.cn/showarticle.php?actiontype=4& id=143, accessed 23 August 2015.
21. http://xzmc.university-hr.cn/showarticle.php?actiontype=4& id=143, accessed 23 August 2015.
22. http://www.chinanews.com/n/2003-12-20/26/383309.html, accessed 25 August 2015.
23. See http://bbs1.people.com.cn/post/11/0/1/130013621.html, accessed 26 August 2015.
24. http://bbs.tianya.cn/post-62-576193-1.shtml, accessed 15 September 2015.
25. See Chap. 6 for details about the function of the ORUT.
26. For example, in 1991, the Liaoning Provincial healthcare system set up a health personnel's ethics evaluation system aiming at rooting out *sheng, leng, ying, ding,* and *chi, na, ka,* and *yao* within the year (Anonymous 1991).
27. This concept is indebted to Elliot Freidson (1986).
28. It was reported on *Jiankang bao* that a surgeon of Tianjin People's Hospital declined a hundred *yuan* wrapped in an envelope given to him by the relatives of a patient whom he hospitalized for stomach cancer (Huang 1981).

29. During the Great Leap Forward and the Cultural Revolution, intellectuals were vehemently attacked for embracing the idea of "private ownership" of knowledge and attempting to sell their skills and knowledge for a good price rather than putting them in service of the people. In the early 1980s, the criticism was redressed, not because "private ownership" was permitted but because it was believed that most intellectuals had already been properly transformed ideologically or there was no such thing as "private ownership" of knowledge as a market for knowledge did not exist. See *Renmin ribao* (People's Daily), 1 April 1958, p. 7; 11 March 1976, p. 3; 30 January 1977. p. 2; 18 February 1983, p. 5.

BIBLIOGRAPHY

Anonymous. 1991. Liaoning jianli weisheng hangye zuofeng kaoping tixi (Ethics evaluation system in health care is established in Liaoning Province). *Jiankang bao (Health News)*, 16 June, 1.

Anson, Ofra, and Shifang Sun. 2005. *Health care in rural China—lessons from HeBei Province*. Hants, UK: Ashgate.

Bloom, Gerald, Leiya Han, and Xiang Li. 2001. How health workers earn a living in China. *Human Resources for Health Development Journal* 5(1–3): 26–38.

Bourdieu, Pierre. 1986. The forms of capital. In *Handbook of theory and research for the sociology of education*, ed. John G. Richardson, 241–258. New York: Greenwood Press.

Cao, Haidong, and Jiandong Fu. 2005. Zhongguo yigai 20 nian (20 years of Chinese health reform). *Nanfang zhoumo (Southern Weekend)*, 4 August. Accessed 2 December 2009. http://big5.southcn.com/gate/big5/www.southcn.com/tech/yylt/ygzl/200510240473.htm.

Cao, Xuebing. 2011. The Chinese Medical Doctor Association: a new industrial relations actor in China's health services? *Relations industrielles/Industrial relations* 66(1): 74–97.

CCP General Office. 2012. Guanyu jinyibu jiaqiang dang guan rencai gongzuo de yijian (Advice on further strengthening the Party's control of talent work). Accessed 25 August 2015. http://politics.people.com.cn/n/2012/0926/c1001-19120416.html.

Center for Health Statistics and Information, Ministry of Health. 2010. *Zhongguo yi huan guanxi diaocha yanjiu (Research on relationship between doctors and patients in China 2008)*. Beijing: Chinese Xiehe Yike Daxue Chubanshe (Chinese Union Medical University Press).

Chai, Huiqun. 2014. Gongli yiyuan chuangshou qianguize (The latent rule of revenue generation in public hospitals). *Nanfang zhoumo (Southern Weekend)*,

20 February. Accessed 29 September 2015. http://www.infzm.com/content/98222.

Chen, Enjia. 1979. Beijing shiji yiyuan weisheng jishu renyuan gongzi fuli qingkuang de diaocha (An investigation of the wages and benefits of health technicians in Beijing municipal hospitals). *Jiankang bao (Health News)*, 21 October, 1.

Chen, Mingyuan. 2006a. *Zhishi fenzi yu Renminbi shidai (Intellectuals and the era of Renminbi)*. Shanghai: Wenhui Chubanshe (Wenhui Press).

Chen, Qisan, and Yibin Liu. 2003. Gongchandang yuan de dianfan: ji quanguo 'kangfei' youxiu dangyuan Liu Yingxia (The mdoel of Communist Party members: Liu Yingxia, the National Party Member of Excellence of 'Fighting SARS'). *Rednet* (4 July). Accessed 16 May 2008. http://news.rednet.cn/c/2003/07/04/436004.htm.

Chen, Tan. 2007. *Danwei shenfen de songdong: Zhongguo renshi dang'an zhidu yanjiu (The loosening of work-unit identity: a study of Chinese personnel archive system), Shehui zhuanxing yu gonggong zhengce (Social transition and public policy)*. Nanjing: Nanjing University Press.

Chen, Xie. 2006b. Fansi 'hongbao' xianxiang de cunzai jichu ji duice (Reflection on the foundation of 'red packet' phenomenon and policies dealing with it). *Zhongguo yixue lunlixue (Chinese Medical Ethics)* 19(1): 55–57.

China Health Year Book Editorial Board. 1983. *China health year book 1983*. Beijing: Renmin Weisheng Chubanshe (People's Health Press).

———. 2004. *China health year book 2004*. Beijing: Renmin Weisheng Chubanshe (People's Health Press).

Chongqing Municipal Health Department. 2003. Lizu gangwei, wusi fengxian, zuji 'feidian' (Hold on to the post, sacrifice selflessly, fight 'SARS'). *Chongqing weisheng xinxi (Chongqing Health Bulletin)* 2003 (42). Accessed 16 May 2008. http://www.cqwsj.gov.cn/Html/2003-05/00002754.html.

CMDA. 2015. Zhongguo yishi zhiye zhuangkuang baipishu (White book of Chinese doctors practicing state). Accessed 27 August 2015. http://www.cmda.net/xiehuixiangmu/falvshiwubu/tongzhigonggao/2015-05-28/14587.html.

Cong, Zhiguo. 2004. Shengyang Zhongyiyuan 'erci jixiao kaohe fenpei' zhengduan diaocha (Investigation of 'redistribution according to second performance assessment' of Shenyang TCM Hospital). *Huasheng chenbao (Huasheng Morning Post)*, 7 June. Accessed 17 July 2007. http://news.sina.com.cn/c/2004-06-07/01593389284.shtml.

Dai, Jianyun. 1995. Jiufeng xian cong 'zhao shuren kan bing' shi (Redressing unhealthy trends from 'seeing doctor through acquaintances'). *Jiankang bao (Health news)*, 19 December, 2.

Dang, Xuan. 1995. Kun Yi Fu Yi Yuan tichu guifan fuwu jiyu (The First Affiliated Hospital of Kunming Medical College regulated service phrases). *Chuncheng wanbao (Spring city evening news)*, 11 September, 2.

Deng, Puping. 1981. Ju shou bingren liwu shou zanyang (Praised for refusing patients' gifts). *Jiankang bao (Health News)*, 26 January, 1.

Deng, Xiaoping. 1983. *Deng Xiaoping wenxuan: 1975–1982 (Selected works of Deng Xiaoping: 1975–1982)*. Beijing: Renmin Chubanshe (People's Publishing House).

———. 1993. *Deng Xiaoping wen xuan (Selected works of Deng Xiaoping)*, 3 vols. Vol. 3. Beijing: Renmin Chubanshe (People's Publishing House).

———. 1995. *Selected works of Deng Xiaoping*, vol II, 2nd edn. Beijing: Foreign Languages Press.

Deng, Yuzhen. 2005. Jinian Bai Qiuen shishi ji 'jinian Bai Qiuen' wenzhang fabiao 65 zhounian zuotanhui (Forum in memory of the 65th anniversary of Bethune's death and the publication of 'On Memorizing Norman Bethune'). *Zhongguo yiyuan (Chinese Hospitals)* 9(1): 31.

Diao, Shuqin, and Yun Xia. 2015. Xiang zhen weishengyuan yiwu renyuan dui yihuan guanxi ji yiliao jiufen renzhi fenxi (Analysis of village and township medical staff's perceptions of doctor-patient relationship and medical disputes). *Zhongguo nongcun weisheng shiye guanli (Chinese rural health service administration)* 35(5): 592–595.

Ding, Hansheng, Hongyun Xin, and Yan Yang. 2015. Bianzhi de shishi feifei (The rights and wrongs of staff quota). *Jiankang bao (Health News)*, 15 June, 6.

Duan, Yali. 2007. Yisheng jishu jiazhi bi bu shang xiaoshi gong (The value of doctors' techniques is lower than the hour rate of casual workers). *Jiangkang bao (Health News)*, 8 March. Accessed 12 May 2007. http://www.ah.xinhua. org/ahjk/2007-03/08/content_9452670.htm.

Editor. 1982. Weisheng Bu tichu wu xiang juti yaoqiu (Ministry of Health put forward five concrete requirements). *Jiankang bao (Health News)*, 4 March, 1.

Eggleston, Karen, and Winnie Yip. 2004. Hospital competition under regulated prices: application to urban health sector reforms in China. *International Journal of Health Care Finance and Economics* 4: 343–368.

Freidson, Eliot. 1986. *Professional powers: a study of the institutionalization of formal knowledge*. Chicago and London: The University of Chicago Press.

Fu, Donghong. 1993. Duzhe xi "hongbao" (Readers analyse "red packets"). *Jiankang bao (Health news)*, 31 August, 2.

Ge, Yanfeng, and Sen Gong. 2007. *Zhongguo yigai: wenti, genyuan, chulu (Chinese health care reform: problems, reasons and solutions)*. Beijing: Zhongguo Fazhan Chubanshe (China Development Press).

General Office of the State Council. 2015a. Guanyu chengshi gongli yiyuan zonghe gaige shidian de zhidao yijian (Guiding advice on comprehensive trial reform to urban public hospitals). Accessed 22 August 2015. http://www.gov.cn/ zhengce/content/2015-05/17/content_9776.htm.

———. 2015b. *Guowuyuan guanyu jiguan shiye danwei gongzuo renyuan yanglao baoxian zhidu gaige de jueding (The State Council's resolution on the reform to the*

pension system for the personnel of administrative and institutional work-units).
Beijing: Renmin Chubanshe (People's Publishing House).

Gong, Xianzhong. 1981. Li fa yu qunzhong jiandu (Legislation and supervision by the masses). *Jiankang bao (Health News)*, 29 October, 2.

Gu, Edward. 2001. State Corporatism and the Politics of the State-Profession Relationship in China: A Case Study of Three Professional Communities. *American Asian Review* XIX(4) (Winter 2001): 163–199.

Gu, Xin, Mengtao Gao, and Yao Yang. 2006. *Zhenduan yu chufang: zhi mian Zhongguo yiliao tizhi gaige (China's health care reforms: a pathological analysis), Social development and public policy series.* Beijing: Social Science Academic Press (China).

Gu, Yining. 2003. Zhejiang dui 32 jia yiyuan diaocha biaoming, yiyuan shoushufei guodi yaojia taigao (Investigation of 32 hospitals in Zhejiang shows: surgical fees are too low while drug prices are too high). *Zhejiang zaixian (Zhejiang Online).* Accessed 11 September 2007. http://news.tom.com/1002/2003927-425584. html.

Guo, Yuli, and Qi Jiang. 1995. Xiao hongbao xianxiang de shehuixue fenxi (A sociological analysis of the little red packet phenomenon). *Zhongguo weisheng jingji (Chinese Health Economics)* 14(10): 57–58.

Han, Xu. 1981. du "shou na tingzhenqi bu ran hui fengqi" xiang dao de (A thought on "Holding stethoscope but not contaminated by unethical practices"). *Jiankang bao (Health news)*, 22 March, 2.

He, Xiaoxia, and Tao Yuan. 2010. Qian xi gongli yiyuan bucheng jizhi de zhuanbian (Preliminary analysis of the transformation of compensation mechanisms in public hospitals). *Zhongguo yiliao qianyan (National medical frontiers of China)* 5(3): 85.

He, Xingdong. 1981. Haozhao "xuexi Bai Qiuen" yiyi zhongda (The call for "emulating Bethune" has great significance). *Jiankang bao (Health News)*, 29 March, 2.

Hsiao, William C.L. 1995. The Chinese health care system: lessons for other nations. *Social Science and Medicine* 41(8): 1047–1055.

Huang, Chang, Dongjiao He, Xiaofang Deng, Nenghai Bin, Rongrong Lei, and Ligui Zhong. 2009. Guangxi xiang zheng huanzhe dui yihua guanxi renzhi de diaocha fenxi (Investigation and analysis of village and township patients' perception of doctor-patient relationship in Guangxi). *Guangxi yixue (Guangxi medical journal)* 31(1): 106–107.

Huang, Hanrong. 1981. Yan shou jilu ju shou liwu (Follow the discipline strictly and refuse gifts). *Jiankang bao (Health News)*, 22 October, 2.

Huang, Yan. 2014. Mou yuan menzhen 2012–2013 nian tousu yuanyin fenxi ji duice tangao (Analysis of outpatient complaints in a certain hospital between 2012 and 2013 and suggestions). *Xiandai yiyao weisheng (Journal of Modern Medicine and Health)* 30(20): 3186–3187.

Huang, Zemin. 1993. Huashuo hongbao (Speak about red packets). *Jiankang bao* *(Health news)*, 17 April, 1.

Ji, Jinghong, and Yingcheng Wang. 2005. Zi pu yiyuan 'kaidan ticheng' shi yu zhigong diu gongzuo (Over ten staff members reporting 'commission for prescription' in their hospital lost jobs). Xinhuanet.com. http://news.xinhuanet.com/employment/2005-10/20/content_3652737.htm. Accessed 25 October 2016.

Jiang, Jingbao. 1993. Beijing zhuazhu zhongdian zhengsu yifeng (Beijing: specify the emphases and rectify medical ethics). *Jiankang bao (Health News)*, 27 August, 1.

Jiang, Zemin. 2006a. *Jiang Zemin wen xuan (Selected works of Jiang Zemin)*. 3 vols. Vol. 3. Beijing: Renmin Chubanshe (People's Publishing House).

———. 2006b. Lingdao ganbu yiding yao jiang zhengzhi (Leading cadres must pay attention to politics). In *Jiang Zemin wen xuan (Selected works of Jiang Zemin)*, edited by CCP Central Committee The Editorial Committee on Party Literature, 455–459. Beijing: Renmin Chubanshe (People's Publishing House).

Jin, Qinghan, Likun Pei, and Fangkun Zhou. 2006. Xian yiyuan jizhen yihuan jiufen fenxi ji duice (Analysis of medical disputes in the emergency department of county hospitals and suggestions). *Zhonghua yiyuan guanli zazhi (Chinese journal of hospital management)* 22(1): 52–53.

Kang, Miao, Jianguo Dong, and Gang Jiang. 2015. 'Youse yanjing' wei zhai, minying yiyuan zaoyu 'boli men' ('Tinted glasses' not removed, private hospitals blocked by 'glass door'). *Jingji cankao bao (Economic Reference)*, 11 August. Accessed 21 August 2015. http://www.jjckb.cn/2015-01/11/c_134501504.htm.

Lai, Fangjie. 2013. Xiao yue qi, Sichuan zhigong gongzi nian zhong jiang ke yu qiye jiti xieshang (From next month, employees in Sichuan can collectively bargain with enterprises for their wages and end-of-year bonuses). *Huaxi dushi bao (West China Metropolitan), 18 January*, 7.

Law of the People's Republic of China on Medical Practitioners. 9th Congress, 3rd Session, 26 June 1999.

Lei, Wei, Yue Gao, and Baohua Li. 2014. 920 li menzhen tousu yuanyin yu tezheng fenxi (Analysis of the reasons and characteristics of 920 outpatient complaints). *Zhongguo yiyuan guanli (Chinese Hospital Management)* 34(1): 63–65.

Leng, Mingxiang. 2002. Shichang jingji tiaojian xia yi huan guanxi ji yide xianzhuang diaocha fenxi (Investigation and analysis of the state of doctor-patient relationship and professional ethics under market economy). *Nanjing yike daxue xuebao (shehui kexue ban) [ACTA Universitatis Medicinalis Nanjing (Social Science)]* 2: 135–139.

Leng, Mingxiang, and Zhengguan Li. 2008. Wu sheng shi yi huan guanxi yu yide yifeng xianzhuang genzong yan xi (A followup investigation and analysis of doctor-patient relationship and professional ethics in five provinces and cities). *Zhongguo yiyuan guanli (Chinese Hospital Management)* 28(7): 40–43.

Leng, Rong, and Zuoling Wang, eds. 2004. *Deng Xiaoping nianpu: 1975–1997 (A chronicle of Deng Xiaoping's life: 1975–1997)*. 2 vols. Vol. 2. Beijing: Zhongyang Wenxian Chubanshe (Central Archive Publishing House).

Li, Fen, Chunlin Jin, Hai Lin, Fu Chen, and Yumei Peng. 2011. 2002–2009 nian Shanghai shi gongli yiliao jigou jingji yunxing zhuangkuang feixi (Analysis of the economic operations of Shanghai public medical organizations between 2002–2009). *Zhongguo weisheng ziyuan (China Health Resources)* 14(5): 290–296.

Li, Guojun. 2009. Dui yiyuan yi huan guanxi guanli xianzhuang de diaocha fenxi (Investigation and analysis of the hospital's management of doctor-patient relationship). *Zhongyiyao guanli zazhi (Journal of Traditional Chinese Medicine management)* 17(9): 808–810.

Li, Hongli, and Xiaohong Sun. 2013. Jiceng yiyuan menzhen tousu xiangguan yisu ji duice (Related factors in outpatient complaints in primary hospitals and suggestions). *Shuli yixue zazhi (Journal of mathematical medicine)* 26(5): 552–553.

Li, Ming. 2005. Yisheng weishenme 'lengmo wuqing' (Why are doctors 'callous and emotionless'). *Jiankang da shiye (Big health vision)* 4: 56.

Lin, Zhangjie (ed). 1999. *Lun xinshiqi Zhongguo de zhishi fenzi wenti (Issues about Chinese intellectuals in the new era)*. Shanghai: Shanghai Jiaotong Daxue Chubanshe (Shanghai Jiaotong University Press).

Liu, Hong. 1991. Weisheng bumen 'jiufeng' chu chengxiao (Achievement of 'rectifying unhealthy trends' in health agencies). *Jiankang bao (Health News)*, 27 August, 1.

Liu, Lanbiao, and Jiming Cai. 1998. Zhongguo nao ti laodong de shouru chabie: Shizheng fenxi he jiazhi panduan (Income differences between physical and mental labor in China: An empirical study and value judgement). *Nankai jingji yanjiu (Nankai economic study)* 5: 10–16.

Liu, Wei (ed). 2003. *Feichang zhanshi: kang 'feidian' yi hu renyuan fangtan lu (Extraordinary fighters: interviews with medical and caring personnel fighting 'SARS')*. Fuzhou: Fujian Kexue Jishu Chubanshe (Fujian Science and Technology Publishing House).

Liu, Xia. 2010. Pinyong zhi cuisheng de xin nanti (New problems arisen from contracting system). *Renmin luntan (People's tribune)* (28). Accessed 25 August 2015. http://paper.people.com.cn/rmlt/html/2010-10/01/content_644141.htm.

Liu, Xingzhu, Yuanli Liu, and Ningshan Chen. 2000. The Chinese experience of hospital price regulation. *Health Policy and Planning* 15(2): 157–163.

Liu, Zhexuan. 1983. Women shidai de yide de jiben tezheng (The basic characteristics of medical ethics in our times). *Yixue yu zhexue (Medicine and philosophy)* 10: 28–30.

Lu, Jichun, and Yinong Fan. 1981. Shehui zhuyi yide hexin (The core of socialist medical ethics). *Jiankang bao (Health News)*, 23 August, 3.

Lu, Zhaofeng, Xiaoyan Wang, and Jian Zhang (ed). 2010. *Yi huan guanxi xianzhuang, yuanyin ji duice yanjiu—quanguo shi chengshi yi huan guanxi diancha yanjiu baogao* (A study of the current state, reasons and solutions of doctor-patient relationship—A research report on the investigation of doctor-patient relationship in ten cities across the country). Beijing: Zhongguo Shudian (Chinese Bookstore).

Ma, Benliang, et al. 1979. Women zai shenghuo shang cunzai shiji kunnan (We have real difficulties in [daily] life). Jiankang bao (Health News), 21 October, 1.

Meisner, Maurice. 1999. *Mao's China and after: a history of the People's Republic*, 3rd edn. New York: Free Press.

Milton, David, Nancy Milton, and Franz Schurmann (ed). 1977. *People's China: social experimentation, politics, entry on to the world since 1966–72, China Readings 4*. New York: Penguin Books.

Min, Jie, and Xingxin Wang. 2007. Wanshan nongcun zhongxin yiyuan "kaidan ticheng" diaocha (Investigation of "prescription for commission" in the rural central hospital of Wanshan). *Zhongguo qingnian bao (China youth)*, 7 February. Accessed 29 September 2015. http://zqb.cyol.com/content/2007-02/07/content_1670176.htm.

Ministry of Finance, National Planning Commission, and Ministry of Health. 2000. Guanyu weisheng shiye buzhu zhengce de yijian (Advice on funding policy of health enterprise). http://www.mof.gov.cn/zhengwuxinxi/caizhengwengao/caizhengbuwengao2000/caizhengbuwengao20004/200805/t20080519_21530.html. Accessed 28 September 2015.

Ministry of Health. 1981. Guanyu jiejue yiyuan peiben wenti de baogao (Report on solutions for hospitals suffering financial losses).

———. 1985b. Guanyu weisheng gongzuo gaige ruogan zhengce wenti de baogao (Report on Several Policy Issues Concerning Reforms of Health Work). Accessed 2 June 2016. http://www.china.com.cn/law/flfg/txt/2006-08/08/content_7060220.htm.

———. 1985c. Yiliao weisheng shiye danwei gongzuo renyuan gongzi zhidu gaige shishi fang'an (Implementing plan for the wage reform for the working staff of medical and health institutional work-units). In *Renshi gongzuo wenjian xuanbian (Selected documents on personnel work)*, edited by Policy Study Office of the Ministry of Labour and Personnel, 357–374. Beijing: Ministry of Labour and Personnel.

———. 1988. Yiwu renyuan yide guifan ji shishi banfa (Implementing measures and codes of medical practice for medical personnel).

———. 1993. Guanyu yanjin xiang huanzhe shouqu hongbao de tongzhi (Circular prohibiting taking red packets from patients).

————. 1995. Guanyu jinzhi yiwu renyuan shoushou 'hongbao' de buchong guiding (Supplementary regulations prohibiting medical personnel receiving red packets).

————. 2003. Renshi Bu, Weisheng Bu, Jiefangjun Zong Zhengzhi Bu lianhe zhuishou Deng Lianxian, Ye Xing, Liang Shikui, Chen Hongguang, Li Xiaohong wu wei tongzhi "Bai Qiuen jiangzhang" (Ministry of Personnel, Ministry of Health and the General Political Department of the People's Liberation Army jointly confer posthumously the "Norman Bethune Medals" to Deng Lianxian, Ye Xing, Liang Shikui, Chen Hongguang and Li Xiaohong). *Weisheng renshi xinxi (Health Personnel Bulletin)* 2003(5). Accessed 22 April 2008. http://www.moh.gov.cn/newsshtml/401.htm.

————. 2007. Guanyu jianli yiwu renyuan yide kaoping zhidu de zhidao yijian (shixing) [The guidelines for establishing the medical professional ethics evaluation system for medical personnel (provisional)]. Accessed 16 September 2015. http://www.moh.gov.cn/mohbgt/pw10802/200804/19298.shtml.

Ministry of Health, Ministry of Finance, Ministry of Personnel, State Price Bureau, and State Taxation Office. 1988. Guanyu kuoda yiliao fuwu youguan wenti de yijian (Suggestions on issues of expanding medical services). Accessed 14 November 2015. http://edu.xz.gov.cn/ws/flfg/030100121310.htm.

Ministry of Health, Ministry of Finance, and National General Bureau of Labour. 1979. Guanyu jiaqiang yiyuan jijing guanli shidian gongzuo de yijian (Suggestions on the experimental work of strengthening hospitals' economic management). http://law.lawtime.cn/d551886556980.html. Accessed 14 November 2014.

Ministry of Health, State Administrative Bureau of Traditional Chinese Medicine, Ministry of Finance, and State Planning Commission. 2000. Guanyu chengzhen yiliao jigou fenlei guanli de shishi yijian (Implementing opinions concerning the management of urban medical institutions by categories). Accessed 25 October 2016. http://www.nhfpc.gov.cn/yzygj/s3577/200804/7bf456a7868c4e1898d24deaeb119bfd.shtml.

Ministry of Organization, Ministry of Health, and Ministry of Personnel. 2000. Guanyu shenhua weisheng shiye danwei renshi zhidu gaige de shishi yijian (Implementing proposals on deepening the reform of the personnnel system in the health institutional work units). In *Weisheng shiye danwei renshi zhidu gaige peitao wenjian huibian* (A compoilation of supporting documents on reform to the personnel system of health institutional workunits), 37–43. Beijing: Zhongguo Fazhi Chubanshe (Chinese Legal Press).

Ministry of Organization, and Ministry of Personnel. 2000. Guanyu jiakuai tuijin shiye danwei renshi zhidu gaige de yijian (Advice on speeding up the progression of the reform of the personnel system in institutional work-units). In *Weisheng shiye danwei renshi zhidu gaige peitao wenjian huibian (A collection of supporting documents on reform to the personnel system of health institutional work-units)*, 44–51. Beijing: Zhongguo Fazhi Chubanshe (China Legal Press).

Ministry of Personnel, and Ministry of Finance. 2006a. Shiye danwei gongzuo renyuan shouru fenpei zhidu gaige fang'an (Reform Plans for income and redistribution system for institutional work-unit personnel). Accessed 25 October 2016. http://www.mot.gov.cn/sj/renshijys/zhengcefg_rjs/gongzigl_rjs/201412/t20141230_1752961.html.

———. 2006b. Shiye danwei zhuanye jishu renyuan jiben gongzi taogai biao (Schedule of basic wages for specialized technical personnel in institutional work-units). Accessed 10 October 2007. http://jgdw.nuaa.edu.cn/jgdw_nuaa_edu_cn/images/20070329143727683.doc.

National Development Planning Commission, and Ministry of Health. 2000. Gaige yiliao fuwu jiage guanli de yijian (Decision on the reform of the administration of medical service prices). Accessed 2 June 2016. http://www.nhfpc.gov.cn/zhuzhan/wsbmgz/201304/2565dbbdefeb4a5199c4fc7c8f9306b0.shtml.

National Health and Family Planning Commission. 2013. Jiaqiang yiliao weisheng hangfeng jianshe "jiu buzhun" ("Nine no's" to enhance the construction of professional ethics in medical and health industry). Accessed 29 September 2015. http://www.nhfpc.gov.cn/jcj/s7692/201312/09bd7a8be8f8420d91997a0041aa868e.shtml.

———. 2014. *Zhongguo weisheng he jihua shengyu tongji nianjian (Yearbook of health and family planning statistics in China)*. Beijing: Zhongguo Xiehe Yike Daxue Chubanshe (Chinese Union Medical University Press).

National Statistics Bureau. 1986. *Zhongguo tongji nianjian (Chinese statistics yearbook)*. Beijing: National Statistics Bureau.

Ouyang, Hongliang. 2005. Yisheng jie yiliao heimu zao tongshi baofu da cheng yangwei beipo cizhi (Doctor who revealed medical black curtain was beaten up by colleagues to impotence in retaliation and forced to resign). *Xiaoxiang wanbao (Xiaoxiang evening news)*. Accessed 29 September 2015. http://opinion.people.com.cn/GB/35560/3133875.html.

Pang, Changfa. 1980. Xing yi ershi nian jianchi bu shouli (Practicing 20 years and never taking gifts). *Guangming ribao*, 20 December, 2.

Qiu, Dingrong, Ping Xia, and Xiuqin Yuan. 2013. Mou zhongyiyuan 2010–2012 nian menzhen huanzhou tousu qingkuang fenxi (Analysis of outpatient complaints in a certain TCM hospital between 2010 and 2012). *Zhongguo zhongyiyuan xiandai yuancheng jiaoyu (Chinese medicine modern distance education of China)* 11(13): 150–151.

Qiu, Xiangxing, Zhiyan Gao, Yinong Fan, Shaopeng Wu, Zhaoyang Xu, Jichun Lu, Xiang Xia, and Zizhen Zhu (ed). 1983. *Yide xue gailun (An introduction to the study of medical ethics)*. Beijing: Renmin Weisheng Chubanshe (People's Health Publishing House).

Qu, Yinghe. 2010. 'Guanxi jiuyi' qu xiang xia yi huan hudong guanxi yanjiu (Study of interactions between doctors and patients from the perspective of orientation of 'relational hospitalization'). PhD, Faculty of Philosophy and Social Science, Jilin University.

Qu, Yinghe, Yipeng Tian, and Xiangmei Zhou. 2010. 'Guanxi jiuyi' xianxiang de diaocha yu fenxi (An investigation and analysis of the phenomenon of 'seeking medical services through guanxi'). *Yixue yu Zhexue (Medicine and philosophy)* 31 (2): 32–33 & 52.

Saich, Tony. 2011. *Governance and politics of China. 3rd ed, Comparative government and politics.* Houndmills, Basingstoke, Hampshire; New York: Palgrave Macmillan.

Schmitter, Philippe C. 1979. Still the century of corporatism? In *Trends toward corporatist intermediation*, ed. Philippe C. Schmitter, and Gerhard Lehmbruch, 7–52. London: Sage.

Sha, Rula. 2015. "Hongbao" xianxiang yuanyin fenxi yu sikao (Analysis and consideration of the reasons behind "red packet" phenomenon). *Zhongguo weisheng zhiliang guanli (Chinese health quality management)* 22(3): 94–97.

Shanghai Research Institute of Dialectics of Nature, ed. 1981. *Yide lunwen ji (Collected articles on medical ethics).* Shanghai: Journal of Medicine and Philosophy Press.

Shao, Jianxiang, Min Chen, and Changcui Chen. 1998. Yi huan jiaoliu yu yiliao jiufen fangfan (Doctor-patient communication and the prevention of medical disputes). *Zhongguo weisheng zhiliang guanli (Chinese health quality management)* 6: 40.

Sidel, Victor W., and Ruth Sidel. 1973. *Serve the people: observations on medicine in the People's Republic of China, The Macy Foundation Series on Medicine and Public Health in China.* New York: Josiah Macy, Jr. Foundation.

Su, Juxiang. 1994. Weisheng Bu Renshi Bu shouyu Zhao Xuefang "Bai Qiuen Jiangzhang" (Ministry of Health and Ministry of Personnel awarded Zhao Xuefang the "Bethune Medal"). *Jiankang bao (Health News)*, 27 March, 1.

Sui, Yongqi, and Fengshan Zhang. 1981. Tan yide (On medical ethics). *Yiyuan guanli (Hospital management)* 2: 28–29.

Sun, Min, Shoujun Zhou, Chuanhua Deng, and Tianshan Zhu. 2008. 226 li menzhen yiliao tousu yuanyin fenxi yu sikao (Analysis and consideration of the reasons of 226 outpatient medical complaints). *Jiangsu weisheng shiye guanli (Jiangsu healthcare administration)* 19(3): 12–13.

Sun, Zhonghe, and Changchun Cao. 2012. Yiwu renyuan shouru shuiping ji gongzuo manyi du de xianzhuang fenxi (Analysis of the current state of medical workers's income levels and work satisfaction rates). *Xibu yixue (Medical journal of West China)* 24(1): 205–206.

Tang, Xiangyue. 2004. Ta weihe likai zhe jia yiyuan? (Why he left this hospital?). *Guangming ribao (Guangming Daily)*, 16 December. Accessed 12 August 2007. http://www.gmw.cn/content/2004-12/16/content_149521.htm.

Tang, Xiangyue, and Jing Li. 2003. Weimin yisheng Hu Weimin (Hu Weimin: the doctor for the people). *Guangming ribao*, 1 August 2003. Accessed 29 September 2015. http://www.gmw.cn/01gmrb/2003-08/01/10-9B26E6D5C325522848256D7400839A63.htm.

The World Bank. 1997. *Financing health care: issues and options for China, China 2020*. Washington, DC: The World Bank.

Unger, Jonathan, and Anita Chan. 1995. China, Corporatism, and the East Asian Model. *The Australian Journal of Chinese Affairs* 33: 29–53.

———. 2015. State corporatism and business associations in China: a comparison with earlier emerging economies of East Asia. *International Journal of Emerging Markets* 10(2): 178–193.

Wang, Shaoguang. 2003. Zhongguo gonggong weisheng de weiji yu zhuanji (The crisis and hope of Chinese public health). *Bijiao (Comparison)* 7. Accessed 22 April 2016. http://www.usc.cuhk.edu.hk/wk_wzdetails.asp?id=2330.

Wang, Wei. 2008. Nanjing: Shiye danwei quanmian zhankai gongzi jiti xieshang (Nanjing: Collective wage bargaining unfold across all institutional work-units). *Gongren ribao (Workers' daily)*, 27 June, 1.

Wang, Yankun. 1998. Dangqian yiyuan hongbao xianxiang de chengyin yu duice (The reasons and countermeasures against the current red packet phenomenon in the hospital). *Jinzhou yixueyuan xuebao (Journal of Jinzhou Medical College)* 19 (4): 69–70.

Wang, Huawei, and Huiting Xu. 2006. Tiantai xian bufen yiyuan yi huan guanxi de diaocha he fenxi (Investigtation and analysis of the doctorpatient relationship in some hospitals in Tiantai County). *Chongqing yixue* (Chongqing medicine) 35 (14): 1330–1332.

Wong, V.C.W., and S.W.S. Chiu. 1998. Health-care reforms in the People's Republic of China. *Journal of Management in Medicine* 12: 270–286.

Wu, Hao. 2001. Kunming: Huanzhe yiyuan qiujiu 120 shijian you jieguo (Kunming: The outcome of patient seeking help from 120 within the hospital). Accessed 16 September 2015. http://www.people.com.cn/GB/shehui/47/20010401/430302.html.

Wu, Huiting. 2006. Chengshi jumin shiye zhong de yihuan guanxi—500 fen wenjuan de diaocha yu sikao (Doctor-patient relationship envisioned by urban residents—survey and thinking based on 500 questionnaires). *Yixue yu zhexue (Medicine and philosophy)* 27(9): 17–19.

Wu, Ping, and Yan Lin. 2006. 919 li yiliao tousu fenxi (Analysis of 919 medical complaints). *Zhonghua yiyuan guanli zazhi (Chinese journal of hospital management)* 22(12): 837–839.

Xi, Jinping. 2014. *Xi Jinping, the governance of China*. First edition. Beijing: Foreign Languages Press.

Xiao, Zhongen, Bi Luo, and Zhuanghui Li. 2009. Bojie 'shuren shehui' de fanfu nanti (Solve the hard anti-corruption question of 'acquaintance society'). *Zhongguo jiancha (Supervision in China)* 14: 31–33.

Xie, Zhengjun. 2006. Hunan Changning Zhongyiyuan liu yisheng jukai huikou yao shouru jing bi menwei di (Six doctors from Hunan Changning TCM Hospital who refuse to prescribe drugs offering kickbacks receive incomes lower than gate keepers). Xinhuanet.com. Accessed 12 August 2015. http://news.xinhuanet.com/health/2006-07/26/content_4880333.htm.

Xu, Huaijin. 1981. Tantao yixue lunli shuli yide xinfeng (Explore medical ethics and establish new ethical practice). *Jiankang bao (Health News)*, 2 July, 1.

Xu, Peng. 2006. 'Hongbao' xianxiang de zhidu jingji xue fenxi (An institutional economic analysis of the 'red packet' phenomenon). *Zhongguo weisheng ziyuan (China Health Resources)* 9(4): 147–149.

Xu, Shuangyan, Ou Zhimei, Su Wei, Lijuan Chen, Qin Lin, Xianglin Wu, You Zhou, and Wu. Jun. 2009. Chengdu Shi gongli yiyuan yihuan guanxi pubian renzhi diaocha fenxi (Investigation and analysis of general perception of doctor-patient relationship in the public hospitals in Chengdu). *Zhongguo weisheng shiye guanli (Chinese Health Service Management)* 12: 806–808.

Xu, Xiuju. 2009. Gongli yiyuan bucheng jizhi yanjiu de yanjiu (Study of the evolution of compensation mechanisms of public hospitals). *Zhongguo yiyuan (Chinese Hospitals)* 13(6): 27–31.

Yan, Wei. 1998. Anhui pushu zhengzhi weisheng hangfeng (Anhui takes action to rectify ethics in health care). *Jiankang bao (Health News)*, 5 August, 3.

Yang, Jie. 2011. The politics of the Dang'an: Spectralization, Spatialization, and New liberal Governmentality in China. *Anthropological Quarterly* 84(2): 507–534.

Yang, Jingqing. 2008. Medical practice in the non-public sector in China. *Journal of Asian Public Policy* 1(3): 346–351.

Yang, Lirui. 1998. Yuanzhang tan yan: Yiliao fuwu taidu hen cha! Kun Yi Fu Yi Yuan jiang jixu gaijin (The director frankly admitted: Medical service attitudes are poor! The First Affiliated Hospital of Kunming Medical College will continue to improve). *Kunming ribao (Kunming daily)*, 9 January, 1.

Yang, Shizhong. 1981. Wang yisheng zuofeng lianjie ju bu shou li (Dr Wang practices honestly and refuses gifts). *Jiankang bao (Health News)*, 8 March, 3.

Yang, Shuqing. 1985. Baoding wu suo yiyuan tuiwei weizhong bingren zhishi yanwu zhiliao (Five hospitals in Baoding city shunned critically ill patients; treatment delayed). *Jiankang bao (Health News)*, 6 June, 1.

Yang, Xingyun. 2007. Shenzhen yigai xinzhao: zhen liao jiage neng jiang buneng zhang (New move of health reform in Shenzhen: diagnostic and treatment prices can go down but cannot go up). *Jingji guancha wang (The Economic Observation*

Net) (9 July). Accessed 9 July 2007. http://www.eeo.com.cn/eobserve/Politics/by_region/2007/07/09/75625.html.

Yu, Chongsheng. 2006. Qian guize xia de shuren shehui (Acquaintance society under informal norms). *Renmin luntan (People's tribune)* 10: 8–11.

Zhang, Danqi, Yong Lu, and Xiong Zhang. 2006. Shouru shuiping yingxiang zeye quxiang (Income levels influence career paths). *Zhongguo weisheng chanye (Chinese health industry)* 11: 80–81.

Zhang, De. 1980. 'Yanwang yiyuan' bian le yang ('Hell hospital' changed). *Chuncheng wanbao (Spring City Evening News)*, 23 September, 2.

Zhao, Hengwen. 2005. *Yiliao jiufen de lilun yu shijian (Theories and practice of medical disputes), Tertiary medical college health law textbooks.* Changsha: Zhongnan Daxue Chubanshe (Zhongnan University Press).

Zheng, Yefu. 2004. *Zhishi fenzi yanjiu (A study of intellectuals).* Beijing: Zhongguo Qingnian Chubanshe (Chinese Youth Publishing House).

Zhong, Shi. 1982. Yiyuan buzheng zhi feng de qingkuang diaocha (An investigation of unhealthy trends in hospitals). *Shehui (Society)* 3: 40–44.

Zhou, Enlai. 1951b. Guanyu zhishi fenzi de gaizao wenti (Issues about remoulding intellectuals). In *Zhou Enlai xuanji (Selected works of Zhou Enlai)*, 59–71. Beijing: Renmin Chubanshe (People's Publishing House).

———. 1956. Guanyu zhishi fenzi de baogao (Report on issues concerning intellectuals). In *Zhou Enlai xuanji (Selected works of Zhou Enlai)*, 158–189. Beijing: Renmin Chubanshe (People's Publishing House).

Zhou, Qiren. 2008. *Bing you suo yi dang wen shui? (Who should be consulted about illness?).* Beijing: Beijing University Press.

Zhou, Tingyu. 2005. Weishengbu: Du jue yiyuan sheng, leng, ying, ding, tui xianxiang (Ministry of Health: Root out the phenomena of distance, coldness, brusqueness, confrontation, and shunning). China.com.cn. Accessed 15 September 2015. http://www.china.com.cn/chinese/news/853770.htm.

Zhu, Hengpeng. 2014. Zhongguo gongli yiyuan ming bu fu shi (Chinese public hospitals are unworthy of the name). *Jiankang jie (Health World).* Accessed 22 August 2015.

Zhu, Youdi. 2010. *Da guo yigai (Health reform in a large country).* Beijing: Shijie Tushu Chuban Gongsi (World Book Press).

CHAPTER 5

Transactions of Red Packets in the Hospital

In the previous chapter, I examined the institutional settings in which forces derived from the institutions inherited from the command economy and those brought about by the economic reforms mutually offset the efforts of each other and restrain the advancement of professionalism toward a state that the government would like to see. In this chapter, I will turn to the practice as it unfolds at clinical level. That is, how red packets are transacted between patients and doctors in the micro-setting of hospitals. Although the institutional arrangements of the healthcare system provide the hotbed of informal payments, what happens in real life is more complicated than a macro analysis of institutional persistence and change could capture. In the meantime, a glance at what is going on in the hospital will doubtlessly help us understand better how the institutions influence the behaviors of individuals in the course of medical encounter.

This chapter, which contains three sections looking at giving, taking, and declining red packets respectively, draws on data collected from empirical as well as documentary sources. The bulk of the data comes from three focus groups that I conducted in 2005, and 20 interviews between 2005 and 2006. The participants of the focus groups and interviews were Chinese medical professionals who were working or studying in Australia when the interview took place. Some of them had settled in Australia and were employed in health or medical institutions, while others were visiting scholars in Australian medical institutions.[1] The reason to conduct the group and individual interviews in a place outside of China was based on the concern that red packets were, and still are, a highly sensitive issue.

© The Author(s) 2017   187
J. Yang, *Informal Payments and Regulations in China's Healthcare System*,
DOI 10.1007/978-981-10-2110-7_5

Doctors I approached in China were reticent about issue, as the practice was (and still is) illegal. Removed from the direct locus of the practice, doctors I interviewed in Sydney, Australia were far more open and communicative. The interviews produced rich data that could substantiate reliable reconstruction of the practice in Chinese hospitals.

All respondents had worked in 3A hospitals in China before. This fact has two implications. Firstly, 3A hospitals monopolize most of the overseas training opportunities in China. That may explain why it was easier for the researcher to recruit participants who had had work experiences in 3A hospitals. Secondly, the findings of the empirical investigation may not be representative of entirety of the Chinese healthcare workforce. But the limitation is not likely to affect the validity and generality of the outcome. Since the most qualified medical professionals concentrate in 3A hospitals, these hospitals become the places where red packets most often occurred.

Documentary data drawn from a variety of sources are also used to triangulate or provide alternative views to those discovered in the interviews.

GIVING RED PACKETS

Whether voluntarily given and solicited, red packets come from patients. Therefore, it is essential to understand first why patients give. Patients may have a broad range of motives that compel them to give. As far as this research is concerned, however, doctors' perceptions of the motives are more relevant because how they perceive will decide whether they take or decline red packets. But before exploring why patients give, I shall look at whom they give in the first place.

Who Are Given Red Packets?

Patients do not give red packets to every doctor they see. The respondents of the research noted that in general, patients with medical conditions that needed surgical interventions and/or needed to be hospitalized tended to give red packets to treating doctors. Outpatients and, in most cases, inpatients with chronic conditions that needed to be hospitalized for a long period or frequently did not often give red packets. Doctors' specialties and professional ranks were another determinant, according to the respondents. In terms of specialties, doctors involved in surgical procedures, such as surgeons, obstetricians, and anesthetists, were far more likely to be offered monetary red packets. Patients usually did not give red packets to internists, pediatricians, TCM doctors, and those of other specialties who did not involve in surgical procedures, even if their conditions might require long periods of hospitalization. These doctors depended mainly on drug kickbacks for informal incomes. A respondent [HDS], who was an internist, insisted that the red packet was not an issue in the Chinese healthcare system, for, speaking from his own experiences, he was given one or two red packets in average each year and they were small in value. Another respondent commented, "Everyone is worried when it comes to the use of scalpel" [CCX]. In-kind gifts were more popular in non-surgical specialties. Several respondents with non-surgical backgrounds noted that patients were more likely to thank the staff of the whole unit by offering fruit, soft drinks, and so on.

In terms of ranks, the respondents agreed that patients usually offered red packets to surgeons of middle and higher ranks (Responsible Doctor and above) who had the authority to perform operations independently, while junior surgeons who only provided assistance in operations were rarely given red packets. Some respondents further pointed out that in the public hospitals that they had worked in, medical procedures were usually allocated centrally by the unit to surgeons according to the degrees of complexity of patients' conditions. After knowing who their chief surgeons were, patients would give red packets to them. If patients wanted to involve senior surgeons to perform operations that were not complex enough to involve the latter, they needed to give red packets to the latter to replace doctors of lower ranks assigned to the operations. A respondent [WYY] commented, "The higher professional levels, the likely the doctors are offered red packets. Patients are more interested in those who hold the scalpel, but care less about their assistants." The work experiences of two respondents conformed to this comment. Both of them were Resident Doctors (i.e., beginning rank of doctor), and reported they had never been offered a single red packet.

One respondent [CXL] in Focus Group 2 noted that in her unit, patients even had to give red packets to the head nurse, because she was in charge of bed allocation. Red packets to the head nurse could help patients get wards with better conditions, or get beds in ordinary wards earlier when they were ready to be transferred from the expensive ICU ward. However, this was possibly not common, because other respondents were surprised on hearing that.

Some respondents believed that patients also gave red packets to ward doctors who were in charge of administration of medication and change of bandage, as a respondent [CXL] said,

> Nowadays, in terms of giving gifts, the situation is like this: [you] must give the chief operator; then the ward doctor. The ward doctor changes bandage for you. In ear-nose-throat units like mine, changing bandage is very complicated. If he changes bandage for you every day, [and] if he changes bandage carefully, your [wound] may heal faster.

Another respondent [YPP] noted that patients knew of the competence of each doctor and chose to give red packets only to those they believed could solve their acute problems.

When Is the Red Packet Given?

In terms of timing, red packets fall obviously into two categories: those given before the critical medical intervention is delivered, and those given after. To facilitate discussion, the two categories are termed here as "the pre-treatment red packet" and "the post-treatment red packet." Pre-treatment red packets are far more common than post-treatment red packets, and are usually in the form of cash. A respondent [ZFG] reported that some patients might follow up pre-treatment red packets with post-treatment red packets if they were satisfied with the outcome. However, the majority of red packets were given before the major medical intervention. As respondent WYP noted, if there were ten patients offering red packets to doctors who declined, only one patient would possibly reoffer red packets after the treatment and the size of these red packets were much smaller.

How Are Red Packets Given to Doctors?

Red packets and gifts are delivered through two means: *guanxi* and "cold offer." The giving of red packets relies heavily on *guanxi*. The respondents reported that a large number of their patients gave them red packets and gifts through people they both knew. "They can always find someone in the hospital they know through their networks, from whom they can make acquaintance with treating doctors and give the red packets to doctors in person or through the people they know" [YJL]. "If they don't know anyone in the hospital, they can first make acquaintance with nurses or even ward aides, and then give red packets to doctors through them" [WYP].

"Cold offer" refers to red packets given to doctors by patients that the doctors do not know before. Several respondents reported that they had been cold-offered red packets. Usually the patient gave red packets by stopping the doctor somewhere in the hospital, or in the doctor's office. Otherwise, patients or their relatives asked for the address of the treating doctor. If the doctor intended to take the red packet, he or she would disclose address. Otherwise, they would not disclose. One respondent [ZXJ] said that a patient followed her to her home and forced a red packet into her hand. Another respondent [CXL] reported a situation in which the patient's father insisted she take the red packet by kneeling in front of her in public. A respondent's account of cold-offered red packets is illustrious.

> [At that time] I had lower qualification and shorter record of service; after all I was only a Responsible Doctor. But when I was on night shift, I was usually the highest rank of available doctors....I feel that sometimes patients would chase you to give you [red packets], you know. They were...afraid that you wouldn't dare to take, so they followed you. For example, if I went to the toilet, they would follow me into the toilet. They would slip [money] into a small envelope... "well, doctor, here is an expression [of gratitude]...you work very hard," they would say. [WYY]

According to the respondents, red packets given through *guanxi* were the dominant pattern of giving in major hospitals. Usually, doctors were very cautious about cold-offered red packets. The caution may force the patient to build up the *guanxi* network first so that the red packet would not be turned down by the doctor. The accounts of the respondents indicated the existence of two types of *guanxi*: one was composed of existing friends, acquaintances, and relatives, and the other was of newly made acquaintances. The "old" *guanxi* was more reliable and helpful, because the participating actors of the network relied on long-term connection (even friendship) to exchange benefits and favors. While the "new" network could be developed into long-term stable relationship, it was more focused and practical and, more importantly, costly. Several respondents reported that in their hospitals some staff members, mainly supportive and administrative staff, were involved in networking for patients who had no acquaintances in the hospital. They received payment from patients for making arrangements with treating doctors. A respondent [LWX] observed,

> This kind of people are disgusting. We call them "resellers" (*erdao fanzi*). I have a feeling that they add fuel to the fire with regard to the red packet phenomenon, because he would put the patient up: yes, you must give. He scares the patient first. The reason is, if he doesn't scare the patient, for they are basically not from surgical departments, they are not front-line surgeons...it can be said that they don't have any qualification to receive red packets, but they make rich from this [i.e., red packets]. But doctors take the risk, do the job, and so it is reasonable [for them to take red packets]...But for them, I feel that they are the most despicable group of people. They really are. Sometimes we don't take [red packets], for we fear, or we feel we don't want to, but they have already taken the red packets. As a result, the patient would say, "Well, look, somebody has taken. Please do take." That makes us really uncomfortable.

Another respondent [ZKY] noted,

> In fact, speaking from my experience, some middlemen in my hospital, their grey incomes are no less than some of us doctors. Imagine that he keeps 20 percent from [the red packet] given to each surgeon [through him]...if there are many patients...since he is a middleman, some of them may have very good relationship [with doctors in the] hospital...not only your general surgery unit, [but also] your cardiac surgery unit, and all surgery units, he knows all the doctors. Therefore these middlemen, the red packets they get...some of them may be even worse, taking 50 percent, even more than half, [before they deliver the patients' red packets] to you doctor.

These stories were confirmed by media investigation. It was reported that in 2004 when the government launched a campaign targeting red packets, patients were worried that doctors would not take their red packets. Under these circumstances, "red packet brokers" emerged helping patients to get their desired doctors. These "brokers" were mainly supportive staff of a hospital, such as securities and mailroom staff. (According to the respondents, even a lift operator could play as a "middle person.") Their job was to make acquaintance for patients with doctors and deliver red packets to the latter. At the same time, they collected some fees for building the bridge. A part-time "broker" was reported to have said, "I am still helping people. Acquaintances and friends come to you for help, how can you turn them down? But I feel guilty for keeping troubling doctors. So [if it involves] some compensation, both sides would feel comfortable. Both sides know me. For this familiar face of mine, they aren't concerned about unpleasant things." This "broker" was alleged to know dozens of specialists very well, and to be "able to arrange specialists' consultation and treatment, to get hospital beds sooner, and to organize operations sooner." According to the same report, a specialist of internal medicine of Beijing 301 Hospital (a military hospital) confirmed that some supportive staff members would bring acquaintances to see doctors frequently and possibly charged patients fees for making the arrangement. But the specialist said that the "brokers" would not share the fees with doctors. Doctors, under the pressure of *guanxi*, usually had no choice but to meet the requests of "brokers" (Li 2004).

What Are Given as Red Packets?

Red packets are not limited to cash. The respondents reported a wide range of goods or other benefits serving the purpose of red packets. Among the in-kind "red packets," the most common form was meals. Meals were regarded as a form of informal payments in this research for the reason that they could be more costly than red packets. The MOH explicitly prohibits doctors from receiving patients' invitations to dinner, categorizing meals as a form of inappropriate offerings as red packets (Ministry of Health 2004a).

The respondents reported that meals were a very common offering in hospitals. A respondent [WYP] noted that in the early 1980s when the red packet was not common, meals were more often offered to doctors to serve the function of red packets, especially in county-level hospitals. In spite of the popularity of red packets in recent years, meals continue to be a fundamental means to socialize with doctors. The respondents reported that doctors usually avoided meals before surgery for they were usually expectation-ridden, and would be happy to go to dinner with the patient's relatives and/or middleperson (patients were usually not well enough to join) after the surgery. The doctor usually brought a group of colleagues, subordinates, or nurses to dinner. The payer's money was thus used to help the doctor lubricate interpersonal relationship with colleagues and subordinates. Two respondents from Group 2 noted that wealthy patients or government officials were usually asked to take the doctor and his or her colleagues to dinner in expensive restaurants. "For example, there are those tycoons, or those we know they are officials. Sometimes we would say, 'Well, if you want to thank us, fine, take all the staff of the unit to dinner.' This is common. Now that he can afford it. . .for him, he perhaps pays out of public funds. . ." [LJL]. It was in this circumstance that meals could be more costly than red packets. But respondents insisted that dinning was a norm of socializing deep-rooted in Chinese culture and should not be regarded as a form of red packets.

Patients from rural (usually poor) areas seeking medical treatment in cities usually had not enough resources to afford even formal payments. The red packets they gave are usually insignificant in terms of monetary value. In many cases, they tended to offer local produce instead of red packets. A respondent [CXL] from north China reported a patient who had been too poor to offer a meal to him but felt obliged to offer something, had bought him several kilograms of *baozi*, a kind of Chinese pie. Other in-kind gifts included soft drinks, fruits, sweets, and so on. Generally speaking, in-kind gifts were usually given after the treatment but could also happen before the treatment. The problem with in-kind gifts was that the patient was usually under the pressure to buy them for the staff of the whole unit, including doctors, nurses, and even aides. Respondents also reported new forms of red packets, such as a piece of valuable information about a stock in the share market, or a business opportunity.

How Much Is Given in the Red Packet?

The amount of a red packet is determined by several things: the specialties, ranks and reputation of the doctors, complexity (or categories) of surgery, grades of hospitals, local wage levels of health professionals, economic conditions of the patient, and timing. Timing is the most important determinant of the amount of the red packet. As mentioned above, only one out of ten patients would give red packets again if their pre-treatment red packets were declined by the doctor, and the amount was barely half the pre-treatment ones. In one sense, pre-treatment red packets were transacted more or less in light of market rules, although this was an informal market.

Understandably, the more complex and time-consuming an operation was, the bigger the red packet the patient was likely to offer. Specialties such as heart surgery, neurology, and hepatology attracted bigger red packets than other specialties, such as general surgery. In economically better-off regions, such as those coastal provinces, major metropolitan cities, and special economic zones, the wage levels for professionals were higher than their counterparts in inland or less developed regions. Patients in these regions tended to offer bigger red packets than in economically less developed regions. Patients' individual economic conditions also determined whether they had the capacity to give red packets and the amount.

Most respondents claimed they had no idea what informal market rates for red packets were, but they noted that through various channels patients were always able to find out the informal price tag for a certain category of operations or services. It is especially so in cities like Shanghai, where "people are smart in calculating how much is enough for different kinds of operations" [WJH]. When deciding the amount of red packets, it was reasonable for the patient to ensure it was not too little as to insult the doctor and to be declined, and not too big as to hurt his or her wallet. The above respondent reported that in 1998 in Shanghai, the red packet for a minor operation was between 100 and 200 *yuan*, and 1000 to 2000 *yuan* for a major operation. Now the 100–200 range did not exist anymore. The minimum amount of a red packet for a minor operation was between 300 and 500 *yuan*, while for a major operation involving an Associate Chief Doctor and above would cost 3000 to 5000 *yuan*. The informal prices were confirmed by a media report, which revealed that in Nanjing in 2004, the starting price for a major brain surgery and chest surgery was 1000 *yuan*, 2000 *yuan* for a Chief Doctor, and 3000 to 5000 *yuan* for a reputed specialist. The red packets for minor procedures like appendectomy and cholecystectomy were between 500 and 1000 *yuan*. The red packets for caesarean section were priced between 400 and 2000 *yuan*, while spontaneous delivery cost a 500 *yuan* red packet (Tao 2004).

Why Do Patients Give Red Packets?

Patients have different purposes they expect to achieve with red packets. Doctors need to detect what their purposes are and calculate whether they are able to meet these purposes before they decide whether to take a red packet or not. A major means that helps doctors to detect the purposes of red packets is when they are given. In general, pre-treatment red packets are driven by givers' concerns and anxiety, while post-treatment red packets are generally an expression of gratitude.

For doctors, post-treatment red packets are much less problematic in moral terms and carry much less risk than pre-treatment ones. The respondents of the research almost unanimously agreed that post-treatment red packets were motivated by gratitude on the part of the patient, and should be regarded as gratuities. However, significantly fewer patients would offer red packets after the treatment or services and they only offered if they were particularly satisfied with the outcome of treatment. Moreover, what were offered were usually not hard cash, but meals to doctors and nurses involved in the treatment, or gifts of small monetary value, such as fruit, soft drinks, sweets, or banners embroidered with grateful words. In other words, post-treatment red packets constituted only a minor part of the phenomenon and were less controversial in the eyes of takers and perhaps health authorities.

In comparison, pre-treatment red packets are far more widespread, frequent and substantial, and are compelled by a wide range of purposes among which gratitude plays a negligible role. The respondents frequently used the phrase "buying peace of mind" to indicate the overarching purpose for giving red packets before major medical interventions. The phrase implied the uncertainty and anxiety felt by patients when seeking medical services in the public healthcare system. Red packets were thus given to quell anxieties and to increase certainty. Then what made patients feel uncertain and anxious? According to the respondents, a major concern of the patients was doctors' commitment and the quality of their services.

Ensuring Commitment and Quality

When seeking medical attention, patients naturally expected that doctors were committed and the service they provide was of high quality. But what patients usually encountered in public hospitals was bureaucracy and indifference. Patients had reasons to worry that doctors were not committed and the quality of their services were not up to standard. As a result, patients gave red packets to motivate doctors for commitment and quality. This was what the majority of the respondents believed. As one respondent [WJH] noted,

> Patients don't trust doctors completely; don't believe doctors would serve them and care for them out of heart. Patients feel that only red packets can demonstrate that they care about doctors, and doctors would reciprocate.

What was suggested in this comment was the role that particularism plays in the doctor–patient relationship. According to the respondents, giving the red packet to establish friendship with doctors was a common purpose of patients. A respondent [LWX] believed that the red packet could turn the doctor–patient relationship into friendship which could have binding force on the doctor.

I feel that for the doctor, if you take the red packet, the doctor-patient relationship can be greatly improved. From the point of view of the patient, he would think that you treat him like friend. Under this circumstance, if there is a minor problem [i.e., malpractice] in the treatment, he is perhaps more tolerant and understanding. On the contrary, if you don't take it, …it becomes a hostile relationship. They would think, "OK, you're afraid of my red packet, or [you] don't want to take my red packet. Then we are no friends any more…"

Another respondent [ZZT] commented to the same effect,

… I feel that in many situations, the patient [gives the red packet] in the belief that it makes socializing easier, and gets the doctor and the patient on good terms.

Committed, particularistic services are the preferential services that are usually equated to quality services. This is at least partially true. The Chinese healthcare system is marked by high malpractice rate and health professionals' poor attitudes toward patients, attributable to bureaucratic medicine and intense workload, especially in major hospitals. Several respondents confirmed the heavy workloads they had to cope with in Chinese hospitals and the link between workloads and poor attitudes. For example,

We were required to see 20 outpatients in an hour. That is two to three minutes a patient. People outside [my office] had to wait in a line for several hours. When he [i.e., the patient] came in, he would say, "I have been waiting outside for three hours, four hours." But as you see, I was now seeing a patient for only two or three minutes. …When it came to his turn, he would say "how come you sent me away in two to three minutes." My prescription was ready when he was still describing [his symptoms]. But you see, if I had not been that fast, did you not have to wait longer outside? [ZXJ]

This situation is equally applicable to doctors looking after inpatients and surgeons in major hospitals. With the breakdown of the three-tier referral system, patients can choose whichever hospital they like, and they are more likely to choose major hospitals which usually have better resources. This has put great pressure on doctors in major hospitals. Under this pressure, it is understandable that doctor's attitudes may not be always pleasant. Accordingly, the red packet is paid to ensure that the doctor will commit sufficient time, attention, and perhaps, more importantly, good attitude to the patient. That is, patients consider doctors' temporal and mental commitment as a major part of service quality. In the above discussed scenario, a red packet to the ward doctor could increase the frequency of bandage change and might lead to quick recovery, but higher frequency of bandage changing would increase the workload of the doctor and was thus a preferential service that was not provided to those who did not give red packets. A respondent [WJH] noted that surgeons usually do not like to perform major operations on Friday to avoid the trouble of ward visit during the weekend. When a red packet is given, however, the surgeon might agree to do it and visit the patient in the weekend. The red packet could be deemed as compensation for the loss of surgeon's public holiday, but more importantly, it was a reward for doctors' efforts to provide prompt and preferential services.

Patients usually expect more attention from families and doctors for psychological reasons. In the words of a respondent [ZKY], "He wants medical attention that surpasses ordinary patients. To this end, he intends, through giving the red packet, to acquire a kind of special services, better quality services." Another respondent [ZFG] commented that the patient "wants the doctor to pay more attention to him, to be more concerned about him." Red packets could apparently help patients and their relatives to achieve this purpose, engaging doctors for particularistic, preferential services.

In short, with red packets, patients intend to turn their relationship with doctors into one of particularism and hope that the latter would honor their friendship rather than treating them as subjects of impersonal, bureaucratic medicine. Such a concern seems to derive from a belief that doctors are likely to be committed to the treatment and recovery of those who enjoy particularistic relationship with them while treat others with indifference. To this connection, red packets are an initiative on the part of patients to build up particularistic trust between them and doctors. On the part of doctors, taking red packets becomes a token of trust and a guarantee of reciprocation of quality services.

Involving Senior Specialists
For resourceful patients, red packets (usually coupled with *guanxi*) can give them more choosing power and beat the system. Engaging doctors they prefer is a way to exercise this choosing power. Patients are usually not allowed to choose their doctors or nominate their surgeons in the public healthcare system.[2] They have to accept whatever doctors are available or

assigned to look after them by the bureaucratic system. To bypass the "blind" system, patients offer red packets to highly qualified specialists that they prefer to ensure their involvement in the medical process. This is also associated with the patient's concern about quality. Senior doctors can apparently provide better therapeutic and surgical services than junior doctors. The respondents commented that the supply of highly qualified surgeons was scarce in China, while there was a huge demand for their services. Red packets were apparently a shortcut to their services. Patients with substantial material and social resources apparently had considerable choosing power. They could use their network and the red packet to secure the services of senior or eminent doctors in the first place.

Jump the Queue
Jumping the queue is another area where red packets can buy patients further choosing power. In spite of the expansion of healthcare sector since the beginning of reform era in late 1970s, quality health resources, including quality doctors, are still comparatively in shortage. The collapse of the three-tier referral system exacerbates the situation as patients can virtually seek medical services from whatever hospitals they want to. This puts great pressure on highly qualified specialists in major hospitals, who usually have long waiting lists. Red packets to these specialists can help the patients to skip waiting lists and receive treatment or surgeries earlier. For patients who travel long distance to another city for medical treatment, earlier treatment can have significant implication on finance, as well as on the chance of recovery. According to the respondents, a major function of the red packet was to ensure the patient to receive operation earlier. As a respondent [ZXJ] noted,

> For example, in cardiac surgery, the children with congenital heart disease have a long waiting list, but he [i.e., the surgeon] can let you have operation first, and let him have later. Of course, this is in the situation of non-emergency. In emergency, I reckon that doctors don't do that in general...but in the case [of non-emergency], it is like [what] cancer patients [face] in China. Every cancer hospital has a long waiting list. Then there is the issue of who receive operation first. But cancer can't wait...

A respondent [ZZT] reported that the patient usually had to wait one or two weeks before he or she could be allocated a bed in one of the Beijing 3A hospitals. The long waiting time forced patients, many of whom traveled from afar, to seek special channels to get hospitalized sooner, and to get the best doctors.

Assurance of Curability

Recovery from illness is the ultimate purpose for patients to seek medical attention. For patients with serious conditions, whether they can recover becomes the biggest unknown and uncertainty and makes them and their relatives anxious. In this circumstance, the red packet can be intended as seeking assurance of curability.

> The patient has a mentality. Without giving the red packet, he feels uncertain. After giving the red packet, he feels assured: my condition perhaps has some hope. The doctor will be committed. [ZXJ]

This could impose pressure on the doctor, who tended to decline red packets loaded with unrealistic expectations. This will be discussed later.

Addressing Status Imbalance

In the patient–doctor relationship, doctors hold a powerful position over patients, who depend on doctors' intervention of their bodies for recovery to normal physical and social state. Patients, being on the receiving end of the relationship, seek to redeem their status and increase their power in the relationship by offering red packets to doctors who are on the giving end of the relationship. Red packets as contribution to doctors can redress the status and power imbalance by turning patients from passive receiver into givers. Consequentially, the doctor's services are not "favors" anymore, but reciprocation. This mentality is particularly common among patients from poor rural areas seeking medical treatment in urban areas. They already feel powerless in cities. Facing medical professionals, they feel even more overwhelmed. Giving red packets or other gifts in kind can help them regain some self-respect and status. Two respondents from Group 1 and 2, who were both from Shangdong Province in north China, reported cases in which patients from poor rural areas offer them local produce. "Such gifts you must take. Otherwise it is too insulting. They would feel you despise them" [LXH]. A scenario reported on media seems more illuminating. When asked why she gave a 1500-*yuan* red packet to an anesthetist in spite of economic hardship, a female patient from the countryside who was receiving an operation in a major hospital in a major city, said, "We're despised by urban residents. If we gave less, doctors would despise us more" (Jin and Xiao 2004).

Following Suit

Patients are not always pro-active and purposeful when giving red packets. Many of them give just because everyone else gives. As doctors tend to engage in more positive interpersonal interactions with hospitalized patients who give red packets, their particularistic attitudes would send an implicit signal to other patients in the same ward, and may pressure the latter or their families into giving red packets. A respondent [ZKY] noted,

> ...back in China...usually four patients, sometimes six or even eight patients, share a ward. Patients communicate with each other. It is especially so in surgical wards. Patients would discuss. If one of the patients says "I have given a few hundred *yuan* red packet before the operation," or the like, it can influence other patients. Other patients would think, "If I don't give, the surgeon may not [treat me as committed]."

Another respondent agreed that the longer and pleasant interactions that doctors engaged with red packet givers would demonstrate the effect of the red packet to other patients in the same ward. "He [i.e., other patients] would think, 'You have given, and the doctor treats you very well. I haven't given. Will the doctor treat me badly?' He would think like that. They [i.e., patients] influence each other" [ZYT].

Solicited

Most patients voluntarily give red packets to doctors, whether they are purposeful or follow suit. However, there are cases in which doctors may explicitly or implicitly solicit red packets or other benefits from patients. The respondents observed that in major hospitals, doctors were unlikely to openly demand red packets, but they may hint at red packets by exaggerating the severity of the illness and therapeutic complexity. A respondent [LWX] commented,

> In large hospitals, I don't see many doctors who solicit red packets. Basically, patients come and take the initiative to give [red packets]. Because they are large hospitals and patients are many, there are a lot of problems concerning his [i.e., the patient] operation and the timing of operation. And after communicating with other patients, he would understand. It seems that in large hospitals [like the one I worked in before], I didn't see any doctor who

solicited red packets. Perhaps there are [doctors soliciting red packets] in small hospitals, but there are few in large hospitals.

However, routine explanation of the risk of therapy or surgery by doctors and anesthetists can be misinterpreted by patients as an implication for red packets, as the following discussion in Group 1 indicates,

> LWX: The doctor is fine. I feel that the anesthetist is very scary. When it comes to him, he would say you [i.e., the patient] could possibly die on the operating table. On hearing this, the patient would. . .100 percent give. I feel that this is popular in surgical units.
> ZXJ: But he must tell you the risks. For example, before you sign the consent for operation form, he has to tell you anyway what may possibly happen.
> ZKY: Death.
> ZXJ: Accident. Anesthetic accident. Even in foreign countries there exist the same issues, for you have to sign several agreements before the operation. But when you talk to the patient—of course the doctor speaks from the medical perspective about what may possibly happen—the patient would not interpret it as such. The patient perhaps considers it from another point of view.
> LWX: Yes. He feels that the doctor is suggesting something.
> ZXJ: True.
> LWX: [This doctor] is scaring me [i.e., the patient].
> ZXJ: True, true. But from the medical point of view, the possibilities do exist.

Misinterpretation as described above reflects patients' deep mistrust of the bureaucratic system and public doctors. To make things worse, some medical professionals do take red packets delivered at this junction, exacerbating patients' perception that such activity as explaining risks is embedded with rent-seeking intent. And patients seem to have a good reason to believe so, as dropping hint has become a social norm.

Explanations of Red Packet Giving Provided by the Respondents

In the course of interviews, the respondents attempted to dig deeper to explain the motives of red packet giving. Many reduced the giving to social norm and/or culture, while a few used supply-demand theory to explain the practice.

Social Norm

Lack of trust and using red packets to lubricate the social wheel apparently has a broader social base. Respondents agreed that the emergence of the red packet in the healthcare system was only a small part of the widespread practice of informal payments in almost every sphere of the society where certain public power was involved. Rent-seeking was a social norm. Fundamentally, all the motives discussed above were rooted in this rent-seeking norm. The respondents in Group 2 confirmed that all public services in China came with informal price tags, which were covered by individuals' informal payments, as demonstrated in the following discussion.

> LJL: They [i.e., patients] give us [red packets]. Then who do we give? We give school principals. In your [i.e., the researcher] next project, you should ask how much money a principal takes.
> . . . . . .
> CXL: ... Before I came [to Australia] my child started junior middle school. I haven't met her Class Supervisor, but I have already sent in a gift through an acquaintance. That is to say, whatever school my child goes, I have to leave something for the teacher; I have to give gifts to the Class Supervisor.
> . . . . . .
> CXL: ... But in China, when your child goes to the kindergarten, do you not give red packets? How about primary school? Middle school? You have to give. I have to give gifts to my child's teachers.
> LJL: And you can't shun it. They'll call you.
> CXL: My daughter is just a little girl. How naughty can she be? But her teacher calls, complaining my daughter. What can I do?
> . . . . . .
> CXL: I would say this problem is actually a problem of the society. He [i.e., the patient] feels, "now my life is in your hands"; he feels that now dealing with any work-unit in the society, as long as you need a favor from someone else, you have to give. Now that my life is in your hands, I have to give even more....We have to give [red packets] when our children go to [public] childcare or schools. This is a universal social phenomenon. He [i.e., the patient] would feel that this is a social phenomenon, a very common social phenomenon. Now his life is in your hand, ... of course he is more concerned...

This description conforms to the so-called "minor corruption" theory first elaborated by Zhang Mingshu (2005). According to this theory, "minor corruption" is a redistributive system that the society creates spontaneously. The system brings an individual's income up to the level of his ability, education, job, and, more importantly, power. For example, if a doctor wants to send his son to a good school, he has to give a red packet to the teacher. The teacher who wants to improve his housing has to bribe the official of the housing bureau. If the housing official transgresses traffic rules, he has to bribe the traffic policeman. When the traffic policeman gets sick and hospitalized, he has to give a red packet to the doctor. Thus, the doctor, the teacher, the official and the traffic policeman, and many other people who wield some power, occupational or administrative, form a cycle from which they make extra incomes to compensate their usually low wages. The existence of this cycle consolidates the red packet giving as a social norm. Under the pressure of this social norm, patients naturally believe that without red packets as an incentive, no public employees, including doctors, would function.

Cultural Motivations

Traditional culture was another origin that many respondents believed the red packet practice came from. A respondent [LJL] stated, "'Giving away money to avoid disaster.'[3] We Chinese like to use money to offset disasters, feeling that after giving money to doctors, I am saved." Especially in Cantonese areas, offering red packets has a long tradition and is deeply embedded in local culture. In Guangdong province, red packets are distributed before treatment for good luck and on discharge from hospitals as celebration. A respondent [HDS] noted that, "in Guangdong, there is the custom of giving red packets. Economy (in Guangdong) is...better developed. In business, or interpersonal interaction...they are accustomed to monetary transactions."

Shortage of Quality

Three respondents [ZZT, YSN, and WJH] referred to supply-demand theory to explain the red packet. These respondents claimed that there was a shortage of quality resources in Chinese healthcare system, including technical and human resources, the best of which were usually concentrated in 3A hospitals. The concentration gave 3A hospitals a high market position. As a respondent [YSN] responded to the question why the patient gave the red packet.

> It is because the scarcity of doctors and medicine...in comparative terms. It is not scarcity of doctors and medicine in real terms. Doctors are not scarce. Nowadays, there is no genuine scarcity of medicine. It is only in comparative terms... Patients have a mentality when seeking medical services. That is, they

hope to get the most reliable, most trustworthy, and at the same time the most medically competent, don't they? This is a common mentality. Under this circumstance...senior doctors in 3A hospitals, in the eyes of the populace, represent the highest level of medical skills...Because of this common perception, they want this type of doctors. As a result...this type of doctors...they don't have three heads and six arms, do they? I'm talking about the problem from the perspective of patients' demand...There is high demand for these doctors. This circumstance prompts the doctor to take some benefits from [the patient]. From the perspective of patients, they are willing to get the opportunity [of being treated by the most eminent doctors] through this method [i.e., giving red packets]. This is market demand. At the end of day, giving red packets reflects market demand...If there are many patients seeking treatment, and they all want it as soon as possible, and the resources is relatively scarce—I mean the comparatively good hospitals—then the problem emerged.

The respondent emphasized here the shortage of the supply of senior doctors, which was fueled by the patient's expectation of high quality services, had reinforced the market position of senior doctors. But the public healthcare system did not follow the market rules, due to the over intervention of the government and the absence of formal bargaining mechanisms between the medical profession and the state. Consequentially, the patient was left to follow the hidden "market" rules and buy scarce services out of pocket informally.

Taking Red Packets

Doctors have different considerations when they face red packets. In the first place, they need to establish a general justification for taking red packets before they decide whether to take individual red packets. The most compelling reasons that the respondents cited to justify taking red packets were that it took longer for them to obtain medical degrees, they usually had heavier workloads, and faced high risks in practice, but they were paid at such low rates that were completely incommensurate with their hard work.

The respondents observed that, compared with other professions, medicine was much more demanding in terms of education and practice. To get a degree in medicine, one required longer training than students of other majors and had to maintain on-job training and study throughout the life. They noted that usually an undergraduate medical degree took a student at least five years to complete, one year more than the common four-year model for other disciplines. For those who wanted a career in 3A hospitals, undergraduate degrees were absolutely not enough. A Master's degree and then a Doctor of Medicine degree was a must to survive the fierce competition in leading hospitals. All in all it took an ambitious student at least 11 years to complete the study of medicine.

When in practice, medical professionals usually have to cope with heavy workload. This is especially so for doctors of major hospitals in major cities. As all the respondents came from 3A hospitals, it was not a surprise they complained about neck-breaking workloads, as discussed above. Other sources confirmed the situation. A survey on doctors and nurses in Guangdong Province showed that the pressure of overwork was ubiquitous (Lin 2007). The survey, which had been conducted by Guangdong Provincial Research Centre between September and October 2007, showed that 73 percent of doctors and nurses worked overtime often. A total of 20 percent claimed that they had to do over 20-hour overtime every week. Over 70 percent reported that they just expected a whole day off every week. In response to the question "what they want to do most at present," 46 percent of doctors and 58 percent of nurses chose the answer that they wanted "to have one day of quality family time;" 22.3 percent of doctors and 17.2 percent of nurses said they wanted a decent sleep (Li et al. 2007). The survey conducted by the CMDA in 2014 produced similar results. Doctors informed that their predominant pressure came from heavy workloads. Over 52 percent of the investigated claimed an average of 40 to 60 work hours per week, and over 32 percent worked more than 60 hours a week. Medical staff of level 3 and level 2 hospitals had much longer work hours than their colleagues in health institutions of lower levels (CMDA 2015).

Apart from heavy workloads, medical professionals have to cope with high risks in practice. According to the respondents and other sources, medical professionals generally faced two major types of risks: one was medical malpractice and the other was physical assault.

Malpractice is a latent risk to all medical professionals and can result in litigation and huge compensation, which may cause significant damage to their professional reputation and career. In the Chinese healthcare system, malpractice, or even patients' complaints, represent significant career risks and, more importantly, monetary losses on doctors, as they are usually not insured against malpractice and healthcare errors. Hospital-centered medical liability insurance first appeared in China in the late 1980s as an experimental and elective insurance for health organizations (Wu and Yuan 2008). In 2007, the MOH, together with China Insurance Regulatory Commission, issued a guideline on the promotion of medical liability insurance in an attempt to tackle medical risks, protect the rights of both hospitals and patients, and construct a harmonious doctor–patient relationship (MOH, State Administration of Traditional Chinese Medicine, and China Insurance Regulatory Commission 2007). The insurance products designed under this guideline, however, were not well accepted by hospitals. They complained that what they really needed was a third-party mediating mechanism which both patients and hospitals could rely on for peaceful solutions of disputes. But insurers, usually charging hospitals substantial premiums for their products, kept themselves aloof from medical disputes and set a very low ceiling on compensations for malpractice (Deng and Deng 2011; Ban et al. 2007). As a result, hospitals did not feel particularly motivated to purchase liability insurance.

The mounting tension between hospitals/doctors and patients forced the health authorities to step up their efforts to address increasing numbers of incidents of violence against medical staff and organizations. In 2014, the National Health and Family Planning Commission, joining hands with China Insurance Regulatory Commission, Ministry of Treasury, Ministry of Law, and State Administration of Traditional Chinese Medicine, issued a decree which made medical liability insurance compulsory for hospitals and demanded that all level 3 hospitals and 90 percent of level 2 hospitals purchase liability insurance by the end of 2015. A third-party mediating mechanism was also introduced in parallel to insurance (National Health and Family Planning Commission et al. 2014). But the effect of the policy is yet to be assessed.

Up to 2015, hospitals usually resorted to other mechanisms to compensate patients for malpractice or just to settle disputes which may not be caused by malpractice. One mechanism was to set up a mutual fund for medical dispute compensation. For example, a major hospital in Shengyang (capital city of Liaoning Province) deducted 2 percent of each staff member's salary and pools in a mutual liability fund to finance the damages of malpractice (Ge 2001). Bozhou First People's Hospital in Anhui Province, however, financed its mutual medical liability fund by deducting a percentage from the individual unit's monthly bonus pool in light of its risk index.[4] But a more widely used mechanism was sharing the costs of compensations between the hospital, the unit where the malpractice complaint or dispute occurred, and the individual doctor who was the culprit of malpractice or dispute. In recent years, more and more hospitals established accountability systems to cope with increasing number of disputes related to malpractice and service quality and the ensued compensations, and adopted different schemes for compensation sharing. For example, Danyang People's Hospital in Jiangsu Province adopted a very structured scheme detailing levels of accountability and ratios of compensation sharing. Doctors who are responsible for disputes share 60 percent of the total amount of compensation if it is less than 10 thousand *yuan*, 50 percent of a compensation between 10 and 20 thousand *yuan*, 30 percent between 20 to 50 thousand *yuan*, 5 percent between 50 to 100 thousand *yuan*, and 2.5 percent above 100 thousand *yuan*.[5] Apart from sharing damages, individual doctors are also punished administratively, such as postpone of promotion, suspension of licenses, and so on. Some hospitals even punish all doctors in the unit for the mistake made by a single doctor, as what the administration of the Third People's Hospital of Yibin (in Sichuan Province) did to the staff of its gynecological and obstetrician unit. In 2012, an obstetrician was sacked for a malpractice which caused brain failure of a newborn baby. The malpractice lawsuit was settled with a compensation to the baby's family of 490 thousand *yuan*. While sharing 70 percent of the amount, the hospital administration demanded every doctor and nurse of the unit to share the remaining 30 percent, and deducted 400 *yuan* from their salaries for 15 months until their shares were fully paid. But the sacked obstetrician did not pay any compensation for what she had done. She just lost her job.[6] Such schemes may have significant impact on doctors' incomes, and, more importantly, on their careers.

In close relation to malpractice disputes and compensations are the increasing number of medical litigations which exacerbate the career risk of medical professionals. With the enforcement of inversion of the burden of proof in malpractice litigation in 2002, the hospital is required by law to prove innocence if sued for malpractice, while the patient who sues the hospital does not need to raise evidence to prove the hospital guilty of malpractice (Supreme Court 2001). Users of the healthcare system are encouraged to take legal action against hospitals and doctors if they believe or claim they are victims of malpractices. But the law puts great pressure on the doctors and hospitals. The respondents complained that they received less protection from the work-unit system now and had to deal with litigation themselves without much help from their hospitals.

WXX: . . . Hospitals are all like this. If something happens to your patients, and they sue you, you have to go to court yourself.
WWH: That's right. True. It is [so].
WXX The hospital doesn't protect you. It's not like here [i.e., Australia], where the hospital will represent you . . .

. . .

WXX: We have a low rank doctor. It may be because of some minor incident. That patient was nasty and sued the doctor. That doctor . . . The Unit of Medical Affairs called . . . and he had to go to court.
ZZT: This is what they call "one foot in hospital, and the other in court," as everyone says.

These comments indicate that hospitals as public work-units now provide less protection for their staff, exposing them directly to state organs. This is what public doctors are not used to. As public organizations executing state functions, work-units used to provide an enclave for their employees, protecting them from direct intervention of the state and giving them opportunities to settle conflicts, disputes, and other issues within and through the network of work-units. This protection still exists for work-units in other sectors, such as universities, but seemed diminishing in the health sector. The disappearing of the protection inevitably increases career risks of doctors.

Physical abuse is another mounting threat to doctors. Documentary data show that in recent years the number of physical assaults on doctors has been on the rise. Reports of doctors being brutally murdered are not few. In 2005, an eminent doctor was murdered by his patient for not being able to cure the latter ten years ago (Cheng and Su 2005). A major hospital in Sichuan Province had to hire bodyguards for six senior doctors whose life was under the threat from patients, because the latter were not satisfied with the outcome of treatment (Fu 2004). According to the 2007 survey of health professionals in Guangdong, 72.4 percent of doctors and nurses reported that they had the experiences of being abused by patients. 93.5 percent of the abuses were conducted verbally; 38.5 percent were in the form of threat; 9.3 percent were physical assaults. Some nurses reported having been sexually harassed by patients (Lin 2007).

The respondents of the research were not unfamiliar with incidents of physical assault. Respondent CCX reported that in the late 1990s he had been physically assaulted by a patient. He had to request hospital security to get the patient to answer for it. The security managed to have the patient to pay the respondent 250 *yuan* as compensation. The respondent spent

200 *yuan* to treat the security to a dinner to thank the latter. A few other respondents reported incidents in which their colleagues were physically assaulted. Several respondents of Group 3 discussed the issue as follows,

> HDS: Here [in Australia], doctors are powerful. If they say your case is not an emergency, they can refuse to see you [as emergency]...Back in China, he [i.e., the patient] quarrels with you. If he quarrels, you are finished ...
> WXX: That's not quarrelling. He swears at you, and you can't talk back.
> ZZT: North-easterners [i.e., residents of northeast China] are aggressive. Such things happen often. That is, patients beat up doctors. You can do nothing about it.
> WWH: True. In my place, [patients] chase [doctors to beat them] all over the building and down the corridors.

It is reported that some hospitals even set up "grievance award" for doctors who are physically or verbally abused and swallow the abuse without fighting back (Geng 2007).

Compared with other professions, Chinese doctors usually spend extra time in universities to qualify for their medical degrees, work harder to survive their demanding workloads, and face considerable risks that have significant adverse implications on their incomes and career. As discussed above, however, their incomes are comparatively low. The doctors I interviewed also confirmed this. When asked whether they thought their official incomes matched their efforts, all respondents asserted that they absolutely did not match. A respondent [ZZT] noted,

> In Beijing, on average, [someone with a] PhD [degree] probably earns an income between eight thousand and twelve [thousand *yuan*], even higher. But [public] hospitals only pay [a junior doctor with a doctoral degree] one thousand odd, or two thousand odd. Not enough for rental...[In Beijing] rental costs you two thousand to three thousand *yuan* per month.... As a [junior] doctor, you make only around one thousand odd, two thousand odd *yuan*...and many hospitals don't provide dormitory [for junior staff]. He [i.e., junior doctor] can't even afford rental...

A respondent [ZXJ] complained that "[t]oo much is expected from doctors, and too little is paid to doctors." Another respondent [CCX] revealed that in late 1990s the compensation he received from his hospital for working overtime on an operation was worth only four eggs.

The findings reveal that formal incomes of doctors across China can vary tremendously due to different wage and compensation schemes adopted by hospitals and the level of economic development of the region. Among the respondents, only two respondents from Group 2 explicitly expressed satisfaction with their official incomes. One of them [ZYT] was from Guangdong, an economically well-off province in China. The respondent's hospital had just undergone a wage reform which greatly increased salaries of medical staff. As an Associate Chief Doctor, the respondent noted that the hospital paid her more than 100,000 *yuan* annually. According to this respondent, the reform was very likely an initiative of the hospital administration and was limited to her hospital only. The other respondent [LJL], a pediatrician of Associate Chief Doctor rank from Beijing, claimed that she could bring home between 200,000 and 300,000 *yuan* annually, and was quite happy about her income. She said, "We live a good life. I don't feel we're poor. We live in luxurious apartment and have a car at home." This particular respondent reported that in her unit, there were three Chief Doctors who were qualified for "special needs" outpatient consultation. The consultation fee for each visit was 200 *yuan*. "Conservatively speaking, they can earn 10,000 *yuan* a month from consultation fees alone."[7]

These two respondents seemed exceptional among the respondents. On hearing the incomes they made, other respondents from the same group were astonished. A surgeon [CXL] of Associate Chief Doctor rank from Shandong Province said that she made less than 50,000 *yuan* annually altogether, although she worked in a major and reputed hospital. An Associate Chief Doctor of internal medicine [HDS] from Beijing reported that the normal gross income for a doctor of Chief Doctor or a rank lower (i.e., Associate Chief Doctor) was between 30,000 and 50,000 *yuan* a year. He claimed that he himself earned only around 50,000 *yuan*, and was shocked to hear that a senior doctor in Zhuhai in Guangdong Province could make 80,000 to 90,000 *yuan* every year. But even an annual income of 50,000 *yuan* was enviable. A dental surgeon of Associate Chief Doctor rank from Shanxi Province [WWH] claimed a monthly salary as low as 1400 *yuan* (i.e., around 16,800 *yaun* annually) without any additional income. Such a low rate of salary sounded unbelievable to other respondents, but WWH insisted that was her real income.

The difference of formal incomes can be attributed to several reasons, the ultimate of which is the difference of fees and redistribution schemes each hospital adopts. In spite of the strict regulation of service fee rates, hospitals have been given limited autonomy to determine the rates and fees of a restricted range of services. For example, the rates of diagnostic tests and surgical procedures that are set by the authority are usually set below the costs, but hospitals are allowed to charge higher fees for the use of new technology and equipment to recover costs. This leads the hospital to encourage, and, in some cases, force the doctor to prescribe high-tech tests, linking their incomes with provision (Liu et al. 2000; Ministry of Health 1985a, 1989). The rates of consultation fees of doctors are definitely set by the government. The hospital does not have any power to change them. But the MOH allows, since the mid-1980s, the hospital to set up special service units targeting upper-end market (Ministry of Health 1985b, 1989; National Development Planning Commission and Ministry of Health 2000). The hospital in which respondent LJL worked was apparently aggressive in utilizing the autonomy permitted by policies and enlisting the support of relevant government agencies, setting higher specialist consultation rates for special needs. Other hospitals were perhaps not as bold. A respondent [LTQ] from Guangxi reported that the consultation fees for the same kind of services was only 3 to 5 *yuan* in his hospital, while another respondent [ZYT] noted that the special consultation fee was 30 *yuan* in her hospital, 10 *yuan* of which went to the specialist.

The findings show that their dissatisfaction with their incomes resulted from comparison with other occupations and medical professionals in developed countries. Some respondents seemed extremely unhappy about the fact that they earned no more than the workers of hospitals' rear-service department.

> [Workers of the rear-service department] have higher bonus than us. How much risk do we have to take? How many days do we work? From Monday to Sunday, we don't have a single day off. I have never had a whole day rest . . . The money you make for the hospital all goes to them . . . It is always like this. [LXH]

Another respondent [LJL] complained that a worker of her hospital's rear-service department who looked after the bicycle shed earned more than a junior doctor. Even the two respondents who were satisfied with their incomes joined other respondents in claiming that doctors' incomes were low and did not match their labor.

Considering all the efforts they put into their practice and the risks they faced, most respondents agreed that red packets were reasonable compensations for their low incomes and it was morally justifiable for doctors to take them as long as they did not solicit. The comment made by a respondent [ZKY] was representative.

> If the current incomes of medical professionals are reasonable, reasonable for this social class, then I must say taking red packets is reasonable. Because most of the time red packets are a kind of compensation for the underpaid labor of medical professionals. Perhaps from certain point of view, taking red packets is not reasonable. But should doctors not have some kind of extra incomes? From this point of view, it is reasonable [for doctors to take red packets].

However, justifying red packets is one thing, while taking them is another. Doctors apparently have many considerations when deciding whether to take red packets. Generally speaking, doctors are likely to take them in several circumstances, especially those offered through *guanxi.*

Red Packet Offered Through Guanxi

Some respondents noted that it would be insulting to turn down a red packet offered through social connections. Red packets of this type were usually deemed as *renqing*, namely, personal favor and gift. It was a "social debt" engaging both the taker and the giver. *Renqing* was culturally motivated networking practice and always involved gifts in all kinds. For doctors, turning down *renqing* offered through *guanxi* could have at least two implications: either the doctor did not intend to help, which was humiliating and could result in the breakdown of friendship, or the doctor, agreeing to help, intended to leave the giver in debt of gratitude, which givers did not usually find comfortable. A respondent [ZKY] noted, "[Red packets] introduced by acquaintances are hard to decline. Not only he asks you a favor, but also you will possibly ask him a favor in the future."

There was another consideration: red packets given through *guanxi* were safe, for the givers were very unlikely to report them. Apart from one respondent in Group 2, all other respondents who had been given red packets before admitted that they would take red packets offered through *guanxi.* In that exceptional case, the respondent [WWH] claimed that it was her principle not to take any gifts from friends and relatives in any situation. Her claim was apparently a surprise to other respondents, who said that *guanxi* red packets could not be turned down.

Post-Treatment Red Packets

As mentioned above, post-treatment red packets are mainly motivated by gratuity and the intention to establish long-term friendship. Red packets of this kind, as well as gifts in kind, are given when patients are satisfied with the treatment. Compared with pre-treatment red packets, they are usually less in monetary value and more relaxing in nature. Generally speaking, doctors take them as patients' acknowledgement and gratitude of the efforts they have put into the treatment and satisfaction with the outcome. The respondents also noted that these red packets were safe, because no patient would report them to authority. Of course, much fewer patients gave red packets or any in-kind gifts of significant monetary value after the treatment. As a respondent [ZXJ] stated,

> If the patient is grateful, and I am fully committed—for example he had a serious condition but has recovered—if he wants to thank me, I would possibly ask him to buy something for [the staff of] the unit, so the staff can share . . .

Confidence

As discussed above, some patients give red packets to ensure the curability of their diseases. Taking the red packet is therefore an indicator of the curability of the disease and the doctor's confidence to cure it. If the doctor has the confidence, he or she is likely to take the red packet before the operation, even if it is cold offered. A respondent [LJL] observed,

> If [the surgeon] feels a hundred percent about an operation, such as [removing] appendix, say, the operation is foolproof, and the money is not much. Then just take it.

However, some respondents maintained that no doctor could be a hundred percent sure about even the simplest operations, and they should exercise caution when taking red packets.

Assuring the Patient

The major purpose of giving red packets before treatment is to obligate the doctor. To this end, taking red packets can apparently assure the patient that the service and the quality they request are guaranteed. A respondent [LKB] reported a few scenarios in which new rich individual proprietors became aggressive if their red packets were turned down. As a result, the respondent found it more practical to take red packets to assure patients that he would commit to their treatment.

> If patients give me red packets, generally, I will take them. Why? When doing an operation, if I take the patient's red packet, the patient will feel assured. This is my observation in my work from a junior doctor to senior doctor. After taking the red packet, I will work harder to serve the patient. Patients are grateful. If I don't take red packets ... I am scared ... He might stab me, or give me trouble. Those individual proprietors are barbaric. They don't have much education. He gives you red packet. Do you take it or not? If you don't, you don't respect a pal. [LKB]

Peer Pressure

In a workplace where everyone takes red packets, those who refuse them can be regarded as breaking unspoken rules and be isolated. Peer pressure can force a doctor into taking red packets to avoid being isolated. Several respondents confirmed the existence of this informal norm.

> Since every doctor takes, and every patient gives ... If one doctor declines the red packet, he is considered by his peers as "not one of us" and finds himself socially excluded. [WYY]
>
> You work in a [surgical] team. The patient gives everyone a red packet according to his/her rank. If you decline, you would make others feel they have lower moral standards. So it is impossible for you not to take. [LWX]

The extent of peer pressure was closely associated with the ethos of units and hospitals. Respondents reported that red packets were more common in some units or hospitals than in others, depending on whether unit heads or hospital managements were serious about discipline.

Gifts of Small Monetary Value

Doctors tend to accept gifts of small monetary value regardless of the timing of giving. These gifts are usually gratuities in nature and intended as lubricant for interpersonal relationship. Turning down these gifts is insulting. These gifts are usually in kind rather than cash. Respondents commented that taking in-kind gifts was not only justifiable, but was also recommended:

> WBN: Generally speaking, if [the gift is meant for] building up friendship, it represents good-will. It doesn't mean ... you are bought off. If somebody suddenly gives you a lot of money, you have to be cautious about his intent. But if it's just a roasted duck, a pack of cigarettes, or a pack of leaf tea, you can be assured that it is only for interpersonal communication. It doesn't mean that ... I'm pressured into doing something unwillingly.
> ...
> WXX: If they're small things for interpersonal communication, and you turn them down, some patients can be unhappy ...

IMPACT OF RED PACKETS

Red packets are mostly given before the treatment and are meant to exercise some influence on the behaviors of doctors. In this sense, pre-treatment red packets are basically manipulative in nature. They are intended to beat the system and provide doctors a monetary incentive to improve quality and attitudes. Then can patients achieve their purposes with red packets? To what extent can red packets change doctors' behaviors? What impact can red packets make?

Impact on Quality

The major purpose of red packets is to motivate the doctor and to ensure the quality of services. Quality can mean several things to patients: competent doctors, quality treatment, responsiveness, and particularistic attitudes. The involvement of competent doctors concerns change to treatment and surgical arrangements and will be discussed in the following section. This section will look at what impact the red packet has on the quality of treatment and the attitude of the doctor toward the patient.

The ultimate concern of a patient is the quality of medical intervention. Most respondents, however, noted that the red packet had little impact on the quality of the technical core of treatment, such as the technical standards of surgery itself. All the surgeons, the respondents asserted, would perform the operation in their best capacity. Quality was where surgeons earned their reputation. The higher quality of the operation, the more patients the doctor could attract and hence more informal incomes. No surgeon would jeopardize their professional reputation by deliberately delivering a poor quality operation just because the patient had not given a red packet. The discussion in Group 2 quoted below is illustrious,

> LTQ: In reality, I don't think that the red packet can make a big difference. At the end of the day, in medicine, the quality is decided by [the doctor's] medical skills. It is the skills, not his attitude.
> . . .
> LTQ: When we discuss the red packet issue, we always concentrate on [the issue of] attitude. In reality, whether a patient can be cured, whether an operation can be successfully done, and whether a disease can be cured, is decided by skills, by medical skills. In terms of medical skills, he [i.e., the doctor] does what he should do.

> LXH: Be his attitude as good as they come, if he doesn't have the skills, he can't do it well.
> LTQ: Right. At the end of the day, you complain he doesn't smile to the patient. But that doesn't influence the quality of the surgery, and his treatment protocol. No. That's what I believe . . .
> LJL: I agree.
> LTQ: I think this [i.e., giving red packets] is wrong. It is going into the wrong door. Wrong. In reality, he [i.e., the doctor] does what he needs to do. It's the same regardless of red packets and *guanxi*, isn't it? How the treatment should be carried out? How the operation should be performed? What program should be followed for patients of internal medicine?. . .I believe the majority of doctors would not let these things influence their medical decisions. No.
> . . .
> LTQ: Two factors decide patient outcomes. One is the skills of the doctor. The other is the disease itself, isn't it? If the disease he has can't be cured, even if he is really willing to give [a red packet]. . .even if he is given five-star services, they can't solve his problem.

The rest of the respondents, although not many, seemed assured that red packets had impact on treatment quality, but their opinions were divided on whether the quality was improved or compromised. Some believed that after taking red packet, the doctor may exercise more caution in the operation. A respondent [LKB] observed,

> Yes, the doctor will be more cautious. For example, for a simple operation, he would give more consideration to possible complications. He will consider more... [The doctor] will definitely exercise caution with saturation, the

process of surgery, and so on. He will consider more, such as anesthesia and so on.

Other respondents claimed that the psychological pressure of the red packet on the surgeon were likely to compromise the quality. Red packets were meant to personalize the doctor–patient relationship. Without the red packet, a public doctor would assume responsibility directly to the public healthcare system and the work-unit rather than the patient. As long as the behavior of the doctor was within the boundary of the tolerance of the hospital, he or she did not find particular incentive to be responsible to the patient. That was what the red packet, and *guanxi*, was meant to change: to engage doctors personally rather than the impersonal institution, and to hold them accountable directly to the patient in addition to the work-unit. But the commitment to the patient as an individual doctor instead of a representative of the public work-unit, according to some respondents, were likely to put extra psychological pressure on the doctor, and might have adverse impact on their performance in surgery. The red packet was not merely an informal payment to compensate the low salary of the doctor. It is embedded with high expectations for better-than-normal services and guarantee of success. The high expectations could make doctors nervous when delivering treatment. As one respondent [ZXJ] noted, "With normal patients, things would not go wrong. However, [if the patient gives a red packet] things go wrong. The doctor is too nervous."

Another respondent [WYP] observed that the red packet could prompt the surgeon to compromise the effect of a surgery in order to avoid risk and embarrassment. After taking red packets, surgeons felt .that they were personally held responsible for the quality and outcome of surgery. Under this pressure, they become very cautious as not to take any risk in the operation. The respondent gave an example,

> This patient has a tumor, but it grows near major blood vessels. If you [i.e., the surgeon] take the red packet before the surgery, during the course of surgery, you probably would not remove the whole tumor. In fact, this [tumor] can be entirely removed, but there is a risk. Blood vessels might break and result in the death of the patient. Under this circumstance, [the red packet] compromises the effect of the surgery ... However, the patient was not aware of the compromise.

While it could barely change the most critical procedure and the technical core of an operation, the red packet could apparently improve the quality of post-surgery treatment and doctors' attitudes. The frequency of change of dressing was where the red packet made a major difference.

The change of attitudes was also evident. Doctors tended to treat patients who offered red packets as "private" patients, paying more visits, smiling more, and having longer conversations with them more often. This was widely acknowledged among respondents. Respondent WJH commented that the surgeon who took a red packet took more care of the patient after the operation. When doing ward visits, the surgeon would stay longer and have longer conversation with the patient, and check the patient more carefully. According to this respondent, red packets could definitely bring positive changes to surgeons' attitudes toward patients. For a surgeon with a busy schedule and many patients to look after, red packets decided who he would consider first and more. Generally speaking, however, surgeons would not delay the treatment to the extent of detriment to the patient.

Whether doctors would change their clinical behaviors and become more responsive to red packet givers, according to some respondents, was at individual doctor's discretion. A respondent [YSN] observed,

Although giving red packets doesn't guarantee you'll get better services, patients and their relatives would believe: they'll get comparatively good treatment. It all depends on whether the doctor who takes the red packet...is willing to take more responsibility...This is an individual issue. This can't be generalized. But speaking from the general perception, people feel they will get better services. Otherwise, nobody would give the red packet again.

Another respondent [WYP] commented that some doctors viewed red packets as what they deserved naturally and did not reciprocate with better services and attitudes.

Because of the asymmetry of knowledge, the patient is unable to make a sound judgment of the quality of treatment. What they can see and feel are those more superficial, such as the frequency of bandage changing and smiling faces. As a vice president of a Beijing hospital commented on media, patients were misled, for 99 percent of doctors would definitely not compromise their techniques even if they were not given red packets (Tian 2008).

Red packet givers, however, are not completely passive in terms of ensuring quality. Engaging eminent doctors is usually an active step toward positive assurance of quality.

Impact on Surgical Arrangements

Changing surgeons is one of the positive outcomes that a red packet can achieve. Some affluent and/or resourceful patients intend their red packets to secure not only quality services, but also the best surgeons, which usually mean senior specialists. Once taking red packets, senior surgeons usually feel obliged to do operations in person. But in general red packets alone usually are not as powerful as to commit senior surgeons. They have to be used with *guanxi*. In other words, *guanxi* is more compelling than red packets. Senior surgeons can turn down a red packet, but they can hardly turn down those offered through *guanxi*. A respondent [CXL] observed,

> You don't dare to take red packets unless they are given through middlemen [that you're familiar with]. Right? But the situation is, at present, some middlemen come to you. They don't give you red packets. But you have to do operations for [the patients they refer]. [If they want] you to do tonsillectomy, [you have to]. You know. You know your students are want so badly [to do it in order to graduate from the school], but you can't help. You have to do it ... You're obliged by acquaintances. You can't help...They [i.e., acquaintances] request senior doctors to do it. What can you do? This has nothing to do with red packets.

The consequence of the buying power of red packets is that senior surgeons have to do operations of both high and low levels of complexities, depriving junior surgeons of opportunities to perform medical procedures. One of the respondents [ZKY] quoted red packet as his major reason to come to Australia, for he had been deprived of many opportunities to practice.

> If a Chief Doctor takes the red packet...because surgery is a complicated procedure, involving a chief operator and assistants. Then, [if the patient] doesn't give the red packet, junior doctors, within the surgical team...would have more opportunities to practice. If [the patient] gives the red packet, the most senior doctor probably wouldn't give it [to junior doctors]. Because he fears...if the operation screws up, the patient would question: I gave a red packet, how come [the operation] screwed up. He [i.e., the senior doctor]

would give it more consideration. To this end, he would not hand the operations over. That is why, after a few years working in hospitals, I hated red packets so much. Because I experienced too much; because the more red packets, the less practicing opportunities for junior doctors.

Another respondent [LWX] commented that because of the red packet, junior doctors were left with nothing to do but to write medical records.

However, respondents also reported that senior surgeons might not completely deprive junior doctors or their students of practicing opportunities. A respondent [CXL] noted, "In my hospital, a lot of senior doctors take red packets but let their students to exercise with scalpel." Another respondent [LJL] agreed, "He [i.e., the senior surgeon] will be definitely in the operating theater [to supervise]. The only thing is that when it comes to operation, the patient doesn't know who is doing [the operation]. It might be his [i.e., the senior surgeon's] student, who might be the chief operator. But he has to be present, because he has taken the money. Otherwise, he wouldn't take the money. If he takes the money, he has to take the responsibility."

Red packets led to the concentration of surgeries into the hands of senior surgeons. The implication for junior doctors was not only the loss of practicing opportunities, but also less income. The respondents also pointed out that with the commercialization of healthcare, surgeons' performance wages were partly linked to the number of operations they performed. Without operations to do, their income could decline considerably.

Impact on Incomes

The impact of red packets on doctors' incomes depended on several things: the doctor's specialties and professional ranks, regions, and the doctor's willingness to take. Understandably, respondents' comments on this issue varied.

Respondents reported that surgeons mainly relied on red packets for informal incomes, while doctors of internal medicine relied on drug kickbacks. The higher the professional ranks, the more red packets the surgeon could receive. Reputation was another determinant of the number and amount of red packets. A respondent [ZZT] noted that in northeast China, giving red packets was popular. Surgeons usually did not bother to check their pay slips. They lived on red packets. Another respondent [WJH] believed that red packets had a "definite and extreme impact on doctors' incomes. That is why red packets can't be stopped. Without red packets and drug kickbacks, doctors' salaries are just slightly higher than manual workers' and much less than other professions and officials."

DECLINING RED PACKETS

Red packets are not official payments and taking them is illegal. Although doctors believe it is morally justifiable for them to take and they do take under many circumstances, there are also a number of considerations that deter them from taking red packets. The circumstances under which doctors take them have been discussed above. Here I will examine the concerns and circumstances that prevent doctors from taking them.

Deterrents against Taking Red Packets

Illegality is the uttermost reason deterring doctors from taking red packets. Since red packets given through *guanxi* are unlikely to be turned down, it is usually the red packet that is cold offered before treatment that is declined by the doctor. A respondent [ZKY] said that he never took red packets from patients that were not introduced by acquaintances. Another respondent [ZYT] shared the same view, "The key thing is whether we know them or not. If we don't [know them before], we don't take [the red packets they give], honestly."

Declining cold-offered red packets is motivated by several concerns, including the potential risk and trouble of being reported and caught for taking red packets, the pressure generated by patient's unrealistic expectation, lack of confidence in the outcome of operations, concerns about personal reputation and professional integrity, or the red packet being overly manipulative.

Potential Risk and Trouble

In China's healthcare system, patients and doctors mutually do not trust each other. While patients do not believe that doctors are fully committed to the treatment and use personal incentive to motivate the latter, doctors fear that patients would report them to authority for taking red packets. As will be discussed in the next chapter, 99 percent of red packet givers do not report their doctors. One percent, however, still represents a potential risk which can entirely ruin the career of a doctor. This risk heightens considerably if patients are not satisfied with the outcome of treatment. A respondent [CXL] elaborated the concern.

I don't take red packets most of the time. Even if you feel 100 percent about an operation, the result can't be guaranteed. You know, if patients really complain ... For those of my age, we are serious about reputation ... Probably some [colleagues] may argue about your professional competence. Some may say you are competent, and some may not. But you don't expect to have trouble in this regard... After all, our career is at a stage of rising ...
...
I feel that taking red packets is risky. It has nothing to do with the wealth of the giver. If he has a nasty personality, the richer he is, the more trouble he can bring you. When he makes trouble, it's not about money. Perhaps he just wants to ruin your reputation.

To this end, if doctors felt that a medical condition was incurable, they would not take any red packets, especially those with terminal diseases. A respondent [ZYT] pointed out that no doctor would dare to take red packets given by patients with terminal cancer who insisted on excision, for the result of surgery could not be satisfactory. By the same token, lack of confidence also cautioned doctors against taking red packets.

Unrealistic Expectations

By giving red packets, patients expect not only commitment of doctors, but also, in many cases, a guarantee of success and curability. While doctors perhaps find it less difficult to live up to patients' expectations of commitment, expectations of success and curability can be unrealistic and create psychological burden on doctors. A respondent [LJL] said,

Patients would think that after spending this money [i.e., red packets], you [i.e., doctors] can turn them...like [those receiving] cosmetic surgery, into a princess [in fairy tales]. It's not like that. Surgery and medical treatment are just the same.

Some respondents commented that the pressure imposed by unrealistic expectations could be very strong. "If patients demand too much, doctors would decline their red packets, because they know they can't meet the demands. These doctors at least have some sense of responsibility" [YSN].

Integrity and Self-respect

Some respondents pointed out that professional integrity played an important role in their decision to decline red packets. This concern was represented in a respondent's comments on her decision not to take red packets.

> For one thing, it's immoral to take red packets. It's to hit a person when he's down. Taking red packets is taking advantage of patients. Furthermore, I have a faint heart. I feel that taking red packets is to let patients use you like a dog and is detrimental to your self-respect. If they ask, "doctor, can you prescribe this? Can you prescribe that?," you know, how can you refuse? I considered it carefully, and I never took a single red packet. [WYY]

A respondent [WBN] noted that he asked his colleagues in surgical units before. Some surgeons told him that if they felt that they would lose dignity after taking red packets, they wouldn't do. The red packets would become a psychological burden on them. Respondent WYP commented that some doctors do not like the feeling of being bought off by patients.

Tight Supervision
Respondents pointed out that doctors tended to decline red packets when there was a government campaign targeting professional misconducts in the healthcare system [YPP], or the administration of the hospital was extremely serious about discipline and investigated and punished red packet takers. It was also noted that the ethos of a hospital or a unit within the hospital had great influence on doctors' attitudes toward red packets, as demonstrated in the following comment.

> In my place, there are two affiliated [teaching] hospitals. They have different systems. One hospital is strict about red packets, and has strict rules. If doctors are found [taking red packets], they will receive punishments of certain kinds. The red packets in this hospital, …[doctors] don't dare to take. Nobody dares to take. But in the other hospital, red packets are endemic. [OYL]

The comment indicated that if the hospital was serious about red packets and willingly to punish takers, doctors were likely to decline red packets.

Sympathize with Poor Patients
Illegality was not the only thing that would prompt doctors to decline red packets. Respondents mentioned that in their work they frequently encountered people with inadequate economic means. Motivated by various reasons, however, they also joined the givers of red packets in order to commit

doctors to their or their beloved's treatment. The respondents agreed that a doctor should not take any red packets in cash from poor patients because it was immoral, and they insisted that they always declined red packets from the later. A respondent [LTQ] exemplified,

> For example, he needs 3000 *yuan* to treat his disease, but he has raised only 1500 *yuan*. Now he wants to give you a 150-*yuan* red packet. Do you take it? Of course not. He doesn't even have enough money for treatment. How can you [take his red packet]?
> Another respondent [ZKY] spoke from his own experiences.
> I saw a lot indeed. For example, I was going to do an emergent operation, an emergent appendix removal operation. Some of the patients were from countryside, or peasant workers. I could see clearly [how much they had] in their wallets when they pull out 200 or 300 *yuan*, and thrust it into your hand. Even if I couldn't return it immediately, I would do after coming out of operation theater.

Some respondents reported that in the work they not only declined red packets from poor patients, but also tried to help them financially. A respondent [LKB] claimed that in his hospital doctors would donate money to patients from rural areas to help them pay hospitalization expenses. Doctors who took their red packets would return them when they were discharged from the hospital. As indicated before, respondents did not feel anything wrong to get rich patients or patients with government positions to buy gifts for the whole staff of their units or take them to dinner. One respondent [LJL] even used the work "*zai*" ("fleecing") to indicate that the officials and rich people deserved being "fleeced." However, the same respondent also noted that when treating economically disadvantaged patients, doctors would provide minimum services and prescriptions to the extent of not comprising treatment effect in order to help patients save, still less taking their red packets. This "helpful" and moral act of declining poor patients' red packets and offering them "affordable" treatment has other implications, that is, doctors provided medical services based on means rather than needs. Such unprofessional conducts were praised if they were intended to help the poor but condemned if meant for overcharge or over-provision.

Implications and Consequences of Declining Red Packets

For doctors, declining red packets is not always easy. While declining red packets offered after treatment may be interpreted by patients as a symbol of high moral standards, declining a pre-treatment red packet can cause misunderstanding. Red packets have become an indicator of willingness to serve and ability to serve. Therefore, declining a red packet bears all the implications of either unwilling to or incapable to provide the desired services. Patients needing surgical interventions are especially sensitive to surgeons' declining of their red packets. According to the respondents, patients could interpret, or misinterpret, doctors' intent to decline red packets before surgery in several ways.

Lack of Confidence and/or Competence

The ultimate reason for patients to give red packets before surgery is to seek assurance of quality and outcome. Taking red packets is thus to assure patients and is thus taken as demonstration of doctors' competence and confidence. To that end, declining red packets is likely to be viewed as lacking competence and confidence. One respondent [CXL] reported two cases in which her patients chose to transit to other hospitals because she declined their red packets.

> CXL: If you solicit, that's wrong. But what about [you take] passively? The patient would say, "Now you aren't confident to take my red packet, you must be afraid of taking responsibility of doing the operation."
> . . .
> Once I had a patient. After being admitted to hospital, he said, "Please arrange discharge for me" . . . At the end, the issue went to the Inpatient Section. Your patient leaves without having the operation. The [authority of] Inpatient Section inquired, "Why did the patient leave without having operation." I was embarrassed . . .
> ZYT: True. Our patients would do that. "You're afraid of taking my red packet. Is it because you're incompetent?"
> CXL: Patients don't trust you.
> ZYT: Incompetent. Especially in Shantou in Guangdong. If you don't dare to take my red packet, you're incompetent to do the operation.

Respondent CXL believed that the patients in question became suspicious about her ability to do the operations or willingness to do them and decided to have surgery done in other hospitals. The hospital that CXL worked for eventually required the respondent to explain. Similar incidents happened twice to this respondent, as she claimed.

In other words, being offered red packets are regarded by doctors as an indicator of competence. Surgeons can opt to turn them down, but one can imagine the embarrassment of a surgeon who has never been offered a red packet. A media report disclosed that many patients mistakenly assumed that the reasons for doctors not taking the red packet were because they were either incompetent or the red packet was too small. Patients did not believe that doctors were afraid of being caught (Li 2003). A story published on *Jiankang bao* complained that a model doctor was nearly sacked for turning down red packets (Xi 1993). Patients whose red packets had been declined by this surgeon complained to the management of the hospital about the "apparent" incompetence of the surgeon. "The relatives of the patient said, 'You didn't dare to take the red packet, which means you're technically incompetent.' They want to engage a trustable doctor to treat their beloved." The management advised that if the surgeon was confident about the outcome of the operation, he should take red packets to assure patients. Otherwise, the surgeon had to resign. The surgeon gave in to the pressure.

Insulting and Disrespectful
Since red packets are always intended, at least partially, as gifts, declining them would be interpreted as disrespectful. As mentioned before, patients also use red packets to address imbalance of status. Therefore, declining red packets can be interpreted as denying patients' attempt in this regard. A respondent [LWX] recounted a complaint against her made more than ten years ago. She declined a patient's red packet before the surgery because she just started her career in medicine and was afraid of taking one. After the surgery, the patient, unsatisfied with the result, wrote a lengthy complaint letter to the unit head. One of the complaints the patient made against this doctor was about her being so arrogant and disrespectful as not to take his red packet. Apparently, this patient felt offended.

Increased Anxiety
As discussed before, giving red packets was intended to buy "peace of mind," namely, to buy assurance. Turning them down would apparently drive givers anxious and prompt them to take irrational actions. Several respondents observed that declining red packets in surgery definitely made patients more anxious. They may think that doctors rejected because the red packets were too small [WYP]. Such conjecture on the part of patients could press them into offering bigger red packets and put doctors into a more difficult situation. Declining red packets may also make patients think their conditions were incurable.

In general, patients needing surgery are very likely to become anxious if their red packets are declined. However, patients who do not need surgical interventions are usually more positive about it. A respondent [LXH] commented that patients would respect doctors of internal medicine if they declined red packets. Another respondent [CXL] from the same group pointed out that sometimes inpatients gave red packets probingly. If doctors declined, the inpatients were happy to take them back, feeling that the doctors had higher standards of professional integrity.

Physical Assault
Patients view the act of taking red packets as a token of commitment, responsibility, and competence. By taking red packets, doctors assure patients of their commitment and competence, and hence win the trust of the latter. If doctors decline red packets, patients can become suspicious and anxious and perhaps do not trust doctors. The worst form of patients' mistrust is physical assault on treating doctors.

Physical abuse of doctors has been discussed. That represents the risk that doctors have to face in daily practice. The incidents of physical assault to be discussed here particularly resulted from declining red packets, as respondent LKB recounted,

> We have a story. In our Cancer Specialty Hospital, an old grandpa had a stomach cancer. They invited a very reputed doctor from our general surgical unit. This doctor is a Chief Doctor, and a model worker of the city. He has very high political standards. [The patient's] son was studying in the US. On hearing his father to have an operation, he came back and gave [a red packet of] eight thousand US dollars to the doctor. But the Chief Doctor didn't take it. He promised he would do his best to perform the operation ... He didn't take the eight thousand US dollars ... Unfortunately, after the operation, the old grandpa—the operation was beautifully done—suffered copious bleeding for unknown reasons, and died three days later. The patient's relatives chased the doctor to beat him. The doctor was too scared to come to hospital. [The relatives] said that "you didn't take our red packet, so you failed the operation, screwed the operation." But the Chief Doctor had very high integrity, and the operation ... it was beautifully done. You can tell from this scenario whether you should take or not? Taking red packet is to buy peace of mind, and is to assure the patient. For patients also want to buy peace of mind.

Media reports also confirmed that returning red packets was likely to lead to physical assault on doctors. Tang Youguan, whose father had received six operations in a hospital, was not satisfied with the outcome. In the course of the operations, Tang gave red packets three times to Ji Weiguang, chief surgeon of the second, third, and sixth operations of Tang's father. Ji declined all of them. Tang thus suspected that Ji, as well as other surgeons, was not committed to the treatment and stabbed Ji to death (Chen and Sun 1995).

Another incident saw a surgeon murdered by his patient's son for declining the latter's red packet. According to a report, in 1990, the son of a terminal cancer patient gave Shen Sixuan—an eminent surgeon—a red packet before the surgery of his mother, but the surgeon declined it. Three years later, the patient died. The son, Ge Zhiguo by name, who was a long-time cancer patient and had given gifts and red packets to every doctor that had treated him, believed that Dr. Shen rejected his red packet because it was too small. As a result, Dr. Shen was not committed to his mother's treatment and operation, which consequently led to his mother's death. In 1999, Ge stabbed Dr. Shen to death (Zhao 1999). This is only an extreme case, for the murderer was a cancer patient who was probably in despair after prolonged, painful but fruitless treatment. But the scenario reflects the tension and extreme distrust in the doctor–patient relationship.

Declining and Returning Strategies

Because of the sensitivity involved in declining red packets in surgery, organizational or individual strategies are developed to cope with the issue. Usually, doctors take red packets before surgery in order to reassure patients and return them at a certain point in the course of treatment. The respondents identified two methods of returning. One was to return through organizational arrangement, and the other through personal arrangement.

Organizational Arrangement

A respondent [ZYT] noted that in her hospital, doctors handed red packets to head nurses of their units before surgery, providing that the doctors were willing to hand them in. Head nurses were responsible for returning red packets to patients respectively right after the patients were sent back to wards from operating theaters. "The head nurse would tell the patient that the operation is successful. Here is your red packet. We are not allowed to take red packets. Our hospital doesn't allow us to take." However, this practice was not without problem. Another respondent [LTQ] from the same group questioned that returning red packets immediately after surgery would prompt patients and their families to suspect that the operation was not successful. Doctors returned red packets through head nurses because they screwed up and did not want to be held accountable personally.

Personal Arrangement

Findings from the investigation show that it was more common for doctors to employ personal coping strategies. A respondent [CXL] said that she usually took red packets first, and then returned them to patients' relatives at the door of the operating theater after patients themselves were already in the theater.

> I used to do the same [i.e., returning red packets after operation]. But later on, a doctor in my hospital was in trouble...I feel that it is too dangerous [to return after operation]...So now I return it at the entrance of the operating theater, rather than returning after operation. Because I think, if you [i.e., the patient] have an accident in the surgery, I'm not to blame, you know. Now I tell patients' relatives, "Don't give me pressure. I'm returning your red packet, and you must take it back. Don't give me pressure. If I make any mistake in the operation, it's because of your red packet."

Other individual strategies were not as blunt as that of this respondent. A more popular way of returning red packets was to send red packets to the fees unit, which used them to offset the official charges to be paid by the patients who gave the red packets. However, the respondents agreed that doctors who sent red packets to the management could be viewed in the eyes of colleagues as having "political aspiration," namely, aspiring to career mobility by demonstrating being more politically disciplined than others.

Empirical findings presented above show that a great majority of red packets are given before the major treatment is delivered. Patients are impelled to give before treatment for various purposes, but the most dominating ones are to seek quality and quicker services.

The Chinese healthcare system is not short of supplies of basic medicine and services, but of quality services. Patients perceive quality as consisting of temporal, physical, and human dimensions, usually equating it to faster services in major hospitals of major cities by senior medical professionals. Apparently, the shortage is accentuated, if not created, by the demand of patients, which is attributable to at least two major factors. The first factor is the improved economic conditions of the general public after years of economic reform, which gives them more purchasing power. As such, they can afford choices and afford some kind of initiative in their medical encounters. In other words, the improved economic conditions allow general public to buy options, power, control, and certainty when seeking medical services in the public healthcare system.

The second factor is patients' deep distrust in bureaucratic medicine. It is not that patients do not trust doctors' professional authority; they do not believe doctors would follow the ideology of "serving the people wholeheartedly" and practice universal particularism in practice. In other words, patients have confidence in modern medicine, be it Western-style medicine or TCM, and in doctors' professional power derived from their mastery of medical knowledge and skills. Otherwise, they would not seek medical services from them. But they do not believe that doctors would practice beyond bureaucratic norms. Therefore, they pay extra to buy doctors' particularistic "wholeheartedness" in order to circumvent bureaucratic medicine. In addition, red packets can serve as an incentive for individual doctors to beat the bureaucratic system on patients' behalf, so that the latter can jump the queue or engage senior doctors.

As the findings indicate, patients in fact do not trust all the state functionaries. In China's bureaucratic system, rent-seeking activities have become a norm. On the one hand, ordinary employees of the state service, administrative, and governing organs do not usually have any bargaining power against the state. The respondents' comments on their workload indicate exactly the lack of bargaining power. These doctors cannot negotiate work terms with their hospitals but have to accept what is imposed on them. To cope with heavy workloads, they have developed a work style resembling assembly line, and exercised indifference to individual needs and expectations of patients. On the other hand, they wield monopolistic state power and authority, together with professional power and authority, on the recipients of their functions. Consequently, a cycle of minor corruptions comes into being, with the medical profession a link on the cycle. From the perspective of patients, they seem to have a clear idea of the standard services they expect or predict the bureaucratic medicine can provide. Any initiatives to change the standard for better incur additional payments, and the payments have to be arranged informally.

Red packets are a response to the shortage of quality, but the outcome of the red packet as a means of quality control is mixed. It can be identified that red packets represent at least two types of tactics of private and informal quality control. The first pattern is to use red packets to "buy" top specialists and time to ensure that patients are attended by competent doctors in a timely manner, namely, involving eminent doctors and/or jumping the queue. This is a pro-active tactic. Timely service by eminent doctors can apparently increase the accuracy of diagnosis and the efficacy of treatment. But it requires the patient to command substantial financial and/or social resources to beat the system. *Guanxi* thus plays an important role. Patients with fewer resources may be compelled to take the second tactic. They do not have *guanxi* and/or other resources (including economic resources) to involve eminent doctors, but give red packets to treating doctors assigned to them by the system to incentivize quality.

The findings show that red packets can change doctors' behaviors and attitudes, and have positive impact on the general quality of medical services, but to what extent that the core technical quality of treatment can be altered seems uncertain. As most of the respondents confirm, the technical standards of treatment are the bottom line of responsibility and professionalism in their position as bureaucratic doctors. Surgeons are very unlikely to risk their career and intentionally perform an operation in breach of technical standards and procedures just because patients do not give them red packets. They will not compromise their skills and knowledge input in the technical core of treatment. But a few other respondents claim that the core quality can be altered, though very unlikely drastically, if treating doctors exercise more attention and caution to details of the core components of treatment or the core procedures of surgery. The outcome of excessive caution, however, may not always guarantee high quality and be beneficial to the patient. Because of the asymmetry of information, patients are incapable of judging the quality of the technical core of treatment. Consequently, patients tend to judge the quality by external indicators that are comprehensible to them, such as the seniority of doctors, words of mouth, smiling faces, frequency of visit, attitudes, frequency of change of dressing, and so on. In other words, red packets are unlikely to have significant impact on the technical quality of treatment, but they can surely improve doctors' responsiveness and attitudes and quality of non-major services. That is to say, what red packets can buy is largely limited to additional values of medical services.

Nonetheless, red packets can change doctors' behaviors and attitudes to the extent that the doctor–patient relationship is personalized to benefit patients. Personalized doctor–patient relationship subverts the bureaucratic medicine, in which bureaucratized doctors are held more responsible for the bureaucratic system than for patients. Although patients face individual

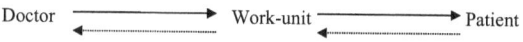

Fig. 5.1   Payment and responsibility structure in bureaucratic medicine

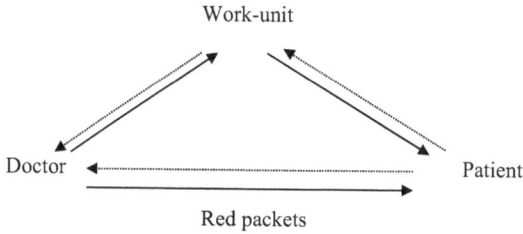

Fig. 5.2   Payment and responsibility structure in a red packet transaction

doctors when seeking services from state-run medical facilities, they in fact deal with an impersonal system rather than doctors. The following diagram illustrates the payment line (dotted lines) and the responsibility line (concrete lines) of bureaucratic medicine (Fig. 5.1)

As we can see, in the public healthcare system, patients cannot reach doctors directly. Between them is the impersonal work-unit accountable for the Party-state. Through red packets, however, another dimension is added to the relationship (Fig. 5.2)

With red packets, patients reach and hold doctors accountable directly. But the cost is obviously higher, for patients have to pay the work-unit and the doctor at the same time. The doctor, upon receiving more incomes from the patient directly, is exposed to the patient directly as well. The direct exposure to patients makes some doctors uncomfortable and prompts them into declining red packets.

There are many circumstances under which doctors would not take red packets. These include doctors' technical concerns (e.g., curability), the pressure of unrealistic expectation, professional integrity, and so on, especially when givers are "strangers." Red packets can give patients more power and control in the doctor–patient relationship. To this end, the declining of red packets is intended, on the part of doctors, to maintain the relationship status quo. Patients can perceive it as doctors' refusal to relinquish any power to patients and to take direct responsibility for the latter. In other words, patients intend to press doctors into exercising particularistic medicine and to engage them into contractual relationship by giving the latter red packets. The refusal can be interpreted as an attempt to continue to practice impersonal bureaucratic medicine, which features indifference to patients' interests and institutional protection of doctors' practice, be they competent or not. Consequently, patients may feel that their attempt to increase or ensure quality is not heeded by doctors. Understandably, uncertainty and anxiety ensue. As a result, frustrated patients may choose several options. If resources permit, they may opt out and buy certainty with another doctor and perhaps in another institution. Or they may try other means to make sure that doctors accept their red packets, by, for example, increasing the amount of red packets or deliver them through *guanxi*. Those who have least resources may have no choice but to wait in anxiety. In extreme cases, the frustration may drive the patient into resorting to violent power to change the doctor–patient relationship, through physical assault or even murder.

From the perspective of power relations, it can be argued that the distrust between the doctor and the patient prompts the latter into empowering themselves by buying power with red packets. The lack of trust apparently makes patients believe that doctors would not serve their interests spontaneously, and only private informal payments can ensure their commitment. The distrust in doctors' professionalism and the thrust to buy power over doctors has worsened the phenomenon of red packets. As a result, declining red packets may be more detrimental to the doctor–patient relationship than taking them.

Notes

1. A three-letter code is assigned to each respondent to facilitate a clear representation of their views.
2. The respondents reported that the "patients choose doctors" scheme was not welcome in their hospitals. See Chap. 6 for further discussion.
3. "Give away money to avoid disasters" (*po cai mian zai*) is a Chinese idiom.
4. http://www.ahbzyy.com/Newsshow.asp?id=109, accessed 30 October 2015.
5. http://wmdw.jswmw.com/home/content/?5240-771711.html, accessed 30 October 2015.
6. http://sc.sina.com.cn/city/xwgz/gdxw/2012-10-26/09173102.html, accessed 31 October 2015.

7. I suspect that the income that this respondent alleged to make probably includes informal incomes. Since pediatricians did not have much red packet income (this had been confirmed by other respondents), informal incomes were likely to be generated from drug kickbacks and moonlighting.

BIBLIOGRAPHY

Ban, Rongming, Haiping Deng, and Shi Bai. 2007. Yiliao fengxian fendan jizhi de qidai he zhanghai (Expectation of and impediment to medical risk sharing mechanism). *Yiyao jingji bao (Medical and Pharmaceutical Economy)*, 25 May, A3.

Chen, Ju, and Changlin Sun. 1995. Xueran 'hongbao': guanyu Wugang Eryuan Ji Guangwei san tui hongbao fan zao da de caifang (Blood stained 'red packet': an investigation of Ji Weiguang of the Second Hospital of Wuhan Steel Co. who was physically assaulted for returning a red packet three times). *Jiankang bao (Health News)*, 10 January, 3.

Cheng, Gong, and Yongtong Su. 2005. Ming yi bei sha weihe yipian jiaohao? (Why the murder of a reputed doctor is widely acclaimed?). *Nanfang zhoumo (Southern Weekend)*, 25 August. Accessed 2 June 2016. http://news.163.com/05/0825/12/1S0KCO140001124S.html.

CMDA. 2015. Zhongguo yishi zhiye zhuangkuang baipishu (White book of Chinese doctors' practicing state). Accessed 27 August 2015. http://www.cmda.net/xiehuixiangmu/falvshiwubu/tongzhigonggao/2015-05-28/14587.html.

Deng, Ya, and Shixiong Deng. 2011. Wo guo yiliao zeren baoxian zhidu gaige tanxi (Reform our country's medical liability insurance). *Yixue yu shehui (Medicine and Society)* 24(3): 22–24.

Fu, Yang. 2004. Yisheng yao kao baobiao baohu: yi huan guanxi mianli xinren weiji (Doctors need protection of bodyguards: doctor-patient relationship faces crisis). *Chengdu wanbao (Chengdu Evening Post)*, 25 February 2014. http://jk.scol.com.cn/04/0225/14/5C5A200ED31D8577.html.

Ge, Suhong. 2001. Yisheng de zhiye fengxian yinggai youshui lai fendan? (Who should share the risks of the medical profession?). Xinhuanet.com. 30 April. Accessed 2 June 2016. http://www.XinhuaNet.com.

Geng, Baowen. 2007. Yiyuan fa 'weiqu jiang' nanyi huanhe yihuan guanxi (Hospitals giving 'grievance award' cannot alleviate tense doctor-patient relationship). *Gongren ribao (Workers Daily)*, 8 January. Accessed 2 June 2016. http://acftu.people.com.cn/GB/67585/5258233.html.

Jin, Yonghong, and Jingdan Xiao. 2004. Zhiji yijie guai xianzhuan zhi hongbao (Face-to-face with an abnormal phenomenon in health care: red packets). *Jiankang bao (Health News)*, 21 April, 5.

Li, Guojun. 2004. Hongbao jinling cuisheng 'yisheng jingji ren' (Ban on red packets gives birth to 'doctor brokers'). *Renmin wang (People's Net)*, 5 July. Accessed 2 June 2016. http://www.people.com.cn/GB/14739/14740/21470/2618242.html.

Li, Heng, Duanyu Tu, and Xi Huang. 2007. Ba cheng duo yisheng zinu bu yuan congyi (Over eighty percent of doctors' children do not want to be doctors). *Guangzhou ribao (Guangzhou Daily)*, 27 July, A8. Accessed 10 June 2010. http://gzdaily.dayoo.com/html/2007-07/27/content_4639.htm.

Li, Honghe. 2003. Shaoze wubai duoze shu qian, tan mi yi huan "hongbao" heidong: song hongbao bili gaoda 75.8% (Five hundred at least, can reach thousands; exploring the black hole of "red packets": as many as 75.8% [of patients] offer red packets). *Shenghuo shibao (Life Times)*. Accessed 2 June 2016. http://www.gmw.cn/01shsb/2003-04/11/37-6BC70EA9CE2F54B448256D04000BA008.htm.

Lin, Jie. 2007. 'Guangdong Sheng yihu renyuan jingsheng zhuangkuang diaocha baogao' fabu, da bufen yihu renyuan chuyu gaodu jinzhang zhuangtai ('Report on the survey of the state of mind of medical and nursing personnel in Guangdong Province' published: the majority of medical and nursing personnel are under high pressure). *Zhongguo qingnian bao (China Youth)*, 30 November, 7.

Liu, Xingzhu, Yuanli Liu, and Ningshan Chen. 2000. The Chinese experience of hospital price regulation. *Health Policy and Planning* 15(2): 157–163.

Ministry of Health. 1985a. Guanyu shixing daxing yiliao jianyan shebei youchang zhanyong de tongzhi (Circular about the trial of paid use of large medical examination equipment). In *Chinese health year book 1986*, edited by Chinese Health Year Book Editorial Board, 217. Beijing: Renmin Weisheng Chubanshe (People's Health Publishiung House).

———. 1985b. Guanyu weisheng gongzuo gaige ruogan zhengce wenti de baogao (Report on Several Policy Issues Concerning Reforms of Health Work). Accessed 2 June 2016. http://www.china.com.cn/law/flfg/txt/2006-08/08/content_7060220.htm.

———. 1989. Guanyu kuoda yiliao weisheng fuwu youguan wenti de yijian (Advice on issues related to the expansion of medical and health services). In *Chinese health year book 1990*, edited by Chinese Health Year Book Editorial Board, 51–53. Beijing: Remin Weisheng Chubanshe (People's Health Publishing House).

———. 2004a. Guanyu jiaqiang weisheng hangye zuofeng jianshe de yijian (Advice on strengthening the construction of good practice in health professions). Accessed 17 September 2010. http://www.moh.gov.cn/publicfiles/business/htmlfiles/mohbgt/pw10405/200804/26860.htm.

Ministry of Health, State Administration of Traditional Chinese Medicine, and China Insurance Regulatory Commission. 2007. Guanyu tuidong yiliao zeren baoxian youguan wenti de tongzhi (Notification regarding issues related to the promotion of medical liability insurance). Accessed 31 October 2015. http://www.china.com.cn/policy/txt/2007-06/29/content_8458520.htm.

National Development Planning Commission, and Ministry of Health. 2000. Gaige yiliao fuwu jiage guanli de yijian (Decision on the reform of the administration of medical service prices). Accessed 2 June 2016. http://www.nhfpc.gov.cn/zhuzhan/wsbmgz/201304/2565dbbdefeb4a5199c4fc7c8f9306b0.shtml.

National Health and Family Planning Commission, Ministry of Law, Ministry of Finance, China Insurance Regulatory Commission, and State Administration of Traditional Chinese Medicine. 2014. Guanyu jiaqiang yiliao zeren baoxian gongzuo de yijian (Advice on enhancing the work of medical liability insurance). Accessed 30 October 2015. http://www.nhfpc.gov.cn/yzygj/s3589/201407/65d55251804c408581a4e58db41f4bc7.shtml.

Supreme Court. 2001. Guanyu minshi susong zhengju de ruogan guiding (Supreme court rules of evidence in civil suits). Accessed 2 June 2016. http://www.china.com.cn/chinese/PI-c/92700.htm.

Tao, Sunjin. 2004. Hongbao, rang yisheng youzou zai tianshi yu mogui zhijian (Red packets let the doctor wandering between angels and devils). *Jinling wanbao (Jinling Evening Post)*, 13 April. Accessed 2 June 2016. http://news.xinhuanet.com/newscenter/2004-04/13/content_1417309.htm.

Tian, Ye. 2008. Liu cheng shoufangzhe song guo hongbao (Sixty percent of the surveyed gave red packets). *Shengming shibao (Life Times)*, 20 January, 24. Accessed 2 June 2016. http://paper.people.com.cn/smsb/html/2008-01/29/content_40932296.htm.

Wu, Haibo, and Jie Yuan. 2008. Cong zhidu queshi kan dangqian wo guo yiliao zeren boxian de fazhan juxian (Lack of institutions and the developmental limitation of our country's medical liability insurance). *Guowai yixue—jingji weisheng fen ce (Foreign medicine—health economics)* 25(3): 139–142.

Xi, Liang. 1993. Bushou hongbao, xian zao jiepin (Nearly sacked for turning down red packets). *Jiankang bao (Health News)*, 17 August, 2.

Zhang, Mingshu. 2005. Guanyu 'xiao fubai' lilun (Theory of minor corruption). *Lingdao wencui (Leadership Digest)* 11: 107–112.

Zhao, Liyuan. 1999. Jushou hongbao jiu sharen (Murdered for rejecting a red packet). *Dushi shibao (Metropolitan Times)*, 24 January, 4.

CHAPTER 6

Rein in Red Packets

In the previous chapters, I discussed how institutional persistence and change have jointly created an institutional setting in which red packets have emerged. In this chapter, I will look at the governing of red packets which also relies on both old and emergent institutions.

Taking red packets is illegal. That alone should suffice to prevent doctors from taking red packets. Since the early 1980s, numerous national and local policy initiatives, regulatory mechanisms, and systematic reforms have been implemented in an attempt to rein in red packets, but the practice seems to have taken root. Its prevalence has generated an impression that the government has not done much to contain the phenomenon. Students of informal payments blame the endemic practice on government's failure to establish a comprehensive regulatory and governing structure, and its failure to introduce competition and market mechanisms into the healthcare system. They thus advance that the government must strengthen its regulatory frameworks and governing mechanisms, and incorporate market elements and competition into health reform (Yan 1994; Li and Tong 1995; Wang 1998, 2005a; Kong 2004; Chen 2006; Xu 2006; Lu 2011). However, what existing studies have not explored adequately are the regulatory and governing efforts that the Party-state has put in to fight informal payments, and have not analyzed to what extent the efforts have failed, and why they have failed. Scholars have excessively focused on how the practice has been controlled or should be controlled within hospitals. Inadequate attention has been paid to the broader governing structures established by the Party-state, and how medical professionals and patients have responded to the

© The Author(s) 2017
J. Yang, *Informal Payments and Regulations in China's Healthcare System*,
DOI 10.1007/978-981-10-2110-7_6

regulatory and governing efforts of the Party-state. The impact on red packets of the market elements that have been introduced into the healthcare system is also under-studied.

As in other arenas of the Chinese healthcare system, the governance of red packets relies on both institutions inherited from the old command economy regime and those emerged from the market reform. In general, two major approaches to tackle the issue can be identified. The first is the disciplinary approach, which features campaigns and administrative devices to battle against the red packet head-on. The second is the market approach, which represents an attempt to empower the patients by giving them more choosing power. These approaches have not altered the general landscape of governance in which power and control are continuously exercised hierarchically and societal input is almost negligible. In the course of implementation, all these approaches have met overtly or covertly resistance.

Disciplinary Approach

The disciplinary approach refers to the exercise of a type of extralegal coercive power and the intervention by a range of associated administrative apparatuses that the CCP has long employed to control subordinates and maintain order. The disciplinary function of the Party-state is predominantly carried out by the CCP's disciplinary inspection commission, an institution whose history can be traced back to the Central Supervisory Commission of the CCP established in 1927.[1] Although the red packet is illegalized in law, the practice is largely dealt with by discipline rather than by law. Its governance is predominantly led by Party organs assisted by government agencies.

The regulatory and governing structure dealing with red packets is extremely complicated. Several CCP and government organs are involved in regulating inappropriate conducts in healthcare. In Chinese political terminology, red packet transaction is defined as a form of "unhealthy trends," which means it is not as serious as corruption, but is morally, politically, and legally incorrect. A major disciplinary body of this category of misconducts is the "Office of Rectifying Unhealthy Trends" (ORUT) established in 1990. "Unhealthy trends" is defined by the ORUT as widespread and frequently occurring inappropriate administrative or service conducts performed by government agencies and public service work-units and their employees. These conducts, referred to as "passive corruptions," infringe the legal and appropriate interests and rights of citizens, legal persons, and social groups. According to the website of the ORUT, rectifying unhealthy trends in medical services is one of its major tasks.[2]

The ORUT is a government unit of ministerial rank and is directly responsible for the State Council, but it is staffed by officials from and is physically located in the Ministry of Supervision (MOS) (State Council 1990). The MOS, re-established in 1986, supervises and disciplines the conducts of public servants, and is responsible for the investigation of corruptions (Bezlova 2007). In 2007, the Minister of Supervision was appointed as the Director of the ORUT,[3] indicating that the latter was a ministerial unit and parallel to the MOS administratively. Although structurally it is a division of the Ministry, headed by the Minister and reporting directly to the State Council, the ORUT gains extra power and resources that other divisions in the Ministry do not have. The ORUT is set up to regulate and discipline the behaviors of ordinary public employees in various sectors and occupations, such as healthcare, education, public security, and transport, as well as serious issues, such as pollution and environmental protection. But the administration of these sectors and/or occupations is usually the jurisdiction of other ministries, such as the Ministry of Health, the Ministry of Education, the Ministry of Public Security, and the Ministry of Transport. Under the direct administration of the State Council, the ORUT can exercise power embedded with the authority of the State Council. When it comes to setting up tasks for rectifying corrupt or unhealthy conducts in a sector or an occupation, the involved ministries would not feel that they are ordered around by another ministry.

These government agencies, however, are not independent, but under the leadership and supervision of the CCP. In the Party-state, the government and the Communist Party are so intertwined that it is impossible to separate the Government from the Party, but the CCP always dominates and controls the government. Anti-corruption and unhealthy trends have been deemed as instrumental in protecting the legitimacy of the government as well as the CCP. As a result, the Central Commission of Discipline Inspection (CCDI) of the CCP Central Committee is charged with the responsibility to investigate corruption of the CCP members (Bezlova 2007). Since many doctors are Party members, the CCDI is thus involved in fighting "unhealthy trends" in healthcare. It is not only focused on the misconduct of public employees and civil servants with CCP membership, but is also heavily involved in the investigation of non-member employees and the formation of action plans for all the sectors and occupations. In 1993, CCDI joined office with the MOS, which means the functions and tasks of CCDI were performed through the MOS. In Chinese political terminology, this is called "the same set of men and horses with two signboards." But the MOS is under the leadership of the Secretary of CCDI. As in 2015, Wang Qishan, who is a member of the Standing Committee of the Political Bureau of the CCP, is the Secretary of CCDI, while Huang Shuxian, Minister of Supervision, serves as the second Deputy Secretary of CCDI. The arrangement indicates that the Minister of Supervision only ranks third in this administrative and power structure.[4]

All the three agencies—the CCDI, MOS, and ORUT—have branches in other ministries and provinces, cities, counties, and state-owned work-units, constituting a disciplinary and supervisory complex. These agencies supervise and investigate local officials and public employees and are responsible for the implementation of the anti-corruption plans and schemes formed by the headquarters. Within the MOH are the ministerial Commission of Discipline Inspection, the ministerial Department of Supervision, and the ministerial Office of Rectifying Unhealthy Trends. These establishments are either dispatched by their headquarters to station in the MOH or staffed by ministerial officials or employees. While the first two are established units within the administrative structure of the MOH, the latter is usually a task force, whose function and duties change in accordance with new anti-corruption tasks set by related authorities. Locally, each of the provincial, municipal, and county health administrative agencies has a discipline inspection unit dispatched from discipline inspection commissions of equivalent administrative levels. The head of the inspection unit stationed in these agencies also sits in the CCP committee as one of the vice-secretaries, a position that usually has more political power than that of an administrator at the same level. Some agencies are also equipped with supervision offices representing the authority of supervision. The discipline inspection unit and supervision office are combined into one office and staffed by the same officials (see, e.g., Zhejiang Health and Family Planning Commission 2015). The task force of rectifying unhealthy trends (RUT) is usually headed by the first responsible person of the administrative arm (not the CCP arm) of a work-unit (Ministry of Health 2010). In the MOH/ National Health and Family Planning Commission (NHFPC), the minister usually serves as the head of the leading group of rectifying unhealthy trends.[5] This complex of discipline-supervision-RUT is replicated in all provincial, municipal, and country health bureaus.

Major hospitals are also required to replicate the disciplinary-supervisory-RUT complex to investigate and discipline corrupt and informal economic activities of their staff. The commission of discipline inspection (CDI) is by rules headed by one of the vice-secretaries of the CCP leadership of the hospital, who may or may not be the director of the hospital's office of discipline inspection and supervision, an established unit in all major national and local hospitals. While some hospitals have relatively fixed ORUTs in their management structures, others have special task forces formed according to the requirements of specific campaigns launched by the central disciplinary complex, particularly the central ORUT. For example, the secretary of the CDI of the Guangdong People's Hospital, a major hospital in the province, is one of the vice CCP secretaries who sits on the hospital's administrative board and oversees the joint disciplinary-supervisory office.[6] The hospital has a resident Discipline Inspection and Supervision Office in its administrative structure and is led by a director under the supervision of the secretary of CDI. The hospital does not have an ORUT, but has organized several task forces to carry out campaigns targeting different malpractices and misconducts as required.[7] As we can see, the organizational structures governing misconducts in the healthcare system constitute a series of hierarchical complexes in which the CCP dominates at every administrative level from the central government down to the hospital. Such an institutional design ensures that policies made by the CCDI can be carried through to the end.

The MOH/NHFPC holds a ministerial meeting every year discussing anti-corruption and disciplinary issues and making policies and action plans. Since 2004 the meeting has been called the Working Meeting of Discipline Inspection, Supervision, and Rectifying Unhealthy Trends, and has been combined with the MOH's Annual Working Conference, which decides the work foci of the year. The decisions of the conference are then communicated to health administrations in provinces, cities, and counties, which in turn hold local conferences to "absorb" the decisions and formulate local action plans for its medical facilities to carry out. However, in the course of communicating ministerial instructions through local government agencies to work-units and in the process of implementing these instructions, the original intents can be compromised or bent or even changed to accommodate local interests.

Discipline and Supervision in the Eyes of Doctors

Front-line doctors are usually not clear about the complex structure of disciplinary and supervisory governance in the hospital, and are usually disdainful of disciplinary actions. The doctors that I interviewed noted a variety of disciplinary bodies within their hospitals but complained they were too complicated and beyond their understanding. Apparently, every respondent was aware that red packets were investigated by some unit in their hospitals, but most of them were not sure what exactly that disciplinary unit was and how it worked. They named a few, including CCP committee, the CDI, the Unit of Medical Affairs, or a special task force under the supervision of the CCP committee, which were not off mark. Some particularly complained about the work of the CDI, as indicated in the following conversations.

> LJL: The hospital has a special commission of discipline inspection.
> . . .
> ZYT: Yes, all our [hospitals] have.
> . . .
> LTQ: In my place, we have "rectifying unhealthy trend" posts.
> LJL: A small group of people are doing this specially.
> LTQ: I don't know what it is meant to be. They are a kind of posts . . . "rectifying unhealthy trends" posts. It is installed there . . . A desk is set up at every entrance, and a person sits there.
> ZYT: They are [working for] the Commission of Discipline Inspection.
> LWX: Those people live on doctors.
> LTQ: Of course . . .
> CXL: Because of the red packets, many new jobs have been created. Many new lazybones have to be fed.
> LXH: Commission in the hospital aside, let's talk about commissions of discipline inspection in other places first. What is a commission for? The commission just means wining and dining.

The cynicism was obvious in these comments. Respondents believed that the creation of a particular body within the hospital to discipline red packet takers was nothing more than granting power to a group of non-professionals to abuse. The comments on the commission of discipline inspection indicated that this anti-corruption device was itself corrupt in the eyes of doctors.

Investigation of Red Packets

The complex governance structure in a hospital carries out many functions. A major one is to investigate unhealthy trends, including red packets. Unhealthy trends are mostly investigated internally by resident disciplinary and supervisory complex. According to the doctors I interviewed, hospitals employed different measures to contain red packet transactions. For example, patients were warned at the point of admission to hospital not to give red packets to doctors. On being discharged from the hospital, they were requested to complete a survey about the quality of services, including whether they had given red packets to doctors. Such survey and inquiry were also arranged through telephone or correspondence. A respondent [YPP] disclosed that her hospital would send disciplinary staff to visit doctors' homes and check if there were signs that they had become rich quickly.

Documentary data indicate that encouraging patients to report their doctors taking red packets is a major investigation device. The MOH demands that hospitals install report boxes and set up grievance hotlines. Complaints must be processed by a specific unit or appointed staff (Ministry of Health 2004c). Surveys of outpatients, inpatients, and discharged patients must be administered regularly. A system of follow-up investigation must be established (Ministry of Health 2004b). Local health authorities also require hospitals to set up significant rewards for informers. For example, Jilin Provincial Health Department decrees that hospitals must reward informers up to 10,000 *yuan* for turning in the takers of red packets and drug kickbacks (Jilin Provincial Health Department 2005). Fujian Provincial Health Department requires hospitals to pay informers up to 50,000 *yuan* for reporting red packet and drug kickback takers (Fujian Provincial Health Department 2003). Some hospitals even have their own rewards for reporting. For instance, Shenyang Hospital of Orthopedics offers free surgery if patients report red packet takers (Ge 2006).

During the 2004 campaign which extended into 2005, hospitals were required to carry out internal investigation and self-rectification, and set up three-tier responsibility systems. The systems demands a series of responsibility contracts to rectify inappropriate conducts to be signed between the hospital and the community, the hospital and its units, and the unit and individual doctors (Ministry of Health 2004b). The internal investigation and self-rectification referred to the internal processes of investigating, educating, reporting, and disciplining without involving external government and CCP agencies. According to the working plan of Jianye Health Bureau, an administrative division of Nanjing, the capital city of Jiangsu Province, internal investigation and self-rectification included using internal inspection units to "observe publicly and investigate secretly" (*mingcha anfang*) every clinical unit and doctor (Jianye Health Bureau 2005). In other words, health authorities encouraged hospitals to "spy" on their doctors.

During major campaigns against unhealthy trends, external forces are also involved in the investigation. In fact, these were the major tactics used by the MOH and the CCDI in their blitz on hospitals in Beijing and Tianjin in the 2004 Campaign. A special task force composed of officials from both the MOH and the CCDI was formed to inspect hospitals in these cities. Quoted below was the inspecting methods described in a newspaper report,

> Yesterday [i.e., 22 November 2004] patients seeking medical services in Youyi Hospital would receive, in the lobby of the outpatient building, a questionnaire inquiring "whether doctors take red packets or overcharge," marking the beginning of the first ever nationwide campaign for rectifying unhealthy trends organized by the Ministry of Health and the Office of Rectifying Unhealthy Trends of the State Council. It is alleged that rectifying inspectors will search clues and traces of doctors taking red packets through organizing focus groups for patients and special public inspectors, circulating patient questionnaires, examining prescriptions and medical records, interviewing discharged patients, and so on... Inspectors can interview patients directly in wards and outpatient offices (Li and Zhao 2004).

As external investigation involves extra resources and duplicates the work of internal investigation mechanism, it is not often used. When used, it only serves for auxiliary and exemplary purpose. The majority of investigation is carried out by internal mechanisms.

The effectiveness of these mechanisms of investigation, however, is not commendable. In spite of the rewards and encouragement, however, patients do not seem particularly motivated to turn their doctors in. For example, for seven months after the enforcement of the rewards mentioned above, the Health Department of Fujian Province received 33 reports across the whole province. Among them, only two were evidenced and rewarded (Gao 2004a). The respondents of my research also confirmed patients' non-cooperation, and unanimously agreed that investigation of red packets was difficult and usually fruitless. Firstly, red packet transactions were under-the-table deals between patients and doctors. If patients did not report, it would be very hard for a third party to detect. Normally, patients would not report on their doctors as long as they were satisfied with the services. A respondent [LKB] commented,

[The management of] my hospital is willing to investigate, but can't find anything. Why? Our hospital … gives lots of questionnaires to every patient, but patients wouldn't say they have given [red packets]. Even if I [i.e., the patient] have, I wouldn't say I have taken. He [i.e., the patient] can't possibly admit having given.

Patients were even less likely to report red packets given through *guanxi.* "If it is given through friends, [patients] wouldn't want to lose the relationship for the sake of some money. Furthermore, as they [i.e., other respondents in the group] said, [patients] probably need to use [the doctors] in the future. So, for long-term purposes, [patients] wouldn't [report]" [ZZT].

The respondents noted that if doctors solicited red packets, and their performance did not live up to the expectations of the patients, or there was a medical accident, patients were likely to report their doctors taking red packets.

Secondly, as a respondent pointed out, even if patients reported, doctors could easily deny taking red packets for the secrecy of giving and taking [CCX]. This was confirmed by documentary sources.

As red packet transaction is a deal between two persons, it is difficult to investigate. Patients all complain about doctors taking red packets, but when you request them to provide evidence, 99 % of patients would not provide any information. When there is a medical dispute and the patient reports, the doctor would say, "Where is the evidence? The patient is framing me." Investigators can hardly collect evidence. (Li and Zhao 2004)

According to the same source, in early 2004, the Municipal CCP Committee of Beijing and Beijing Health Department employed public inspectors to carry out secret investigations in 17 hospitals, and interviewed 344 patients or their relatives privately. Among them, only seven, or 2.1 percent of them, reported giving red packets, the total amount of which was 6300 *yuan.*

The investigation in other cities encountered the same problem. For example, during the 2004 Campaign, *Xiandai kuaibao* (*Modern Express News*), a local newspaper of Nanjing, set up a hotline for readers to recount their experiences of giving and taking red packets (Li and Zhang 2004a). One complaint is illuminating,

> Mr Wu: My father had a heart operation in a hospital last year. Under the suggestion of my friends, I gave the doctor a 2000-*yuan* red packet. The outcome of the operation was just so-so. After [my father was] discharged from the hospital, I wrote two letters to the hospital's "good practice office" to report this doctor for taking [the] patient's red packet. But the letters were anonymous, and didn't tell when and how much. I was afraid that the doctor could guess it was I who complained. Since my father has to receive follow-up check-ups in the hospital every other month, how do I dare to offend these doctors? I know the "good practice office" could hardly carry out investigations in response to my letters. What I wanted to do was just to vent my anger.

Another reader seems stoic,

> Mr Zhu: I gave red packets before, and I thought about reporting. On second thoughts, what's the point? No matter what motivated me to give, I gave of my own accord. Doctors didn't snatch them from my pocket. How could you report red packets that you gave of your own accord? In addition, even if the hospital managers investigate and ask me to provide evidence, what evidence can I provide? The doctor who took the red packet could deny it all. When taking red packets, doctors didn't give me receipts or other evidence. So I say there is no point to report. Reporting is just giving vent to your anger, and is completely useless.

The same report stated that 99 percent of complaint letters received in some Nanjing hospitals were anonymous. So were the complaints made through the hotline. When the operator of the hotline asked complaining callers for their names, identities, and the names and work-units of the doctors that they reported to have taken red packets, over 90 percent of the callers refused to provide. The reasons the callers gave were all the same. Firstly, giving and taking red packets became a norm. Secondly, patients did not have evidence. Thirdly, they might have to see the same doctor in the future and could not afford offending them.[8]

Apparently, patients are not happy to give red packets, but in the meantime, they cannot and do not intend to report their doctors for taking them. As one respondent [LWX] noted, "If people don't report, the authority doesn't investigate." Consequently, despite the involvement of multi-government and CCP agencies, the multi-levels of the responsibility system, special task forces, and numerous harsh methods used for investigation, the effect is extremely limited. The complaining users of the public healthcare system that the government and the CCP undertake to protect are forced to ally themselves with doctors who "abuse" them. They know that a greedy doctor is better than no doctor.

Punishing Red Packet Takers

According to government documents and laws, the punishment for taking red packets is severe. The "Law of the People's Republic of China on Medical Practitioners" (1999) stipulates that it is illegal for doctors to exploit their positions to solicit or illegally receive goods from patients or obtain other inappropriate interests. Transgressors will inflict warning, suspension of practice from six to twelve months, revocation of their license, up to criminal charges as punishment, depending on how serious the transgression is. In 2004, the MOH demanded that medical work-units must discipline medical professionals against taking red packets and drug kickbacks and other inappropriate conducts. Punishments included open criticism, ineligibility for good performance and promotion of that year, suspension of post or employment, up to dismissal.

On the basis of the instructions of the central government, local health authorities formulated specific rules of punishment. For example, the Shanghai Municipal Health Department decreed that health professionals taking red packets and/or drug kickbacks with a monetary value of less than 1000 *yuan* would receive a warning. The transgressor would be suspended from practicing for six up to twelve months for taking red packets and kickbacks of 1000 to 5000 *yuan*. If the value of red packets and/or kickbacks exceeded 5000 *yuan*, or the doctor was caught for taking red packets and/or kickbacks more than twice, or the act had a serious consequence, the health professional would have his or her license rescinded (Shanghai Municipal Health Department 2004). In Nanjing, the punishment was more severe. The Nanjing Municipal Health Bureau decreed in 2004 that any doctor who was caught for taking one red packet would be suspended from work, and would have his or her practicing license revoked if they were caught for taking red packets twice (Li and Zhang 2004b).

It is interesting to notice that middle persons are punished in some places. For example, the Xiacheng Health Bureau, an administrative district of Hangzhou in Zhejiang Province, decreed that workers of medical work-units who played as the middle-person in taking and delivering red packets and gifts to doctors, or pocket part of money and goods given to doctors, would be punished in accordance with the same rules for red packet takers (Xiacheng Health Bureau 2004).

With few givers willing to report their doctors, however, the punished are even fewer. As mentioned above, the disciplinary-supervisory complexes resident in hospitals are responsible for implementing policies and supervising staff in the hospital. But the work of the complexes is greatly compromised by their double-loyalty, or "dual leadership" (Gong 2008, p. 149; Guo 2014). On the one hand, a hospital disciplinary-supervisory complex is appointed by the local government and is responsible to the complex resident in the local health authority or that of the local government or both. On the other hand, a hospital complex is not an independent third-party unit, but part of the formal administrative structure of the hospital. Its positions are staffed by employees of the hospital. The director of the complex sits on the hospital's administrative board and the CCP committee, which means the director is at the same time responsible for the hospital management. His or her work is under the leadership of the hospital CCP committee. The disciplinary capacity of the complex is considerably limited by such an administrative structure. Moreover, the hospital disciplinary staff members are on the hospital payroll, and receive bonuses and other welfare entitlements from the hospital. That means their personal interests are bound to the economic performance of the hospital, and it is in their interest not to interfere with the hospital's efforts to pursue revenues and not to offend the major contributors to its coffer. This dilemma has posed difficulties for the hospital disciplinary complex to perform its duties. For example, senior surgeons are usually in high demand and thus have higher informal price tags than middle-rank and junior surgeons. They usually take more red packets than other surgeons, and at the same time contribute more to the hospital's revenue. Furthermore, senior surgeons are usually the responsible persons of their units and are involved in the management of the hospital (Chen 2002). Consequently, hospitals and their disciplinary complexes are unwilling or unable to investigate their senior medical professionals for taking red packets (Peng 2004).

The doctors I interviewed evidenced that hospitals were generally reluctant to punish their doctors for taking red packets, especially prominent surgeons. Hospitals relied on these doctors to attract patients. The more patients, the more revenue for the hospital. Some respondents reported that hospitals would cover up for prominent surgeons who took red packets. As a respondent [LWX] commented,

The most famous [doctors] in a hospital are usually the top red packet takers. They are never punished. Such as those famous osteologists in our [hospital], it is obvious they take red packets. Other doctors take one thousand [*yuan*]; they take three thousand, five thousand. The hospital treasures them. If something happens, the hospital settles it for them. It won't let them suffer ... because they are the signpost of the hospital. The hospital uses them to attract patients. How would the hospital let them suffer even the least? In fact, the more senior you [i.e., the doctor] are, the safer [you are]. The more [red packets doctors] can take, the safer they are.

Hospitals do punish red packet takers, especially when there is a campaign targeting red packets or unhealthy trends. According to the respondents, punishments included suspension of prescription right, delay of promotion or even demotion, working in supportive sections or medical records unit for some time, withholding bonus, and so on. The punished, however, were usually junior or middle-ranked doctors, and were usually troublemakers in the eyes of the hospital management. "They will be punished anyway. Punishing them for taking red packet is just an excuse" [LWX]. Another respondent [ZKY] noted,

Therefore, those who are caught for taking red packets in a hospital are usually scapegoats. There are many cases reported to the hospital management or the Party committee. For example, there are twenty. But only one or two are actually publicized. [The doctors] perhaps are punished for some other reasons than taking red packets. Taking red packets is just what is publicized ... They are scapegoats for the red packet issue ... For a real prominent surgeon, even if he takes red packets and is caught, the hospital will protect him ...

A respondent [GYC] indicated that even the government was not serious about punishing doctors for taking red packets,

If doctors had higher social status, and higher pay, and are caught for taking red packets, you could punish them severely, or revoke their licenses. [In that situation], I don't think doctors would feel it worthwhile to take the risk. But now [with low social status and low pay] if you catch one and revoke his license, who else can you find to work for you? At the end of day, [red packets] can't be rooted out. Everyone is taking them.

However, under extreme political pressure from higher-level party and government agencies, some health authorities and hospitals are impelled to take inappropriate measures to fight "corruption." The national anti-corruption theme of 2006 was anti-corruption in business. In the healthcare system, it translated into combating drug kickbacks and other misconducts in pharmaceutical purchase and sales (Ministry of Health and State Bureau of Traditional Medicine Administration 2006). In the self-inspection and self-rectification stage of the campaign, local health authorities set up bank accounts and urged doctors to send drug kickbacks, as well as red packets, to the accounts to avoid serious disciplinary actions. If they were caught in the external inspection stage for taking red packets and drug kickbacks without surrendering them to the anti-bribery account, they, as well as the hospital and its management, would face serious punishment. Under-standably, the amount of "bribes" sent to the accounts was used as an indicator of how seriously local health authorities and hospitals took the campaign and whether hospitals would be exempted from serious external inspection (Ministry of Health 2006). The administrators of a hospital in Chengdu, Sichuan Province, worried about the "achievement" of their anti-business corruption efforts, demanded that every doctor in the hospital must contribute to the anti-bribery account set up by the local health authority. Unit heads were ordered to contribute at least 500 *yuan* and ordinary doctors at least 300 *yuan* (Gao 2006). The doctors, although extremely unhappy and complaining to the media, had no choice but to abide by this command. A leading hospital in Zhenjiang, Jiangsu Province, was also alleged to have demanded that its doctors meet "red packet" quotas (Liu 2006).

It must be pointed out that in the entire network of governance, there is no role and position for any medical professional associations at any level. CMDA is completely excluded from the disciplinary-supervisory-RUT complex and is not involved in the disciplining of unhealthy trends in any way. Its voices representing its members are generally muffled and ignored. In 2004, the CMDA attempted to defend the act of doctors' taking red packets during the peak of anti-misconducts campaign, but its voice was completely drowned in the extensive criticisms of the profession in media and ignored by the authority, in spite of the fact that the voice was orga-nized by the president of the CMDA, who was former Vice Minister of Health (Yan 2004). Professional associations have been completely power-less and non-existent in the entirety of the disciplinary approach.

The disciplinary approach is exercised through extensive and complicated governance networks involving both CCP and governmental organs, dominated by the Party authority, but its effect is very limited. In comparison, the market approach seems more effective.

Market Approach

Apart from disciplinary measures, the government and hospitals also strived to find more productive solutions to the problem of red packets. As mentioned earlier, the state investment in healthcare and the healthcare system have been in decline and are considerably inadequate. In the meantime, the wage reforms in the healthcare system have failed to raise the official incomes of doctors. Low income has a significant demotivating effect on doctors' morale. The authorities are not unaware of this. For various reasons, including a superstitious belief in market and economic growth (Wang 2003), however, the government was convinced that market and competition, rather than increase in investment, is the right way to motivate doctors and improve the quality of services and efficiency. The market principles that the government has followed to improve the efficiency of healthcare and the performance of medical professionals are to give more power to users of medical services and to introduce competition into public hospitals by linking doctors' incomes to their performance. Two policies have been particularly adopted to increase the power of users, to stimulate competition among doctors, and to contain inappropriate conducts. One is to let patients to choose their doctors for "free," and the other is to allow patients to choose their surgeons by paying extra fees.

"Patients Choose Doctors" and Internal Competition

Previously, patients did not have the right to choose the doctors. They paid a small registration fee to get a number to see a doctor in a particular unit in a hospital, but they did not know who would see them until their numbers were called. The "patients choose doctors" (*bingren xuan yisheng*) scheme, initiated by the MOH in 2000, was promoted in the public healthcare system to give patients more power over doctors and to compel doctors to compete with each other for the patronage of patients. As the MOH (Ministry of Health and State Bureau of Traditional Medicine Administration 2000) stipulated,

> "Patients choose doctors" is to grant patients full choosing rights over medical services. It is a major reform of the doctor-patient relationship. The

implementation of "patients choose doctors" should stimulate fair and orderly competition in every sector and on every post, improve attitudes, and increase medical service quality, skills and efficiency.

What is emphasized here is the market-style competition between doctors within the hospital. To facilitate patients' selection of doctors, hospitals are required to publicize doctors' photos, professional titles, specialties, and other information. Outpatient units are required to be staffed by doctors of middle and higher ranks in order to increase the rate of first-time accuracy of diagnosis. In inpatient units, doctors of various ranks are organized to form medical teams for patients to choose from (Ministry of Health and State Bureau of Traditional Medicine Administration 2000).

In fact, patients had had some choosing power before 2000 under other schemes, such as "special need consultation" (*texu menzhen*) or "specialist consultation" (*zhuanjia menzhen*). The difference lies in that patients have to pay extra fees. Additionally, the "patients choose doctors" scheme is more inclusive through involving doctors of middle rank, while the other two schemes are only open to senior doctors. More importantly, the "patients choose doctors" scheme is supposed to be universal, which means patients are given power to make selections and decisions in almost every aspects of their treatment.

The impact of this scheme on doctors is supposed to be that their performance decides their incomes. The more patients choose them, the more income they have. Therefore, doctors have to improve their service quality and attitudes to attract and keep more patients in order to earn more. The scheme seems reasonable and effective, as demonstrated in two hospitals—Chongqing Surgical Hospital and Tianjin No. 3 Central Hospital—which have been acclaimed as model hospitals in this regard.

Both hospitals implemented the scheme almost for the same reasons: lack of competition, which resulted in low efficiency, low morale, and tense doctor–patient relationships. Chongqing Surgical Hospital allowed patients to choose their doctors in 1993, the first hospital which did so. The management of the hospital abandoned the egalitarian "big rice bowl" and remunerated each doctor or surgical team according to their workloads, integrity, and degrees of patient satisfaction. More work, more pay; better work, better pay. Doctors were no longer paid in light of their professional ranks. A senior doctor could be employed as a senior doctor but paid at the rates for middle-rank or even junior doctors, while a middle-rank or junior doctor could be paid at the rates for higher-rank doctors. The difference was decided by their performance. Doctors were therefore pressured into competing with each other for patients by improving their skills, service quality, and attitudes (Zhao 2001).

Tianjin No. 3 Central Hospital enacted similar policies in 1998 and went even further. Up to 2000, 21 doctors were laid off because of low selection rate by patients; 93 doctors were transferred to other posts (most possibly non-medical). The competition between doctors differentiated their incomes dramatically. It was reported that for doctors of the same ranks in the same unit, the highest income could be seven times the lowest (Han 2000). A patient was reported to comment on the change of services and attitudes as follows,

> Previously everyone paid the same for outpatient consultation, but those having *guanxi* all ended up in the offices of experts. We commoners had to settle with any doctors we happened to encounter. There was no room for choice. It's very unfair. Now patients can choose doctors. I feel balanced. Since everyone pays the same, everyone should get the same. And in the inpatient section, once you choose your responsible doctor, you don't have to worry about following and begging the doctor. On the contrary, doctors will come to visit you often. We don't have to worry about being left out in the cold. Now I feel that it is not the patient who pleases the doctor, but the doctor seemingly "pleases" the patient (Han 2000).

With all the seeming benefits, there was little wonder that the MOH reaffirmed seven years later that "patients choose doctors" was the direction of reform. Wang Longde, Vice Minister of Health, is reported to have asked these rhetorical questions in a health conference, "What do we demand patients to follow our arrangements for? Why do patients have to accept whatever ward doctors they meet by chance when hospitalized?" (Guo 2007). The comment indicated the belief of the top health officials that as long as empowered patients dominated the doctor–patient relationship and doctors competed with each other for the patronage of patients, the quality of medical services and doctors' attitudes toward patients would naturally improve.

Many doctors I interviewed reported that this scheme had been implemented in their hospitals and seem to have produced positive results. Respondents reported two mechanisms that were adopted in their hospital to stimulate internal competition. One was bed allocation schemes, and the other was evaluation of patients' satisfaction. Both were associated with doctors' incomes.

The respondents noted that there were two ways of allocating hospital beds to doctors. One scheme was to assign a fixed number of beds to each doctor and to link doctors' floating wages to the turnover rate of beds. As one respondent [WXX] remarked,

> For nowadays, a doctor has only two beds. Then to make more profit, I have to treat more patients, and do more operations. I need to do my best to increase the turnover rate of patients. [Therefore], I do surgery well so that patients can be discharged sooner. And I can admit new patients.

The same respondent commented in another context that the services and attitudes of doctors in her hospitals had been improved tremendously. "Before I dress patients down, but now I wouldn't dare."

The other scheme was to pool all beds. Competing with each other for the use of these beds, doctors were pressed to provide quality services to attract patients and occupy as many beds as they can. One respondent [CXL] noted,

> We don't divide beds now. Previously, after you were promoted to Associate Chief Doctor, you could lead a team and were given a certain number of beds. Now beds are not allocated [to staff]. Patients come to you and stay on the beds [of your responsibility] all the time. You can have twenty beds, or even half of the beds of the unit. If no patient comes to you, you don't have a single bed.

A hybrid scheme was to allocate a fixed number of beds to each doctor, but a doctor who had more patients than his or her beds could accommodate was given access to his or her colleagues' beds, providing they were not occupied [LXH].

A respondent [WWH] reported that the allocation of beds in her hospital is more rigid. Other doctors did not have access to the beds under their colleagues' responsibility, even though they were not occupied. But the "patients choose doctors" scheme did create pressure on those doctors with less satisfactory performance. Doctors trusted by patients had long waiting lists for their beds, while their colleagues might have unoccupied beds for a lengthy period.

Such competition has differentiated the incomes among doctors and has caused tension. A respondent noted that in her hospital some doctors had operations every day, while others did not have a single operation in a month and their incomes suffered as a substantial portion of their wages was linked to the number of patients they treat. The competition apparently strained the collegial relationship, as these respondents commented,

> LTQ: Some hospitals fix the number of beds [for each doctors], and some hospitals don't. In some units of some hospitals ... if all patients choose you, you can use all the beds. If other [doctors] are unable to admit any patients, they have no work to do.
> CXL: Now you are under great pressure. After teams being formed, if no one asks you to do operations, then doctors under your leadership have no operations to do. Doctors under your leadership give you big pressure. "I joined in your team, and I don't have a single operation to do." The responsible doctors are anxious, and doctors under them are anxious, too.
> CXL: You're in a team ... If patients come to me to do operations, then my team has a lot of bonuses to redistribute. But his team has no operations all day, and then it has no bonus to pay. So nowadays the doctor is under great pressure.

Performance wages (usually in the form of bonuses) are also linked to patients' satisfaction rates. Some respondents reported that patients were requested on discharge of hospitals to complete a survey to rate their satisfaction anonymously. Doctors received their bonuses in proportion to satisfaction rate.

> If you have low satisfaction rate, that means patients will not come back to your unit ... The beds [assigned to you] are directly linked to your bonus. Without patients, where do you earn money? So nowadays, doctors are very polite to patients [LXH].

"Patients choose doctors" policy, however, is not universally accepted. Some respondents reported that it was strongly resisted in their hospitals. A respondent [HDS] from Beijing said that in his hospital outpatients could choose doctors, but inpatients were assigned to each doctor by nurses. Documentary data seems depicting an even gloomier situation. In spite of Wang Longde's alacrity, hospitals do not seem as enthusiastic. According to media reports, many hospitals have phased it out. For example, it is reported that all major hospitals of Nanjing embarked on the program in 2001, but six years later, only two were still running it (Zhou and Chen 2007). The reasons are manifold, but market failure is central to the poor outcomes of the scheme.

Stiglitz (2000) notes two fundamental market failures in the healthcare sector: one is imperfect information, and the other limited competition. They have a causal relationship. Central to the identity and qualification of the medical profession is a body of abstract and complex knowledge which doctors acquire through prolonged training. Patients do not have that expertise. The asymmetry of information indicates that patients simply cannot assess and evaluate doctors' advice and "must rely on the doctor' judgment as to what medicine is required or whether an operation or other procedure is advisable" (Stiglitz 2000, p. 309). The imperfection of knowledge limits patients' choosing power and reduces "the effective degree of competition" (Stiglitz 2000, p. 309).

Chinese patients also face the constraint of imperfect information. As a result, the choosing power promised by the "patients choose doctors" policy is very limited. For one thing, the Chinese healthcare system does not have general practitioners as gatekeepers. Patients have to make self-diagnosis first and then decide which medical specialties they need to go to for further diagnosis and services. Although in many cases self-diagnosis may bring patients to the right doctors, in more circumstances it may not. In the hospitals, patients have to decide which specialty they have to go to and choose doctors from the unit of that specialty from the very beginning. If the self-diagnosis is not accurate, their selections may land them in the wrong hands. Even if they make the correct self-diagnosis and come to the right unit, many patients cannot exercise their choosing power properly by merely looking at the photos of doctors and reading their brief biographies put up on the wall. For many patients, the choosing power is redundant. It was reported that some patients even complained why they had to make the choice (Gao and Yang 2003), while some others tended to choose the good looking ones (Zhu 2002; Zhang 2000).

Moreover, limited by imperfect information, patients do not have the knowledge to make sound judgment of the technical core of medical services. The easiest way for them to judge quality is by the professional ranks of doctors. As a result, for the same amount of consultation and service fees, most patients choose doctors of senior ranks (Zhou and Chen 2007; Xiong 2000). They even consult senior specialists for minor conditions, such as a common cold or fever (Zhang and Xu 2007). This puts great pressure on senior doctors and in turn gives them more power over patients.

To guarantee quality, as requested by the "patients choose doctors" scheme, they have to spend longer times with patients to ensure the accuracy of diagnosis. That means they may have to see fewer patients every day. This in turn pushes up the demand for their services and creates a long waiting list. To jump the queue, patients still have to give red packets and/or use *guanxi* to get their consultation and operations earlier. Otherwise, patients have to settle for less prominent doctors or whatever doctors are available.

While the benefits of the internal competition scheme to patients are largely limited, its adversary impact on career development and incomes of doctors and damage to the collegial atmosphere between them constitute a grave concern for hospital managers. The "patients choose doctors" scheme empowers the former in such a way as that their demand must be met unconditionally and without delay. The workload of senior doctors thus increases drastically due to high selection rates, leading to work fatigue, drop of quality, and inadequate time for professional development (Zhu 2002; Yuan et al. 2003). In the meantime, the workload of lower rank doctors reduces considerably in some hospitals, which is detrimental to their career development, as the advancement of their medical skills is hindered by lacking in practice (Yuan et al. 2003; Li 2000). Lack of patients can have significant adversary impact on the incomes of middle-rank and junior doctors as doctors' floating wages are linked to their selection rates by patients (Gao and Yang 2003). What the hospital management is more concerned than the inequality in incomes is the damage to the collegial atmosphere and solidarity within the organization. In many hospitals, some nurses are appointed as patient advisors, channeling patients to appropriate departments and doctors. There have been reports that doctors complained against these nurses for not recommending enough patients to them (Gao and Yang 2003). As colleagues become rivals, cooperation among them becomes rare as they fear that their patients are "lured" by their colleagues (Gao and Yang 2003; Li 2001).

Apparently, the "patients choose doctors" scheme has not helped stamp out red packets. This may explain why the "patients choose doctors" scheme was implemented in 29 provinces and major cities in 2000, while in 2004 the MOH still had to launch a major campaign targeting red packets. For hospital management, the scheme caused more troubles than solving them. In the mid-2000's, the scheme was largely abandoned by hospitals, although a few, such as the Tianjin No. 3 Central Hospital, continued to operate it (Anonymous 2009).

"Operation by Nomination"

While "patients choose doctors" gives patients choosing power without extra charges, "operation by nomination" (*dianming shoushu*) allows patients to buy choosing power with extra payments. Unlike the former, which placed emphasis on equal access to quality medical services through competition among doctors, "operation by nomination" was intended to differentiate patients, offering better, preferential services to the well-off. In many ways, it has been considered as a major initiative to "formalize" informal payments and a "policy exit" for the otherwise institutionally besieged hospitals that faced drastically decreased government finance but little leeway in pricing their own services (Yuan 1995; Wang 2006b; Yan 2006; Guo 2008; Ding 2003).

The "operation by nomination" scheme emerged in the late 1980s as part of special medical services encouraged by a MOH decree, which permitted hospitals organizing higher quality but expensive special medical services to meet the elevated needs and demands of well-off patients (Ministry of Health 1989; Chen and Wang 2010). This intent was reinforced by a 1992 decree which further liberalized the pricing for special medical services (Ministry of Health 1992; Chen and Wang 2010). Special services became a major source of revenues for hospitals to make up the loss derived from providing basic services (Xu and Gu 2010; Zeng et al. 2014). But throughout the 1990s, the "operation by nomination" scheme was not properly regulated, leading to the widely abuse of the scheme (Yin 1993).

The first major step toward regulating "operation by nomination" was initiated by the Beijing Municipal Commission of Development and Reform and Beijing Health Department, which formally included "operation by nomination" fee schedule in the "unified medical service fee standards" handbook in 2001 (Li 2006). As in other schemes of specially needed services, such as specially needed outpatient consultation and specialist outpatient consultation, only senior surgeons (i.e., Associate Chief Doctor and above) were qualified to participate in this scheme. The nomination fees were redistributed between the hospital, chief surgeons, anesthetists, assistants, and nurses. Before it was abolished in 2006, nomination fees were charged at the rate of 50 percent of the basic cost of an operation and capped at 800 *yuan*. These special services were limited to 30 percent of the annual amount of surgeries of a hospital and should be limited to the most complicated surgeries (Beijing Price Bureau and Beijing Municipal Health Department 2001).

In spite of the government's attempt to formalize red packets and to give hospitals a policy window to increase revenues (Meng and Liu 2004), the scheme was problematic. The majority of the respondents I interviewed claimed that the scheme had never gained popularity among surgeons, because surgeons had to pay tax for "nomination fees" and they had to share with the hospital, other members of the surgical team, including nurses. The comments of two respondents from Group 1 were particularly revealing.

> LKB: In the past they [i.e., his hospital] experimented with it, but it was hard to set up [fee] standards for different doctors.
> . . .
> LKB: Firstly, it is detrimental to internal solidarity. Secondly, patients don't know whether Doctor Zhang is better or Doctor Wang is better. They can only judge doctors by the level of fees. If that doctor costs one thousand *yuan*, they won't have a doctor of two hundred *yuan* to do operation. So, it's hard; unfair distribution . . .
> LWX: And in fact . . . in comparison, chief operators get less, but in reality, they do most of the work, and take the biggest risk. At the end of the day, even nurses of the operating theater have a share in the money.
> LKB: This is egalitarianism.
> LWX: Yes. But within the group, everyone, including anesthetists and so on, has a share. In fact, except for nurses who benefit, doctors are not happy. For example, previously, anesthetists have their money [i.e., red packets], and chief operators have their money. Now everyone has a share. Not only the hospital takes away a part of it, nurses also have a share. So no one [i.e., the doctor] is keen. Eventually, it was dropped, was left as that. It was left as that in our hospital.
> LKB: We tried for three months, and then dropped it.

Furthermore, as only senior surgeons were qualified for the scheme, patients tended to pay for senior doctors to do even the least complicated surgery. Consequently, junior and middle-rank doctors were deprived of opportunities to do surgery. Since the number of surgeries a surgeon performed decided his or her floating wages, this practice then had a significant impact on the incomes of lower rank surgeons and created tension.

The Beijing Health Department claimed that in spite of the benefits of the scheme, its disadvantages were greater. Firstly, hospitals had administered surgeries by categories and degrees of complexity, and allocated them to surgeons of relevant ranks accordingly. Under the "operation by nomination" scheme, specialists, professors, and chief doctors were nominated to do all kinds of operations, regardless of the degrees of complexity, in order to meet the requirements of patients. As a result, they did not have time to do ward visit, to discuss complicated and critical cases, and to train junior doctors. Meanwhile, junior and middle-rank surgeons were deprived of opportunities of performing surgeries, which were detrimental to their professional development and incomes. Secondly, the scheme differentiated the incomes between surgical units and non-surgical units, and had adverse impact on the job selections of medical personnel. Thirdly, it increased economic burdens on patients (Beijing Municipal Health Department 2006). The policy also encouraged patients from outside Beijing to seek medical services in Beijing, for they could nominate their surgeon without having *guanxi* first. These patients burdened Beijing's healthcare system and prolonged the waiting lists of senior surgeons (Li 2006). But what was not mentioned by health authorities and official media was the political controversy of the scheme. Unlike the "patients choose doctors" which demanded doctors to serve patients better and equally, the "operation by nomination" scheme encouraged hospitals to differentiate patients and treat them unequally, which was entirely contradictory to the ideology of "serving the people." This may explain why the central health authority continued to promote the "patients choose doctors" scheme while the Beijing Municipal Government took the initiative to abolish the "operation by nomination" scheme in March 2006 (Beijing Municipal Commission of Development and Reform and Beijing Municipal Health Department 2006).

It is interesting to notice that the "operation by nomination" scheme, in an attempt to formalize informal payments, failed to root out red packets. It is said that even if patients paid formal nomination fees to desired surgeons and their teams, they still had to pay extra money informally to chief operators and anesthetists (Wang 2006a; Li 2006). There are two possible reasons for this. Firstly, the nomination fees were capped. The maximum amount of nomination fee that an operation can be charged was only 800 *yuan*, and it had to be shared between the members of a surgical team, as well as the hospital and the unit. The hospital usually took 50 percent, and another 25 percent went to the unit. The rest was shared in the team (Li 2006). Chief operators thus did not feel particularly motivated, as the scheme did not seemingly make significant changes to the incomes of surgeons (Wang 2006b). Secondly, the nomination fee was formally charged by the hospital. Although part of the fee went to the pocket of the surgeon, it was regarded by the patient as a bureaucratic arrangement and thus did not serve the purpose of motivating doctors privately. Giving red packets was intended to personalize the doctor–patient relationship. As discussed before, the public had a customary distrust of the bureaucratic system and its employees and believed that only personalized relationships could obligate them. This mentality compelled savvy patients to continue to give red packets even if they had paid extra fees for the special services. Consequently, despite nomination fees, red packets had never disappeared (Yuan 1995; Zhang 2006; Yang and Ding 2006).

But the policy had merits. It did give patients the power to choose eminent doctors who were otherwise unavailable if patients did not have *guanxi*. A survey shows that 40 percent of patients opposed the abolition of nomination fees. They had two concerns. Firstly, although the scheme failed to root out the red packet, it at least formalized part of it. With the abolition of the scheme, patients feared nomination fees would just turn back into red packets under the table again. Secondly, and more importantly, patients felt that they lost their choosing power. This might have a greater impact on non-Beijing patients who usually did not have any *guanxi* to help them obtain the services of eminent doctors in Beijing, even with cash in hand (Fang and Wang 2006; Fang and Guo 2006; Li 2006; Wang 2006b).

As with the "patients choose doctors" scheme, the "operation by nomination" gave patients more choosing power only to reinforce the professional power and market position of high-ranking and renowned surgeons. These reforms unintentionally increased demand for their services and tensed the relationship between them and their colleagues of middle and junior ranks. But its effect on red packets is very limited.

Discipline and market are the major approaches that have been employed by the government and hospitals to address the issue of red packets. They are the offspring of institutional persistence and institutional changes respectively. The former is attributable to authoritarianism and the CCP's insistence on its leadership, while the latter is the corollary of an emergent institution—market. However, as indicated above, both approaches have failed to contain informal payments.

The failure of the disciplinary approach lies in its structural flaw and doctor–patient collusion. The disciplining of red packets is carried out through a sophisticated administrative complex dominated by the CCP organs with government agencies playing a secondary and supportive role, without any input from the CMDA—the utmost "representative" of the medical professions. The complex exists at every level of healthcare governance and exercises its most direct disciplinary power in hospitals. Due to flaws in institutional design, the power and efficiency of the complex are compromized by dual leadership and conflict of interests. On the one hand, the disciplinary unit of a hospital is subject to the leadership of the CCP committee of that hospital and cannot play an independent disciplinary and supervisory role within the work-unit. On the other hand, the incomes and welfare of the disciplinary and supervisory officials and staff of a hospital are bound to its economic well-being. As a result, the disciplinary and supervisory complex has neither the power nor the incentive to discipline informal payments within the hospital.

The administration of the public hospital is ambivalent toward red packets. The old role of public hospitals as functionaries of the Party-state remains. They are required to execute the Party-state orders in the work-unit, and support the disciplinary complex to control misconducts and malpractices. However, with the decreasing state budget and increasing economic and administrative autonomy, the management of hospitals has gained more and more independence from the state and more control over internal affairs. The economic interest of the hospital becomes the prime goal of the management. To protect their interests, hospitals tend to defy the government's disciplinary efforts and protect patient-attracting senior doctors from being investigated and punished for taking red packets. The dependent disciplinary complex is generally powerless in preventing the management of the hospital from doing so.

To make things worse, even patients, who are the victims of informal payments, do not willingly cooperate with the health authority in combating red packets. A major feature of the disciplinary approach is to grant patients political and legal power to report their doctors for taking red packets. Patients are reassured of their rights to services that are conferred by the health ideology of "serving the people." But the vast majority of patients choose, willingly or unwillingly, to relinquish this power and continue to subject themselves to the power of doctors, even if they are extremely unhappy about giving red packets.

The market approach seems to have produced a more positive effect on controlling red packets than the disciplinary approach, but its outlook is not optimistic. The major thrust of this approach is to empower patients. While "patients choose doctors" works on the ideology of "serving the people" with a market twist, "operation by nomination" allows patients to buy extra power with formal additional payments. Both schemes associate doctors' incomes with the quality of their performance. Previously doctors relied solely on the work-unit for livelihood and welfare benefits. Now they are economically dependent on patients to a substantial degree. Doctors are thus compelled to improve their responsiveness, attitudes, and quality of services to win over patients. The rising patient's power has put pressure on doctors and increased the latter's accountability. As a result, the medical profession seemingly no longer dominates the doctor–patient relationship. Patients are gaining power over doctors.

The change in the power relationship, however, is not all good news for patients. Due to market failures, patients tend to use their newly gained choosing power irrationally, and easily surrender their choosing power to senior doctors, especially senior surgeons. Senior doctors are consequently in high demand. The medical profession is polarized. At the upper end of the power spectrum are the prominent doctors of some specialties who continue to exert dominating power in their relationship with patients. At the lower end are the junior and middle-rank doctors and doctors of other specialties and of lower level hospitals who are losing power to patients. In general, patients continue to stand in awe of the professional power of doctors and in most of the time would not dare to challenge it even if they are not happy about having to give red packets. On the contrary, to compete with each other for the temporal, physical, and mental resources of senior and prominent doctors and their preferential services, patients still have to give red packets. The only difference may be that with the choosing right and increased buying power on the part of patients, red packets now concentrate more in senior doctors than before. The polarized incomes created great tension between senior doctors of lucrative specialties and doctors of other specialties and/or of other ranks. The tension is poisonous to the collegiality and solidarity in hospitals. As the findings indicate, both the "patients choose doctors" and "operation by nomination" schemes are abandoned either by hospitals or by the government for the reason that they seem to have brought more harm than benefits to the healthcare system, patients, medical work-units, and the profession.

Up to date, all the anti-red packet efforts seem to have entered a vicious circle. Patients are empowered by the Party-state to protect their interests, but they readily succumb to the monopolistic and professional power of doctors and hence strengthen the position of the latter. Although the majority of patients are apparently not willing to give red packets, they nonetheless give and do not report their doctors. They virtually collude with doctors in red packet transactions, which subvert the state's attempt to protect their interests. The collusion forces hospitals to tolerate doctors taking red packets and undertake particular efforts to protect eminent doctors from the Party-state's disciplinary power in order to protect the economic interests of the work-units. Consequently, in terms of the control of red packets, the Party-state is rendered "powerless" in its relationship with the medical profession.

NOTES

1. http://cpc.people.com.cn/n/2013/0904/c75234-22804679.html, accessed 11 November 2015.
2. http://www.mos.gov.cn, accessed 15 November 2015.
3. http://www.gov.cn/xxgk/pub/govpublic/mrlm/200803/t20080328_32222.html, accessed 12 November 2015.
4. http://www.ccdi.gov.cn/xxgk/ldjg/, accessed 12 November 2015. Since 2012, the administrative rank of ORUT has been reduced to a Bureau rank (*ju ji*) unit within the MOS and the Minister no longer concurrently holds the position of the Director of ORUT.
5. Between 2009 and 2012, Chen Zhu, the Ministry of Health, served this post.
6. See http://www.e5413.com/Framework/NewsList.aspx?did=2&bid=7&sid=11&nva=1&minnva=3, accessed 21 October 2012; http://www.gdghospital.org.cn/NewsMessage-5613.aspx, accessed 15 November 2015. In 2015, many hospitals removed information on CDI and the disciplinary and supervisory office and did not replace with new information, perhaps due to the uncertainty which resulted from the unprecedented anti-corruption campaigns and reforms to the disciplinary and supervisory governance structure launched by incumbent President Xi Jingping and Wang Qishan, Secretary of CCDI.
7. See http://www.e5413.com/Framework/NewsList.aspx?did=2&bid=246&sid=248&nva=3&minnva=0, accessed 21 October 2012.
8. See also (Zhang 2004).

BIBLIOGRAPHY

Anonymous. 2009. "Bingren xuan yisheng" zhiji gaishan yi huan guanxi (The system of "patients choose doctors" improves doctor-patient relationship). *Zhongguo jingji shibao (Chinese Economic Times)*, 9 April, 4.

Beijing Municipal Commission of Development and Reform, and Beijing Municipal Health Department. 2006. Guanyu jinyibu guifan he quxiao bufen yiliao fuwu xiangmu shoufei de tongzhi (Circular about further strengthening the regulation and cancellation of the rates for some medical service categories). Accessed 1 December 2015. http://www.bjpc.gov.cn/tztg/200602/t111328.htm.

Beijing Municipal Health Department. 2006. Ren ren xiangyou jiankang tingli (Everyone deserves healthy hearing). Accessed 2 June 2016. http://www.bjhb. gov.cn/gzfwq/zhfw/wsaqts/200603/t20060306_3614.htm.

Beijing Price Bureau, and Beijing Municipal Health Department. 2001. Guanyu guifan feiyingli yiliao jigou texue yiliao fuwu xiangmu he shoufei biaozhun de tongzhi (Circular on the standardization of the categories and rates of specially needed medical services in non-profit medical organizations). Accessed 1 December 2015. http://law.lawtime.cn/d434230439324.html.

Bezlova, Antoaneta. 2007. China: Bureau of Corruption Prevention lacks teeth. In *Global Information Network*. New York: Global Information Network.

Chen, Fangfang, and Hongman Wang. 2010. Wo guo texue yiliao fuwu de lishi guiguo (A historical reflection on our country's special medical services). *Zhongguo yiyuan guanli (Chinese Hospital Management)* 30(10): 33–35.

Chen, Jianlin. 2002. Dui yiyuan "hongbao" xianxiang de sikao yu zhanwang (A consideration and anticipation of the "red packet" in the hospital). *Zhonghua yiyao huicui zazhi (Journal of Chinese Medical Essence)* 1(4):58–59, & 96.

Chen, Xie. 2006. Fansi 'hongbao' xianxiang de cunzai jichu ji duice (Reflection on the foundation of 'red packet' phenomenon and policies dealing with it). *Zhongguo yixue lunlixue (Chinese Medical Ethics)* 19(1): 55–57.

Ding, Xinggang. 2003. Jiaqiang "dianming shoushu" de guanli (Strengthen the management of "operation by nomination"). *Zhongguo weisheng shiye guanli (Chinese Health Service Management)* 2: 81–82.

Fang, Fang, and Ying Guo. 2006. Jingcheng yiyuan quxiao 'diandao fei', da shoushu huanzhe hai xiang zhao zhuanjia (Beijing hospitals abolish 'nomination fees'; patients still want to nominate specialists for major operations). *Beijing yule xinbao (Beijing Entertainment News)*, 2 March. Accessed 6 February 2008. http://society.people.com.cn/GB/1063/4158348.html.

Fang, Fang, and Rongrong Wang. 2006. Yiyuan buxu zai shou 'diandao fei', huanzhe: quexiao le zenme zhao mingyi? (Hospitals are not allowed to charge 'nomination fees'; patients: how can them get eminent doctors?). *Beijing yule xinbao (Beijing Entertainment News)*, 24 February. Accessed 6 February 2008. http://society.people.com.cn/GB/41158/4139622.html.

Fujian Provincial Health Department. 2003. Jiangli jubao 'hongbao' 'huikou' yougong renyuan zanxing banfa (Provisional measures of awarding informers of 'red packet' and 'drug kickback' takers). Accessed 4 February 2008. http:// www.fjphb.gov.cn.

Gao, Hongmei, and Mingcai Yang. 2003. Qianlun zonghexing yiyuan shishi "bingren xuan yisheng" de li yu bi (The advantages and disadvantages of implementing "patients choose doctors" in comprehensive hospitals). *Zhongguo weisheng shiye guanli (Chinese Health Service Management)* 8: 470–471.

Gao, Jianjin. 2004a. Wei he 'zhongshang' zhi xia wu 'yongfu'? (Why big awards' failed to encourage 'informers'?). *Guangming ribao (Guangming Daily)*, 6 April. Accessed 24 February 2008. http://www.gmw.cn/content/2004-04/06/content_8848.htm.

Gao, Zhu. 2006. Chengdu jing you yiuan xiada shangjiao 'hongbao' zhibiao (A Chengdu hospital goes as far as to set quota for 'red packets' surrender). *Gongren ribao (Workers' Daily)*, 7 September, 1. Accessed 1 February 2008. http://www.grrb.com.cn/template/10002/file.jsp?cid=0&aid=265376.

Ge, Suhong. 2006. Shenyang yi jia yiyuan guiding huanzhe jubao yisheng shou hongbao shoushu mianfei (A hospital in Shenyang make a regulation that patients who report doctors taking red packets will receive free surgery). Xinhuanet.com, 15 February. Accessed 1 January 2008. http://society.people.com.cn/GB/41158/4108905.html.

Gong, Ting. 2008. The party discipline inspection in China: its evolving trajectory and embedded dilemmas. *Crime, Law and Social Change* 49(2): 139–152.

Guo, Yong. 2014. Zhongguo jijian jiancha paizhu zhidu yanjiu (A study of the system of dispatched discipline inspection and supervision in China). *Guojia Xingzheng Xueyuan xuebao (Journal of Chinese Academy of Governance)* 2: 112–116.

Guo, Yonggang. 2007. Weisheng bu Fu Buzhang Wang Longde: bingren xuan yisheng shi yiliao fuwu gaige de fangxiang (Vice Minister of Health Wang Longde: patients choose doctors is the direction of medical service reform). *Zhongguo qingnian bao (China Youth)*, 16 April, 7. Accessed 1 January 2008. http://zqb.cyol.com/content/2007-04/16/content_1734166.htm.

Guo, Youde. 2008. Wo guo yiliao weisheng gaige jianzhan yu zhanwang (The progress and outlook of our country's medical and health reform). *Zhongguo weisheng ziyuan (China Health Resources)* 11(4): 151–153.

Han, Lintao. 2000. Qinli 'bingren xuan yisheng' (Experiencing 'patients choose doctors'). *Jiankang shibao (Health Times)*, 7 September, 1. Accessed 13 November 2005. http://www.people.com.cn/GB/paper503/1391/220927.html.

Jianye Health Bureau. 2005. 2005 nian weisheng xitong hangfeng jianshe gongzuo jihua (2005 work plan for the construction of good practice in the health care system). Accessed 31 January 2008. http://www.njdj.gov.cn/jydj/Adx/mainarticle.jsp?article_id=62273.

Jilin Provincial Health Department. 2005. Guanyu jiangli jubao shou shou 'hongbao' 'huikou' yougong renyuan de zanxing banfa (Provisional measures about awarding informers of 'red packet' and 'drug kickback' takers). Accessed 4 February 2008. http://www.cc.jl.gov.cn/.

Kong, Guipiao. 2004. Dujue 'hongbao', shi gaishan yihuan guanxi de guanjian zhiyi (Eliminating 'red packet' is one of the keys to improve doctor-patient relationship). *Zhongguo xiandai linchuang yixue (Chinese Journal of Clinical Medicine)* 3(8): 92–93.

Law of the People's Republic of China on Medical Practitioners. 9th Congress, 3rd Session, 26 June 1999.

Li, Benfu. 2001. Bingren xuan yisheng de shishi yu tantao (Implementation and discussion of patients choose doctors). *Yixue yu zhexue (Medicine and Philosophy)* 22(3): 8–10.

Li, Chun, and Xing Zhang. 2004a. Hongbao: women shi zenme gei de (Red packets: how did we give them). *Xiandai kuaibao (Modern Express News)*, 16 April. Accessed 30 January 2008. http://news.xinhuanet.com/newscenter/2004-04/16/content_1422385.htm.

———. 2004b. Nanjing xiang yiliao waifeng kaidao, shou hongbao yici dai gang, liangci kaichu (Nanjing takes action against unhealthy trends in medicine: suspension from work for taking red packets once, and dismissed for taking twice). *Xiandai kuaibao (Modern Express News)*, 13 April. Accessed 30 January 2008. http://news.xinhuanet.com/newscenter/2004-04/13/content_1414987.htm.

Li, Chunhui. 2006. Beijing weihe jiaoting 'diandao fei', huanzhe fanchou (Why did Beijing call an end to "scalpel nomination fees"). *Renmin ribao (People's Daily)*, 20 April, 15.

Li, Gang, and Xinpei Zhao. 2004. Weisheng bu, Guowu yuan Jiufeng ban zuo qi yancha Jingcheng yiyuan hongbao (Ministry of Health and the Office of Rectifying Unhealthy Trends of the State Council started to meticulously investigate red packets in Beijing hospitals). *Beijing qingnian bao (Beijing Youth)*, 23 November, A3, A. Accessed 17 November 2013. http://news.xinhuanet.com/fortune/2004-11/23/content_2250541_1.htm.

Li, Weimin, and Xianfang Tong. 1995. Weisheng hangye 'hongbao' xianxiang de chansheng, weihai ji zhili duice (The emergence, hazards and rectification of 'red packets' in the healthcare system). *Lanzhou xuekan (Journal of Lanzhou)* 6: 43–44, & 62.

Li, Xiaofeng. 2000. "Bingren xuan yisheng": yi shou hao ting nan zou de qu ("Patients choose doctors": a melody that is good to hear but hard to play). *Beijing ribao (Beijing Daily)*, 22 November 10.

Liu, Jinsong. 2006. Yisheng jiao 'hongbao' bei xiada renwu zhibiao? (Doctors are given quotas for 'red packets' surrender?). *Xiandai kuaibao (Modern Express News)*, 24 October, A13. Accessed 1 February 2008. http://www.kuaibao.net/html/2006-10/24/content_49194068.htm.

Lu, Zhengrong. 2011. Qianxi 'kanbing song hongbao' ji zhili duice (A study of 'giving red packet for medical treatment' and policies dealing with it). *Zhongguo yiyao zhinan (Guide of Chinese Medicine)* 9(24): 360–362.

Meng, Zhaoli, and Yuanyuan Liu. 2004. Shoushu dianming fei shi hongbao de hefahua? Huanzhe dao di gai bu gai gei? (Surgical nomination fees are legalized red packets? Should patients give or not?). Accessed 19 December 2010. http://news.xinhuanet.com/newscenter/2004-12/19/content_2353580.htm.

Ministry of Health. 1989. Guanyu kuoda yiliao weisheng fuwu youguan wenti de yijian (Advice on issues related to the expansion of medical and health services). In *Chinese health year book 1990*, edited by Chinese Health Year Book Editorial Board, 51–53. Beijing: Remin Weisheng Chubanshe (People's Health Publishing House).

———. 1992. Guanyu shenhua weisheng gaige de jidian yijian (Several suggestions on deepening health reform). In *Chinese health year book 1993*, edited by Chinese Health Year Book Editorial Board. Beijing Renmin Weisheng Chubanshe (People's Health Publishing House).

———. 2004b. Guanyu zai quanguo yiliao jigou zhong kaizhan xiang shehui fuwu chengnuo huodong de shishi fangan (Implementing plan for carrying out activities of undertaking to provide [quality] services to the society). Accessed 1 February 2008. http://www.moh.gov.cn/newshtml/7822.htm.

———. 2004c. Quanguo wensheng xitong kaizhan jiuzheng yiliao fuwu zhong buzheng zhifeng zhuanxiang zhili shishi fang'an (Implementing plans of specific projects rectifying deviant practices in medical services in nation-wide health system). Accessed 2 December 2007. http://www.law-lib.com/law/law_view.asp?id=83318.

———. 2006. Li Xi zuzhang chuxi bufen sheng qu shi weisheng ting ju jijian zuzhang zuotanhui bing qiangdiao zhuyi chaban ju bu zi cha zi jiu anjian (Group Leader Li Xi attended the discussion meeting for group leaders of commissions of discipline inspection of some provincial, regional and municipal health authorities and drew attention to the investigation of cases of refusal to conduct self-inspection and self-rectification). Accessed 2 June 2015. http://www.medste.gd.cn/wsgl/ArticleShow.asp?ArticleID=244831.

———. 2010. Guanyu jinyibu jiaqiang he wanshan weisheng jiufeng gongzuo zerenzhi de yijian (Circular on further strengthening and improving the responsibility system of the work of rectifying unhealthy trends in health care). Accessed 14 November 2015. http://www.nhfpc.gov.cn/jcj/s7692/201007/74dd96644bec4c47bdb99289e6b6c33f.shtml.

Ministry of Health, and State Bureau of Traditional Medicine Administration. 2000. Guanyu shixing bingren xuanze yisheng cujin yiliao jigou neibu gaige de yijian (Advice on promoting 'patient chooses' doctor in order to advance internal reform of medical institutions). Accessed 17 November 2014. http://www.law-lib.com/law/law_view.asp?id=15429.

————. 2006. Guanyu kaizhan zhili yiyao gouxiao lingyu shangye huilu zhuanxiang gongzuo de shishi yijian (Implementing plans for special project combating business bribery in the purchase and sales of pharmaceuticals).

Peng, Yuzhu. 2004. "Yiliao hongbao" xianxiang de sikao yu zhili jianyi (Consideration and suggestions on governing "medical red packets"). *Jiangsu weisheng shiye guanli (Jiangsu healthcare administration)* 15(6): 110–112.

Shanghai Municipal Health Department. 2004. Guanyu benshi yiwu renyuan shou shou 'hongbao' 'huikou' wenti de chuli guanding (Penalties for medical personnel taking 'red packets' and 'drug kickbacks'). Accessed 31 January 2008. http://www.smhb.gov.cn/website/b/32056.shtml.

State Council. 1990. Guanyu sheli Guowuyuan jiuzheng hangye buzheng zhifeng bangongshi de gongzhi (Circular of the General Office of the State Council on the establishment of the State Council Office for Checking Unhealthy Tendencies in Business Activities). *Gazette of the State Council of the People's Republic of China* 28: 1053–1054.

Stiglitz, Joseph E. 2000. *Economics of the public sector*, 3rd edn. New York: W.W. Norton.

Wang, Hongxia. 2005a. Yiwu jie hongbao xianxiang de zhili duice (Measures against red packets in healthcare). *Zhongguo yixue lunlixue (Chinese Medical Ethics)* 18(3): 11–13.

Wang, Shaoguang. 2003. Zhongguo gonggong weisheng de weiji yu zhuanji (The crisis and hope of Chinese public health). *Bijiao (Comparison)* 7.

Wang, Shujun. 2006a. Beijing Shi ge yiyuan quxiao shoushu dianming fei: haoshi neng fou ban hao? (Beijing hospitals abolish surgical nomination fees: can a good thing be well done?). *Renmin ribao (People's Daily)*, 16 March, 5.

Wang, Sihai. 2006b. 'Shoushu dianming fei' bei jiaoting: dui huanzhe shi fu shi huo? ('Surgeon nomination fee' is put on halt: good or bad news to the patient?). Xinhuanet.com, 1 March. Accessed 9 March 2016. http://news.xinhuanet.com/focus/2006-03/01/content_4241894.htm.

Wang, Yankun. 1998. Dangqian yiyuan hongbao xianxiang de chengyin yu duice (The reasons and countermeasures against the current red packet phenomenon in the hospital). *Jinzhou Yixueyuan xuebao (Journal of Jinzhou Medical College)* 19(4): 69–70.

Xiacheng Health Bureau. 2004. Xiacheng qu weisheng xitong hangfeng jianshe jiandu chuli zanxing guiding (Provisional rules for supervision of good practice construction and penalties in Xiacheng health care system). Accessed 31 January 2008. http://www.hzxc.gov.cn/portal/html/20041205000280/20050712000263.html.

Xiong, Xiaoyan. 2000. Chengdu 'bingren xuan yisheng' si da kunhuo (Four major confusions in 'patients choose doctors' program in Chengdu). *Sichuan qingnian bao (Sichuan Youth)*, 30 October. Accessed 23 September 2010. http://www1.peopledaily.com.cn/GB/channel1/10/20001030/292829.html.

Xu, Jing, and Wen Gu. 2010. "Te xu" yiliao jizhan gonggong ziyuan yin zhengyi ("Specially needed" medicine encroached public resources and sparked controversy. *Nanjing ribao (Nanjing Daily)*, 13 September, 5.

Xu, Peng. 2006. 'Hongbao' xianxiang de zhidu jingji xue fenxi (An institutional economic analysis of the 'red packet' phenomenon). *Zhongguo weisheng ziyuan (China Health Resources)* 9(4): 147–149.

Yan, Guochen. 1994. Dui hongbao de kanfa ji duice (Attitudes towards red packet and countermeasures). *Yixue yu zhexue (Medicine and Philosophy)* 2: 34–35.

Yan, Lixin. 2004. Hongbao huikou zui yu fei zui: yishi xiehui you hua yao shuo (Red packets and drug kickback—guilty or not guilty: doctor association has a say). *Jiankang bao (Health News)*, 15 September, 5.

Yan, Yang. 2006. Shoushu dianming fei: xiang zuo zou haishi xiang you zou (Surgical nomination fee: turning left or right). *Zhongguo gaige bao (China reform)*, 12 April, 3.

Yang, Chao, and Huayan Ding. 2006. Fa gai wei jiao ting "dianming shoushu" fei (Commission of Development and Reform called an end to "operation by nomination" fees). *Huaxia shibao (China Times)*, 23 February, 6.

Yin, Dakui. 1993. Zai quanguo yizheng gongzuo huiyi shang de baogao (Speech at the National Conference of Medical Administration). *Zhongguo yiyuan guanli (Chinese Hospital Management)* 13(10): 5–12.

Yuan, Changhai, Guifang Gong, Mingzhang Sun, and Yurong Han. 2003. Bingren he yisheng dui "bingren xuan yisheng"de yixiang (Patients' and doctors' preference toward "patients choose doctors"). *Zhongguo weisheng shiye guanli (Chinese Health Service Management)* 1: 16–18.

Yuan, Li. 1995. Shui lai "yiliao" teshu yiliao? (Who come to "treat" special medicine?). *Weisheng jingji yanjiu (Health economics research)* 8: 29.

Zeng, Liangliang, Yahong Li, and Sisi Xiao. 2014. Te xu yiliao tuichu gongli yiyuan yin zhengyi (Specially needed medicine is removed from public hospitals, sparking dispute). *Jingji cankao bao (Economic information daily)*, 16 May, 7, Health.

Zhang, Lizi. 2006. Quxiao dianming shoushu fei—Yisheng ruhe pingshuo (Abolishing fees for operation by nomination—doctors' opinions). *Jiankang bao (Health news)*, 20 March, 3.

Zhang, Xing. 2004. Zhengduan 'jinshou hongbao': zhuanjia danxin zuihou reng shi 'zhi shang tan bing' (Diagnosing 'red packet ban': experts are afraid it is only 'a fight on paper' again). *Xiandai kuaibao (Modern Express News)*, 14 April. Accessed 30 January 2008. http://news.xinhuanet.com/newscenter/2004-04/15/content_1420048.htm.

Zhang, Yingsong. 2000. Bingren xuan yisheng bu yao zouru wuqu (The myth of patients choose doctors). *Jiancha ribao (Supervision daily)*, 4 November 3.

Zhang, Zhaobi, and Bobo Xu. 2007. Bingren xuan yisheng: Quanzhou liu nian shijian diaocha (Patients choose doctors: investigation after six years in practice in

Quanzhou). *Quanzhou wanbao (Quanzhou Evening News)*, 29 April. Accessed 1 January 2008. http://www.qzwb.com/gb/content/2007-04/29/content_2447863.htm.

Zhao, Yongxin. 2001. Bingren xuan yisheng (Patients choose doctors). *Renmin ribao (People's Daily)*, 15 January, 2.

Zhejiang Health and Family Planning Commission. 2015. Zhejiang Sheng weisheng jisheng wei dangzu jiaqiang zhishu danwei jijian jiancha zuzhi jianshe (The leading Party group of Zhejiang Health and Family Planning Commission strengthens the organization and construction of disciplinary and supervisory (offices) in work-units directly under its control). Accessed 13 November 2015. http://www.nhfpc.gov.cn/jcj/xsdtf/201506/05368104099b49d3a43a3d4b99f73c87.shtml.

Zhou, Li, and Yanping Chen. 2007. Nanjing: bingren xuan yisheng zhengce leisheng da yudian xiao (Nanjing: the 'patients chooses doctors' policy is much said but little done). *Jinling wanbao (Jinling Evening Post)*, 17 April. Accessed 9 March 2016. http://www.js.xinhua.org/xin_wen_zhong_xin/2007-04/17/content_9808586.htm.

Zhu, Huihong. 2002. Bingren xuan yisheng li bi fenxi ji duice sikao (Analysis of the advantages and disadvantages of patients choose doctors and solutions). *Zhongguo yiyuan tongji (Chinese journal of hospital statistics)* 9(3): 148–149.

CHAPTER 7

Conclusion

Red packets have been a stigma of the Chinese healthcare system for decades. As the present research reveals, its rise and prevalence is brought about by old institutions inherited from pre-reform era and new institutions established in the reform era. A fundamental difference between the Chinese healthcare system and those in open and democratic societies lies in the absence of an intermediary social structure between individual practitioners and the state. This intermediary structure is an essential precondition for an open political space in which medical professionals can exercise their organizational power and collectively negotiate and bargain with the Party-state who is the ultimate employer of the medical profession.

The intermediary structure was once existent. Before 1949, the medical profession in the Republican era enjoyed considerable freedom of association and could collectively exert countervailing power against the state. As a result, doctors enjoyed significant autonomy to determine their work and economic terms. Since the inception of the PRC, the ideology of the CCP, especially the principle of "serving the people," became the overarching ethics of the entire society and substituted for professional ethics. Under this ideological principle, the medical profession was swiftly turned into a hybrid profession, as its counterpart in the Soviet Union. On the one hand, it lost its organizational power and ceased to be an intermediary social structure between the authoritarian state and individual practitioners. Corollary to that was the loss of control over economic and work terms. The Party-state monopolized the employment of qualified medical professionals and graduates of medical schools. Doctors were no longer able to form associations

© The Author(s) 2017
J. Yang, *Informal Payments and Regulations in China's Healthcare System*,
DOI 10.1007/978-981-10-2110-7_7

to negotiate and bargain with the Party-state, but were allocated by the latter to work-units and served as health and medical bureaucrats responsible for the redistribution of state resources. On the other hand, however, with the nationalization and bureaucratization of medical human resources, doctors gained bureaucratic power. An inevitable consequence of the bureaucratization was the emergence of bureaucratic medicine which featured indifference and impersonalism toward patients. The Party-state launched many campaigns to rectify bureaucratism in medicine, but once the political fervor faded, bureaucratic medicine returned.

The expansion of healthcare services between 1949 and 1978 further strengthened the bureaucratic power of doctors as distributers of state resources. The healthcare system grew tremendously in quantity terms, but the growth was achieved largely through economical means. Health and medical work-units were called on to expand their services immoderately under the principle of "hard work and thrift" while government investment in healthcare increased only moderately. Medical resources were diffused, leading to the shortage of quality services in urban areas in particular.

Institutionally, the Chinese healthcare system in the pre-reform era resembles that which is prerequisite for the emergence of "inxit" as a coping strategy on the part of doctors. Without a public space for collective actions and open negotiation and bargaining, Chinese doctors' voice was largely blocked. With the absence of a functioning private sector, doctors had no "exit." But informal payments did not appear consequently. An important implication of the "inxit" theory is that the coping strategy is universally applied, which means that doctors expect or take informal payments from every patient seeking medical services in public medical facilities constrained by shortage. For patients who do not give, doctors are likely to provide sub-standard services. In the Chinese healthcare system, however, bureaucratic impersonalism and particularism of acquaintance society had equal impact on doctors' behaviors. As a result, doctors in the pre-reform era did not take "universalistic" informal payments as the "inxit" theory would predict. On the contrary, they were engaged in "particularistic" backdoor medicine and exercised particularism to people from their *guanxi* networks. Backdoor medicine did not exclude gifts of monetary value, but affinity with doctors played a more important role. In spite of the CCP's efforts to promote universal particularism in healthcare and encourage doctors to treat all patients indiscriminately as families, particularism was the norm, and backdoor medicine was widespread.

In the reform era, many old institutions survived. China remains an authoritarian state, with a civil society only in embryonic form. "Serving the people" is further institutionalized as the core of the professional ethics of the socialist medicine. Under this principle, the medical profession is denied organizational power to countervail the Party-state's interference and to openly and collectively negotiate and bargain with the government, which is still the predominant employer of doctors. The profession remains a hybrid one; doctors retain their cadre status and continue to serve as medical bureaucrats in the public sector. Unsurprisingly, bureaucratic medicine persists in no lesser magnitude. Again, in spite of the promotion of treating patients as families, doctors continue to accord particularistic care to patients from their *guanxi* networks.

But market as a new institution has been established across the entirety of the economy. Market-oriented reform has been advanced in the healthcare system, and "hard work and thrift" is abandoned as a way to expand healthcare system. Although the authority continues to uphold Norman Bethune as a role model and demand the doctor to sacrifice selflessly, it has enacted numerous policies that have spurred profit-driven activities. Hospitals and individual doctors are no longer ashamed of pursuing economic ends. Ideologically, medical professionals benefited from the political recognition of their cultural capital, which gives them a favorable market position. But the old institutions prevent doctors from capitalizing their newly confirmed cultural capital. Consequently, a black market has emerged for medical professionals to cash in on their market positions. Red packets become prevalent in such an institutional setting.

The applicability of the "inxit" theory to red packets in the reform era is also limited. Doctors' voice is muffled. A functioning private sector is in its preliminary stage and does not constitute an attractive exit for both patients and medical professionals. But due to the success of the economic reform, residents have more disposable incomes. The market-oriented reform has instilled market principles into both patients and doctors who accept money as a more straightforward and efficient way of exchange than the complicated networks of gift and favor exchanges in the previous era. Particularism consistently plays an important role in doctors' decision to take red packets or not, but, as evidence indicates, the scope of the practice is markedly expanded to include those who have money but do not have *guanxi* in the first place.

The applicability of the "inxit" theory is further limited by the complexity of red packet transactions at clinical level. Empirical findings confirm that red packets are predominantly intended to overcome bureaucratic medicine and shortage of quality, and have to be used most of the time with *guanxi*, a legacy of acquaintance society. Doctors have little control over their salaries and workloads and do not feel morally problematic to take red packets to compensate for their low incomes, heavy workloads, and high risks of practice. But contrary to what the "inxit" theory would predict, doctors do not accept every red packet offered to them. They have many considerations and respond differently to each informal offering. Generally speaking, they tend to accept red packets given through acquaintances and turn down those offered by "strangers" or those overly manipulative or laden with unrealistic expectations. The effect of the red packet is not always clear. It can apparently beat the rigid system of hospitals and give patients opportunities to jump the queue or engage senior doctors they trust. Doctors who accept informal payments usually accord the giver better attitude and more care. But in most cases red packets have barely any impact on the technical core of medical treatment, which, as doctors believe, is more relevant to patients' recovery.

The Party-state is concerned about endemic red packets and views the practice as a threat to its ruling legitimacy. Obliged by its commitment to serving the people, the CCP has made considerable efforts to contain it, drawing on both old and new institutions and employing both disciplinary and market approaches. The market approach has empowered patients but has not successfully reduced red packets. It only concentrates them in the hands of senior doctors. The disciplinary approach draws on the Party-state's coercive power and resources to discipline red packets, and represents an attempt on the part of the Party-state to serve and protect the interests of patients. But for the same purpose of protecting their own interests, patients collude with doctors, though unwillingly to a large extent, and do not report doctors who take red packets to the authority. The hospital management, for the purpose of protecting the interests of the work-unit, usually does not take red packets seriously and is inclined to cover up red packet takers. In this context, it is the government that is rendered "powerless" and can do little about the unhealthy trend in the healthcare system.

In 2015, the government launched a new round of reform to urban public hospitals. The reform emphasizes healthcare as a public good and promises to increase governmental investment. Hospitals are given more autonomy in the management of doctors, and doctors are assured that their incomes will increase. But in terms of the organization of medical professionals, there is no breakthrough. Public hospitals will continue to dominate the healthcare system and function as the major employers of doctors. Free association and professional autonomy of doctors are nowhere mentioned in the reform decree.[1] The old institutions will probably endure even in stronger forms as "de-marketization" and the re-assertion of governmental responsibility and dominance are central to the reform. The medical profession will remain bureaucratized. An open space for collective negotiation and bargaining with the Party-state is still out of sight in the Chinese political system. Given the terms of the reform, it is very likely that red packets as an unhealthy trend will persist in the foreseeable future.

Note

1. See http://www.gov.cn/zhengce/content/2015-05/17/content_9776.htm, accessed 6 June 2016.

INDEX

A

altruism, 34, 35, 74
American Medical Association (AMA), 40
Anglo-American societies, 39, 40, 93
anti-bureaucratism. *See* bureucratism
Armenia, 5
attitudes
  domineering, 99
  service, 114
authoritarian, 29, 40, 41, 44, 51, 57, 77, 141, 263, 275, 277
authoritarianism, 41, 57, 77, 263
autonomy
  economic, 68, 77–9, 83–5, 88, 161
  professional, 72, 79–90, 95, 97, 229
  technical, 88–90

B

bargaining
  collective, 38, 41, 48, 57, 59, 143, 144, 148, 161
  formal, 56, 205

Beiyang government, 70, 71
Beiyang regime. *See* Beiyang government
Bethune, Norman
  Bethune Medal, 140
  Bethune Spirit, 137–40
  On Memorizing Bethune, 80
Bolshevik, 45
Bourdieu, Pierre, 158, 160
bribe, 16, 17, 39, 49, 156, 203, 204, 252
British Medical Association (BMA), 38
Bulgaria, 4–6
bureaucracy
  healthcare, 94
  impersonality of, 104–6
  medical, 93, 102, 115
bureaucratic power, 46, 47, 57, 90, 93, 94, 276
bureaucratism
  in medicine, 101, 106, 276 (*see also* medicine, bureaucratic)
bureaucratization, 44, 45, 90–118, 276